250 YEARS OF
CONVENTION AND CONTENTION:
A HISTORY OF THE
BOARD OF DEPUTIES OF BRITISH JEWS,
1760–2010

250 Years of
Convention and Contention:
A History of the
Board of Deputies of British Jews,
1760–2010

RAPHAEL LANGHAM

To Alfred,

Enjoy.

Rap

VALLENTINE MITCHELL
LONDON • PORTLAND, OR

First published in 2010 by Vallentine Mitchell

Middlesex House,	920 NE 58th Avenue, Suite 300
29/45 High Street, Edgware,	Portland, Oregon,
Middlesex HA8 7UU, UK	97213-3786 USA

www.vmbooks.com

British Library Cataloguing in Publication Data

ISBN 978 0 85303 982 2 (cloth)

Library of Congress Cataloging in Publication Data

Printed by T J International, Padstow, Cornwall

This book is dedicated to the memory of my cousin and lifelong friend Michael Fox ז״ל, a distinguished lawyer and erudite columnist for *Ha'aretz*.
I also dedicate it to my two most recent grandchildren, Jay and Lottie.

Contents

Illustrations

Foreword

The years since the founding of the Board of Deputies in 1760 have seen enormous changes in the nature and composition of British society as well as in Britain's position on the international scene. At the same time, this period has seen revolutionary changes in the nature and composition of British Jewry. The Board has been at the heart of these changes, many of which have been played out in its debates as well as in the elections of its honorary officers.

It is surprising, therefore, that until now there has been no serious attempt to write a history of the Board, and of the way it has influenced the community and in turn has been influenced by it. This gap has been commented on and lamented by many Anglo-Jewish historians and it is therefore with great pleasure that we are able to introduce this history, which will take the story of the Board from its inception right up to the present day.

The Board has, of course, come a long way in this time. When it began there were no staff, only a handful of deputies (whose language was Portuguese), and for the first seventy years there were only very infrequent meetings. Indeed, at one point twelve years elapsed with no meeting being held. The Board made occasional interventions with government, usually concerning overseas matters. Today the Board has regular monthly meetings, a substantial if overworked secretariat, and subcommittees – known as divisions – dealing with education, defence of *shechita*, *brit milah*, burials, provincial communities, antisemitism, discrimination against Jews in employment and at schools, boycotts against Israeli goods, Israel advocacy, government legislation generally, and countless other matters. On average the Board issues several press releases three or four times a week, on matters ranging from religious practice in this country to the situation in Israel, to the problems encountered by Jews and other minorities in other countries.

There have been a number of phases in the history of the Board: the Montefiore era, the domination by the Cousinhood (the small network of aristocratic Jewish families), the takeover by the Zionist caucus, to its present leadership. Similarly, many of the great issues which have impacted on the Jewish community during that period – the emancipation, the Balfour declaration, the great influx of immigrants from Eastern Europe before the First World War and of refugees from Central Europe before the Second World War, the Holocaust and finally the creation of the state of Israel – are reflected in the debates and politics of the Board. Many themes that recur throughout the history are present today: the Board's claim to represent the community to government, the relationship between the Board and other non-representative Anglo-Jewish bodies, antisemitism, and attitudes to Zionism and Israel, as well as the continuing tension between the different religious branches of the community. This history shows how these issues have been handled over the last two-and-half centuries.

How they will be handled in the future, one can only speculate.

Vivian Wineman
President of the Board of Deputies

Preface and Acknowledgements

When I was asked to write a history of the Board of Deputies to commemorate their 250th anniversary I felt flattered and honoured, but I was also delighted because there had been family connections with the Board over many years. My father, Harold Langham, had been a deputy in the 1930s representing Stamford Hill Beth Hamedrash ('Grove Lane'). By coincidence, when he left the Board on enlisting into the army, his successor was Joe Wineman, the father of the present president. Another family member of the Board was my uncle, Samuel Fox, who claimed, correctly as far as my researches have found, that when he was first elected to the Board in 1922, just after his twenty-second birthday, he was the youngest ever deputy. He represented Nelson Street Sphardish for a few years and, many years later, Hendon United from 1950 to 1970. A number of years ago I thought I had been elected to the Board, only to find it was the London Board of Jewish Religious Education and not the Board of Deputies of British Jews.

Many people have helped me with this book. First and foremost is Dr David Feldman of Birkbeck College whom the Board appointed as my adviser. He read and we discussed the drafts of each chapter as they were completed; he encouraged but criticized and his advice was invaluable. My son Eric also read and discussed with me each chapter as it was written and came up with many significant comments and ideas as to restructuring some sections. My other son, Philippe, read the final draft of the whole book, made some very helpful suggestions and in particular recommended the title. Stephen Massil also read the final draft and suggested many valuable changes and improvements. Professor William Rubinstein let me see extracts from his forthcoming *Dictionary of Anglo-Jewish History*, and in particular the biographies of the presidents of the Board contained therein and mainly researched and written by his wife, Dr Hilary L. Rubinstein. Daniel Tilles let me see a copy of his paper on the anti-fascist campaign of the Board in the 1930s, which is due to be published in 2010. To all of these I offer my grateful thanks. I give particular thanks to my friend and shul neighbour Charles Corman. Every Shabbat I was able to sound out ideas with him, in an undertone whilst the *baal Musaf* repeated the *Amidah*.

I have used many primary and secondary sources and these are all listed towards the end of the book and cited where appropriate in the work itself. I am grateful to all these authors, too numerous to mention here.

I interviewed many past presidents and honorary officers of the Board, and to Lord Greville Janner, Eldred Tabachnik, Jo Wagerman, Henry Grunwald, Flo Kaufman (an honorary officer for twelve years from 1997 to 2009) I offer my thanks. I spent many pleasant hours discussing the Board with His Honour Judge Israel Finestein ז״ל, who shared with me his insights into many of the issues dealt with by the Board and the personalities of many past leaders and deputies. It is of great regret that he died just as I was completing this book. Dr Lionel Kopelowitz was extraordinarily helpful with his prodigious memory of many events long past. I am very grateful to him for the time he spared for me. I am also grateful to Vivian Wineman, the current president, not only for his foreword to this book but also for his advice and encouragement as the book progressed. I must also thank Michael Whine, the defence director of the Board and a director of the Community Security Trust, for putting me right on the complicated issue of defending the Jewish community in Britain from external threats. Sandra Clark, the administrative director of the Board, was a tower of strength and knowledge, forever obtaining material for me and pointing me in the right direction.

I owe particular thanks to Heather Marchant of Vallentine Mitchell, whose advice was invaluable. She kept me on the straight and narrow, but put up with some of my idiosyncrasies. For example, I have a particular antipathy against inserting a hyphen after the anti in antisemitism. Vallentine Mitchell use a hyphen in all their works in accord with the *Oxford Dictionary for Writers and Editors*, but she made an exception in my case. I must also thank Helen Grubin for compiling the index.

Most of the photographs in this book are from the Board's own collection. Some are from the *Jewish Chronicle* and I am grateful to them for giving permission for their reproduction. A few are by particular photographers, whose names are given in the captions, and I thank them all for giving permission for reproduction.

Finally, and most important of all, I have to thank my wife Dolly for her strong support. She put up with me disappearing for hours to my study and pacing up and down, whenever an idea occurred or I had to consider how to write about a particularly difficult matter. We did not cancel any holidays, but I am sure I spoiled them by taking my laptop and the files on the book with me.

In conclusion, I must emphasize two points. First, the work, the comments and conclusions are mine alone and I am responsible for any errors or omissions. Secondly, I have had total freedom in writing this book and no one has tried to influence me in one direction or another.

Raphael Langham
Chanukah, 5770
December 2009

Abbreviations

ADC	Aliens Defence Committee
AJA	Anglo-Jewish Association
AJC	American Jewish Conference
AJEX	Association of Jewish Ex-Service Men and Women
ANL	Anti-Nazi League
AR	Annual Report of Board of Deputies
Board	Board of Deputies of British Jews
BOD	Archives of the Board of Deputies
BUF	British Union of Fascists
CBF	Central British Fund for World Jewish Relief
CBJO	Co-ordination Board of Jewish Organisations
COJO	Conference of Jewish Organisations
Conjoint	Conjoint Foreign Committee of the Board and the AJA
CRIF	Conseil Representatif des Juifs de France
CST	Community Security Organisation
EJC	European Jewish Congress
EZF	English Zionist Federation
JACOB	Jewish Aid Committee of Britain
JC	*Jewish Chronicle*
JFS	The Jews' Free School
JLC	Jewish Leadership Council
JNF	Jewish National Fund
Joint	Joint Foreign Committee of the Board and the AJA
JPC	Jewish People's Council Against Fascism and Anti-Semitism
JRSO	Jewish Restitution Successor Organisation
LCC	London County Council
PRO	Public Records Office
STV	Single Transferable Vote
TAC	Trades Advisory Council
TNA	The National Archives

UCAR	United Campaign Against Racism
UNA	United Nations Association Jewish Affiliates Coordinating Committee
UNESCO	United Nations Economic and Social Council
UNRRA	United Nations Relief and Rehabilitation Administration
WCJE	World Council of Jewish Education
WJC	World Jewish Congress
WZO	World Zionist Organisation

Introduction

On 3 November 1760, the leaders of the Bevis Marks Synagogue in London established a committee to (a) prepare and issue a loyal address to King George III, who had just ascended the throne, and (b) thereafter to deal with the most urgent matters that affected the community. This committee evolved into what we know today as the Board of Deputies of British Jews ('the Board'). As it developed, the Board had to change and adapt as political, social and demographic changes occurred in Britain. It also had to adapt as the British Jewish community was transformed, not only by its increase in size from 1881 onwards, as the community was overwhelmed by the influx of Jewish immigrants from Eastern Europe, but also as the community itself changed from an almost entirely religious group in 1760 to the myriad of ways in which Jews define their identity and are perceived by the outside world in twenty-first-century Britain.[1]

The mission statement of the Board, as published in its Annual Review for 2008, reads: 'The Board of Deputies of British Jews exists to promote and defend the religious rights and civil liberties of British Jewry. As the community's democratically elected cross-communal organisation, the Board connects with government, media and wider society, providing a unique means through which all British Jews can be heard and represented.'[2]

Most, but not all, synagogues and many Jewish institutions in Britain are represented on the Board by deputies who are elected for a three-year term. Those Jews not represented are either members of synagogues that have chosen not to be represented on the Board or are not members of represented synagogues or institutions. In the same way as the non-Jewish world in Britain considers the chief rabbi to be the spiritual head of British Jews, even though many Jewish congregations do not accept his authority, so the president of the Board is considered the lay head. On Sunday 17 May 2009, Vivian Wineman was elected president of the Board. That evening he received an email from the prime minister congratulating him on his election. Government and the media recognize other Jewish institutions or organizations, but they see the Board as the paramount one. Whilst the British government and others consult with other Jewish organizations on some issues, it is only the Board that they consult on *all* issues relevant to the Jewish community in Britain.

The Board has often been called the 'Parliament of the Jews'. It is not a parliament in the sense of legislating, but it is in the sense of a forum where deputies can express views on any issues affecting Jews in Britain. The Board generally holds eight plenary sessions a year where members of the public and the press can attend, but most of its work is conducted by four divisions – Community Issues, Defence and Group Relations, International, and Finance and Organisation, chaired by the three vice-presidents and the treasurer. There are five honorary officers and a permanent staff headed by a director general.

Until the 1930s, the leadership of the Board, primarily its presidents and other honorary officers, was drawn from the 'Cousinhood'. This soubriquet was first coined by Chaim Bermant in his book *Troubled Eden*.[3] He refers to a group of about two hundred upper- and upper-middle-class Jewish families linked by marriage and whose wealth came primarily from finance related activities. They included the Cohens, Franklins, Goldsmids, Henriques, Josephs, Mocattas, Montagus, Montefiores, Rothschilds, Samuels and Sebags. It must be appreciated that the members of this group, although related, were heterogeneous in their views and often had strongly conflicting opinions on many issues. Leading the Board was and is not a sinecure and representatives from these families, as well as all subsequent honorary officers, sacrificed a great deal of their time in the interests of the Jewish community in Britain. For some it was *noblesse oblige*; for others it was the prestige; for many it was a sense of responsibility; and for some it was a mixture of all of these reasons. The success or otherwise of the activities of the Board depended, and still depends, to a large extent on the efforts and abilities of the president and the other honorary officers, as well as the permanent staff. Likewise, representations often depend on the man making them and some presidents have been more successful in this regard than others. Success in approaching government and officials is often in proportion to the standing of those making the approach. The book includes some discussion on many of the former presidents of the Board, but there is none on any past president who is still alive.

This book relates not only the history of the Board, but also describes, sometimes in great depth, the issues and events that involved the Board both in Britain and overseas. It is essentially in narrative form, a descriptive rather than an analytical history, but many of the matters dealt with in the body of the work include some analysis. The chapters are in chronological order and the breaks between chapters tend to be what I have seen as a turning point in the history of the Board. The final chapter brings the narrative up to date, considers which current issues might prove of significance to future historians and looks back over the last 250 years. The latter part of Chapter 5, the whole of Chapter 6 and the early part of Chapter 7 were difficult to write because they were contemporary with my own life and it was important not to confuse history with memory and personal opinions on the various community disputes that arose during these years. Each chapter, except the first and last, is in three parts – background and developments within the Board, home issues and foreign affairs. The reader who is only interested in a history of the Board itself and not with the matters it dealt with needs only read the introduction and part one of each chapter. The issues dealt with within each part of each chapter are thematic and in chronological order from when they first occurred, but each issue is generally followed through to its conclusion before reverting to the next matter. There are four appendices. Appendix 1 is the first constitution of the Board agreed in 1836. The constitution has been amended on no fewer than fifty occasions since 1836. The original constitution had twelve clauses and the current one thirty-eight clauses, six appendices, one annex, one schedule and twenty-nine standing orders. The second appendix gives the number of deputies in triennial periods; Appendix 3 lists the past presidents, and Appendix 4 lists the past senior officials.

The practice of Judaism in Britain displays a continuum from non-adherence to any ritual to complete observance of Halacha in all its minutiae. There is a comparable range for synagogues, although it does not follow that all members of a synagogue are homogeneous in their observance. There are no synagogues for Jews who do not adhere to any ritual, although some of these Jews attend synagogues from time to time. Most historians and surveys have categorized synagogues into three broad groups with varying nomenclature. I have used 'Strictly Orthodox', 'Central Orthodox' and 'Progressive'. Strictly Orthodox includes the Machzike Hadath, the Adath Yisroel and members of the Union of Orthodox Hebrew Congregations. Various adjectives have been used to qualify this group such as 'right-wing', 'ultra-orthodox', 'haredi' and 'fundamentalist', but I prefer not to use such adjectives which in many cases are inappropriate. Central Orthodox includes the United Synagogue, the Federation of Synagogues, the Spanish and Portuguese Synagogues, the other Sephardi synagogues and most of the independent provincial synagogues. Progressives are the Reform and Liberal synagogues. For the purpose of this book it has not been necessary to categorize the Masorti synagogues or the Belsize Square and other Conservative synagogues, although they are becoming an increasingly important group in the community. The Orthodox Group on the Board comprised essentially deputies representing Strictly Orthodox synagogues.

The available material is immense. Apart from secondary sources, the primary sources are daunting. The indices to the archives of the Board encompass more than 500 A4 pages, Jewish newspapers from the 1840s onwards have written reams about the Board (for example, a search in the online *Jewish Chronicle* archives found 24,500 entries mentioning the words 'Board of Deputies'), and the National Archives (formally the Public Records Office) has hundreds of files of correspondence between the Board and the government. The Board has been involved in an overwhelming number of matters ranging from very large issues that had a bearing on all Jews in Britain or elsewhere to minor issues involving just one or two individuals. I have had to be selective in what to include. My selection is entirely subjective – either material of interest to me or that which I consider particularly significant. The two do not always coincide. I apologize in advance to any reader whose favourite event or issue is either not included or dealt with much too briefly.

Raising finance to cover the cost of its activities has been a perennial problem for the Board. In fact, at its first meeting the newly formed committee asked its parent, the *Mahamad* of Bevis Marks, for a budget to cover expenses.[4] There was no formal answer to this request and it was repeated on at least two later occasions. There were occasions when the Board could not take the action it would have liked to have done for financial reasons. Moses Montefiore addressed this issue of finance in 1835 when he incorporated in the first constitution of the Board a provision that the expenses of the Board should be met proportionately by all member congregations, but the congregations forced him to place a monetary limit on their costs.[5] The methods of financing the Board have changed over the years to meet changing conditions, but the important point is that despite many financial crises the Board has survived for 250 years. This is to the credit of the hard work, determination and creativity of the Board's treasurers. The main source of finance for the Board has been for most of its period of existence what is now termed the 'Communal Levy'. For synagogues this is generally paid by individual members, and for most synagogues it is voluntary.

On very many occasions, the president of the Board is asked to arbitrate in disputes, often between congregations in the same town and sometimes in disputes between individual Jews, not always with success. These disputes tend to be ones where it is not appropriate to use a Beth Din or when one or both of the parties does not want to do so. This form of arbitration is encouraged by the Board even though it could place quite an onerous burden on the president or other honorary officers. In more than one of its annual reports, the Board pointed out that dragging local differences, often very petty, to the courts reflected badly on the Jewish community and it appealed to communities to seek arbitration by the president. Furthermore, the archives are full of correspondence between the Board and individuals, where those individuals had asked the Board to intercede on problems they had with their employers, government institutions and so on, generally because of their being Jewish or trying to observe the Sabbath and Festivals. Some matters were clearly antisemitic in origin; others arose for different reasons, such as ignorance or not wanting to employ observant Jews because of the difficulties the employers conceived could arise. The Board always tried to deal with these, but not always with success. In the interests of space, I have decided not to include in this book descriptions of most of these matters.

From its inception, the Board became involved in matters affecting Jews in foreign countries. Following Sir Moses Montefiore's successful visit to the Middle East in connection with the Damascus Blood Libel, Jewish communities throughout the world contacted the Board whenever crises occurred. These included violence against Jews, particularly following ritual murder accusations and the frequent attacks on Jews in Morocco and pogroms in Russia. There were also laws and decrees against Jews, such as the ukase in Russia in 1843 that required much of the Jewish population to move, and the 1866 law in Romania that removed all citizenship rights from Jews. Legal and similar cases against Jews also involved the Board, such as the kidnapping of Edgardo Mortara in 1858. The Board always reacted positively to these appeals, generally by contacting the Foreign Office and asking it to take action to alleviate the situation, but frequently the Board became involved directly with the country concerned and even, particularly during the Montefiore era, sending representatives to the country concerned. Sometimes the Board was successful and on other occasions failed despites its efforts. The help the Board received from the British government depended on the government's relationship with the country concerned and the political situation at the time. For example, it suited the government's policy to be very supportive over Damascus and Mortara but less so over the pogroms in Russia. In many such cases, particularly of violence against Jews, the Board not only took appropriate political action but also instituted appeals for the victims. In this book there is only room to discuss a few of these episodes, and I have chosen the most well known.

The work of the Board is much more and much wider than dealing just with major events affecting Jews in this country and overseas. A significant volume of what could be termed routine work is carried out daily, not only by the honorary officers and deputies, but also by the chief executive and the staff. Legislation has to be scrutinized, meetings attended, Jewish issues throughout the world observed and, when appropriate, action has to be taken, *shechita* and all aspects of Jewish observance have to be protected, medical issues such as *brit milah*, organ transplants and post-mortems have to be monitored, and individuals given help and advice, marriage secretaries have to be registered, disused cemeteries must be maintained, antisemitism combated, Jews and Jewish premises defended from physical attack, interfaith forums attended and answers given to a myriad of questions from and regarding Jews in Britain – the list is endless.

At the end of 1964, the Board established a research unit to investigate the demographic features of British Jewry.[6] This unit has proved to be of significant value to the community and its very many reports of essential use to researchers and historians of British Jewry. In 1976, on the initiative of Ruth Winston-Fox, the chairman of the Education and Youth Committee, the Board established a travelling exhibition called *The Jewish Way of Life Exhibition*. The object is to explain Jewish religion, culture and history to non-Jews (now aimed primarily at primary and secondary school children), but also to remind Jews who visit the exhibition of their heritage.[7] It is now a three-way partnership by the Board, World ORT and the Pears Foundation. Since its foundation, the exhibition has been set up in hundreds of venues throughout Britain, such as museums, schools, synagogues and community centres. The exhibition has its own website (www.jwol.org.uk) and a CD-Rom is available free to all schools in Britain. In recent years, inter faith activities have come to assume an important part of the Board's work. The Board has represented the Jewish community on the Inter Faith Network since it was founded in 1987. The President of the Board is a vice-chair of its executive committee. In 2005, the Board decided to formalize and extend their involvement in inter faith issues by employing a full-time Inter Faith Officer. In 2008, the Board launched 'Shared Futures', a schools-linking programme that brings together Jewish faith-schools with non-denominational schools, and schools of other faith groups. The Board also initiated a major study into Jewish involvement in inter faith activities in Britain resulting in the publication in 2009 of a report entitled 'Communities in Conversation'. The Board has taken many other such initiatives: some have only lasted a few years and others are still ongoing.

The Board of Deputies has been in existence for 250 years. There is only one Jewish institution in Britain, other than synagogues, that is older. This is the Initiation Society (*brit milah*) that was founded in 1745, fifteen years before the Board.

NOTES

1. See, for example, the *Jewish Chronicle* [JC], *New Year Supplement*, 5770, 18 September 2009, pp.2–5.
2. *Annual Review of the Board of Deputies* (AR), 2008, p.1.
3. Chaim Bermant, *Troubled Eden* (London: Vallentine Mitchell, 1969), pp.62–73.
4. BOD, Minute Book 1, p.1.
5. Ibid., pp.24–25.
6. *JC*, 25 December 1964, p.1; AR, 1964, p.17.
7. *The Jewish Year Book, 2009* (London: Vallentine Mitchell, 2009), p.xxiv.

1 The Early Years, 1760–1828

In 1760, there were about 10,000 Jews in England divided between Sephardim, who lived almost exclusively in London, and Ashkenazim. The Sephardi community was in the main originally from Spain and Portugal, having escaped from those two countries or having moved from the already established Sephardi communities of Amsterdam and elsewhere. Many of them, even on arrival in London, were already merchants of some substance. They referred to themselves as the 'Nation' or the 'Portuguese Nation' and referred to the Ashkenazim as Dutch or German Jews. They were relatively affluent compared with the Ashkenazi community which was established much later, in the 1690s, and mainly by poor Jewish refugees, most from the German states in Central Europe but some from Holland and elsewhere. By 1760, however, the Ashkenazim had not only grown numerically so that they far outnumbered the Sephardim, but a number of their leading families had become wealthy and could meet the Sephardim as social and financial equals.[1]

Most Jews were poor, some impoverished and others living just above the poverty level. They were badly educated and occupied mainly in street and similar trades. Crime was rife. There were, however, skilled craftsmen, artisans and shopkeepers and the wealthier Jews were merchants, dealers in precious stones, brokers or engaged in other ways in finance and commerce. They were limited in choice because some occupations and many professions, including teaching, medicine and law, were not open to them. This was essentially because entry often required swearing an oath, which included the words 'on the true faith of a Christian', and sometimes it was necessary to receive the Holy Sacrament. These disabilities applied to all persons who were not members of the Church of England and thus impinged on Catholics and Nonconformists as well as Jews. Jews could not attend most universities because entrance or graduation required an oath containing the non-acceptable words. Those eligible to vote in parliamentary elections could not do so, because it was necessary to take an oath before voting. On the other hand, there were no specific anti-Jewish laws or statutes or special taxes on Jews as there were in many other countries. A few restrictions applied to Jews but not to Catholics and Nonconformists. For example, Jews were not admitted to the freedom of the City of London until 1832 and consequently could not engage in retail trade there, although they could beyond the city's boundaries. There were also a number of numeri clausi, including, until 1830, a limit of twelve on the number of Jewish stockbrokers.[2]

Jews, even the wealthier ones, tended to keep a low profile. This stemmed partially from feelings of insecurity, but also from what they thought was expected of Jews in England. In 1664, the Jewish community had been concerned that the Conventicle Act of that year, which prohibited assemblies for prayer except in accordance with the liturgy of the Church of England, might apply to them. The Act was aimed at Nonconformists but the Jews were uncertain and petitioned the king, Charles II, who referred the matter to the Privy Council. On 22 August 1664 the Privy Council assured the Jews that they might 'Promise themselves the effects of the same favour as formally they had had, so long as they demeane themselves peaceably and quietly with due obedience to his Majesty's laws and without scandal to his government'.[3] This had been reiterated in 1685 when, in connection with the arrest of thirty-seven Jews under an anti-Catholic law, James II instructed the Attorney General that 'His Majesty's intention being, that they should not be troubled on this account, but quietly enjoy the free exercise of their religion, whilst they behave themselves dutifully and obediently to his government' and to stop all proceedings.[4] Thus it is not surprising that the practice among Jews was to try to take a low profile in public.

There were three major synagogues in London. Bevis Marks served the Sephardi community, and the Great in Duke's Place and the Hambro in Magpie Lane near Fenchurch Street served the Ashkenazi community. (Strictly speaking, the Duke's Place Synagogue was only formally named 'the Great' when it was rebuilt in 1790.) There was little contact between the two communities, even when it came to contact with the government. An example of this occurred in 1744 when Empress Maria Theresa of the Austrian Empire issued a decree expelling all Jews from Prague with effect from 1 January 1745. An appeal from the Bohemian Jews was sent to foreign Jewish communities eliciting their support, and representatives from Duke's Place Synagogue sent a petition to King George II, who instructed the British ambassador in Vienna to intervene and obtain a repeal.[5] The Sephardi community either were not asked or declined to participate in the petition. However, the Ashkenazi and Sephardi communities jointly created a fund for refugee relief. This is one of the first examples of British Jewry coming to the aid of overseas Jews through political and charitable activities and probably the first example of cooperation between the Ashkenazi and Sephardi communities, albeit for charitable and not political purposes.

However, this cooperation was not followed up immediately. In 1746, the Sephardim established a committee to look after the interests of the Jews of England and to represent them in discussions with government and other authorities. It is not clear but doubtful whether the Ashkenazim were asked to participate and it is also unclear whether the committee saw themselves as representing all Jews in Britain or just the Sephardim. In 1753, as a result of lobbying from this committee, the Jewish Naturalization Bill, commonly called the 'Jew Bill', was enacted by Parliament, giving foreign-born Jews the right to apply to Parliament for naturalization without the then existing prerequisite to receive the Holy Sacrament. These foreign-born Jews needed to be naturalized in order to own property. The Act was only permissive and of limited application in that each naturalization would still require an individual Act of Parliament, and thus only the wealthy could take advantage of it. Nonetheless it gave rise to a huge, and mainly antisemitic, clamour. For a few months in 1753 it was the major topic of political discussion in England and aroused unprecedented publicity. Rumours abounded and it was suggested that Jews would convert St Paul's to a synagogue and circumcise their tenants.[6] Voltaire remarked on the clamour as 'le cri de la nation' against further rights to the Jews.[7]

As a result of the clamour, the Act was repealed on 20 December 1753.[8] Horace Walpole wrote: 'the Jew Bill which superstitious bigots in the Commons repealed under the influence of a fanatical mob, thus demonstrating how much the age, enlightened as it is called, was still enslaved to the grossest and most vulgar prejudices'.[9] As soon as the Act was repealed all manifestations against Jews disappeared. As David Katz has written: 'After the Jew Bill had been repealed and the parliamentary elections of 1754 decided, the entire case was very nearly forgotten, and had no effect whatsoever on the status of Jews in this country.'[10] Or, as Voltaire put it, 'les Juifs se contentèrent d'être riches et libres'.[11] It was not until 1826 that the requirement to take the sacrament was abolished. The Sephardi committee that had been established to represent them to government was dissolved following the failure of the Act.

On 25 October 1760, George II died and was succeeded by his grandson George III. Most Jews in London were probably indifferent to this, but not so the leaders of Bevis Marks. Just over a week later, on 3 November, the *Mahamad* and elders of the Bevis Marks Synagogue resolved to establish a Committee of Deputies (from the Portuguese word *Deputado* meaning delegate or representative) and resolved:

> That seven Gentlemen of this body be appointed. That it be left to them to consider what should be done on the present occasion to testify to His Majesty (Geo III) our homage; and thereafter to deal with the most urgent matters which present themselves in connection with our Nation. And that the said gentlemen should not seek for new privileges for such nation without first communicating the matter to the Elders. And that the said gentlemen have power to confer with any persons whom they should think necessary. But that no business be transacted unless three of the said gentlemen be present.[12]

The seven were Jacob de Moseh Franco, Benjamin Mendes da Costa, Jacob Nunes Gonsales, Moseh de Joseph da Costa, Joseph Jesuran Rodrigues (also known as Joseph Salvador), Isaac Jesurun Alvares and Isaac Fernandes Nunes. This committee evolved into what we now call the Board of Deputies and thus these seven can be considered the first members of the Board of Deputies. It is very likely that the name derived from the 'London Board of Protestant Dissenting Deputies' that was created on 9 November 1732 by various Nonconformists to make representations to the government.[13] This Protestant committee included in its objects the support of the claims of British Jews to be relieved of similar disabilities.[14] In 1831 it petitioned both Houses of Parliament to repeal any laws that included civic disqualification for Jews and supported all the bills for Jewish emancipation.[15] As mentioned in the Introduction, this committee, initially of the Bevis Marks Synagogue, will be referred to in this book as 'the Board' unless the context decrees otherwise although, strictly speaking and for the pedantic, the name Board was first used in a letter in 1817. From about 1836 the term Board of Deputies was used frequently in the minutes and correspondence, but it was not until 1871 that the term was introduced into the constitution.

The Board met for the first time on Wednesday 19 November 1760 (11 Kislev 5521), under the chairmanship of Benjamin Mendes da Costa, who can thus be considered the first president of the Board. Benjamin Mendes da Costa was a merchant and philanthropist. He was born to former Marrano parents in Amsterdam, became a naturalized Englishman in 1725, and from 1730 to 1762 was a member of the *Mahamad* of Bevis Marks and for some years its president.[16] At its first meeting the Board resolved that a dutiful address should be presented to King George III to mark his accession and the death of His late Majesty, George II. Subsequently a deputation from the Board met with the Lord Chamberlain (the Duke of Devonshire) and asked him to assure His Majesty of the loyalty of the Portuguese Jews and to convey to him their congratulations.[17]

There was nothing unusual in this, in that on the accessions of George I in 1714 and George II in 1727 similar addresses had been presented. It is also likely, although no records are extant, that an address was conveyed to Queen Anne on her accession in 1702, particularly as she was considered a good friend of the Jews, having visited the original Sephardi synagogue in Creechurch Lane during Passover 1681. What was unusual was the reaction of the Ashkenazi community. They had not commented on the previous loyal addresses that had also omitted them, but this time they appear to have been furious.

Aaron Franks, the senior warden of the Great Synagogue, went to Bevis Marks on 7 December to lodge a formal complaint. As a result, a special meeting of the Board was called and Aaron Franks as well as Levy Salomons of the Hambro Synagogue were invited to attend. In its defence the Board explained that what had been done was according to precedent but, as the address was in the name of the Portuguese Nation, it was up to the others to submit their own address.[18] Alternatively, both communities could jointly present a loyal address to the new king's mother and other members of the royal family. This was agreed by the Ashkenazi representatives, who also suggested that in future each 'nation' or community should inform the other what it was doing in public affairs. The Board agreed to this but proposed that the Ashkenazim should create a similar committee to its own for this purpose. On 11 December, Aaron Franks (for the Ashkenazim) and Joseph Salvador (for the Sephardim) went to the palace, kissed hands with some members of the royal family, and expressed the humble devotion of both of their communities.

Another meeting of the Board was held on 14 December 1760, at which it was informed that the Ashkenazim had created a new committee to be called the 'German Secret Committee for Public Affairs', and its members were Aaron, Naphtali and Moses Franks, Michael Adolphus representing the Great, and Henry Isaac, Levy Salomons and Abraham Elias representing the Hambro. It was agreed that in all public matters of interest to the two communities (or nations), each committee should communicate with the other, and that the Board would report to the *Mahamad* what had happened and also request that it should have leave to spend money if necessary. The resolution, which was conveyed by letter to the Ashkenazi committee, read: 'Resolved that whenever any public affair should offer that may interest the two nations, we will on our parts communicate to the Board of the Dutch Jews' Synagogues what we may think proper should be done, and what we desire the said gentleman may do the same and make a minute thereof.'[19]

This was not a decision to combine the two committees, nor an agreement to always speak with one voice, nor even an agreement to discuss and agree the attitude or response of the Jewish communities. It was merely an agreement by the two bodies to tell each other what they were doing.

For the next seventy or so years, the Board met very infrequently and it seems the Secret Committee did not meet at all, or if it did it met in secret, as no records seem to exist. Stephen Massil has suggested that between the mid-1760s and the late 1780s, Naphtali Hart Myers and Naphtali Franks, wardens of the Great Synagogue, made representations to government and other persons of importance and influence and thus acted as a sort of two-man Board of Deputies of the Ashkenazim.[20] They involved themselves in the notorious Chelsea murder case whereas the Board itself did not, as the culprits were Ashkenazim.[21]

The early years of the Board itself included the first occasions for what proved to be some of the most enduring features of the Board. One was its concern in the affairs of Jews in foreign countries, particularly when they faced crises. Secondly, from its very early days the Board tried to insist that it was the sole representative body of the Jews in Britain and confirmed this in its first constitution in 1835, but this self-proclaimed monopoly did not always receive complete acceptance within the Jewish community. Thirdly, there were arguments, disputes and controversies between different members, groups and factions both within the Board and between the Board and individuals or groups outside the Board.

Finally, in the first few years the Board decided on a number of occasions to take no action or a rather low-key action on matters brought to its attention. This practice continued and has often led to very sharp criticism, and the Board has frequently been accused of 'keeping its head down below the parapet'.[22] One reason is that it seems to have inherited at the outset the long-standing Anglo-Jewish stance, as mentioned above, that Jews had nothing to fear if they kept a low profile and were law-abiding and peaceable.

The first foreign affairs issue tackled by the Board, towards the end of 1760, was a letter from the Jewish community in Jamaica. They complained that they were being ill-treated, that there was an order for them to serve in the militia and also a proposal to levy a special tax on Jews. With regard to service in the militia the Board responded that 'so long as martial law was in force, it was their duty to obey without question such orders as were published, even though it involved the desecration of the Sabbath'. It is not clear if the haham was consulted on the latter point. By happy chance the governor of Jamaica was in London and some members of the Board were able to meet with him, and he told them that he had already issued instructions to relieve the Jews of the proposed special tax, and promised to give added security to Jewish life and property in the island. A success for the new Board. Not so a few years later in 1766 when the Jews of Minorca asked the Board tointercede on their behalf, as they were not permitted to build a synagogue. The Board saw the colonial secretary, but without success.[23]

The Board did not meet again until 1778. At this time it was enlarged by three extra members: Moses Isaac Levy was appointed vice-president and secretary, a new post, and Joseph Salvador's name appeared for the first time as president. Joseph Salvador was born in London, the son of a wealthy Dutch merchant. He was very active in the campaign in 1853 for legislation to enable Jews to be naturalized without having received the Holy Sacrament; he served as a warden of Bevis Marks and was the first secretary of the Board and its second president.[24] It was at this stage that the records were written in English and not Portuguese, although some of the early minutes were translated in the Minute Book into English. In 1778 there was also a disagreement with the Ashkenazim who wanted the Board to support them in an application for relief from an Act impressing men into the king's service. The Board considered that an application for a general exemption of Jews was ill-advised, although there was nothing to prevent individuals applying for exemption. This was during the American War of

Independence and, although the Board had not involved itself, Jews participated in the General Fast on 13 December 1776, to wish success to the British army against the rebels in America. They saw it as an opportunity to demonstrate their loyalty to George III, and the haham, Moses Cohen D'Azevedo, preached a special sermon seeking 'Divine Assistance on behalf of His Majesty's Arms, that he may obtain victory and success'.[25]

In 1783 the wardens of Bevis Marks asked the Board to address the king on the American peace, but the Board refused, resolving 'that Peace or War being political concerns addressing would be taking a part in matters we ought to avoid, but an address may be proper when the subject relates to the King's person or family'.[26] This was an interesting distinction but not always adhered to subsequently. For example, on 8 May 1856 the Board congratulated Queen Victoria on the Peace following the Crimean War. It is necessary, however, to put this earlier refusal in context. For example, in 1787 the leaders of the Rome Jewish community enquired about the status of Jews in England and the reply indicated that the Jewish political position was one characterized by privileges rather than rights, and the Board was clearly anxious not to prejudice that position in any way. Furthermore, the American war was divisive in Britain.

In 1789 we have confirmation from the minutes of the Board that the Ashkenazim, who sometimes were present at meetings, were there only by invitation. A meeting was held to agree to send an address to King George III on his recovery from an illness.[27] Eleven years later, in 1800, the Board again met with representatives of the Ashkenazim to agree to send an address to the king on his escaping an assassination attempt. The king seems to have been doubly lucky on the day in question, 15 May 1800. In the morning, whilst reviewing the Grenadier Guards, a rifle was accidentally fired and the bullet hit a man standing about twenty yards from the king. In the evening the king attended a performance at the Drury Lane Theatre and a man called Hadfield stood up from the front row and fired a pistol at the king. Two bullets passed just above his head and lodged in the woodwork of the royal box. It later transpired that Hadfield missed his aim because a man near him pushed his arm just as he was firing. The man was a Jew, David Moses Dyte, whose son became honorary secretary to the Jewish Blind Society and his grandson surgeon to the Jewish Board of Guardians.[28] Dyte refused any honours, but asked to be given the monopoly of selling opera tickets. In their address to the king, the Board forbore to mention that it was a Jew who had saved his life.[29]

A disagreement developed in 1802 between some senior members of the Ashkenazi community and the Board. It was in connection with a scheme to merge together by Act of Parliament all Jewish charities in London. A new edition of Patrick Colquhoun's *Treatise on the Police of the Metropolis* drew attention to what he considered the endemic criminal activity of poor Jews, particularly those belonging to the Dutch (i.e. Ashkenazi) synagogues, and even went so far as to suggest that there was a code of corrupt commercial ethics to which all Jews subscribed. He described the poor Jews' situation as dire and that often their choice was between starvation and crime.[30] Joshua van Oven, who was honorary physician to the Great Synagogue, published a letter he had written to Colquhoun defending these poorer Jews and proposing a scheme to alleviate their position. In essence the proposal was to create a Jewish poor relief board that would have the powers to build hospitals, w rkhouses, trade schools and an old-age home. This was to be financed out of the poor rates paid by Jewish householders. In this proposal van Oven was strongly supported by Abraham Goldsmid, a leading and wealthy member of the community, and indeed Colquhoun was enthusiastic and gave great assistance in developing the plan.

The Ashkenazim petitioned Parliament for such an Act and the Board, on behalf of the Sephardi community, counter-petitioned. The Sephardim did not wish to be included, primarily because they thought they would have to bear a disproportionate share of the cost, but also they did not want to be considered part of the same political body as the Ashkenazim, nor did they wish to be associated with them in the public eye. They wanted a clause to be inserted such that the Sephardi community would be excluded from the provisions of the Act. Their letter to the lawyer responsible for drafting the Board's petition is of interest because it demonstrates the attitude of the Sephardi community towards their Ashkenazi brethren – they set out their differences, demographically, financially and in religious custom, and also noted that proportionately they had fewer poor members than the Ashkenazi community and that these were well looked after.[31] Some senior members of the Ashkenazi community were also opposed to the plan. They were concerned that it would give the rich great powers over the poor and would l a step towards the *kehilla* system in Central and Eastern Europe, which they deplored and considered inappropriate and unnecessary in Britain. Because of the opposition the scheme was abandoned. As a consequence of this reversal, Abraham Goldsmid and his brothers founded the Jews' Hospital in Mile End, which opened in 1806. This catered for the elderly as well as the young and comprised an old-age home and a trade school. It moved to Norwood in 1866, merging with the Jews' Orphan Asylum to create The Jews' Hospital and Orphan Asylum in 1876, becoming known throughout the Jewish community as Norwood.

It seems that in 1805 the Board decided to extend an olive branch to the Ashkenazim. It wrote to the wardens of three London synagogues (the Great, the Hambro and the New), inviting them to appoint representatives of their congregations. It read:

> We, the undersigned, appointed by the elders of our Portuguese Jew nation, by the appellation of Deputados, for the purpose of watching all Acts of Parliament, Acts of Government, laws, libels, addresses, or whatever else may affect the body of Jews, are desirous of acting with complete unison in all public concerns, therefore deem it necessary to assume the liberty of soliciting that your congregation in concert with the others will be pleased to appoint such gentlemen as you may think proper under the same denomination, that we may request their attendance as occasion requires, and have the pleasure of joining in all transactions that may concern us as one body. Should you think proper to comply with our recommendation, we beg you will transmit us the names of the gentlemen so appointed.[32]

Discussions with the Ashkenazim must have been difficult or long, or both, as there is no further correspondence or reference to this invitation until a meeting on 10 May 1812 of the governing body of the Great Synagogue where three 'deputados'[33] were appointed. The Board did not meet between 1805 and 1812, and the minutes of the 1812 meeting indicate that representatives from the Ashkenazi congregations were now members of the Board and not just 'in attendance'.[34] Their first 'deputies' were Moses Samuel, Samuel Samuel, Moses Levy Newton, Joseph Cohen, N. Hart, Levy Salomons, M. Salomons, Gabriel Cohen and G. Levien. So, at last, the Board became representative of all the main synagogues in London.

Antisemitism was alive and well in London at the beginning of the nineteenth century, and on two occasions the Board discussed this. Neither incident was of any great moment, but illustrates the Board's involvement and concern with such matters. The first occasion was in 1805 when the Board discussed what it considered a libel published in the *St James's Chronicle* and its lawyer was instructed to demand a retraction and apology and, failing that, to commence proceedings.[35] In November 1804 the paper had published a letter suggesting that the cause of a deadly fever epidemic in Gibraltar was the filth of the Jews living there and that anyone visiting the Jewish districts in London would find that 'the followers of Moses are the most nasty and filthy people under the canopy of Heaven'. The letter suggested the Jews 'should have a town to themselves ... and to wear a mark whenever they came into the city'.[36] The paper refused to retract and Counsel's advice was sought to ascertain the grounds for an action for libel. No further mention is made of this event in the minutes.

In 1817 a resolution was passed that steps should be taken 'to do away with the aspersion on the Jews with regard to the validity of their oath' made by John Ingram Lockhart, MP for Oxford, in the House of Commons. He claimed that Jews often made false oaths and suggested 'their Rabbies [*sic*] should enlighten and instruct these Jews on the subject of oaths'.[37] Regrettably, there are no records of what action was taken, but it is interesting to note that the resolution was only passed by seven votes to five.[38] What is surprising is that the Board never reacted to the antisemitic speeches and writings of William Cobbett – in particular the articles in his publication *Political Register*, where he always referred to the City of London as 'Jew Wen' and thought it a pity that England could not return to the sensible policy of Edward I and make the Jews wear badges.[39]

It seems from the absence of any records that the Board did not try to attend or make representations to the government regarding the Congress of Vienna in 1815, although representatives from Jewish communities in other countries did attend to plead for Jewish emancipation. Lucien Wolf was of the view that the Board might have felt that it could not raise with the government the question of religious liberty and Jewish emancipation. The British government would not have been prepared to listen to proposals that it should champion Jewish emancipation in Vienna, when its members could not even discuss Catholic emancipation among themselves, as it was a coalition with both pro- and anti-Catholic ministers.[40] The Board did not meet from 1812 to 1817 and at the meeting on 20 February 1817 there seems to have been some sort of internal argument regarding the calling of meetings, possibly because of this time-lapse. It was resolved that independent of the right of the president to call meetings when he thought proper, a meeting could also be called by five members of the

'Board' – the first time that the word 'Board' was used in the minutes, which also referred to 'the United Deputies of the four City Congregations'.[41]

In 1827 Nicholas I, the tsar of Russia, introduced a number of severe anti-Jewish measures. In particular there was one that required all districts of the Pale of Settlement to supply a number of recruits to the army. Each recruit would have to undergo six years of military training followed by service in the army of twenty-five years. There were great protests among Jews in Britain against these measures, including very large public meetings in December 1827 and January 1828.[42] There was neither mention of the Board at any of the meetings nor any mention of the meetings or the action of the tsar in Board minutes. Furthermore, at the January public meeting, mention was made that a notice had just been sent to all Jewish shopkeepers in Petticoat Lane that as they could not obtain the Freedom of the City of London they must vacate their shops. Two issues for the Board, but not taken up by them.

In 1828 Moses Montefiore was elected a deputy.

NOTES

1. Todd M. Endelman, *The Jews of Britain, 1656 to 2000* (London: University of California Press, 2002), Chapter 2.
2. Harold Pollins, *Economic History of the Jews in England* (London: Littman Library, 1982), p.56.
3. Public Records Office (PRO), *Calendar of State Papers, Domestic Series*, 1663–4, p.672.
4. The National Archive, Public Records Office [TNA PRO], PC2/71, p.157.
5. Copy of Decree, the appeal from the Bohemian Jews, the petition to King George II and the letter to the British ambassador in Vienna are in Lucien Wolf, *Notes on the Diplomatic History of the Jewish Question* (London: Jewish Historical Society of England, 1919), pp.7–11.
6. Endelman, *The Jews of Britain*, p.75.
7. Voltaire, *Essai sur les moeurs et l'ésprit des nations et sur les principaux aits de l'histoire depuis Charlemagne jusqu'à Louis XIII, Tome 2* (Paris: Classiques Garrier, 1963), p.63.
8. Davis S. Katz, *The Jews in the History of England* (Oxford: Clarendon, 1996), Chapter 6.
9. Martin Kallich, *Horace Walpole* (New York: Twayne, 1971), p.46.
10. Katz, *The Jews in the History of England*, p.240.
11. 'The Jews were satisfied to be rich and free', Voltaire, *Essai sur les moeurs et l'ésprit des nation*, p.63.
12. BOD, Minute Book 1, p.A; Charles H.L. Emanuel, *A Century and a Half of Jewish History* (London: Routledge, 1910), p.1.
13. Bernard Lord Manning, *The Protestant Dissenting Deputies* (Cambridge: Cambridge University Press, 1952).
14. Sidney Salomon, 'Board of Deputies of British Jews, 1760–1960', *Jewish Affairs*, 15, 11 (October 1960), p.4.
15. Manning, *Protestant Dissenting Deputies*, pp.211–12.
16. William Rubinstein, *Dictionary of Anglo-Jewish History* (Basingstoke: Palgrave Macmillan, 2010) [Forthcoming].
17. BOD, Minute Book 1, p.1.

18. Ibid., p.3. The address stated: 'on behalf of the community of Portuguese Jews'.
19. Ibid., p.8.
20. Stephen Massil, 'Naphtali Hart Myers (1711?–1788): New Yorker and Londoner', unpublished paper presented to the Jewish Historical Society of England on 17 December 2009.
21. Ibid; Raphael Langham, *The Jews in Britain: A Chronology* (Basingstoke: Palgrave, 2005), p.46.
22. Stephen Brook, *The Club: The Jews of Modern Britain* (London: Constable, 1989), Chapter 16.
23. BOD, Minute Book 1, pp.4–5.
24. Rubinstein, *Dictionary of Anglo-Jewish History*.
25. I. Abrahams, 'Hebrew Loyalty under the First Four Georges', *Transactions of the Jewish Historical Society of England*, 9 (1918–20), p.120.
26. BOD, Minute Book 1, p.18.
27. Ibid., p.19.
28. James Picciotto, *Sketches of Anglo-Jewish History*, revised and edited with a prologue, notes and an epilogue by Israel Finestein (London: Soncino Press, 1956) p.269.
29. BOD, Minute Book 1, p.26.
30. Patrick Colquhoun, *Treatise on the Police of the Metropolis*, 6th enlarged edn (London: Mawman, 1800).
31. See BOD, Minute Book 1, p.27 and final pages (unnumbered).
32. Ibid., p.28.
33. Archives of the United Synagogue, London Metropolitan Archives, ACC/2712/GTS/00/2.
34. BOD, Minute Book 1, p.31.
35. Ibid., p.27.
36. *St James's Chronicle*, 13–15 November 1804, p.4.
37. *Hansard*, Vol. 36 (1817), p.821.
38. BOD, Minute Book 1, p.32.
39. John W. Osborne, 'William Cobbett's Anti-Semitism', *The Historian*, 47 (1984), pp.86–92; Simon Schama, *A History of Britain, Volume, 1776–2000: The Fate of Empire*, paperback edn (London: BBC, 2003) p.102.
40. Wolf, *Notes on the Diplomatic History of the Jewish Question*, p.12.
41. Ibid., p.32.
42. *The Times*, 2 January 1828, p.2.

2 The Montefiore Era, 1828–1874

By 1830 the number of Jews in Britain had increased from about 10,000 in 1760 when the Board was founded to about 30,000, two-thirds of whom lived in London. Most of this increase was through immigration and the majority were economic migrants, though some had fled persecution. The social character of the community was beginning to change as the Jews became more affluent, although this was relative since there were still a great number of very poor Jews. Many disabilities remained, in particular oath requirements that included the words 'on the true faith of a Christian'.

Britain had also changed; it was more tolerant of religious minorities such as Nonconformists and Catholics, and political reform was on the agenda. Britain had become a prosperous country and was seen as one of the most powerful countries in Europe.[1]

In the late 1820s, some of the leaders of the Jewish community, sensing these changes, wanted to move faster in removing their disabilities than most members of the Board. They took the view that Jews should be treated as all other subjects and have the same privileges and that these should not depend on religion. Others took a different view and considered that Jews should have certain rights as a privilege, but need not have all rights, particularly if this involved any compromise on orthodox religious observance. The former group included Isaac and Francis Goldsmid, Nathan and Lionel Rothschild and David Salomons. The latter group included Moses Montefiore as well as most members of the Board. There was also a difference of opinion on the pace of changing disabilities, with some pressing for fairly rapid and comprehensive change and others preferring a more gradual approach, particularly as they considered this more likely to be successful. These differences can be seen in the Emancipation and Marriage Law issues discussed below, and curiously had the result of transforming the Board. Its membership remained fairly exclusive, even elitist, but it began to meet more regularly and tried to expand the number of synagogues it represented. An issue emerged that has dogged the Board ever since as to whom it represented and whether its self-assumed role as the spokesman for the Jews of Britain should be exclusive.

1. THE BOARD

Leadership

In April 1835, Moses Montefiore was elected president of the Board. He was born in Livorno, Italy (during a visit there by his parents), on 24 October 1784, but grew up in London, where he made his fortune on the Stock Exchange. He died on 28 July 1885. Montefiore was well connected. He married Judith Barent Cohen, whose sister Hannah was married to Nathan Rothschild. In 1836, Montefiore reduced his business interests and devoted himself to philanthropy and communal politics. He a l his wife visited the Holy Land in 1827 for the first of many such visits, and during this visit he reverted to strict Jewish observance.[2] He was president of the Board from 1835 to 1874, with gaps when others deputized for him during his many foreign travels. He was elected a fellow of the Royal Society in 1836, sheriff of the City of London from 1837 to 1838, knighted in November 1837, and created a baronet in 1846.

Montefiore was loved and idolized by many Jews in Britain and elsewhere. He was a giant of a man both literally and metaphorically and an autocratic leader of the Board, and this very obstinacy often led to him failing to gain the support of his colleagues on some important issues. Indeed, it has been suggested by some historians that, particularly in the latter years of his tenure, he held up changes that were vitally needed.[3] On the other hand, it was during his period of office that the Board emerged from being a lacklustre and lethargic body into a much more dynamic and proactive one. His role as president of the Board and as one of the leaders of the British Jewish community is constantly being reappraised and there is no uniformity in the views expressed.[4]

Representation

One of Montefiore's first acts as president was to form a committee, under his cha manship, to frame the Board's first constitution. This constitution was adopted on 7 March 1836 and is reproduced in Appendix 1. In essence it renamed the Board as the 'Committee of Deputies of the British Jews'; it stated that the Board would be the sole body representing all British Jews; that all congregations of Jews in the United Kingdom could appoint deputies, provided the congregation bore its proper proportion of the expenses of the Board; and that there should be new elections for deputies every five years. Letters were sent to the Western and Liverpool Synagogues, and the president was empowered to invite other synagogues, if they were of sufficient size, to send deputies. It is not clear how many invitations were sent, but the results were not encouraging as only the Western Synagogue in Maiden Lane responded favourably and the provincial synagogues either did not reply or said that lack of funds and the indifference of their members meant they could not join. A second attempt was made in 1838, but with much the same lack of response. The Sunderland Synagogue said it would send a deputy, but shortly afterwards withdrew for financial reasons. The number of synagogues adhering to the Board grew very slowly indeed, four in 1835 only rising to eight by 1850. This was primarily for financial reasons.

The adoption of the constitution was followed a couple of years later by the introduction of by-laws. The Board claimed, correctly, that it was the only representative body of British Jews but it was not very representative. In 1836 there were no provincial congregations with deputies on the Board, and many smaller London congregations were not represented either. Within congregations that were represented, only seat holders could vote and be elected as deputies, and seat holders were only a part of the membership of the synagogues and excluded women. Furthermore, many Jews were not members of a synagogue. This lack of proper representation should also be seen in the context of the times in Britain where the Chartism movement, which demanded more rights and representation for the working classes, was at its height in the period 1838 to 1848.[5]

Montefiore wasted little time in informing the government of the Board's self-adopted powers. On 24 May 1836 the Board resolved that he should write to the Chancellor of the Exchequer that the 'Board of Deputies of British Jews constituted the only official channel of communication for the secular and political interests of the Jews'.[6] The reason the Board wrote to the Chancellor of the Exchequer, Thomas Spring Rice, was because he was the most senior government minister sympathetic to Jewish emancipation and was about to introduce a bill into the House of Commons to this effect.[7] This assertiveness seems to have upset some other leading members of the community and as a result a conference of leading Jewish dignitaries, under the auspices of the Board, was held in early June. The only outcome seems to have been another letter from Montefiore to the Chancellor reiterating that the Board was the only institutional organ that could satisfactorily represent the Jews. It worked, because shortly afterwards the president of the Board was given statutory powers under the Marriage Registration Act of 1836 to certify which Jewish synagogue secretaries or officials could be licensed to certify marriages. It is clear, though, that this restiveness with and within the Board continued, as later in 1836 the Board considered, but rejected, a motion that the deputies should resign and resubmit themselves for re-election on a more popular basis. The issue of some form of accountability must have been on the agenda as it was decided fairly shortly afterwards to publish half-yearly reports to constituent synagogues.

In January 1838 there was a further debate on elections and this time a motion that deputies should resign so as to precipitate new elections was passed by a majority of one. It does not appear to have been acted on as elections were in practice not held until 1841 as envisaged under the 1836 constitution. The demand for a more popular basis for holding elections suggested that dissatisfaction had been expressed with the methods adopted by constituent synagogues for electing deputies and was intended to ask them to consider more democratic methods, perhaps under the influence of the Chartism movement in the country at large.[8] It would seem that some synagogues did not have a proper procedure for proposing and seconding members who wished to stand as deputies, and also that not all seat holders were able to vote. One suspects that in some synagogues the honorary officers chose their deputies and avoided proper elections.

All of this infuriated Isaac Goldsmid, already out of sorts with the Board over its seeming lack of help and support in the emancipation struggle (see below). On 26 September 1838 he wrote a letter to the secretary of the Great Synagogue, objecting strongly to the clause in the constitution that declared the Board as the sole medium of communication with the government on behalf of British Jewry, and pointing out that it did not represent any provincial community. Furthermore, he resented the implication that a member of a synagogue that had deputies was deprived of the right of independent action. He considered the Board too large and unwieldy, with no powers of delegation, and thus unable to deal with urgent matters. He pointed out that the Board often had to ask for amending legislation because it had failed to comment on the bills when they were still under discussion. This was a comment in connection with the issues that arose as a result of the Matrimonial Causes Act of 1835 (see below). He complained that the Board was apathetic concerning emancipation and cited its failure to support him financially in connection with the drafting of bills on the subject.[9]

This letter was forwarded to the Board and Isaac Goldsmid and his son Francis were invited to discuss the letter with Board members, who were conciliatory. On 4 December 1838 they passed a motion that no individuals who were members of a synagogue or of the Board were precluded from exerting their influence with the government for the promotion of their civil rights. This did not go far enough for Goldsmid, who expressed his dissatisfaction and when, in the following year, he was elected a deputy from the Great Synagogue he declined the appointment. He was not finished yet. In 1840 the Board presented a loyal address on behalf of the Jews of Britain to Queen Victoria on her marriage. Imagine its consternation when it discovered that a separate loyal address was presented to Her Majesty by Isaac Goldsmid on behalf of the Western Synagogue. The Board protested to the Western Synagogue that this was an unauthorized act and manifested to the world 'a want of general co-operation and of unanimity'.[10]

The Jewish Chronicle *and the Board*

The *Jewish Chronicle* (JC) was founded in November 1841 but folded in May 1842. It was revived in October 1844 under new ownership and management and from that time there has been a love–hate relationship between the paper and the Board. The comments and opinions of the JC on the Board are important because not only is the JC the Jewish paper of record or, as it used to call itself, 'The Organ of Anglo-Jewry', but its opinion columns and letter pages are one of the main means we have of examining the views on the Board of the community at large, or rather some of the more articulate members of the community. As David Cesarani has pointed out, there was some active opposition to the establishment of the JC, notably from some of the leaders of Anglo-Jewry who resented the idea of public criticism, but also from the paid officials of communal organizations who were afraid of coming under general scrutiny.[11] It is doubtful that Moses Montefiore was among this former group as he supported the project financially and took out ten subscriptions. At first the JC limited itself to a few announcements concerning the activities of the Board, with occasional praise for its actions. In fact its first comment as such on the Board, as opposed to announcements or news items, was on 7 February 1845. After a preamble praising the Board for its exertions on behalf of the community, it then continued by telling the Board that its approach to the emancipation issue was not good or strong enough. The *JC* proposed that all Jews supporting emancipation should sign a petition and that such a petition would carry more weight with the government than representations by the Board. Interestingly, it also proposed that the petition should not emanate from the Board but be prepared by the recently formed Jewish Literary Institute at Sussex Hall.[12] Two weeks later the *JC* claimed some sort of victory in that it stated that its plan had been favourably received by many in the community, including a number of deputies. In practice no such petition was prepared.

In 1847 the *JC* seems to have gone on the warpath against the Board, probably stimulated by restlessness with the Board within the Manchester Jewish community that led to the election of three Mancunian deputies replacing those based in London.[13] From April onwards it published a whole series of letters highly critical of the Board, its structure, its activities and its apathy. There was no response either officially from the Board or from any deputies until on 17 September there was a letter from Jacob Franklin, recently elected as a deputy for the Halliwell Street Synagogue in Manchester, who expressed surprise at the attitude of most deputies who saw their role as solely watching parliamentary proceedings to ensure that no legislation was enacted that might be against the interest of Jews, and he found himself in a minority who saw a much wider role. This letter must have been written as the result of the president using his casting vote against a motion at the Board's meeting on 30 August 1847, proposing that the Board collect statistical returns for all Jews in the British Empire. Another motion, that in order to assist the deputies from provincial communities there should be an annual meeting of the Board in London fixed well in advance, was also rejected.[14] In early October one of the two Manchester synagogues, who had elected deputies for the first time in June 1847, passed a resolution instructing their deputies to request more openness from the Board by agreeing to admit the press and also toextend its activities. These requests stimulated the *JC* to publish a leader in which it expressed this view:

> We deem it highly important to the interests of the Jewish Community of Britain, that some public and above all spirited

demonstration be made, either to awaken the Board of Deputies from the utter listlessness which they manifest for all British Jewish interests, or that the body of the Jews should take into consideration the entire abolition of so useless a board, and a construction of a new one more fitting the time.[15]

The Board did not respond, the Manchester petition was rejected, and no one took any initiative to try to organize a new body. In fact the Board had clearly become unhappy at the actions of the deputies from provincial congregations and at a meeting on 3 November 1847 resolved that, in future, provincial congregations joining the Board would be limited to one deputy each.[16]

However, the Manchester congregation did not give up easily. On 27 April 1848 the Board held a special meeting to consider a new petition from the Manchester New Synagogue.[17] The editor of the *JC* had asked permission to attend that meeting and report the proceedings, but this was refused. In fact the first proposal in the petition was that reporters from the Jewish press should be admitted to meetings of the Board. This was rejected by a large majority. The second proposal was that the Board should collect statistics from all the Jewish congregations in the empire regarding numbers, state of education and schools, occupations, charitable institutions, literary and scientific institutions, form of governance, state and number of impoverished Jews. The grounds for this were that this information was vital so that the Board could act to improve the overall situation of the Jews. This proposal was also rejected.[18] The *JC* reported the meeting even though it was not permitted to have a reporter there. It had explained two weeks previously that it got its information through a member of the Board and pointed out how this made a mockery of the Board's refusal to admit reporters.[19]

The rejection of the Manchester proposals formed the front-page article in the 5 May 1848 edition of the *JC*. This article pointed out that the Board's contention that constitutionally it could only superintend the political affairs of British Jews, but could not organize or regulate the improvement of their social condition, was at variance with the actual words in the constitution that required it to 'deliberate on what may conduce to their welfare'. It contended that the reality was that the Board did not want to get involved and yet there was no other Jewish institution in Britain to which recourse could be had for dealing with social matters. It urged the deputies to extend their powers if they thought it necessary and were certain that they would get the support of the members of their constituent synagogues.[20] This article did not give rise to any correspondence in the *JC* and at first seems to have been ignored by the Board. However, at the beginning of 1849 the secretary of the Board started to collect some basic statistics from the community, on numbers of seat holders and numbers of births, marriages and deaths. It is likely that the reason to start collecting these statistics was not the result of the proposals from Manchester but a report received by the Board in December 1848 from the Registrar General, giving a statistical breakdown of Jewish marriages that were certified in 1846. These criticisms of the Board from letter and leader writers in the *JC* through to disillusioned deputies and communities did not bear fruit at first but clearly influenced opinion among at least some of the leaders of the Anglo-Jewish community.

Enter the Reform

The Board of Deputies was under the ecclesiastical guidance of the chief rabbi and the haham, under a clause added to the constitution in 1841. Thus a member of the Reform West London Synagogue, which had no allegiance to either the chief rabbi or the haham, could not be eligible to become a deputy, or so it seemed. From its establishment in 1842, however, no approach seems to have been made by the West London Synagogue to become a constituent of the Board and elect deputies. In 1853 a by-election for a deputy was held at the Great Synagogue. The successful candidate was Benjamin Phillips, who was to become the second Jewish Lord Mayor of London in 1865. His election programme included removing restrictions on members of the West London Synagogue from participating in communal affairs, and he objected to the secret manner in which the Board's affairs were carried out. The normal triennial elections to the Board were due later in the year and these issues were highlighted by the *JC*; this, for the first time ever, created great interest in the elections. Other issues that emerged were wider provincial representation, the institution of some sort of committee system to enable greater speed in dealing with matters, a more formalized arrangement for convening meetings instead of them being at the whim of the president, a wider franchise for the election of deputies and for representation to be proportionate to membership rather than financial contribution. The Board was seen to be controlled by a small group of London-based 'Jewish aristocrats' and there had emerged many affluent middle-class Jews who wanted a say in its activities.[21]

The results of the May 1853 election speak for themselves. In the 1850 elections, six London synagogues were represented by twenty-six deputies and in 1853 the outcome was the same. However, in the provinces, whereas following the 1850 elections there were only two deputies (both resident in London) representing two synagogues, in 1853 the numbers changed radically to thirty-two deputies representing twenty-nine synagogues.

At one of the first meetings of the new Board on 31 August 1853 'strangers were spied'.[22] These were three deputies elected by provincial communities. All three lived in London and were members of Orthodox synagogues both in London and in the towns they represented. However, they were also members of the Reform West London Synagogue. They were asked to withdraw but refused, and the police were called but did not enter the meeting room. The president left the chair and the deputies dispersed in some disarray. In fact there were four recently elected deputies who were members of the West London Synagogue, but one of them lived in Sunderland and did not attend the meeting of the Board on 31 August. At the next meeting of the Board it was proposed that any member of a congregation which did not conform in religious matters to the ecclesiastical authorities of the Board – that is, the chief rabbi or the principal rabbi of Bevis Marks – should be disqualified. Montefiore expressed sympathy with the motion but, as the debate indicated that opinion seemed evenly divided, he decided to hold a special meeting to consider the matter, at which there might be a fuller attendance.

At that follow-up meeting all the four asked to be admitted and, after a rather acrimonious debate, when it was also alleged that there had been some irregularities in their elections, it was decided by a majority of one to postpone the matter and that a committee of five deputies should meet with five members of the West London Synagogue with a view to effecting a reconciliation between that congregation and the ecclesiastical authorities of the Board. This proved to be a complete fiasco as the West London Synagogue refused to cooperate and meet with the committee. In the meantime, the Hambro Synagogue petitioned the Board against admitting the four.

The points at issue were complex. Technically they involved the constitution of the Board, but at heart they were concerned with the very nature of the Board and how it should operate. Under the then constitution a deputy had to be a *yehid* or *baal habayit*, these terms being understood as being seat holders of a synagogue. However, the four could be barred as they were members of a Reform congregation and the ecclesiastical authorities of the Board did not accept any Reform synagogue as such, and even if they were simultaneously members of an Orthodox synagogue their parallel membership of a Reform congregation meant that they had to be excluded. In essence, the issue was: should the Board follow the guidance of its ecclesiastical authorities in *all* areas or could it be argued and accepted that their writ did not cover this particular area? Was the Board a religious assembly or was it a secular one and only under the guidance of its ecclesiastical authorities when it was dealing with religious matters? Ironically, a parallel was drawn with the parliamentary emancipation debate, where the Jewish lobby was arguing that the wording of the oath (in effect a religious requirement) should be changed.

Meetings followed meetings and the matter came to a head at a meeting on 8 December 1853. The voting on a motion to exclude the four was tied at twenty-three votes for and twenty-three against. Montefiore, as president, exercised his casting vote in favour of the motion. The matter did not end there. There was uproar in the community and much protest at Montefiore's casting vote. Many deputies resigned. In 1855 there was an attempted 'putsch' whilst Montefiore was out of the country. A group of deputies, led by David Salomons, proposed to remove from the president the power to certify marriage secretaries and thereby secure reconciliation with the West London Synagogue to whom the president had refused to issue such a certificate. The coup failed.[23] The disillusionment was reflected in the results of the triennial elections in 1856. In London the number of synagogues electing deputies remained the same at six but the number of their deputies fell from twenty-six to seventeen. In the provinces the fall was even more drastic. The number of synagogues represented fell from twenty-nine to twelve and the number of deputies fell from thirty-two to fourteen. Montefiore remained president for another twenty years.

It took another twenty years before the Board agreed to admit deputies from the West London Synagogue, and in fact at that meeting in December 1873 only one vote was cast against the motion. Moses Montefiore was not at the meeting and he retired from the presidency a few months later. The West London Synagogue, however, refused to accept the invitation on the grounds that some of the clauses in the Board's constitution were inconsistent with the principles on which the synagogue had been founded, primarily the rule that stated that guidance on religious matters should be in the hands of the chief rabbi and the rabbis of Bevis Marks. The West London Synagogue also did not like a clause that effectively gave a veto to any synagogue where the majority of its members disagreed with any action about to be taken by the Board. Although the West London Synagogue refused to appoint deputies, a number of its members became deputies for provincial congregations and there were no objections as there had been in 1853. In December 1885, one month after the death of Sir Moses, the Board amended its constitution to remove the difficulties that prevented the West London Synagogue from joining. Essentially, it added a clause stating that nothing in the constitution should affect the internal affairs of any congregation that was certified under the 1856 Marriage Act, which was the act that gave powers for marriage certification to the West London Synagogue. At the triennial election in 1886 the West London Synagogue returned deputies for the first time, thirty-three years after the 1853 crisis. In the 1887 annual report of the Board this event was called 'a gratifying circumstance'.[24]

It must be mentioned that every issue of the *JC* during the dispute in 1853 carried news reports, letters and sometimes feature articles. There were editorials galore and two supplements were issued, one on the crisis meeting of the Board held on 8 September 1853 (the first Board meeting to which the Jewish press were admitted) and another containing the avalanche of letters the paper had received on the subject. The *JC* was clearly on the side of those that wanted to restructure the Board and supported the admission of the 'four'. Indeed, it can be argued that it was the views of the *JC* on the structure of the Board that led in the first place to the 'manifestos' of those candidates who demanded major changes. It was the *JC* that pointed out that the crisis was ruining the hopes of political emancipation, as 'how could we ask for religious tolerance from Parliament when we did not exercise it ourselves'.[25]

Reorganization
There was another side to the Reform synagogue crisis. Many deputies were highly critical of how the Board was run. Among their proposals was that the Board should delegate some of its powers to committees. In 1854 the Board decided to convert an informal committee established in 1846, which had the task of overseeing matters introduced into Parliament that might affect Jews, into the Law, Parliamentary and General Purposes Committee. This presaged a number of other changes, some requiring changes to the constitution. In 1857 it was decided to appoint, for the first time, a vice-president, a treasurer and

two auditors. These four, together with the president, formed the first honorary officers of the Board. Following complaints from several constituent synagogues, the Board reviewed, in 1858, its method of assessing contributions to meet its expenses. It decided to change from a rather opaque method to determining the subscription per synagogue in proportion to its number of deputies. The number of deputies was also reviewed and it was decided that the six main London synagogues would continue to have in total sixteen deputies, and that any provincial synagogue which wished to be represented could have one deputy provided it had twenty male seat holders. Clearly the Board wanted to ensure that London still had control. These changes took effect from the elections in May 1859.

It is interesting to observe that many of the various proposals for change that had been part of the agenda of those advocating changes at the time of the 1853 elections had now actually been made, not with any great fanfare but slowly and quietly. They included the admittance of the press to Board meetings, increasing the number of honorary officers from one (the president) to five, delegating to committees, and creating ad hoc sub-committees to consider important issues as they arose, and a more equitable arrangement for determining subscriptions by participating congregations. One suspects, although there is no evidence to support this one way or the other, that this was due to the quiet and relentless pursuit of these objectives by a few deputies. There remained some other important demands, including more representation from provincial communities, representation to be proportionate to synagogue membership and greater democracy and openness regarding elections of deputies. This last point was addressed in January 1874 when a revised constitution was agreed that required that election of deputies should be by nomination and ballot, whereas previously there were no formal requirements. It was nearly forty years since dissatisfaction had first been expressed at the Board regarding the methods used by some congregations for 'electing' deputies.

The Anglo-Jewish Association

In 1871 the Anglo-Jewish Association (AJA) was founded. Its objects were to defend Jewish interests throughout the world. One of the reasons for its formation was a weakening of the Alliance Israelite Universelle as a consequence of the Franco-Prussian war of 1870. Another reason was no doubt that a number of its founders, among whom were some prominent members of the West London Synagogue, were dissatisfied with the Board for one reason or another and wanted to establish a new, not necessarily rival, organization. According to Vivian Lipman, the general view at the time was that the Board was under-financed, unduly rigid in procedure, and given so much to the passing of formal resolutions that it was known as 'The Board of Congratulations and Condolence'.[26] The AJA asked the Board to cooperate with it when the occasion might require it, but the Board responded that for over one hundred years it had undertaken the cases of Jews persecuted abroad and intended continuing to do so, and thus saw no reason to cooperate.

In 1873 the Board changed its constitution to emphasize this point by inserting a provision that the Board should exert its influence in favour of foreign Jewish communities and individuals suffering from wrong or oppression or misfortune. It had always done this without such a provision. However, it added a rider that the Board might cooperate for such purpose with any bodies, persons or institutions – a sort of constitutional olive branch to the AJA. Overtures by the AJA were reopened in June 1876, but came to nothing, mainly as a result of opposition from a majority of deputies. Their objections included the view that the Board must reserve to itself the power of independent action as it was purely a British body but the AJA was closely identified with foreign bodies, and that the Board was representative of the majority of Jewish congregations in Britain whereas the AJA represented only those who subscribed to its funds.[27]

In 1877, following the triennial election of a new Board, it was decided to reopen discussions with the AJA.[28] This was in part to remedy an anomalous – and with the benefit of hindsight, some would now say ill-advised – situation, particularly as some of the leading and most influential figures in the Jewish community were members of the AJA but not the Board, and the main spokesmen in the House of Commons on Jewish 'foreign' issues were members of the Reform synagogues, and thus precluded from being deputies.[29] Agreement was reached in April 1878 when the Board joined with the AJA to form the Conjoint Foreign Committee (Conjoint), consisting of seven representatives from each of the two parent bodies.[30] If there was agreement all well and good, if not the matter was referred to each parent body and if they still disagreed each parent body could make separate representations on the issue. Thereafter, until well into the twentieth century, matters affecting Jews in foreign countries were seldom discussed at Board meetings, except to the extent of discussing reports it received from its representatives on the Conjoint. When the Conjoint was disbanded in 1917 the Board continued its partnership with the AJA in foreign matters through the Conjoint's successor the Joint Foreign Committee (the Joint).

2. HOME ISSUES

Emancipation[31]

In 1828 the Board addressed for the first time actions that could be taken to remove various disabilities of the Jews that made it impossible for them to qualify for certain offices, in particular oaths that included the words 'on the true faith of a Christian'. This was the start of a campaign that was to end in July 1858 with the admittance of Lionel Rothschild to the House of Commons. Although the Board must be credited with supporting the initiative that led to the start of the campaign, its eventual success lay not with the Board but with a few prominent individuals in the Jewish community with the aid and support of many liberals in the wider community. On 28 April 1828, the Board discussed a bill that was before Parliament repealing the Test and Corporation Acts that imposed the necessity for receiving the Holy Sacrament in order to qualify for certain offices. The bill was aimed to relieve Protestant Nonconformists from this requirement; this was against a background of a more tolerant society and the view that they were no longer a threat to the established Church. The Board had hoped, perhaps naively, that the bill would relieve the Jews as well, and decided to petition the House of Lords in order to protect the interest of the Jews. However, the bill replaced the Holy Sacrament obligation by a requirement to take certain oaths for public office including a declaration of loyalty, and in the House of Lords the bishops succeeded in requiring the words 'on the true faith of a Christian' to be added to this oath.[32] As a consequence the position of Jews was worsened. It is uncertain whether this amendment was added specifically against Jews or more generally against non-Christians including atheists and deists.

In 1829 a bill was enacted that gave Catholics full relief, but it seems that although there was a lot of pressure for toleration it was much more in response to political demands from the Irish. In February 1829, Isaac Goldsmid attended a meeting of the Board and explained the various steps he had taken on his own initiative, including briefing a number of peers and MPs who were sympathetic and promised to support measures that might be submitted to Parliament for the relief of the Jews. At a meeting of the Board on 16 April 1829 it was decided to draft a petition for submission to Parliament to be signed by all the deputies as well as Isaac Goldsmid and Lionel Rothschild. It is interesting to note that at that meeting Lionel Rothschild (who was not a deputy but was there by invitation) suggested that the reliefs demanded should give full protection for the holding of land and property as well as the removal of civic and political disabilities and that the petition should only be signed by Jews born in Britain. He also strenuously advised that there should be no publicity for the petition and it should not be published in the press, as any controversy would be fatal to the objectives.[33] A deputation met the prime minister, the Duke of Wellington, who was not prepared to support the measure in view of the great difficulty he had experienced in carrying through the Catholic Relief Bill. Because of the high probability that the bill would be lost and because of the great potential expense, the Board decided not to proceed further.

In May 1830 a new petition was prepared and presented to Parliament. This time a bill was introduced by Sir Robert Grant, a supporter of religious toleration and in particular an advocate for the removal of Jewish disabilities, but was lost at the second reading in the House of Commons. In 1831 Isaac Goldsmid proposed to the Board that it should make another attempt, this time through the House of Lords, but this was rejected on grounds of cost. Nonetheless Goldsmid and his allies went ahead and in 1833 another bill similar to the 1830 one was introduced, again by Sir Robert Grant, which was passed by the Commons but defeated in the Lords. Similar measures to remove all Jewish disabilities and alter the oaths for taking a seat in the House of Commons were introduced ten times between 1834 and 1857. All had a similar fate, passed by the Commons but rejected by the Lords.[34]

The majority of Jews were in fact indifferent to the debate on full emancipation – they had little or nothing to gain and their concerns were elsewhere, primarily economic survival. Neither Moses Montefiore nor the two chief rabbis during the period concerned were at all enthusiastic, mainly because they thought that public office would lead the holder to neglecting his religious duties and to assimilation. There were also Jews who were opposed on the grounds that the Jews were in exile and must await their return to the Promised Land. Furthermore, as far as Montefiore was concerned (and in practice this meant the Board as well), it ranked lower in priority than ensuring that government legislation did not impinge adversely on the maintenance of strict Jewish observance and in assisting foreign Jewries when called on to do so.[35] On the other hand, Montefiore was very active in lobbying for emancipation, particularly in the 1830s,[36] but not through the Board.

Although the Board was involved at the start of the emancipation campaign it did not participate wholeheartedly in the struggle. The leader of the campaign was Isaac Goldsmid and at first he assured the Board he would not take any decisive step, and particularly a public one, without consulting it. However, when in 1831 the Board refused his request for another petition to Parliament their paths began to diverge. In fact there is no mention of emancipation in the minutes of Board meetings between 1831 and 1836 and indeed the Board as such seemed hardly involved until 1845, although it is clear from Montefiore's diaries that he was active and helpful behind the scenes, although rather reluctant.[37] In 1845 two Jewish deputations on the subject of emancipation met the prime minister, Sir Robert Peel. One was led by the Goldsmids and the other was a deputation from the Board led by Montefiore. Whereas the Goldsmid deputation demanded complete emancipation, the Board deputation was prepared to accept just the abolition of municipal disabilities. The Goldsmid deputation comprised essentially members of the Reform West London Synagogue, and David Feldman has concluded that this indicated that they challenged not only the ecclesiastical authority but also the temporal authority within Anglo-Jewry.[38]

The meeting of the deputation from the Board with the prime minister was held on 19 February, and three days later Peel ordered the Lord Chancellor to prepare a bill outlawing all remaining municipal disabilities. This led to an act passed in July 1845 that enabled any Jew to use an acceptable declaration to take up a municipal office. On the same day, and one can assume as a direct result of the Board's representations, Peel appointed a Royal Commission to report on penalties and disabilities in regard to religious opinions as they affected all non-Anglicans, with the exception that the question of those disabilities excluding Jews from Parliament should not be addressed. The Royal Commission reported at the end of May, and was followed a year later by the Religious Disabilities Act 1846 which provided, inter alia:

> That from and after the commencement of this Act Her Majesty's subjects professing the Jewish Religion in respect to their Schools, Places for Religious Worship, Education and Charitable Purposes and the property held therewith, shall be subject to the same Laws

as Her Majesty's Protestant Subjects dissenting from the Church of Britain are subject to, and not further or otherwise.

Up to the passing of this Act in 1846, Jews had been excluded from the benefits of the Toleration Act of 1688 and there had been uncertainty as to how various statutes might impact on Jews, and penalties could conceivably have been imposed on Jews for, among various matters, repairing synagogues, exercising their religion, and so on. In the words of H.S.Q. Henriques: 'After the lapse of more than a century and a half the Jews were formally, by a solemn Act of the legislature, admitted to the benefits of the Toleration Act, and their religion was no longer merely connived at, but was placed under the protection of the law.'[39] Two important pieces of legislation that owe their conception to the efforts of the Board.

Lionel Rothschild was elected to the House of Commons in 1847 but was unable to take his seat because of the oath requirements. As a consequence the Board prepared and submitted a petition to the government signed by all deputies and thirty-three congregations in Britain asking for the same civil rights for Jews as those enjoyed by all other classes of subjects. The bill that followed this was defeated yet again in the House of Lords. With the exception of another very similar petition submitted in April 1857, the Board as such was not again involved in the emancipation struggle, although individual members were. A number of reasons can be advanced for this. The emancipation struggle was ably led by the Goldsmids, Lionel Rothschild and David Salomons, and the Board had a very full agenda of other matters. Secondly, as we have seen, there was little love lost between the Board and Isaac Goldsmid. Thirdly, the Board remained of the cautious view that as the representative and spokesman for the Jewish community it should not outstrip public opinion in its statements and requests. This hearkened back to the low-profile approach adopted as a result of the statements made by Charles II and James II in the late seventeenth century, as mentioned in Chapter 1. When political emancipation was achieved the Board was heavily criticized for its lack of activity in this regard, and even its apathy. James Picciotto, who generally was a great supporter of the Board, went further and in his regular sketch on Jewish history in the *JC* in 1873 he condemned the Board for its timidity and dread of responsibility.[40]

By 1858 most disabilities had been removed, but there remained taking a seat in Parliament. In that year a compromise was reached under which each House of Parliament could decide separately by resolution the form of oath to be taken by a Jew to become a member.[41] Lionel Rothschild had been elected as a Member of Parliament four times between 1847 and 1858, but had been unable to take his seat because of the oath. On 26 July 1858 the House of Commons agreed that he could replace the words 'on the true faith of a Christian' by another appropriate phrase. Lionel Rothschild took the oath (and his seat) on Monday 29 July replacing the unacceptable words by 'so help me elohim [i.e. God]'. This was specific to him and until 1866, when the Parliamentary Oaths Act substituted a new oath not containing the words 'on the true faith of a Christian', which applied to both Houses of Parliament, a resolution had to be passed by the House of Commons in each session to permit Jews to change the words of the oath.[42] Thus from 1866 Jews could enter the House of Lords as well, although it was not until July 1885 that a Jew received a peerage – Sir Nathaniel Mayer Rothschild, the son of Lionel. Incidentally, it was not until 1891 that atheists were able to affirm rather than take an oath in order to be admitted to Parliament.[43]

Although the admission of Lionel Rothschild into the House of Commons on 26 July 1858 is generally taken as the final stage in the emancipation of the Jews in Britain, not all the disabilities had been removed. For example, there remained the oath requirements at a number of universities. At Cambridge it was necessary to swear an oath including the words 'on the true faith of a Christian' in order to obtain a degree and at Oxford it was necessary to take a similar oath in order to matriculate, thus effectively barring entry to professing Jews, and often Nonconformists and Roman Catholics as well. In 1869 Cambridge University conferred a degree on Numa Hartog who was the senior wrangler that year, giving him permission to make an acceptable oath, and at about the same time the Board petitioned Parliament in favour of the University Test Bill that would have the effect of removing all religious tests. It is interesting to note that the Board's case was not specific to the Jewish situation but it argued that university education and also obtaining fellowships should be available to all irrespective of religion. The Bill was enacted in 1871.[44]

Protection of Jewish Religious Observance
The Board has never been slow to take up issues that have a bearing on Jewish religious observance. During the period covered by this chapter many such issues arose. There was an important meeting in May 1834, when the Board formed a committee to frame amendments

to the Poor Law Amendment Bill. The object was to obtain relief for Jewish poor who should be exempt from work on the Sabbath and Holy Days and should be given their own food. In the end this did not prove necessary since it appeared that the Poor Law commissioners would have powers to give the required relief.[45] This was the start of the Board's involvement in trying to secure relief for the Jewish community from having to work, attend schools, and sit examinations on Saturdays and Jewish festivals as well as measures for enabling members of the armed services to keep kashrut and hold sedarim. Indeed, on more than one occasion the Board has been successful in having polling days for both general and local elections changed so as not to coincide with Jewish festivals. This is one of the significant but unsung features of the Board's activities and has been of inestimable value to observant Jews.

In April 1842 the Board was informed that the trustees of a charity, the Bedford Charity, had decided to exclude Jews from its benefits, despite a decision of the Lord Chancellor in 1819 that Jews were eligible. The Board was successful in preventing the exclusion of Jews. The 1842 Income Tax Bill did not include Jewish places of worship among the list of exemptions, and the Board was able to obtain an appropriate amendment, with the support of Sir Robert Peel, the prime minister.[46] In 1847 the Board was informed that a Jewish girl aged 14 in Hobart (Van Diemen's Land and now Tasmania), who was attending a school for children of prisoners, had been forcibly converted. It also received an appeal from Hobart that Jewish prisoners should be exempt from work on Jewish Holy Days. The Board raised these issues with the Colonial Office and although the prisoners' appeal was successful it is not clear what the result was regarding the forced conversion of the girl.[47] In September 1856 the Board received a letter from the official Jewish prison visitor saying that Jewish convicts who had previously been exempt from working on the Sabbath and Jewish holidays were no longer so exempt. Some prisoners had refused to work on these days and as a consequence had been locked in solitary confinement and received only bread and water for some days. It would seem that prison governors had received instructions from the Home Office to order Jewish prisoners to work on the Sabbath. The president of the Board wrote immediately to the home secretary and received a reply that he had authorized prison governors to grant permission for Jewish convicts to abstain from work on their Sabbath and other religious festivals.[48]

In 1859 the Board was informed that the Oxford Local Examinations that year would extend over Saturday, thus making it impossible for some Jews to participate. The matter was raised with the examining body and a satisfactory solution was found. This outcome was used as a precedent for obtaining concessions subsequently from other examining boards and has remained an important feature of the Board's activities ever since.[49]

The Marriage Acts of 1835 and 1836[50]

Until 1836 there were no specific laws in Britain regarding Jewish marriages, and in practice such marriages were recognized. Lord Hardwicke's Marriage Act of 1753, which made null and void all marriages solemnized without the publication of banns, specifically exempted Jewish marriages. In 1835 the Matrimonial Causes Act, also know as Lord Lyndhurst's Marriage Act, reached the statute book and in 1836 the Marriage and the Marriage Registration Acts were enacted. The Marriage Act of 1836 specifically sanctioned Jewish marriages provided both parties were Jewish and provided notice had been given to an appropriate registrar and a registrar's certificate had been issued. The Registration Act gave the power to determine who should be able to register Jewish marriages to the president of the Board. He would have to certify in writing to the Registrar General which secretaries of synagogues could be furnished with marriage registers and designated marriage secretaries.[51] Not only did this give statutory recognition to the Board, but also it gave immense power to the president. It became the practice of the presidents to consult with the chief rabbi or other suitable religious authority as to whether or not a synagogue requesting marriage powers for its secretary was to be considered 'a synagogue of persons professing the Jewish religion'. In the absence of such recognition the president refused to ask the Registrar General to certify that synagogue's secretary as a marriage secretary. This gave rise to many disputes between synagogues and the Board.

The Matrimonial Causes Act of 1835 made void all marriages within the prohibited degrees of consanguinity or affinity. These were not defined in the Act but it was taken that they incorporated into British law the Ecclesiastical Law rules. They included prohibitions against a widower marrying his deceased wife's sister, a widow marrying her deceased husband's brother, and between an uncle and his niece. None of these marriages were prohibited by Jewish law and thus there could be a conflict between British law and what would be permissible for a Jewish religious marriage.

Late in the day the Board became concerned as to whether or not this Act applied to Jews. It should have raised this issue as the bill was progressing through Parliament, but it did not. This was, in fact, one of the criticisms of the Board levied by Isaac Goldsmid in his letter mentioned earlier. It had not so much taken its eyes off the ball; it had not had them on the ball in the first place. At a meeting of the Board on 7 March 1836 it was considered that the Act applied to Jews and, as a consequence, it was resolved that they should seek exemption so that Jewish marriages might be valid even though they infringed the prohibited degrees. A committee, chaired by the president, Moses Montefiore, was appointed to put effect to this, but appears to have done nothing. Subsequently, as a result of the two 1836 Marriage Acts, some deputies considered that the 1835 Act did not apply to Jews after all, and in December 1836 it was decided to press for a bill to remove all doubt. The committee assisting with the Emancipation Bill arranged for a bill to be introduced into the House of Commons in June 1837. The aim of this bill was to make it clear that Jewish marriages could only be voided by consanguinity or affinity if they were in breach of Jewish law. The chances of the bill succeeding were very slight, particularly in the House of Lords, and the Board authorized Montefiore to consider submitting a petition as well, but in practice he did not do so, although it is clear from his diaries that he made strenuous efforts to get the bill passed. It was in this connection that he wrote in his diary on 9 July 1837 that 'I am most firmly resolved not to give up the smallest part of our religious forms and privileges to obtain civil rights.'[52] In the event the bill was lost as a result of the prorogation of Parliament on 17 July 1837.

It was difficult for Montefiore. He could not gather a lot of support at the Board for his views on this issue, particularly as many deputies were of the view that Jews should not seek any exceptional status in this regard, essentially as it would draw unnecessary attention to the differences of Jews from other members of society. There was also the group who considered the Act did not apply to Jews. Their view was strengthened by Counsel's opinion on a specific case. The chief rabbi had refused to perform a marriage ceremony for an uncle and niece that was complicated by certain proposed property arrangements. The Board had referred this to Counsel and he opined that if the marriage was valid in Jewish law it would be upheld in the courts and that the 1835 Act did not apply to Jews.

In the 1840s the issue emerged again at the Board, partly because it was perceived that the climate of public opinion was becoming more favourable to Jewish emancipation and partly because the new chief rabbi, Nathan Marcus Adler, was a strong proponent of the view that Jews should be able to marry in accord with their own laws.[53] On 6 May 1844 the Board appointed a committee to obtain the best possible legal advice on the subject, and it sought opinions from the Attorney General and two eminent ecclesiastical lawyers. The Attorney General declined to advise on the grounds that he was limiting himself to matters connected with his office, but the other two were of the view that Jewish marriages within the prohibited degrees would not be valid. As a result the Board wrote to all synagogues warning them not to carry out any marriages within the prohibited degrees until a successful legal case or new legislation permitted this.[54]

Matters came to a head in 1850. Jonas Spyer, a Jewish solicitor, consulted four eminent counsel as to whether his daughter could marry her uncle. All four counsel, who included the two who had given their view in 1844, were of the opinion that the courts would uphold the marriage if it were valid in Jewish law. The chief rabbi was then approached and consented, subject to the agreement of the Board. A special meeting of the Board was held on 4 December and, after a particularly long debate and despite all of the weighty opinions in favour of the marriage, it was decided by eleven votes to two not to depart from its 1844 policy. This caution was justified as the Registrar General wrote to Montefiore a few weeks later stating that in the unanimous opinion of the Queen's Advocate, the Attorney General and the Solicitor General the proposed marriage would be invalid in British law whatever its status in Jewish law.[55]

Another attempt at clarification and change in the law was made in 1855. The Registrar General was conducting a survey into areas where it might be desirable to reform the marriage laws. He asked the Board a number of questions relating to Jewish marriages and in particular the frequency with which Jews contracted marriages outside the permitted degrees, if at all and, if it were viewed that such marriages were prohibited by the act, whether this was regarded by the Jews as a grievance that should be remedied.[56] The chief rabbi was asked to help and stated that he knew of only eight such marriages, all solemnized abroad. However, he thought Jews would consider it a boon if they were able to marry within all the degrees allowed under Jewish law. The Board resolved that in any future marriage legislation, Jews should be specifically exempted from the provisions of the 1835 Act. It is of interest to note that the Board petition on this issue asked for the law to be amended so as to legalize these marriages for everyone and not just for Jews. This petition was sent to the Registrar General, but no action was taken. The Board decided that it now had to wait until there was a judicial decision on the issue.

It had to wait a long time, until 1900 when in *De Wilton v. Montefiore* (1900 2 Ch.489) the judge ruled that Jewish marriages were governed by the matrimonial causes law.[57] Ironically the Montefiore in the case was Joseph Gompertz Montefiore, a son of Moses Montefiore's sister Abigail. His father was Benjamin Gompertz, the first Jewish actuary in Britain. Joseph Montefiore had married his niece, not in Britain but abroad because of the doubt. The niece was on his mother's side and thus was a grand-niece by marriage of Sir Moses. In 1907 marriage with a deceased wife's sister was legalized; in 1921 marriage with a deceased husband's brother was legalized; and in 1931 marriage with a niece or nephew by marriage was legalized.

Opinion on this and other issues was changing very fast among leading Jews, including some deputies. Many were of the view that Jews should be subject to the same rights and privileges as all other Nonconformist citizens, but should have no special privileges other than any specifically required in order to observe their religion. This became apparent when in 1857 the chief rabbi, supported by the Board, was successful in including in the Matrimonial Causes Bill a clause which would have exempted Jewish divorces requiring dissolution by the civil divorce court to be established under that act, thus implicitly recognizing the validity of Jewish divorce. This clause was dropped by the government as a result of pressure from Lionel Rothschild and David Salomons, at least partly, it would seem, because they were concerned that any legal recognition of the special position of Jews might harm their attempts to enter Parliament. After two heated debates the Board asked the government to restore the clause, but the government refused.[58] In 1858 the Board sought and received Counsel's opinion on the bearing of the act on Jewish divorces granted by the Beth Din – that is, through a *get*. The opinion was that these were valid, and persons so divorced could remarry under British law. However, in 1866 the Registrar General, after asking certain questions of the Board regarding a *get* in a particular case, concluded that such a divorce would not be valid under British law.[59] As a result, since 1866 no *gittim* have been granted without a prior divorce decree through the courts. There is no such thing as a 'free lunch'. As Geoffrey Alderman has pointed out, there was a cost to emancipation, particularly in the religious sphere, and the self-imposed requirement that a Jewish religious divorce had to be preceded by a civil one (on which the requirements could differ) is one of the prices paid.[60]

To complete the picture there was also the issue of 'stille chuppas' (quiet marriages) – that is clandestine or illegal marriages. These were Jewish marriages which were performed from time to time without registration under the 1836 Act, either because of ignorance or secretly because they did not meet the requirements of British law. In December 1847 the Board circulated all synagogues warning of the dangers of such marriages.[61] This became an ongoing problem, particularly following the large immigrations from 1881 onwards, and it is discussed in the next chapter.

The Reform Movement[62]

On 15 April 1840, sixteen members of Bevis Marks and eight members of the London Ashkenazi synagogues met to discuss certain dissatisfactions they felt with the current synagogue set-up. They were concerned with the distance of the synagogues from where they lived, the length of the services, their inconvenient hours, and the absence of religious instruction in the synagogues. There was probably a bit more to it than just this. Isaac Goldsmid, as we have seen, was very dissatisfied with the Board's approach on the emancipation issue and from about 1831 had been threatening to establish a new synagogue independent of the Board, and this move could have been the culmination of the spat between the Goldsmids and the Board and in particular with Moses Montefiore.[63] Thus it could be argued that, in part at least, the policy of the Board led to the establishment of the reform movement. The group decided to form itself into a new congregation, with a new place of worship to be called the West London Synagogue of British Jews. It would be established in the western part of London,[64] with a revised service at more suitable hours, and where religious instruction would be available.

The Board was not involved at first, so it would seem, as there is no mention in its minutes or other archived documents during the period. However, at a meeting of the Board on 20 May 1841, a letter from the chief rabbi and the principal rabbi of Bevis Marks was read out. This letter deprecated the establishment of a 'dissenting' synagogue which, it was claimed, would depart from traditional Jewish laws and observances. The Board was urged to take measures to defend the current position, because if the community became disunited a weakening of the Board's influence would develop. It appears, according to the diaries of Sir Moses Montefiore, that there followed many heated discussions at the Board, and many deputies refused to acknowledge the authority of the ecclesiastical chiefs – or at least, not on this issue.[65] Nevertheless, at a meeting of the Board with the chief rabbi on 9 November 1841 it was resolved that a *herem* on the new congregation promulgated by the chief rabbi and the Beth Din of Bevis Marks should be communicated to all London synagogues. Under its terms all faithful Jews were prohibited from having any contact with any seceders. According to James Picciotto there is some evidence to suggest that the chief rabbi, Solomon Hirschell, and Rev. Meldola, the senior rabbi of Bevis Marks, were conciliatory and reluctant to take this step, but were forced by the more recalcitrant lay leaders of the main synagogues, who presumably did not want anyone to secede from their benign authority![66]

On 22 January 1842 the *herem* was read out in all synagogues, and on 27 January 1842 the West London Synagogue of British Jews opened. It immediately applied to the president of the Board for his certification of the appointment of the synagogue's secretary as its marriage secretary. This was referred to the chief rabbi, who objected, and as a result the president refused to issue the certificate. He obtained counsel's opinion which confirmed he had exercised his discretion properly, in that he had sought and obtained the views of the chief rabbi and Beth Din. The West London then asked if he would rule that the new synagogue 'was a Synagogue of persons professing the Jewish religion', even though he might not consider it the right kind of Judaism. The Board refused to comply.[67] Members of the West London Synagogue who wished to get married did so by a civil ceremony before a registrar followed by a religious ceremony in their synagogue. Ten years later a clause was included in the Dissenters Chapel Act that recognized the West London Synagogue secretary as a marriage secretary and empowered the leaders of the West London Synagogue to certify as marriage secretaries the secretaries of other Reform synagogues. In fact the original clause in the bill was a more general one which would apply to any synagogue and only required twenty householders to certify the appointment of a marriage secretary. The Board strongly objected to this clause, as it would effectively remove its power of appointment of marriage secretaries for Jewish communities. The clause was amended so that it applied only to the West London Synagogue, and this amendment was approved by both the Board and the chief rabbi.

The efforts of the West London Synagogue to join the Board were discussed earlier, but it did not seem to be bound by the Board's view that it had the monopoly on representing the views of British Jews to government. As already mentioned, in 1845 a deputation consisting in the main of members of the West London congregation saw the prime minister to try to persuade him that the piecemeal approach to removing the remaining Jewish disabilities, as was the policy of the Board, was inappropriate; they were looking for full emancipation. The *JC*, in commenting on this meeting with the prime minister, mentions that the note that this delegation left with the prime minister had made the point that the Board did not represent *all* British Jews.[68] It cannot be a coincidence that a few weeks later, in its letter to Rabbi Dr Nathan Adler welcoming him as the new chief rabbi, the Board stated that it represented *nearly* the whole of the Jewish community in Britain.[69]

Cemeteries[70]

Jewish cemeteries are a matter that has frequently exercised the Board. In 1843 the Internment Bill threatened to interfere adversely with Jewish cemeteries, and the Board successfully lobbied the home secretary on this issue.[71]

A major issue erupted in 1850. A report of the Board of Health on burials in London stated that there were various abuses connected with burials and made a number of proposals. The report recommended the establishment of a commission to control all cemeteries; private cemeteries were to be closed, all internments were to take place in national cemeteries and existing graveyards were to be transferred outside city boundaries. A Metropolitan Internment Bill, incorporating most of these measures, was introduced early in 1850. The Jewish community was alarmed by this bill, which could mean that the management of Jewish funerals could fall into the hands of non-Jewish officials and could lead to the violation of its religious burial laws. A deputation of the Board went to see the home secretary, and they also issued a memorandum giving full details of Jewish burial requirements and their customs, and explained how the proposed measures could violate these requirements. Furthermore, they pointed out that the abuses that had been highlighted by the report did not occur for Jewish internments. Whilst they did not oppose inspection by the health authorities, they wished to retain Jewish cemeteries intact and leave internment regulations to their own congregations. In effect they

wanted total exemption from the bill.[72] The home secretary was sympathetic but refused to grant exemption. The Board resolved to continue to pressurize the government and formed a much-strengthened
subcommittee including David Salomons and Lionel Rothschild; it also
issued a new memorandum which was sent not only to the home secretary but also to the president of the Board of Health who had initiated
the whole matter. The subcommittee met with these two, but again
with no success. Undeterred, it approached John Abel Smith, an MP
who was one of the staunchest supporters of emancipation in Parliament, and he agreed to intervene on its behalf. This proved successful
and an amendment was proposed and agreed, that religious denominations would be allocated separate portions within the new national
graveyards with separate burial facilities, and that existing Jewish
cemeteries would not be closed.[73]

There was an ironic postscript. In 1852 the new Conservative
government repealed the Internment Act.[74] The immense efforts of
the Board were thus in vain, but it had put a marker down with the
Home Office and the Board of Health that in the area of burials and
cemeteries there was a Jewish point of view that should not be ignored.
Furthermore, the Board itself remained involved in the whole question
of Jewish cemeteries. In particular it assumed responsibility for the
supervision and maintenance of disused Jewish cemeteries and has continued this practice to the present day. In 1898 an honorary inspector of
cemeteries was appointed and at about the same time a specific Disused
Cemetery Fund was established.

Education[75]

Until the early nineteenth century the state had had no real involvement in education: it was an area that was seen as the province of the
religious authorities. Education was not compulsory and standards
were not laid down. The first public grant to schools was made in 1833
as a result of an Act of Parliament and it was limited to Anglican and
Nonconformist schools. The act established an Education Committee
of the Privy Council and an inspectorate was appointed in respect of
schools receiving state aid. Annual public expenditure on education
rose from £20,000 in 1833 to more than £800,000 in the 1860s.[76]

In 1847 education appeared for the first time on the Board's
agenda. It was not education as such which exercised the minds of the
deputies, but rather its financing. Roman Catholic schools had just
been given state aid in the form of grants and the Board approached

the Education Committee of the Privy Council for similar consideration for Jewish schools. There was a shortage of qualified Jewish teachers which meant that their salaries were high and this was a difficult burden for the community to bear.[77] The case was on the grounds of civic equality and the 1846 Religious Disabilities Act which gave legal recognition to Jewish schools, places of worship, and educational and charitable funds. This was unsuccessful partly because the Privy Council was wary of supporting non-Christian religious instruction or at least appearing to support it.

In 1851 the Board was persuaded to take the matter up again by the Manchester Hebrew Education Society on behalf of the Manchester Jews' School.[78] This school, established in 1838 and at the time with sixty pupils, had had its application for a grant turned down by the Education Committee of the Privy Council on the grounds that the council did not have power to assist Jewish schools. The Board's case was that in Manchester there were a number of free schools that were aided by a special rate levied on local rate-payers, including Jews, and that the tuition in the Jews' school had been particularly commended by the school inspectors. Long and difficult negotiations took place, but in the end the council agreed that it would be prepared to accept applications for grants from Jewish schools for purposes other than for buildings. The requirements were that the average attendance at a Jewish school should reach a required level (which for the Manchester school was fifty boys and forty girls), that at least part of the Holy Scriptures should be read daily, and that the instruction of secular subjects should be open to government inspection.[79]

The Education Committee of the Privy Council preferred to deal with a single representative body for all schools of a particular denomination and asked the Board to provide evidence that it was the appropriate body. The Board sent to the committee copies of resolutions adopted by several synagogues in 1850 which included a statement that 'the Board was the only medium of official communication with the government'. This evidence was accepted by the committee, notwithstanding that it was with regard to synagogues and not Jewish schools.[80] In fact there was not a representative body for Jewish schools at that time and the Privy Council appointed the Board as the official channel through which a Jewish school could apply for state aid. The committee stated that it would prefer proposals for state aid by Jewish schools to be in a common format and it sent the Board sample applications that had been used by other denominations,[81] and as a consequence the Board decided to draft a model trust deed as a standard for Jewish schools. This draft included a clause requiring that religious instruction in Jewish schools had to be under the control of the ecclesiastical authorities of the Board, that is, the chief rabbi or the haham.[82]

A requirement regarding control of religious instruction was not included in the sample documents sent to the Board by the committee and thus was not strictly necessary in the model deed to be used by Jewish schools. Gerry Black, in his book on the history of the Jews' Free School (JFS) in London, considers that this might have been an attempt by the chief rabbi, aided by Sir Moses Montefiore, to exercise some control over Jewish schools.[83] This draft was agreed at a Board meeting on 9 May 1852, at which many of the more 'liberal' deputies were absent, and passed by twelve votes to five. The JFS in London and the Manchester school objected to the clause that religious instruction had to be under the control of the chief rabbi, as did a number of synagogues, but Bevis Marks, the Hambro and the Western synagogues wanted it retained. Six members of the Board, including Lionel Rothschild, who had not been present at the meeting that had approved the model deed, requisitioned a special meeting to reconsider this clause.[84] The *JC* was firmly on the side objecting to the Board's draft.[85] After further heated and acrimonious discussions within the British Jewish community, a compromise was reached so that religious instruction had to be under the supervision of the chief rabbi, or of a minister, or of a person appointed by the school's governing committee and supervised by them.[86] This argument illustrates the point that there were powerful forces within the Jewish community that were not prepared to accept the authority of the chief rabbi in some or even all areas. It was another hundred years before the chief rabbi became the ecclesiastical authority for the JFS in London.[87]

This was not the end of the controversy over the model deed. A further clause, required by the Privy Council and only agreed to very reluctantly by the Board, was that a Jewish state-aided school had to be open to non-Jewish children. Thus Jewish children for whom there might be doubts concerning their halachic credentials would be eligible to be admitted to Jewish state-aided schools. Interestingly the Privy Council offered an olive branch in respect of its requirement for a clause to admit non-Jewish children. It withdrew the restriction of not giving grants for buildings.[88] It is important to note that the conditions for obtaining a grant were the same for all schools, irrespective of their religious background.

In 1870 the Board addressed itself to the Elementary Education Bill of that year. The main purpose of the bill was the creation of locally elected School Boards who would have the responsibility to establish Board Schools in their areas, to be financed out of local rates. The Board of Deputies was particularly involved in consultations on the conscience clauses of the bill. It was envisaged that the bill would require non-denominational Christian religious instruction in schools, and this was considered unacceptable for Jewish children. Part of the Board's concern was the activities of the London Society for Promoting Christianity among Jews, who would see this as a great opportunity. The Board advocated that there should be a clause incorporated into the bill that permitted the withdrawal of children from religious instruction on the grounds of conscience and, to facilitate this, religious instruction as such should be at the beginning or at the end of the school day. The Board also wanted a clause stating that Jewish children should be exempt from attending elementary schools on Saturdays and such other religious days as their parents deemed sacred, without forfeiting any benefits. The Board was entirely successful in having appropriate clauses incorporated into the act, mainly due to the efforts of Sir John Simon in the House of Commons.[89]

In 1872 the Board became concerned that when children were committed to industrial schools or reformatories no enquiries were made as to the children's religion. This subject was referred to the Law, Parliamentary and General Purposes Committee. The committee reported that there was a duty to check on the religion of the child, but that there were no Jewish institutions to which the relevant authorities could send Jewish children. The committee had contacted thirty-six institutions throughout the country and in only nine of them were any questions raised as to the religion of a child committed to them, and of these only five made special arrangements so that Jewish children did not have to attend divine service. The superintendent of the institutions suggested that for only a little extra cost per head, Jewish children could be grouped into only a few such institutions where Jewish religious instruction could be carried out. The Board decided to form a joint committee with the United Synagogue for this purpose. Within a year arrangements were in hand for all Jewish children sent to industrial schools to be grouped in an industrial school in Birmingham and for religious education to be undertaken by the Birmingham congregation. The United Synagogue guaranteed the extra cost of fifty pounds a year per child. After all this bother it was found that there was just one Jewish boy in a reformatory and one girl in an industrial school.[90]

Working Hours and Sunday Trading

From the late 1860s the Board became very much involved in various parliamentary bills which would have an important bearing on the work practices of Jews. In 1867 the Hours of Labour Regulation Bill limited the hours that could be worked by women and children in workshops and factories to a maximum of sixty and prohibited their working on Sundays and after 2 p.m. on Saturdays. This could lead to hardship for many observant Jews who closed their workshops on Saturdays and opened them on Sundays and sometimes Saturday nights. A number of Jewish manufacturers petitioned the Board to seek some sort of exemption. This led to many heated debates at the Board. Whereas some deputies argued that this was the sort of issue the Board was created to deal with, many members were concerned that any attempt by the Board to obtain exemptions for Jewish-owned factories could lead to resentment against the Jewish community. In the end the Board voted narrowly in favour of intervening and as a result a memorandum was submitted by the Board to the home secretary. What it sought for those Jewish establishments that were closed on Saturday until sunset were provisions that enabled such establishments to employ any woman or child on Saturday evenings from sunset until 9 p.m. in winter and 10 p.m. in summer, provided that the total number of hours worked by each employee did not exceed sixty in a week. The principle was accepted by the government, but the details led to very long negotiations.[91]

In 1868 some Jewish occupiers of workshops were convicted of infringements under the Factory and Workshop legislation in that they employed persons on a Sunday who were prohibited under the terms of the act. This led to the Board resolving to ensure, yet again, that such Jewish occupiers should not be liable to penalties for employing children or women on Saturday nights. They had support from a recent report of the inspector of factories who had commented on the hardship suffered by Jews under the existing legislation. This report also mentioned that the cigar-making industry in London employed mainly Jewish women and young persons who, before the Factory Act, used to work for a few hours on Sunday mornings. They left early on Fridays and as a consequence of the act did not resume work again until Monday morning. It seems that the quality of cigars made on Mondays were inferior due to the fact that the workers hands had become stiff over the long weekend break and they were clumsy in manipulating the tobacco.[92]

The issue became a cause célèbre in the Jewish community and at the Board. One side arguing that Jewish factories should be able to open on Sundays, on the grounds that whereas the Sunday Trading Bills (see below) might be religiously inspired by the Sabbatarians (a Christian group who advocated no work or trading on their Sabbath Day), the Sunday closing provisions for factories were aimed at limiting the hours worked by women and children. The other side considered that, since all the religious disabilities had only been comparatively recently removed, it would be wrong for the Board to demand further privileges. The Board came under attack for being much too inactive, ineffective and seeking a quiet life, with some vitriolic letters in the Jewish press. The *JC* joined in the debate and was strongly on the side of those seeking exemption, arguing that the threat was not to the Jewish factory owners who could employ Christian labour, but to the Jewish workers who would lose their jobs. Matters came to a head in 1870 when a deputation from the Jewish Tailors' Benefit Society met with the Board and explained how the regulations for late working for those establishments closed on Saturday were insufficient and of little practical value. In the end the Board proposed, and the government accepted at first, an amendment to the Factories Amendment Bill of that year, that in factories that were closed during the Sabbath, work could be permitted until 2 p.m. on Sundays. Regrettably the Select Committee examining the bill, whilst recognizing that Jews had a grievance, recommended that it should not be dealt with in that bill, and it was not.[93]

Sir David Salomons then joined in. He was an MP,[94] and he introduced a bill in 1871 that allowed Jewish-owned factories that were closed on Saturday to employ Jewish women and children on Sundays. This bill was enacted as the Workshop and Factory (Jews) Act 1871 but sadly, despite lobbying by the Board, was limited to workshops and tobacco manufacturers.[95] The Board continued to press its case and was successful in that its recommendations were incorporated in the 1878 Factory Act, which extended the Salomons' Act to all factories and workshops.[96] In 1880 a Jewish tailor was arrested for working on a Sunday and appealed to the Board for help. He was arrested under the terms of the Lord's Day Act, which had been enacted in the late seventeenth century. He had claimed that the Factory Act of 1878 gave him exemption, but this was rejected by the magistrate. However, the magistrate did not impose the statutory fine of five shillings. The Board was unable to help and pointed out that the Factory Act was meant to stop the exploitation of women and young people aged between 14 and 18 and applied only to them. The comment on this in that year's report of the Board read:

> No doubt a hardship is occasioned in most cases in which the Lord's Day Act is enforced against persons professing the Jewish religion who observe the seventh day Sabbath, but such instances are rare, and the magistrate usually takes a lenient view of the case. He did so in the present instance, for he imposed no fine, but simply ordered the defendant to pay the costs; the Board, however, should watch any legislation relative to Sunday observance, or Sunday trading, and will avail themselves of any opportunity that may be found of endeavouring to secure relief for such cases as the present.[97]

In 1880 a Jewish pastry-cook was convicted under the Lord's Day Act for baking and selling bread after the authorized hours on a Sunday. He sought help from the Board, but it was unable to assist him for the same reasons as for the tailor. In its report the Board again drew attention to the fact that the Factory Act only applied to women and young persons, and although admitting that the law sometimes operated harshly on practising Jews, they considered that any action by them to obtain a modification of the law would be inexpedient at that time. No reasons were given.

Sunday Trading Bills, generally introduced by Sabbatarians, and which sought to reduce or even eliminate trading on Sundays, were considered by Parliament from time to time, but all failed to be enacted. In 1855 a public meeting of London Jews was held to protest about a private member's bill that would have prohibited many kinds of Sunday trading. As a consequence a deputation from the Board met with the MP who had introduced the bill and he agreed to introduce a clause exempting Jews.[98] This bill was not enacted. In 1867 a new bill was introduced and the Board held discussions on it with the Jewish MPs and the promoters of the bill. The concern was again that the measure would prohibit trading on Sunday and the Board sought some exemptions for Jewish businesses that were closed on Saturday. The most they were able to obtain was an exemption for butchers licensed by the London Board for Shechita in respect of kosher meat.[99] At that time some non-Jewish butchers had licences to sell kosher meat and it would seem they sold non-kosher meat as well. Not all butchers selling kosher meat were licensed by the London Board; some had licences from other boards including overseas ones and some had no licence at all. In the event this bill did not pass through Parliament, was introduced again in 1868 and met the same fate. It would seem that those against Sunday trading were determined to have some regulations on this enacted and this area developed into a major issue for the Board.

3. FOREIGN AFFAIRS

The Damascus Blood Libel[100]

On 5 February 1840, Father Thomas, the superior of a Capuchin Monastery in Damascus, disappeared, together with his servant. They were last seen near the Jewish quarter of the town, and within a few days a number of Jews were arrested on the grounds that they had murdered the pair in order to use their blood for Passover matzot. Some died and others confessed under torture. After various unsuccessful attempts at rescue, an appeal for help from the Jewish community of Constantinople was forwarded to the Rothschilds in London, who passed it on to Moses Montefiore. He wasted little time and arranged for the acting president, Joseph Henriques, to convene a meeting of the Board on 21 April 1840. Also present at that meeting were Lionel Rothschild, Isaac Lyon and Francis Goldsmid, David Salomons and Adolphe Crémieux, then vice-president of the Consistoire Central des Israelite Français, who had come especially from Paris. The chief rabbi, Dr Hirschell, was unable to attend due to ill health. The Board agreed three important steps. First, a request would be made to the governments of Britain, France and Austria to intercede in Constantinople and Alexandria (at that time Damascus, although in the Ottoman Empire, was effectively under the control of Egypt) to attempt to stop the atrocities. Secondly, a delegation was nominated to request a meeting with the foreign secretary, Lord Palmerston. Thirdly, a committee was established to give publicity to the event and the decisions of the meeting. It did so by means of paid advertisements in thirty-one British journals, dailies (sometimes more than once), weeklies and the provincial press.[101]

The committee met with Lord Palmerston on 30 April, who promised to use his influence with Mohammed Ali, the viceroy of Egypt, and the Turkish government to put a stop to the atrocities. It is clear that the events horrified Palmerston, and the request to intervene suited his foreign policy at the time, which was to force Mohammed Ali out of greater Syria and return it to direct Ottoman rule – a good example of how foreign Jewish crises often got the sympathy of British governments because they suited British foreign policy at the time. However, in this case it would seem that Palmerston felt genuine revulsion, as can be read in the despatches he sent on 5 May to the British representatives in the Middle East.[102] A flavour is given by a letter he wrote on 21 May to N.W. Werry, the British consul in Damascus, who had written that he was confident of the guilt of the Jews. Palmerston's note read in part:

> I have to state to you that I have read with much surprise ... your despatch which relates to the atrocities ... committed on the Damascus Jews, and I have to observe that ... it either proves you to be wholly uninformed of what passes in the city in which you are stationed or else evinces on your part an entire want of those principles and sentiments which ought to distinguish a British agent.[103]

The next meeting of the Board was on 15 June and was attended by all those present at the previous meeting, plus the chief rabbi. An initiative had been taken by the French Consistoire to send a Jewish delegation to the Middle East, and Crémieux, who was to represent France, was in London to obtain support. The meeting persuaded Sir Moses to join the delegation. On 24 June Sir Moses met with Lord Palmerston who promised to give Sir Moses various letters to British officials in the Middle East and to do all he could to facilitate the mission. On this occasion the Board was very proactive and very public in its strategy. Appeals for help and solidarity were sent to all Jewish communities in Britain and abroad. Well-publicized meetings were held throughout the country, supportive resolutions passed and funds raised. The mission was successful, the Jews still in prison were released and the sultan issued a firman concluding that the 'violence to which the Jews had been subjected results from calumny and no more'.[104] The success, although not pyrrhic, was not long-standing. Ritual murder charges against Jews continued to be raised in many places, were often believed in the outside world and proved difficult to overcome; many Jews died as a result. A myth arose that the Damascus case had provided conclusive evidence that ritual murder played a role in the religious practice of at least some Jews, or a secret sect within Jewry.[105] A tomb allegedly containing Father Thomas's remains was erected in the Capuchin monastery in Damascus and in 1866 removed to the Terra Sancta church in the same city. It still has the words 'Assassinato Dagla Ebrei' inscribed on it, despite a promise by representatives of the Catholic Church to Montefiore that the words would be removed.

There is also a rather interesting postscript. Colonel Charles Churchill, who was the British military attaché in Damascus, wrote to Montefiore in June 1841 proposing that the Jews should re-establish themselves as a nation in Palestine.[106] This letter was put on the agenda of the Board but there is no record of any discussion. A further letter was sent by Churchill in August 1842 with a more modest proposal that the Jews should seek permission to appoint an official to reside in Syria with the object of watching over the interests of the Jews residing there. The Board was clearly not particularly interested or enamoured of the ideas and responded that it was precluded from originating any of the measures proposed but, if they should emanate from the general body of Jews in Europe, the Jews of Britain would be supportive. Churchill responded in January 1843 hoping that the Board would take the initiative in obtaining the views of the Jews in other countries of Europe, but the Board decided to drop the matter.[107] Emancipation, not restoration, was the objective of the elite of British Jewry. In fact demands for some sort of Jewish entity in Palestine might have well given ammunition to the anti-emancipationists who might claim that Jews were acknowledging that they were in exile awaiting redemption. Lord Palmerston would have been interested and probably supportive, and thus perhaps the Board missed an opportunity of being one of the first to try to re-establish a Jewish state in Palestine.

Russia[108]

In July 1842 the Board discussed a letter Moses Montefiore had received from a Dr Lilienthal, who was a German Reform rabbi. This letter informed the Board that certain concessions had been granted to the Jews in Russia by the tsar, the object being to raise the status of Russian Jews. A network of Jewish state schools, under the Ministry of Public Education, was to be established and a Council of Rabbis had been appointed to advise on the management of these schools. Moses Montefiore was invited to St Petersburg to attend a meeting of this council, as such a visit would clearly add to its weight and prestige.[109]

The background to this lies in the objects of Tsar Nicholas I, from about 1840 onwards, to change radically the life of Russian Jews, by attempting to bring to a close their isolation in Russian society, to make them more useful to the economy and to reduce their role in the economic life of the peasantry. To this end he appointed a committee to plan appropriate measures and one of its first proposals was the introduction of Jewish state schools which would have a secular as well as a religious curriculum, and at the same time abolishing the traditional Jewish religious schools.[110] These plans were opposed by the Orthodox but well received by the *maskilim* – that is, those who were supporters of the European Jewish enlightenment movement. Dr Lilienthal had been appointed the principal coordinator to the scheme. Appointing a Reform rabbi was hardly the best way of trying to obtain the support of the Orthodox. The reason for Lilienthal inviting Moses Montefiore to Russia was that as a result of his involvement in the Damascus Blood Libel he had become famous throughout the Jewish world. Indeed Lilienthal's letter specifically referred to Montefiore's visit to Syria.[111] It must also be appreciated that educational reform was only one of a large number of measures that were introduced.

Montefiore decided he needed more information before reaching a decision on whether or not to go to Russia. In his reply he welcomed any plans to ameliorate the position of the Jews in Russia, but made the point that they must ensure absolute loyalty to the tenets of traditional Judaism and 'our sacred law'.[112] Clearly his concerns must have been aroused by some remarks in Lilienthal's letter regarding the rather negative attitude to the plans by most Russian Jews. His reply put a dampener on the idea to invite him and the Rabbinical Council met without him.

The council met in April 1843, the same month as a ukase compelling Jews to move inland from Russia's western borders was promulgated. News of this reached the Board in June 1843 in a letter from the Jewish community of Königsberg, East Prussia. This letter referred to the help the Board had given to the Jews of Damascus, and gave details of the ukase. All Jews who lived within fifty *wersts* (about thirty-five miles) of the Prussian and Austrian frontiers would be forced to move into the interior and this would drive half a million Jews from their homes. This letter was considered at a special meeting of the Board held on 13 July 1843. It would seem that Montefiore had acted independently and pre-empted the Board since he informed its members that he had already discussed the matter with the Russian ambassador, who agreed that the decree was a bad measure but advised against taking any public steps as there were still two years before the ukase would take effect. Furthermore, Montefiore had also written to the minister responsible in Russia. On Montefiore's advice the Board decided to keep the issue strictly private and work behind the scenes,[113] the opposite of the action the Board took over the Damascus Affair. Probably the Board considered that as Russia was an ally and one of the most powerful nations in Europe, and as Lord Palmerston had been replaced as foreign minister by the pro-Russian Earl of Aberdeen, it was unlikely to get the support of the British government.

On 19 October 1843 the Board met again to consider a letter from the Russian Beth Din, suggesting that as the brother of the tsar was in London, the Board should organize a petition asking him to intercede with the tsar to get the ukase abrogated. The Board decided that since its president had already written to the Russian government on the matter, and as he had not yet received a reply, it would not be advisable to take any further measures at present.[114] It was about this time that the Jewish press, in particular the *Voice of Jacob*, started criticizing the 'pussyfooting' approach of the Board and pressing for a more publicly active campaign.[115]

Two other meetings of the Board were held on 3 January 1844 and 26 February 1844 to discuss letters received from others regarding the ukase, but on both occasions the Board decided to continue to wait until a response from the Russian government was received. One of the letters considered at the meeting is of interest because it was from a group of non-Jews in Britain who asked for guidance on what they could do to help as fellow countrymen. They later wrote that they were standing by to be of assistance to the Board in whatever action they chose to take including public meetings and signing petitions.[116] This lack of action by the Board led to more criticism in the press. A letter to the *Voice of Jacob* stated: 'The Jews of this country are virtually without a head, without even a leading body.' In the same issue the editor, Jacob Franklin, commented that it was 'devoutly to be wished ... that another body might succeed it, representing not only a larger constituency but invested with power to act in emergencies not provided for in the present constitution'.[117] Clearly not only an opportunity to criticize the Board on its Russian policy, but to raise a more general criticism of the Board itself. Montefiore and Lionel Rothschild met with the foreign secretary on 1 March and reported back to the Board at a meeting on 5 March. The foreign secretary was sympathetic and stated that, although the official intervention of the government was not practicable, its friendly offices would be rendered on behalf of the sufferers.[118]

A little time later it was announced that the tsar had postponed the execution of the ukase. It is idle to speculate what made the tsar take this step, but it is unlikely to have been because of the actions of the Board. However, the Board had an opportunity and took it. In June the tsar unexpectedly visited the queen in London, and at a meeting on 4 June 1844 the Board resolved to present an address to him, thanking him for staying the execution of the ukase and hoping that the halt would remain forever. At that meeting Montefiore asked for power to be able to amend the wording of the address if he considered it appropriate, and it was only his casting vote that gave him this power. Clearly the Board was much divided on the issues but no reporters were present at the meetings and the minutes do not record the debates, so we do not know the details of the argument.[119] The address to the tsar was discussed by Lionel Rothschild and Moses Montefiore, first with the foreign secretary and subsequently with the prime minister who doubted that the tsar would have time to see them. He was right, but the address did reach the tsar, who apologized that due to his visit being so short he was unable to see them. His reply did not indicate whether or not he would ever execute the ukase, but he did send them a donation of fifty pounds to be applied to a Jewish charitable institution as evidence of his favourable disposition to the Jewish people. The *Voice of Jacob*, never missing an opportunity to criticize the Board, thought that it should have coordinated its address to the tsar with that of a group of peers and high churchmen who had likewise petitioned him on the subject.[120]

Regrettably the position of the Jews in Russia became much worse rather than better. The Board held a number of meetings on the issue later in 1844 and throughout 1845, culminating in a meeting on 3 December 1845 to consider a letter from the chief rabbi. The letter pointed out that the deportation of the Jews was now being carried out and the chief rabbi asked the Board to 'signify your wish to Sir Moses' that he should undertake a mission to Russia to try to alleviate the situation. The Board agreed that Montefiore and Lionel Rothschild should hold meetings with the government to discuss the advisability of Sir Moses undertaking a journey to Russia. At about the same time, a delegation from the Jews of Russia visited Britain and met with the Board. At first the Foreign Office advised Montefiore not to go, but he became implacable and they eventually agreed he could go, and with their assistance.[121] The Russian Ambassador in London advised that the visit should be in a personal capacity and not as a representative of the Board. Montefiore made the visit in a personal capacity and left London on 10 March 1846. He did not succeed in having the ukase abrogated or any of the tsar's other anti-Jewish policies reversed.[122]

The Mortara Affair[123]

No sooner had the Jews in Britain celebrated Lionel Rothschild taking his seat in the House of Commons than they received news of an event in Italy that was to have worldwide repercussions. On 23 June 1858, Edgardo Mortara, a 6-year-old Jewish boy, was taken by the Inquisition from his parents' home in Bologna to the House of Catechumens (an institute for new converts) in Rome. They had discovered that when he was a baby he had been seriously ill and was secretly baptized by a maid who feared for his immortal soul. The Inquisition's case was that as he was thus a Catholic he could not be brought up by Jewish parents, as they were unlikely to give him a Catholic education. It was not until 16 July that the first news regarding Edgardo was published in Britain,[124] but it did not cause any great stir. However, on 13 August the *JC* gave more information, and a few days later the Mortara incident was raised at a regular meeting of the Board. One deputy remarked that it was not an uncommon occurrence in parts of Italy and victims seemed to accept the situation as one which could not be rectified. A few members suggested positive action by the Board, but others advocated caution and considered that in the absence of any formal request to the Board, 'it would be little consistent with the dignity of the Board to commit itself to any rash measures'. Although several deputies expressed their indignation and deep regret, the general feeling seemed to be that as the case had not been brought formally to the notice of the Board by the parties concerned, the deputies could not take any official steps.[125]

On 3 September the *JC* expressed surprise at the lack of activity from the Board, but did not have long to wait. The Board had received a letter from Turin in late August calling on the Jewish communities in France and Britain to 'look upon it as a sacred obligation to make an appeal to their respective governments'. The appeal was discussed at the Board meeting on 6 September and a special committee was formed, to be chaired by its president, Sir Moses Montefiore, with full power to take all necessary steps.[126] The committee acted immediately. The next day letters were sent to the foreign secretary and to the British press. The *JC* praised the action of the Board and considered that it 'might be instrumental in the overthrow of one of the most iniquitous institutions disgracing civilization and impeding social and moral progress'.[127]

The Board met on 22 December to consider the report of the committee. The committee had rejected a proposal from Sir Culling Eardley, president of the Evangelical Alliance, that a joint Jewish–Christian delegation should obtain support from Napoleon III and then go to Rome to see the Pope. Napoleon III was very influential with the Pope, and his support would have been very beneficial to any delegation going to Rome. Instead, the Board's committee proposed to send a memorandum to the Pope, to be delivered by an all-Jewish delegation led by Sir Moses Montefiore, and without trying to obtain the support of Napoleon III. The leader in the *JC* of 31 December was supportive of the steps taken by the Board. It made the point 'that the case has directed attention to Jews and has roused strong sympathies in favour of the oppressed. It has also raised the Jewish community in the estimation of the intelligent with their energy and zeal in pursuing the case.'[128]

Montefiore's mission failed. The Pope refused to see him, considering 'it was a closed question'. The *JC* reacted to the failure of the mission by deploring the fact that the Pope refused to see Sir Moses and commenting that 'the Papal government has added insult to crime'. It considered that in the end the visit was a triumph for Montefiore, as it would be one of the last of such cases of Catholics kidnapping Jews and it aroused the sympathy of all men.[129] The French Jewish press were less kind to Montefiore. They suggested that their co-religionists across the Channel had borrowed the worst characteristics of British men – arrogance, individuality and a wish to surmount obstacles alone for glory's sake. They considered that the mission failed because of this egoism and that had the delegation cooperated and visited Paris and met the emperor they would have found support and not made some basic errors.[130]

The failure of the mission, instead of driving the leaders of the British Jewish community to seek other ways and new initiatives to secure Edgardo's release, led rather to a period of inactivity on the matter. In December 1859 the Board wrote to Sir Culling Eardley, who was still pursuing the Mortara case actively, that 'having done all in their power in the Mortara case, they could not attempt to do more, but hoped he would persevere and be successful'.[131] This letter stirred up a hornets' nest. Momolo Mortara, the father of Edgardo, was visiting London at the time hoping to persuade the Board to ask the

British government to support a memorandum he intended submitting
to each representative at the forthcoming peace conference on Italy in
Paris. Initially the Board declined to help.[132] When news of this got
out, a series of articles attacking the decision appeared in the *JC*,[133]
and 450 members of the London and provincial Jewish communities
signed a petition demanding that the Board should support Momolo
Mortara. At its meeting on 26 December the Board bowed to this pressure and changed its mind. A meeting of the Mortara committee was
held a week later on 2 January 1860, a draft of a proposed memorandum to the Congress was approved and the president, Sir Moses Montefiore, was asked to consult with the government.[134] All this proved
to be in vain, because the peace conference was postponed and eventually abandoned.

The recently formed Alliance Israélite Universelle wrote to Sir
Culling and the Board asking them to come to Paris with a delegation
to meet the emperor and raise the issue of Mortara,[135] but this was
rejected by the Board.[136] The *JC* was not happy with this turn of
events, and a leader on 14 December 1860 stated that 'after Cavour
and Garibaldi it was Mortara who rendered the most eminent service
to the Italian cause. It was Mortara that made people see that the Pope
had not changed his spots. The Papacy, in refusing to listen to the voice
of justice, had committed moral suicide.'[137] A few days later the Board
considered a further approach from the Alliance and agreed to a joint
meeting with them on 20 December to consider suggestions to facilitate the release of Edgardo. Sir Moses did not attend that meeting as
he was indisposed, but this was possibly a diplomatic illness. That
meeting was indecisive and was divided on how to respond. The Board
decided it would further consider the Mortara case at an early meeting when the president was present.[138] In late February 1861 the Board
decided, subject to consultations with the Foreign Office, to write on
the subject of Mortara to Victor Emanuel, in the likely event that he
became king of Italy.[139] When he was duly installed, a draft letter to
him was sent to the Foreign Office. The reply said that there was no
point in sending the letter since the king of Italy did not rule in Rome
and had no influence there. The Board decided not to write to the
king.[140] This appears to be the last time that the Mortara affair was
mentioned at a meeting of the Board.

In 1870 Italian troops occupied Rome and Edgardo was free to take
his own decisions. One of his brothers immediately travelled to Rome
and suggested to Edgardo he should revert to Judaism and thus reunite

the family. Edgardo said that he fully wanted the family to be reunited, but the solution lay in their all becoming Catholics. In due course Edgardo became a priest and an ambassador for the Vatican. He retired to an abbey in Belgium and died there on 11 March 1940, a few weeks before German troops invaded Belgium and began rounding up those of Jewish blood. Thus the wheel did not quite turn full circle.

Morocco[141]

The involvement of the Board in the problems of the Jews of Morocco is a complex story. It started in 1859 when news reached the Board that a report had been received from the British consul in Rabat that the Jews in Morocco were in a deplorable condition. The Board sought the intervention of the British Government and the Foreign Office promised that the British Chargé d'Affaires in Morocco would do all he could to alleviate their situation.[142] Later in the year there was a panic-stricken exodus of Jews from Tangier to Gibraltar as a result of the outbreak of a war between Morocco and Spain and some wild tribes using the opportunity to attack Tangier. As a result the Board established a relief fund administered by a Morocco Relief Committee and sent a senior member of the Board, Moses Picciotto, to Morocco on a mission of enquiry with the power to spend funds as he saw fit. He reported late in 1860 and, by 1863, following a further visit to Morocco by Picciotto, about £8,000 of the £14,000 collected had been used to assist the Jews in Morocco. In 1863 there thus remained a balance in the fund of about £6,000 and the Board decided to establish a Council of Administration of these funds, which were invested and could only be used for the benefit of Jews in Morocco. The annual income was used mainly for education and sanitation.

In September 1863 at Safi in Morocco two Jews were executed on what seemed to be a trumped-up murder charge, and two others were imprisoned on the same charge. News of this reached London in early October and was discussed by the Board at an urgently convened meeting on 8 October. The agenda also included a separate case of two Jews bastinadoed (caned on the soles of feet) and imprisoned in Tetuan. The Board considered that, other than getting the Foreign Office involved, it was more likely to get a satisfactory solution if Sir Moses were to visit Morocco. It was reluctant to propose this as Sir Moses was 78, his wife was unwell, and he had only recently returned from a six-month tour of the Middle East, mainly in Palestine. However, when more worrying information reached London, Sir Moses informed the Board that he was willing to go and arrangements began to be made.[143] The Foreign Office, which in the meantime had investigated the matter and had instructed its 'men in Morocco' to try to protect the Jews, was very supportive of such a visit and promised to do all that it could to facilitate it. It pulled out all its stops even to the extent of despatching a naval frigate to convey Sir Moses and his party from Gibraltar to Mogador. The motivation of the British government was both humanitarian and political. Politically Britain and Spain were rivals for influence in Morocco and the Safi affair gave Britain the opportunity to demonstrate to the sultan its power. As David Littman has written: 'Britain's desire was to keep Morocco at peace with Europe by reducing the opportunities for direct foreign interference and to guarantee regular provisions for Gibraltar, as well as maintaining her long-established and privileged economic position'.[144]

Sir Moses visited Spain first, primarily because the events had occurred in towns occupied by Spanish forces. The Spanish minister in Morocco had been opposed to the innocent claims of the Jews, had been particularly cruel to them, and had had two Jewish youths arrested on a minor and not proven charge and subsequently imprisoned in Tangier and publicly bastinadoed. This visit proved successful in that Sir Moses not only saw the queen and the prime minister but also received promises of cooperation. Indeed the Spanish government was determined to be cleared of launching an anti-Jewish crusade and arranged for its minister in Morocco to issue a circular to all Spanish consuls in Morocco that was supportive of Jews. In Tangier Sir Moses was able to obtain the immediate release of the two Jewish youths and an assurance that the two Safi prisoners would be released. He was also instrumental in the establishment of an Anglo-French Jewish school in Tangier. It opened in 1864 with about 7,500 pupils and was administered jointly by the Board and the Alliance.

Montefiore then moved on to Marrakech, returning first to Gibraltar, thence by sea to Mogador and onwards overland. The British naval ship waited for him in Mogador for four weeks to take him back to Gibraltar. His meetings with the sultan proved very successful and the sultan issued an edict that promised security to Jews.[145] Regrettably, those who considered it 'a dead letter' were proved right before too long. It would seem that the old Moorish saying 'to promise is not the same as to perform' has more than an element of truth in it.

Romania[146]

Under the Treaty (1856) and Convention (1858) of Paris, following the Crimean War, the two Principalities of Moldavia and Wallachia remained in the Ottoman Empire, but were guaranteed as semi-autonomous countries by the Great Powers. They gradually became united (as Romania) following the election by both national assemblies of the same prince, Alexandru Cuza, in 1859. Under the Convention of Paris all citizens of the Principalities were to be treated equally under the law, but only Christians could have political rights. These rights could be extended to other religions by legislation. Cuza was fairly liberal and the position of the Jews improved and political rights became close to realization. However, in 1866 Cuza was forced to abdicate, primarily because of his liberal policies, and was replaced by Prince Carol of Hohenzollern-Sigmaringen.[147]

The new prince embarked on framing a new constitution. The Jewish community, aided by the Alliance Israelite and the Board who obtained the support of their governments, tried to obtain equal political rights. Initially this was successful and the Romanian government proposed that religion could not be an obstacle to citizenship and introduced a special clause that Jews would be gradually admitted to naturalization. However, during the debate on these clauses in Parliament there were public demonstrations against granting rights to Jews. The minister of finance announced that the government was withdrawing the clauses relating to Jews: 'we have said that the government does not intend to give the country to the Jews nor give them rights which endanger the interests of Romania in any way'. This excited the demonstrators and it turned into an anti-Jewish riot. A very large synagogue that had just been built in Bucharest was ransacked and destroyed, as were many Jewish houses and shops. The British government protested very strongly, but to no avail. The Romanian government then introduced an infamous clause into the constitution (Article 7) which read: 'The status of Romanian is acquired, retained and lost according to the rules established by civil law. Only foreigners of the Christian religion may become Romanians'. Despite protests from the British and the other Great Powers it was enacted. As if this was not enough it was confirmed later that year that all Jews, even those already resident and born in Romania, would be treated as foreigners. In 1867 it was announced that energetic steps would be taken to expel from the country Jewish 'vagrants' and that Jews no longer had the right to reside in rural areas, to operate hotels and to lease properties. This resulted in many Jews being rounded up and deported.[148]

This situation of the Jews in Romania was debated in the House of Lords on 1 July 1867 and raised by Sir Francis Goldsmid in the House of Commons on 5 July 1867.[149] Following a discussion by the Board, Sir Moses Montefiore, then aged 83, decided to visit Bucharest and ask Prince Carol to change his policy towards Jews. He travelled there in August 1867. He was received by the prince and was assured that the situation of the Jews would improve. It did not. Even whilst Sir Moses Montefiore was there, riots against Jews took place and there were demonstrations against him.[150] Following his visit new expulsions of Jews were ordered and carried out.

In January 1868 a violent anti-Jewish riot broke out in Moldavia. The Jews had been accused of poisoning a candidate to the Chamber of Deputies. Sir Moses wrote to the prince and received a reply from the Romanian foreign minister that it was the Jews themselves who had provoked the incident.

Major anti-Jewish riots broke out again at the beginning of 1872, when a Jew who had been converted to Christianity committed a robbery in a cathedral. The Board raised this matter with the Foreign Office and as a result the foreign consuls (led by the British) issued a collective note to the foreign minister demanding protection for the Jews. The reply stated that this had been done, but shortly afterwards the arrested rioters were released and a number of Jews punished for the robbery of which they were clearly innocent. The consuls again protested. These events gave rise to a debate in the House of Commons on 19 April 1872.[151] At about the same time a special committee of the recently formed Anglo-Jewish Association was established under the leadership of Sir Francis Goldsmid. Some deputies joined this committee but there does not seem to have been any formal representation from the Board. This committee was called the Romanian Committee and worked strenuously on behalf of Romanian Jews. One of its first initiatives was to organize a massive public protest meeting at the Mansion House on 30 May 1872, under the presidency of the Lord Mayor of London.[152] This had a significant effect on public opinion both in Britain and abroad.

In 1876 the Board was informed of negotiations between Romania, Britain and France for a commercial treaty that would have excluded British Jews from trading benefits. It raised the matter with the Foreign Office and was assured that a treaty on the lines proposed would never be accepted by the government.[153] Later in the year the Board received an appeal from the Jews of Romania, saying that they were being expelled from some districts, often with great cruelty and leading to destitution. This was raised with the Foreign Office, which instructed the British consul general to appeal to the Romanian government (which disapproved of these measures, which it said were local), and it dismissed four officials. The Board set up a relief fund for the Jews who were affected by these measures.[154]

At the Congress of Berlin in 1878, the issue of the Jews in Romania came to a head. Prior to the Congress, the Board, through the medium of the just-established Conjoint Foreign Committee, issued a paper to the prime minister, Benjamin Disraeli, setting out the problems that had affected the Jews of Romania and requesting that efforts should be made by the Congress that the Jews of Romania should be given equal rights with all inhabitants.[155] At the Congress, Romania sought recognition from the Great Powers for its independence. Led by Britain, the Congress agreed that the independence of Romania would be recognized, provided that Romania granted equal civic, religious and political rights for the Jews. This posed major problems for the Romanian government, which was faced with a sort of 'Hobson's choice' – that is, either it could give their Jews rights and achieve independence, or else give no rights to their Jews and not gain independence. Following the Congress, and with great reluctance, Romania gradually adopted some measures that gave a semblance of granting citizenship to a few Jews. This was enough for some of the Great Powers, but not for Britain, France and Germany. Unfortunately, Germany was interested in resolving a major financial dispute and when Romania agreed to do so on terms particularly favourable to Germany, it too agreed to recognize the independence of Romania. Britain and France held out for a bit longer but political expediency dictated that they too had to recognize Romanian independence, which they did in February 1880.[156]

Oppression of the Jews in Romania, particularly by the device of treating them as aliens and making naturalization virtually impossible even for those born there, continued and even intensified right up until the First World War. The Board, through the Conjoint, was forever taking action to try to alleviate their position.[157] The Jews of Romania did not become fully emancipated until 1923.

Spain[158]

In 1868, there was a revolution in Spain and the queen abdicated. During the discussions in the Spanish Parliament on a new constitution, there was an acrimonious debate between the Republicans who wanted the total separation of Church and State and the Catholics who opposed this. The Catholics attacked Judaism, which they claimed encouraged heretical ideas, despite there being a complete absence of Jews in Spain. One of the Republicans countered this by proposing that Jews should be readmitted.[159] When news of this reached London, the Board decided to write to the head of the provisional government in Spain, Marshal Serrano, asking for the 1492 expulsion edict to be repealed.[160] This was most likely at the initiative of Haim Guedalla, a deputy and an honorary officer of the Board in his capacity as auditor. He was a nephew by marriage of Moses Montefiore and had accompanied him on his mission to Morocco, which went and returned via Spain. The reply repeated what was already known, that Jews were free to visit Spain, although it also stated that there were no disabilities in Spain for those professing any creed. There was no mention of the 1492 edict at all.

In 1875, the monarchy was restored and a new constitution was under consideration by the Cortes in Spain. The Board felt that this was an opportunity to make another effort to obtain permission for Jews to be readmitted to Spain and practise their religion. Accordingly, they submitted a memorandum, via the Foreign Office, to Alfonso XII, the king of Spain.[161] In this paper, they requested that Jews should be permitted to settle in Spain and be free to profess and practise their religion. There was no immediate answer to this memorandum, but one of the clauses of the new constitution, whilst stating that the Catholic religion was the religion of the state, also stated that no one should be molested or persecuted 'for his particular form of worship as long as he keeps within the bounds of Christian morality'. However, it went on to state that 'no other ceremonies and no other public manifestations than those of the religion of the State shall be permitted'. This rather ambiguous clause alarmed the Liberal Party in Spain and it put down an amendment protecting the public and private exercise of every form of religion. After a discussion which lasted many days the amendment was rejected and the original and ambiguous clause adopted, but not before a minister had stated that dissenters would have the same rights as Catholics. In the meantime, the British ambassador in Spain had consulted the representative of the Rothschild Bank in Madrid (David

Weisweiller, who was the great nephew of Judith Montefiore – Sir Moses's wife), who thought it was better to let sleeping dogs lie and not raise the issue of repealing the 1492 edict at that time. The Board was not happy with the outcome, particularly as some harsh interpretations of the clause began to emerge, but hoped that in due course religious freedom would be secured in Spain to all 'who are prepared to exercise it with prudence and discretion'.[162] This harkened back to what the Board in its early days had seen as the deal under which Jews were able to exercise their religion in Britain. It decided, however, not to take any further steps in this matter for the time being. This was confirmed at a meeting of the Conjoint Foreign Committee on 26 July 1880.[163] However, a year later, in July 1881 the Board received a letter from the Spanish ambassador stating that there was no legal obstacle to prevent Jews settling in Spain, and the constitution, which permitted private religious practice, was more important than the 1492 edict and rendered its repeal unnecessary. This was almost certainly the result of personal correspondence between Haim Guedalla (probably impatient at the Board's lack of action) and the Spanish prime minister.

NOTES

1. W.D. Rubinstein, *Britain's Century: A Political and Social History 1815–1905* (London: Arnold, 1998), pp.xi–xv.
2. Sonia Lipman and V.D. Lipman (eds), *The Century of Moses Montefiore* (Oxford: Littman Library, 1985), pp.15–16.
3. See, for example, Israel Finestein, 'The Uneasy Victorian: Montefiore as Communal Leader', in S. Lipman and V.D. Lipman (eds), *Century of Moses Montefiore*, pp.45–70.
4. For an analysis of Sir Moses's life, see S. Lipman and V.D. Lipman (eds), *Century of Moses Montefiore*. For recent appraisals, see Israel Finestein, 'Sir Moses Montefiore: A Modern Appreciation', *Jewish Historical Studies*, 29 (1988); Abigail Green, 'Rethinking Sir Moses Montefiore: Religion, Nationhood, and International Philanthropy in the Nineteenth Century,' *American Historical Review*, 110, 3 (June 2005); Abigail Green, *Moses Montefiore: Jewish Liberator, Imperial Hero* (Cambridge, MA: Harvard University Press, 2010) [Forthcoming].
5. Stephen J. Lee, *Aspects of British Political History, 1815–1914* (Routledge: London, 1994), Chapter 8.
6. BOD, Minute Book 2, p.105.
7. M.C.N. Salbstein, *The Emancipation of the Jews in Britain: The Question of the Admission of the Jews to Parliament, 1828–1860* (London: Littman Library, 1982), p.73.
8. Rubinstein, *Britain's Century*, pp.64–7.
9. BOD, ACC/3121/A5, pp.33–44.
10. Charles H.L. Emanuel, *A Century and a Half of Jewish History: Extracted from the Minute Book of the London Committee of Deputies of British Jews* (London: George Routledge, 1910), p.33.
11. David Cesarani, *The Jewish Chronicle and Anglo-Jewry, 1841–1991* (Cambridge: Cambridge University Press, 1994), p.9.
12. *Jewish Chronicle* [JC], 7 February 1845, p.94.
13. Bill Williams, *The Making of Manchester Jewry, 1740–1875* (Manchester: Manchester University Press, 1976), pp.158–9.

14. BOD, ACC/3121/A/6, p.68.
15. *JC*, 29 October 1947, p.286.
16. BOD, ACC/3121/A/6, p.91.
17. Williams, *Making of Manchester Jewry*, pp.159–60.
18. BOD, ACC/3121/A/6, pp.125–7.
19. *JC*, 21 April 1848, p.507.
20. *JC*, 5 May 1848, p.521.
21. *JC*, 11 March 1853, pp.177–8; 28 April 1853, p.233.
22. BOD, ACC/3121/A/7, p.195.
23. *JC*, 22 June 1855, p.210.
24. Annual Report of the Board of Deputies (AR), 1887, p.12.
25. Almost every edition of the *JC* from March 1853 until the end of the year had news, editorials, opinion columns and letters on the subject. The two special supplements were on 9 September 1853 and 9 December 1853.
26. V.D. Lipman, *A History of the Jews in Britain since 1858* (Leicester: Leicester University Press, 1990), p.36.
27. *JC*, 16 June 1876, p.169; 23 June 1876, p.187; 30 June 1876, p.198; 21 July 1876, p.278; 28 July 1876, pp.256, 266.
28. *JC*, 22 June 1877, p.2; 13 July 1877, p.6.
29. Israel Finestein, 'Lucien Wolf (1857–1930): A study in ambivalence', *Jewish Historical Studies*, 35 (1996–98), p.241.
30. *JC*, 19 April 1878, p.5.
31. For further reading, see Chapter 1 of Israel Finestein, *Jewish Society in Victorian Britain: Collected Essays* (London: Vallentine Mitchell, 1993); A. Gilam, *The Emancipation of the Jews in England, 1830–1860* (New York: Garland, 1982); Salbstein, *The Emancipation of the Jews in Britain*, Chapter 3.
32. Rubinstein, *Britain's Century*, p.26.
33. BOD, Minute Book 2, p.9.
34. Salbstein, *The Emancipation of the Jews in Britain*, Chapter 3.
35. Ibid., Chapter 4.
36. Green, 'Rethinking Sir Moses Montefiore', p.16.
37. Louis Loewe (ed.), *Diaries of Sir Moses and Lady Montefiore, a facsimile of the 1890 edition* (London: Jewish Historical Society of England, 1983), Vol. 1, p.92.
38. David Feldman, *Englishmen and Jews: Social Relations and Political Culture 1840–1914* (London: Yale University Press, 1994), p.51.
39. H.S.Q. Henriques, *The Jews and the English Law* (Oxford: Augustus M. Kelley, 1908), p.163.
40. *JC*, 5 December 1873, p.549. See also James Picciotto, *Sketches of Anglo-Jewish History*, revised and edited with a prologue, notes and an epilogue by Israel Finestein (London: Soncino Press, 1956), p.120.
41. H.S.Q. Henriques, *The Jews and the English Law* (Oxford: Augustus M. Kelley, 1908), p.292.
42. Ibid., pp.300–1.
43. Rubinstein, *Britain's Century*, p.304.
44. Ibid., p.157.
45. Emanuel, *Century and a Half of Jewish History*, pp.22–3.
46. Ibid., p.45.
47. Ibid., p.53.
48. Ibid., pp.70–1.
49. Ibid., pp.73–4.
50. For further reading, see Israel Finestein, *Jewish Society in Victorian England: Collected Essays* (London: Vallentine Mitchell, 1993), Chapter 2; and H.S.Q. Henriques, *Jewish Marriages and the English Law* (Oxford: Bibliophile Press, 1909).
51. Emanuel, *Century and a Half of Jewish History*, pp.26–7.
52. Loewe (ed.), *Diaries of Sir Moses and Lady Montefiore*, Vol. 1, p.111.
53. N.B. English law did recognize Jewish marriages that had taken place abroad, even if they would not have been valid should they have taken place in England.
54. Emanuel, *Century and a Half of Jewish History*, p.49.
55. Ibid., pp.59–60.
56. Ibid., pp.67–8.

57. *Law Reports* [1900], 2 Ch 489.
58. Emanuel, *Century and a Half of Jewish History*, p.71.
59. Ibid., pp.84–5.
60. Geoffrey Alderman, *Controversy and Crisis: Studies in the History of the Jews in Modern Britain* (Boston, MA: Academic Studies Press, 2008), p.45.
61. Emanuel, *Century and a Half of Jewish History*, p.55.
62. For a full discussion on this see Robert Liberles, 'The Origins of the Jewish Reform Movement in Britain', *AJS Review*, 1 (1976), pp.121–50.
63. Ibid., pp.124–7.
64. Emanuel, *Century and a Half of Jewish History*, p.44.
65. Loewe, *Diaries of Sir Moses and Lady Montefiore*, Vol. 1, p.302.
66. Picciotto, *Sketches of Anglo-Jewish History*, p.374.
67. Emanuel, *Century and a Half of Jewish History*, p.44.
68 . *JC*, 7 March 1845, p.109.
69. *JC*, 25 July 1845, p.209.
70. See Abraham Gilam, 'The Burial Grounds Controversy between Anglo-Jewry and the Victorian Board of Health, 1850', *Jewish Social Studies*, 45 (1983), pp.147–56.
71. Emanuel, *Century and a Half of Jewish History*, p.47.
72. BOD, ACC/3121/A/6, pp.202–7.
73. Emanuel, *Century and a Half of Jewish History*, p.59.
74. Ibid., p.62.
75. See Israel Finestein, *Scenes and Personalities in Anglo-Jewry, 1800–2000* (London: Vallentine Mitchell, 2002), Chapter 2.
76 . Ibid., pp.54–5.
77. Emanuel, *Century and a Half of Jewish History*, p.54.
78. Williams, *Making of Manchester Jewry*, p.207; BOD, ACC/3121/A/7, pp.28–36.
79. Williams, *Making of Manchester Jewry*, p.208; BOD, ACC/3121/A/7, p.50.
80. BOD, ACC/3121/A/7, p.51.
81. Ibid., pp.52–5.
82. Ibid., pp.65, 70.
83. Gerry Black, *JFS: The History of the Jews' Free School, London, since 1732* (London: Tymsder, 1998), pp.80–1.
84. BOD, ACC/3121/A/7, pp.78–9.
85. *JC*, 8 October 1852, pp.6–7; 15 October 1852, pp.10–11; 22 October 1852, pp.16–19.
86. BOD, ACC/3121/A/7, p.113.
87. Black, *JFS*, p.83.
88. Emanuel, *Century and a Half of Jewish History*, pp.63–4.
89. Ibid., pp.92–3.
90. Ibid., pp.94–5.
91. Emanuel, *Century and a Half of Jewish History*, p.85.
92. AR, August 1869, p.18.
93. Emanuel, *Century and a Half of Jewish History*, pp.91–2.
94. He was the second Jewish MP after Lionel Rothschild, and entered the House of Commons following the 1859 general election.
95. Emanuel, *Century and a Half of Jewish History*, p.93.
96. *JC*, 14 April 1876, p.28.
97. AR, 1880, p.17.
98. Emanuel, *Century and a Half of Jewish History*, pp.68–9.
99. Ibid., pp.85–6.
100. For a full description of this episode see Jonathan Frankel, *The Damascus Affair: 'Ritual Murder', Politics, and the Jews in 1840* (Cambridge: Cambridge University Press, 1997).
101. Emanuel, *Century and a Half of Jewish History*, pp.33–5.
102. Extracts can be read in Frankel, *Damascus Affair*, pp.128–30.
103. Ibid., p.130; also PRO, FO 78/410.
104. Emanuel, *Century and a Half of Jewish History*, pp.37–8.
105. Frankel, *Damascus Affair*, p.402.
106. Emanuel, *Century and a Half of Jewish History*, pp.42–3.
107. The correspondence between Churchill and the Board can be found in Lucien Wolf, *Notes*

on the Diplomatic History of the Jewish Question (London: Jewish Historical Society of England, 1919) pp.119–24.

108. See Jonathan Frankel, 'Demanding Leadership: The Russian-Jewish Question and the Board of Deputies of the British Jews, July 1842 – February 1846 (with Documents)', in *Transition and Change in Modern Jewish History: Essays Presented in Honour of Shmuel Ettinger* (Jerusalem: Merkaz Zalman Shazar le-toldot Yiś ra'el: ha-Hevrah ha-historit ha-Yiś re'elit, 1987), pp.xxxi–lxxi; Chimen Abramsky, 'The Visits to Russia', in S. Lipman and V.D. Lipman (eds), *Century of Moses Montefiore*, pp.254–65.
109. Abramsky, 'The Visits to Russia', p.264.
110. Ibid., p.255.
111. Ibid.
112. Frankel, 'Demanding Leadership', p.xxxix.
113. Ibid., p.xlii.
114. Ibid., pp.lvi–lvii.
115. Ibid., pp.xlv–xlvi.
116. Ibid., pp.lvii–lix.
117. *Voice of Jacob*, 5 January 1844, p.64.
118. Frankel, *Damascus Affair*, pp.lx–lxi.
119. Ibid., p.lxii–lxiv.
120. *Voice of Jacob*, 21 June 1844, p.172.
121. Frankel, *Damascus Affair*, pp.lxviii–lxxi.
122. Abramsky, 'The Visits to Russia', p.258.
123. For a full account of the Mortara Affair, see David Kertzer, *The Kidnapping of Edgardo Mortara* (London: Vintage Books, 1997) and Raphael Langham, 'The Reaction in Britain to the Kidnapping of Edgardo Mortara', *Jewish Historical Studies*, 39 (2004), pp.79–101.
124. *JC*, 16 July 1858, p.245.
125. *JC*, 13 August 1858, p.275; 27 August 1858, p.293.
126. BOD, ACC/3121/A/8/290.
127. *JC*, 17 September 1858, pp.316–17.
128. *JC*, 31 December 1858, p.4.
129. *JC*, 29 July 1859, p.4.
130. *Archives Israélites*, December 1859; English translation in *JC*, 16 December 1859, p.7.
131. Loewe, *Diaries of Sir Moses and Lady Montefiore*, Vol. 2, p.107.
132. BOD, ACC/3121/C13/1/1, p.15.
133. *JC*, 9 December 1859, pp.2–5; 16 December 1859, pp.1–2, 5, 7; *JC*, 23 December 1859, p.2.
134. BOD, ACC/3121/C13/1/1/22–23.
135. *JC*, 26 October 1860, p.7.
136. BOD, ACC/3121/A/9/108–9.
137. *JC*, 14 December 1860, p.4.
138. *JC*, 28 December 1860, p.5.
139. BOD, ACC/3121/A/9/131.
140. BOD, ACC/3121/A/9/147–9.
141. For a full account, see David Littman, 'Mission to Morocco', in S. Lipman and V.D. Lipman (eds), *Century of Moses Montefiore*, pp.171–229,
142. Emanuel, *Century and a Half of Jewish History*, p.74.
143. Ibid., pp.79–80.
144. Littman, 'Mission to Morocco', p.192.
145. Ibid., p.190.
146. For a history of the Jews of Romania, see Carol Iancu, *Jews in Romania 1866–1919: From Exclusion to Emancipation*, trans. Carvel de Bussy (New York: Boulder, 1996). Also U.R.Q. Henriques, 'Journey to Romania, 1867', in S. Lipman and V.D. Lipman (eds), *Century of Moses Montefiore*, pp.230–57.
147. Henriques, 'Journey to Romania, 1867', p.231.
148. All of these episodes are recounted in Iancu, *Jews in Romania 1866–1919*.
149. *Hansard*, 3rd Series, Vol. 188, pp.746–51 and 1136–41.
150. Henriques, 'Journey to Romania, 1867', pp.238–44.
151. *Hansard*, 3rd Series, Vol. 210, pp.1585–604.

152. *The Jews of Romania: Report of Public Meeting held at Mansion House on Thursday May 30 1872* (London, 1872).
153. Emanuel, *Century and a Half of Jewish History*, p.104.
154. Ibid., pp.105–6.
155. Ibid., pp.107–9.
156. A copy of the letter from the British government, recognizing Romania, can be found in Wolf, *Notes on the Diplomatic History*, pp.35–6.
157. See, in particular, AR, 1909, pp.50–65; AR, 1913, pp.54–74; AR, 1915, pp.57–65.
158. For more information, see Michael Alpert, 'Dr Angel Pulido and philo-Sephardism in Spain', *Jewish Historical Studies*, 40 (2005), pp.109–19.
159. Ibid, p.108.
160. BOD, ACC/3121/A/010, p.260.
161. BOD, ACC/3121/A/011, p.373.
162. AR, 1877, p.42.
163. BOD, ACC/3121/A/012, p.160.

3 The Cousinhood Period, 1874–1917

In February 1874, Benjamin Disraeli became prime minister at the head of a Conservative government with a good majority. He had been prime minister of a minority government from February to December 1868, when on his appointment he had made his well-known remark to Queen Victoria: 'I have climbed to the top of the greasy pole.' A few months later Sir Moses Montefiore resigned from the presidency of the Board. The coincidence of the closeness of the two dates signifies nothing, but the first event was of great significance for Britain and both events were of great significance to the Jews of Britain. Sir Moses was aged 89 when he retired and he had been president for most of the previous forty years. The next three presidents were all nephews of Sir Moses, and they and the next four presidents were all members of the 'cousinhood' (as described in the Introduction).

The previous fifty or so years had been in the main good for the Jews in Britain. The community had prospered and its numbers had grown to about 60,000. Virtually all the Jewish disabilities (in particular the unacceptable oath requirements) had gone so that most occupations and institutions were open to them, and Jews practically had equal rights with all citizens and a number of exemptions from the law or regulations to facilitate religious observance. However, as the *Jewish Chronicle* (JC) pointed out in a leading article early in 1874, there was no room for complacency – there were difficulties for observant Jews in Sabbath observance and adhering to the dietary laws in certain occupations, and Jews were precluded from attending large public schools such as Eton and Harrow.[1] Numeri clausi operated and there were social exclusions: for example, many of the London clubs did not allow Jews to join. The emancipation issues had reached a satisfactory conclusion with Lionel Rothschild having been able to take his seat in the Commons, and twenty-seven years later his son Nathaniel Mayer became the first Jewish peer and could sit in the House of Lords. The Board had been recognized, both within the Jewish community and by the government, as the spokesman for the Jews in Britain and was consulted on all matters affecting Jews. Whilst it was true that the Board had to take the initiative to raise Jewish concerns whenever legislation seemed to have an adverse impact, nonetheless it was generally successful. This was probably due less to its powers of advocacy and more to the fact that its demands were not seen by the government as having an adverse political impact on the country. On matters affecting foreign Jewry, the Board generally found sympathy and help from the government. Again, this was less because of the humanitarian support for the issues, but more because it was either neutral or supportive to British foreign policy. Where an issue arose in a foreign country where intervention might be against the perceived British interests then help was denied.

Montefiore retired at a good time. Not quite on the horizon was the flood of Jewish immigrants from Eastern Europe that would lead to a major change in the demographic and social make-up of the Jews in Britain and thus give rise to issues within the Board as to how to react to them and how to adapt to accommodate these changes. The number of Jews in Britain rose from about 60,000 in 1870 to 300,000 in 1914. Immigration led to conflicts within the community and thus the Board. Furthermore, immigration began to focus attention on Jews – not so much the total numbers, since the proportion of Jews in Britain has always been well below 1 per cent of the total population, but because of their concentration in certain urban districts like the East End of London.

Britain was also changing. Governments, particularly liberal administrations, were becoming much more concerned with social reform, and legislation in this area began to be introduced. There were significant electoral reforms leading to a much wider enfranchisement, and the concepts of the role of the state began to change. The Jewish issue in British politics moved from constitutional issues such as emancipation to social policy such as how to deal with immigrant aliens. The large number of Jewish immigrants from Eastern Europe led eventually to a royal commission on alien immigration and the Aliens Act of 1905, which for the first time imposed restrictions on immigration into Britain. A popular measure with the general British public, but not among British Jewry.

During the period covered by this chapter, the Board was particularly concerned with maintaining its authority within the Jewish community and trying to remain the sole spokesman for the community in its relationship with the government. There were many challenges to its leadership and often, in order to maintain this position, it had to change its stance on issues, including such matters as holding public meetings to protest against possible restrictions on Sunday trading and protesting against the pogroms in Russia. Other Jewish organizations, such as the English Zionist Federation (EZF) and the B'nei B'rith, often bypassed the Board and talked directly to government, leaving the Board to protest that it was the sole properly *representative* body of British Jewry. As a result, the question of how representative it really was became an issue. When in 1903 the concept of establishing a Jewish settlement in East Africa was proposed by the government, the Board was ignored and the government talked directly to the Zionists.[2] Nothing came of this idea, but the Board records are completely silent on the subject. This lesson was learned by the Zionists and in the lead up to the Balfour Declaration they bypassed the Board, which was seen as dominated mainly by anti-Zionists, and talked direct to government.

This chapter is again divided into three parts. The first considers the internal structure and workings of the Board and how it restructured itself to meet its internal and external challenges. The second part covers the issues the Board dealt with that arose at home and the third part deals with foreign affairs, including the rise of Zionism.

1. THE BOARD

Leadership

Following the retirement of Sir Moses Montefiore, his nephew Joseph Mayer Montefiore was elected president of the Board. He was a stockbroker, treasurer of Bevis Marks and had been vice-president of the Board from 1858 to 1874.[3] The *JC* used the occasion of his election to urge the Board 'to reject its passivity and once more assume its role as the leading body in the British Jewish community',[4] but it seems it was disinclined to do so. This is evidenced by the Board's reaction when in 1876 it was invited by the Alliance Israélite Universelle to attend an International Jewish Conference in Paris to consider action to be taken with regard to attacks on Jews in Turkey and Serbia. This invitation was considered by the Board at a specially convened meeting held on 7 December 1876, and by a majority of seven to four it was decided not to send representatives to this conference.[5] Following this meeting, the Board wrote to the British government informing it of the conference and the Board's decision not to attend, and stating that it would continue to rely on the government to look after the interests of Jews in foreign lands. These actions led to considerable criticism of the Board, not only in the Jewish press but also, judging by the letters published in the press, by many prominent members of the British Jewish community. The *JC* published many letters from deputies who were opposed to the inaction of the Board.[6] The Board's reaction to the invitation contrasted with that of the AJA who took a prominent part in the conference, which earned them many 'Brownie points' in the Jewish community. It might well have been this that led the Board, late in 1877, to reopen discussions for cooperation with the AJA.

If this was not enough trouble for the Board, it was almost immediately faced with what could have been its demise. On 2 January 1877, J.M. Laurence, a member of the Council of the United Synagogue, gave notice that he would be proposing a motion that the connection between the United Synagogue and the Board should be severed.[7] It would seem that the reaction of the Board to the conference invitation was the final straw. The proposal was withdrawn following intervention from Sir Nathaniel Mayer Rothschild, the vice-president of the United Synagogue, who had in the past been highly critical of the Board but this time came to its defence. It was not that he supported the Board on the conference issue, but it was its likely extinction that concerned him.[8]

In 1880, Joseph Mayer Montefiore died and was succeeded as president by Arthur Cohen, a nephew of Sir Moses on his wife's side.[9] Arthur Cohen was a prominent QC, a Liberal MP and the first Ashkenazi president of the Board. He was a distinguished president of the Board during a very difficult period. To a large extent he was responsible, together with the president of the AJA, Henry de Worms, for developing the modus operandi of the Conjoint Foreign Affairs Committee. In this respect, he has been criticized for ceding too much power to the Conjoint, which virtually monopolized the Jewish community's actions and reactions to foreign matters and their relationship with the Foreign Office. This criticism was essentially that the Conjoint was unrepresentative, oligarchic and acted autonomously.[10] In October 1895 Arthur Cohen unexpectedly resigned. His reason was that one of his daughters was about to marry a non-Jew and he considered that this would 'deprive him to a great extent of the authority and influence which the president of the Board ought to have on the Jewish community'.[11] At the Board meeting following his resignation all the deputies who spoke did not agree with the reasons for his resignation, but most accepted it on the grounds that his letter of resignation stated that his decision was irrevocable.

A month after the president of the Board resigned, the president of the AJA also resigned, through ill health. F.D. Mocatta, who was very prominent in the community, and the vice-president of the AJA proposed in a letter to the *JC* that this was an opportunity for the fusion of the Board and the AJA. Clearly, neither body liked the idea as the Board promptly elected Joseph Sebag-Montefiore as its president and the AJA elected Claude Montefiore as its president. A proposal was also mooted in the *JC* that the Board should concentrate on home affairs and the AJA on foreign matters,[12] but, not surprisingly, the Board did not concur and matters proceeded as previously. Joseph Sebag-Montefiore was a nephew and the principal heir of Sir Moses Montefiore. He was a businessman and was knighted in 1896. He is probably best remembered for carrying out his uncle's wishes and burning many of his papers after his death.[13]

In 1903 a new president, David Lindo Alexander, and a new vice-president, Leopold de Rothschild, were elected. David Alexander, a barrister, had joined the Board in 1877 and as president dominated the Board until June 1917 when he resigned following a vote of no confidence. He was a member of the 'old' Anglo-Jewish elite and was the president at a time when the Board's authority was being increasingly challenged by the new Jewish middle class as well as the Jewish immigrants from Eastern Europe. He was constantly being criticized for being out of touch.[14] He was a member of the Cousinhood, but not from the Montefiore family. In fact, in 1895 when Arthur Cohen resigned a number of deputies had tried to persuade David Alexander to stand for president, but he demurred, feeling that a nephew of Sir Moses, Joseph Sebag-Montefiore, had a prior claim. Nepotism was still alive and well.

Representation

In 1881 a letter to the *JC* from someone who signed himself 'Scrutator' highlighted the poor representation of provincial communities on the Board and suggested this was due mainly to the cost of representation, and proposed a change from a charge per congregation to a charge per seat-holder.[15] This point was taken up by the Board and in 1883 a capitation method of assessing subscriptions to the Board for small provincial congregations was introduced. Hitherto all synagogues were required to pay a subscription equal to their proportionate share of the total expenses of the Board, the proportion being the number of the synagogue's deputies divided by the total number of deputies. It was decided that for any provincial congregation with fewer than a hundred seat holders who wished to send a deputy, the subscriptions to the Board would amount to two shillings (equivalent to ten new pence) per seat holder. This heralded the start of major changes in the method of financing the Board. The Board took the opportunity of the review of its constitution to make another important change. For a number of years there had been a lot of pressure from communities in the British Colonies to be able to elect deputies and in 1883 it was agreed that they could do so. In practice it was not until 1898 that a deputy from a colony was elected. He was Henry Bonas of Hatton Garden, London and represented Griqualand West, which was a British territory in the Transvaal and where there were considerable diamond mines.

Five years later the United Synagogue created another crisis for the Board, this time over finance. The issue arose because in 1887 there had been unusually high expenses mainly in respect of the costs of a special album presented by the Board on behalf of the Jews of Britain to Queen Victoria on the occasion of her Golden Jubilee. The United Synagogue did not object to the presentation but was concerned at the lack of financial control. It proposed a change to the constitution by placing a limit on the assessment of each synagogue to £7.50 a year per deputy. There was no such limit in the then constitution and this proposed limit was 50 per cent higher than the most recent assessment of £5 per deputy, so there was quite a margin. This proposal was strongly opposed by the honorary officers, but received a lot of support from many deputies. The debates on the matter at the Board meetings were quite acrimonious, giving deputies the opportunity to air other grievances. In the end a compromise was reached and a limit of £9 a year per deputy was agreed, with certain powers for additional assessments to congregations should expenditure exceed this amount.[16]

Provincial representation remained a problem. Only a handful of provincial synagogues took up the opportunity afforded by the special subscription for communities with fewer than a hundred seat-holders, and some of their deputies were based in London. In fact many provincial congregations were represented by deputies resident in London, essentially because they had difficulty in finding suitable local men who had the time and were prepared to incur the expense of frequent trips to London. Furthermore, a number of London Jews who wished to become deputies arranged to represent provincial congregations based on paying the subscriptions themselves – a sort of 'rotten borough' situation. The problem had been compounded by Board meetings being switched to a Sunday from midweek and this had led to great protests from deputies based in the provinces. As a result it had been agreed that two out of three meetings would revert to midweek. The whole issue of representation was discussed by the Board at a meeting in February 1902 and a subcommittee was formed to consider ways and means of strengthening the representative character of the Board and enlarging the scope of its work.[17]

The committee recommended, among other matters, appointing a second vice-president, extending representation to India and all other British possessions and reorganizing the committee structure. This latter proposal was not agreed, but the most important innovation was the introduction of an annual meeting.[18] The main object of this was to obtain closer relationships with provincial congregations. These congregations were invited to send their wardens or other prominent members to the annual meeting. The annual meeting had no real powers as any resolutions that were passed had to be debated and agreed at subsequent Board meetings. Nonetheless they proved to be very successful, and judging by the minutes enabled many delegates to get rid of a lot of steam. They also gave the honorary officers a very good feel for the views of the provincial delegates and which issues they considered most important.

Following the triennial election in 1904 more deputies were elected and more synagogues represented than ever before. The *JC* attributed this in part to the abilities of the new president and vice-president, but also to the growing importance of a number of communal questions and to the fact that the Board was the only national body where these questions could be discussed.[19] However, as the next triennial elections approached it deplored the ease with which anyone could still purchase representation from some provincial synagogues and, to add insult to injury, it pointed out that after election some deputies did not pay to their congregation what was expected![20]

B'nei B'rith

In 1910, the Board became concerned with the establishment of the First Lodge of Britain of the B'nei B'rith.[21] In other countries the B'nei B'rith had intervened with governments on behalf of Jewish communities and the Board considered that the Lodge in Britain might try to usurp some of its authority in this area. They were particularly concerned because some of the Board's more disaffected deputies, as well as the haham who was often in disagreement with the Board, were among the Lodge's founders.[22]

The Board did not have long to wait, because the Lodge decided to establish a scheme of legal aid for alien immigrants in conjunction with the Home Office, something the Board should have been doing but was not. The Board was forced into action because of this initiative, and an alien's legal aid committee was established jointly with the B'nei B'rith. The Lodge decided to pursue its own path in scrutinizing new or potential legislation affecting Jews and often put forward to government views differing from or even opposed to those of the Board. Examples include supporting Dr Gaster, the haham, in his opposition to the attitude of the Board regarding *shechita* in 1911. Matters came to a head in 1912 in what became known as the 'Russian Passport Question'. The Russian government had been discriminating against British Jews visiting Russia and the Lodge arranged for a petition protesting this to be submitted to all Jewish MPs for onward transmission to the government. The Lodge was encouraged in taking this step as in the United States a petition organized by the B'nei B'rith had succeeded in obtaining the abrogation of the Russo-American Treaty of Commerce for similar reasons. The Board had been involved in this issue for some years, and when asked by the Lodge to cooperate firmly rejected any such cooperation. In the event nothing was achieved because the government considered this to be interference in the affairs of a foreign country, which it would not do at least with regard to one of the 'Great Powers' with whom Britain had certain ties.[23] Other issues where the Lodge differed from the Board and took independent action are mentioned elsewhere in this book. The point is that other Jewish bodies, representative or not, were bypassing the Board and making representations direct to government. Some were issues that the Board had ignored or had chosen not to deal with, and others were where views differed from those of the Board.

In 1911 a National Insurance Bill had clauses that would have a bearing on Jewish Friendly Societies. Instead of asking the Board to make representations on their behalf, the Jewish Friendly Societies, including the B'nei B'rith Lodge, formed a conference of delegates and decided to make a direct appeal to the Chancellor of the Exchequer, David Lloyd George. In fact it would seem that they went out of their way to mislead the Board as to their intentions. Invitations from the

Law, Parliamentary and General Purposes Committee to meet with the conference were ignored and at a meeting of the Board one of the delegates to the conference, who was also a deputy, stated that they had not yet reached a stage where it would be appropriate to meet the committee. However, shortly after this the Board learned of the direct approach from the conference to the government. In fact the Board discovered that an important point in the bill that could have an adverse effect on observant Jews had been ignored or missed by the Friendly Societies, and it made its own representations to the Chancellor of the Exchequer.[24] It is unclear if the Friendly Societies did not think that the Board would be able to make adequate or effective comments, or whether it was a clash of status, *amour-propre* and personalities.

Dissatisfaction

At the annual meeting in December 1908 the president had, as usual, discussed the various issues that the Board had dealt with during the previous year but concluded with a *cri de cœur*:

> Another matter of some importance, viz., the deplorable waste of time which occasionally takes place at the ordinary meetings of the Board, owing to the attitude of a few of the members who seem to take a pleasure in trying to harass the Honorary Officers ... during the past year instances have not been wanting in which certain members of the Board have failed to yield that willing and prompt obedience to the ruling of the Chair ... The result has been that much valuable time has been spent over trivial and insignificant matters which might have been more profitably employed on the more serious and important work of the Board.[25]

Judging by reports of subsequent meetings of the Board those responsible were not moved by this exhortation. But it gives us a clue that something was going on and, as we shall see, there was more to it than just sniping at the honorary officers; there was dissatisfaction with the Board at various levels both within the Board by some deputies and externally as well.

An example of this dissatisfaction manifested itself at the first meeting of the Board following the 1910 triennial elections. At this meeting the honorary officers were due to be elected and a number of deputies complained that they had not been sent a list of those deputies eligible for office nor any invitations to make nominations. The meeting became quite stormy at that point, but in the end the protestors were ruled out of order and the 'old gang' were re-elected. Herbert Bentwich, a deputy, subsequently wrote to the *JC* complaining of what went on and suggesting that 'the rank and file members should organise themselves if the Board is to continue beyond its 150th anniversary as an effective representative institution of the community'.[26] Herbert Bentwich was in fact a thorn in the flesh to the hierarchy of the Board. He was one of the founders of the English Zionist Federation and the B'nei B'rith and seldom missed an opportunity to harangue the Board on almost whatever issue was under discussion. Stuart Cohen has drawn attention to a comment by R.N. Salaman that 'to people like myself, who met him frequently on committees and casually outside them, it was always Bentwich's obstructionist and antagonist attitude which came foremost'.[27]

In fact 1910 and 1911 were not good years for the standing of the Board. Not only were there the post-triennial election complaints and the independent role adopted by the B'nei B'rith Lodge, but its relations with others in the community declined. There were two well-publicized altercations with the haham, one over the Board's evidence to the Divorce Commission and the other on the Slaughter of Animals Bill. Furthermore, the Jewish costermongers and traders in the East End considered that the Board did not properly represent, or even understand, their views on Sunday trading and the costermongers went so far as to make representations themselves to the Home Office, much to the chagrin and embarrassment of the Board. The immigrant Jewish community in the East End of London did not consider the Board was taking a strong enough line against the threat of new anti-alien legislation in 1911. They formed a committee to combat this – at first called the Jewish Protection Society and subsequently, under new leadership, the Aliens Defence Committee (ADC). This committee bypassed the Board and wrote directly to MPs and the government. As the threat of legislation faded away so did the ADC, but the important point remained that the Board could be bypassed and that a more active response to issues than that taken by the Board could be taken by other groups in the community.[28]

In October 1911 there was a blistering attack on the Board in the *JC* by 'Mentor', which was the pen name that Leopold Greenberg, the editor, used for his column 'In the Communal Armchair', which was normally a commentary on matters involving the British Jewish community.[29] There were a number of prongs to his attack. He mentioned some of the matters that the Board would have to deal with on its return from its summer recess, such as alien immigration issues, *shechita*, Sunday trading and outrages in South Wales (Tredegar), and doubted that it would be able to do its work properly because of the way the Board was constituted. He considered that the Board was not properly representative mainly because of the 'rotten borough' system under which most deputies were not truly representative of the community they represented. He suggested that most of these deputies had been allocated to synagogues through the offices of the secretary of the Board and had merely joined that synagogue so as to become its deputy and pay the fees due from that synagogue. Furthermore, these deputies never visited their constituencies to give an account of their stewardship. He went on to write: 'To that extent the Board of Deputies is a sham and a delusion and its glaring inefficiency and impotency – the characterless backbonelessness of its policy on all matters – will endure so long as it remains upon the sand-dune of make-believe.' It does not follow, of course, that lack of true representation leads to inefficiency and ineffectiveness, but that was his argument. He criticized the way matters were dealt with by the Board, normally being delegated to the Law, Parliamentary and General Purposes Committee and with important decisions being taken by the executive, which he considered a 'tiny voluntary oligarchy'. His real bone of contention in this regard, although not actually stated as such, was that whereas Board meetings were open to the press, committee meetings were not.[30]

It must be appreciated that Leopold Greenberg had his own agenda. He was one of the founders of the English Zionist Federation and had resigned from the Board in 1908, partly because he was out of sorts with the Board hierarchy that tended to be anti-Zionist and thus militated against the EZF strategy of infiltrating the leading communal institutions.[31] In fact his opposition to the 'rotten borough' method of electing deputies might well have stemmed from his frustration at not being able to get many pro-Zionists elected as deputies.

The *JC* received and published a large number of letters as a result of the 'Mentor' article, mainly unfavourable to the Board. The attack on the Board was raised at the Board's meeting on 22 October 1911 but the president refused to allow any discussion. As a result a motion was sent to the secretary requesting a special meeting to discuss the matter, but this was ignored. At the same meeting a deputy, S. Rosenbaum, gave notice that at the next meeting of the Board he would move a resolution of censure on the president. He contended that the action of the president in relation to matters such as evidence to the Divorce Commission, the Slaughter of Animals Bill, the Shops Bill, and so on, had had the effect of seriously diminishing the influence and authority of the Board. Clearly the *JC* article had provoked at least one deputy. The censure motion was debated at the Board meeting on 19 November 1911. It was a long, serious and not acrimonious debate and at the end of the discussion the proposer asked leave to withdraw the motion, but this was refused and a vote took place resulting in only two votes for censure and sixty against.[32] A letter to the *JC* signed by a 'Deputy' considered that the wrong issue had been debated by the Board – it was not a question of confidence in the president, but rather what should have been debated was why the Board was no longer trusted by many sections of the community and what should be done to remedy this situation.[33] The few members of the Board who were in favour of change continued the fight. At the Board's meeting on 21 January 1912 a proposal was tabled that a committee should be established to consider what amendments should be made to its constitution and procedures in order to strengthen the Board in carrying out its activities. The arguments put forward by the proposers were essentially that a reform was needed in the methods of electing deputies and in the Board's methods of operation so as to give its members a greater sense of responsibility. The proposal was defeated by twenty-nine votes to fourteen even though it seems from the report of the debate in the *JC* that the case for change was very strong and well presented whereas the arguments against were exceedingly unsatisfactory and unconvincing.[34]

At the annual meeting of the Board held on Sunday 4 February 1912, the president went on the attack against all the criticism that had been going on. His opening remarks included the following:

> It is no more than a bare statement of fact to say that the Board has passed through a year full of incident and grave anxiety and perplexing controversies: (1) It has been confronted with problems phenomenal in their gravity and complexity, and quite unprecedented in there number; (2) The principles, methods and actions have been grievously misrepresented and unjustly and unscrupulously attacked and criticised; (3) It has been subjected to a flood of unmeasured abuse which has added greatly to the sum total of its difficulties and hampered the energies of those responsible for the conduct of its affairs, and (4) It has had to fight against a factious

opposition on the part of a small dissatisfied minority whose methods have been obstructive, discreditable and disloyal.

He then went on to explain and defend the various actions of the Board. The debate was acrimonious and a motion to amend the constitution to improve provincial representation and make other changes was defeated.[35]

The *JC* heralded 1913 in a leader headed 'Wake up Jewry!' which included a reiteration of its case for improving the Board by better representation and proposed that this could be achieved in the forthcoming triennial elections. In March 1913 'Mentor' elaborated on this under the heading 'Will Jewry Wake Up?' and his challenge was taken up by the Manchester synagogues, who convened a conference of their deputies in late April at which it was decided that as far as possible all provincial communities should be represented by provincial men; that they (the Manchester deputies) should form themselves into a permanent local committee; and that other provincial communities should be encouraged to do the same. This was to be the genesis of the establishment of Jewish Representative Councils in a number of provincial centres. This meeting led 'Mentor' to write perhaps his most vituperative attack on the Board and its need for reorganization. Action, though, was on its way. Whether stimulated by the press campaign or not, the president of the Board met with the Manchester deputies and it was agreed to implement some changes. These included speeding up meetings, a requirement that the president should make a statement at each meeting as to the matters dealt with by the Conjoint, a yearly list of the dates of meetings fixed in advance and that the official title of the Board should be changed from 'The London Committee of Deputies of the British Jews' to 'The Board of Deputies of British Jews'. These reforms were all agreed and incorporated into the by-laws. These were all welcomed and considered they would greatly improve the working of the Board, but lack of proper and full representation remained an issue, particularly for synagogues that did not choose or were unable to join the Board and for those Jews who were not members of synagogues.[36]

Another example of what might be considered a consequence of the unrepresentative nature of the Board occurred in July 1914 at a conference of Jewish Trade Unions. It seems that the Board had lobbied Jewish MPs to block a bill, known as the Bakehouse Bill, that would have had the effect of reducing the number of hours worked in bakehouses from twelve hours a day to eight. The Board's case was that if the bill was passed it would increase the price of bread and further-more there would not be sufficient time to bake matzot for Passover. It seems that the Jewish Bakers Union had been on strike for twenty-six weeks in 1913 for a reduction in hours, but was not successful. Furthermore, there were a significant number of unemployed Jewish bakers. The conference complained to the Board that they represented over 10,000 Jewish workers and were never consulted by the Board. Their letter was raised at a Board meeting on 19 July 1914 and the secretary pointed out that he had consulted Messrs Bonn and Co., a manufacturer of matzot. Some deputies protested that he should have consulted both sides and obtained the views of the employees as well before taking action. No response was made to this point.[37] The bill was dropped following the outbreak of the First World War.

The activities of the Board in relation to the war came under a lot of criticism by the Jewish press and other sections of the community, particularly with regard to internment of Jewish aliens and also the conscription of Russian Jews where it was considered by the *JC* to be less supportive than it should have been and virtually left the field open in this regard to the B'nei B'rith. In March 1915 the Board discussed a proposal to admit representatives of the Jewish Friendly Societies as deputies, but this was rejected partly on the grounds that this would create a precedent and would open the door to other sections of the community.[38]

Towards the end of 1915 the Board announced it was convening a conference in January 1916 to consider revisions to the constitution prior to the triennial elections later that year. The results of the con-ference were disappointing to those who wanted change, in that the majority voted in favour of the status quo regarding representation and with no real changes to the constitution.[39] They might, however, have been encouraged in that about one-third of the deputies voted for change, which was a much higher proportion than previously. This might have been an indication of where things were moving. Following the triennial elections in May 1916, 'Mentor' was disappointed that the new Board was much the same as its predecessor and remarked that a number of new deputies had had to ask the secretary of the Board as to which synagogue they represented![40] At about the same time a letter from a deputy, Samuel Daiches, was published in the *JC*, proposing that those deputies looking for changes to the Board should form themselves into a group or party. This seems to have gained some support judging by further letters, but nothing happened.[41] This is a further indication of dissatisfaction with the Board, this time from within. It also can be considered the first of proposals that would lead to groups or caucuses within the Board, as will be discussed later. Samuel Daiches, like Herbert Bentwich, was also a thorn in the side of the Board leadership, participating in most debates and generally opposed to the views of the honorary officers. He was a rabbi and lecturer at Jews' College, a strong Zionist and also one of the founders of the B'nei B'rith.

Censure

The Conjoint had been at loggerheads with the English Zionist Federation for some time, but this had seldom involved the Board directly. Matters came to a head on 24 May 1917 when *The Times* published a letter signed by the presidents of the AJA and the Board, attacking Zionism and stating that their view represented that of Anglo-Jewry.[42] The reaction of many deputies was very hostile, not only those who were Zionists, but also others who considered it was incorrect to state that this was the view of Anglo-Jewry and that the president should have consulted the Board in advance. At the Board meeting on 17 June 1917 the following resolution was tabled:

> That this Board, having considered the views of the Conjoint Committee as promulgated in the communication published in the Times of the 24th May, 1917, expresses profound disapproval of such views and dissatisfaction at the publication thereof, and declares that the Conjoint Committee has lost the confidence of the Board, and calls upon its representatives on the Conjoint Committee to resign their appointments forthwith.

The president announced that he would consider the matter as a vote of censure on the officers. The resolution was proposed by Elsley Zeitlyn and seconded by Neville Laski (who became president of the Board in 1933). The debate was long and acrimonious, but in the end the resolution was passed by fifty-six votes to fifty-one. The president, D.L. Alexander, one of the vice-presidents, H.S.Q. Henriques, and the treasurer, J.M. Levy, immediately resigned their offices.[43]

At the next Board meeting it was decided to sever connections with the Conjoint and this led to the Conjoint being dissolved. Many thought at the time that the vote of censure was a great victory for the Zionists, and indeed it went down in Zionist mythology that it was.

However, Stuart Cohen has shown that there were many other factors at work including dissatisfaction from many deputies, particularly those from provincial synagogues, with the structure and workings of the Board and their inadequate representation. These were only symptoms; at root it was the resentment felt by what has been termed the Jewish middle class at the autocratic and oligarchic leadership of the Board by the older, more established community and their reluctance even to share power. It was the result of the accumulation of discontent over many years and illustrated the tensions at that time within the British Jewish community. Aubrey Newman suggests that the new generations were flexing their muscles and Todd Endelman considers that the vote indicated a shift in the social character of British Jewry and was the start of a transformation in communal governance.[44] As we shall see in the next chapter it was not a revolution as such, but it signalled the beginning of the end of dominance by the old elite.

2. HOME ISSUES

Mass Immigration and Alien Issues

The pogroms in Russia triggered off a mass movement of Jews from Eastern Europe to the west. Most were economic migrants and those who had been denied entry into the professions, universities, civil service and so on, rather than political refugees or those fleeing from pogroms. Between 1881 and 1914 about 120,000 to 150,000 Jews from Eastern Europe settled permanently in Britain, as well as many others who stayed for shorter periods en route to other countries, particularly the United States. Given that the Jewish population of Britain in 1880 was about 65,000 the newcomers swamped the established community and changed its demographic nature. They were mainly Yiddish-speaking and essentially very poor with dissimilar culture and ways of thinking to the established community and, for a significant number, stricter religious practices. Furthermore, modernization had taken a different trend in Eastern Europe to that among Jews in Britain. For example, many immigrants were socialist or anarchist, not movements that would appeal very much to the grandees of the Board. All of this led to friction between the newcomers and the established community.

Non-Jewish opposition to this unlimited immigration and demands for statutory measures to restrict it did not take long to surface. In April 1886 there was a public meeting in the East End urging such measures. The main point at issue was the shortage of adequate housing leading to major overcrowding rather than pressure on the employment market. The Board, though, were slow to respond to these demands and to participating in the debates that had already started within the Jewish community as to how to deal with this influx. Helping and integrating the newcomers was seen as a welfare issue to be dealt with by the Jewish Board of Guardians and other voluntary social organizations. The Board itself did not participate in the debates on how to integrate the newcomers into the community nor the issue of attempting to repatriate many, particularly those deemed unsuitable for one reason or another.

It was not in fact until 1898 that the Board really got involved. The catalyst was a bill that had been passed by the House of Lords that gave power to inspectors from the Board of Trade to prohibit the landing of immigrants who, in the view of the inspector, fell into a number of 'undesirable' classes such as a pauper or a person likely to become a public charge. The bill failed in the House of Commons, but it was enough for the Board to decide to establish an Alien Immigration Committee to compile facts and figures on Jewish aliens. It also arranged for two deputies who were MPs to keep a careful watch on all future legislation dealing with aliens.[45] Tables giving a lot of statistical information on 'Jewish Alien Paupers' were subsequently included as an annex in each annual report of the Board. These tables proved very helpful in enabling the Board to counteract attacks in the press and from other quarters which often exaggerated the numbers of aliens, particularly Jewish, and gave a false impression of their character. The *JC* thought it was about time the Board addressed itself properly to this alien immigration issue and considered that 'these are the days for active, living organizations, and not for ornamental institutions'. There was a riposte the following week in a letter from the secretary to the Board who claimed that the statement was incorrect and the Board had already been much involved in the issue.[46] Both were right: the Board was involved but, judging from the minutes of its meeting, in a rather desultory way.

In March 1902, a Royal Commission on Alien Immigration was established and Lord Rothschild was appointed one of its members. Even before being asked to give evidence, the Board collected and compiled reliable statistics that it considered would be vital in counteracting the contentions of those who were opposed to further alien immigration. These statistics indicated that, if there were problems, they were limited to the East End of London. The Board sought and obtained information on the nature and history of the issues and what steps were already being taken to relieve the overcrowding in the East End. It also collected evidence from employers of foreign Jewish labour as to their utility.[47] The Board perceived its role as the champion of the cause of the alien immigrants before the Royal Commission. It saw the anti-alien movement as powerful, with strong support among the public, and saw that the centre of the movement's attack would be directed against Russian and Polish Jewish aliens. The Board directed a lot of effort to this cause, which was primarily against any statutory imposed restrictions. Not only did it give written evidence to the commission, but also a number of deputies gave oral evidence, and the secretary of the Board gave oral evidence and also attended all the twice-weekly commission sittings. The Board also sought and found witnesses, Jewish and non-Jewish, who were able and prepared to give supportive evidence. The *JC* published a supplement on 27 March 1903, setting out the full case of the Board for no restrictions and the evidence given to the Royal Commission by members of the Board.

The Royal Commission published its report in August 1903. Its conclusions were that aliens were few in number, mainly in the East End of London, and did not take away English jobs. However, its recommendations were harsh and belied its conclusions. Its proposals included strict restrictions on immigration, the establishment of an Immigration Department whose officers would have significant powers of refusing entry to a whole range of persons including categories that would encompass most Jewish immigrants. It also proposed the forcible deportation of immigrants within two years of arrival if they fell into a number of categories including those without visible or probable means of support. Furthermore, if certain neighbourhoods were deemed as overcrowded, immigrants would not be permitted to move there. Lord Rothschild wrote a minority report disagreeing with most of the recommendations. The Board was appalled and published its views in a pamphlet. Essentially it considered the recommendations as unjust and unnecessary, and in particular that it seemed as if the inequitable provisions were directed mainly against Russian and Polish Jews.

In early 1904 the government introduced an Aliens Bill. The Board considered that in some respects this was even harsher than the recommendations of the Royal Commission. The Board prepared a new pamphlet giving up-to-date and accurate statistics on alien immigrants and setting out its main objections to the Bill. The pamphlet was particularly strongly worded and was circulated to all MPs and all synagogues throughout Britain. The Board arranged with Lord Rothschild for a deputation to meet with the home secretary, who assured them that their views would be carefully considered by the government.[48] For a variety of reasons, including vigorous opposition by Winston Churchill, the bill was dropped,[49] but a new bill was introduced in April 1905. Many of the objections raised by the Board to the previous bill remained, but one major concession was that immigrants seeking admission as political or religious refugees could not be refused entry on grounds of want of means. This concession was the result of a personal approach from the president of the Board to the prime minister, Arthur Balfour.[50] A protest meeting, not organized but supported by the Board, was held on 17 March 1905, and the Board issued to all synagogues a pro forma letter to be given to each of their members and to be sent by them to their MP requesting that MP to support the amendments proposed by the Board.[51] Despite all of these objections from the Board and the Jewish community, this bill was enacted without amendment just before a general election, which resulted in a Liberal government replacing the Conservative one. Some historians have criticized the Board because it spent its time and resources in trying to get the bill amended rather than defeated in Parliament or repealed by the incoming Liberal government.[52] In fact some deputies at the time advocated this course, but with the benefit of hindsight it seems highly unlikely that defeat or repeal of the legislation would have been achieved, given that even the proposed amendments were not passed and it was generally considered a popular piece of legislation in the country at large.

The Board was concerned that the officials responsible for implementing the new immigration procedures would be unsympathetic to Jewish immigrants, as they had been appointed by the previous Conservative administration. In addition many of the officials appointed had no training or experience in dealing with the problems affecting Jewish immigrants, such as language. Furthermore, the new legislation did not include the right of appeal against non-admittance or deportation, a condition that had been pressed by the Board. As a result the Board started collecting information and statistics as to the working in practice of the Act. Its fears were alleviated by a letter in March 1906 from the recently appointed home secretary, Herbert Gladstone, to the Immigration Boards instructing it that where doubt existed as to whether or not immigrants were fleeing from political or religious persecution, the immigrant should be granted the benefit of the doubt. Nonetheless, the Board persisted in collecting information regarding the workings of the Act and in October 1906 wrote to the home secretary pointing out some of the shortcomings of the Act, imperfections in its administration and the difficult issues that had arisen.[53] The Board did not receive a reply until February 1907, which it considered unsatisfactory; in particular it failed to answer most of the points raised by the Board, and the Board wrote again to the home secretary but did not receive a response.[54] Correspondence continued with the Home Office throughout 1907 on various individual cases and the Board became so frustrated at the lack of any positive response that in October it circulated to all government ministers a resolution urging the repeal of all the clauses of the Act that created injustice to immigrants.[55]

There is another side to the coin, in that examination of the correspondence between the Board and Home Office officials indicates that the latter were becoming more and more irritated by some of the issues, many of them petty, being raised by the Board with regard to individual cases. The October round robin letter elicited no positive reaction and in February 1908 a petition from the Board and signed by all the leaders of Anglo-Jewry was sent to the prime minister, Henry Campbell-Bannerman. This demanded urgent steps to improve the administration of the Aliens Act in order to mitigate some of the hardships that had arisen and made some specific proposals.[56] The reply dated March 1908 offered little consolation, but was rapidly followed by the resignation through ill health of the prime minister, although one assumes there was no connection between the two. The Board immediately appealed to his replacement, Herbert Asquith, who seemed to be more sympathetic. One important point, namely the provision of receiving homes at the ports of entry, was conceded and the Board was satisfied that if this was implemented it would lead to some improvement in the workings of the Act. Sadly, although a suitable clause was included in the Port of London Bill which enabled the home secretary to require the establishment of a receiving house for immigrants, no steps were taken to implement this. All of this petitioning and correspondence led John Pedder, the Home Office official responsible for the management of the Aliens Act, to describe the Board as hopelessly biased and to advise that it could be discouraged by not replying to its letters.[57]

In 1910 Winston Churchill, who was particularly sympathetic to the plight of the immigrant Jews, became home secretary. The Board immediately wrote to him requesting that he arrange the enforcement of the requirement for receiving houses. The reply was even better than the Board expected. Churchill instituted a committee of enquiry into the most practical way of instituting receiving houses and asked the president of the Board to be a member of this committee. He agreed to an earlier request of the Board that an immigrant should have the right of legal assistance and he was prepared to consider nominees of the Board as additional members of the Immigration Boards. The president agreed to serve on the committee and three deputies were nominated and appointed members of Immigration Boards.

The provision of legal aid to immigrants was likely to be a financial burden and the Board made enquiries as to where help might be found. In Hull and Grimsby the local communities offered help, which left London as the remaining main port of entry. The Board of Guardians was unwilling or unable to help, but the Board heard that the English Lodge of the B'nei B'rith was making arrangements to provide legal aid in London. This gave the Board something of a problem as there were some who feared that the B'nei B'rith was beginning to encroach on the area that had hitherto been a monopoly of the Board, namely making representations to government. Their *amour-propre* was at stake. A joint meeting of the Board and the Lodge was held and an agreement reached that a committee to deal with legal aid should be established, comprising seven members (including the chairman) to be appointed by the Board and six by the Lodge. Furthermore it was agreed that the Board would retain the sole right of making representations to the government and government departments with regard to any issues concerning Alien Immigration.[58] The Committee on Receiving Houses reported favourably with some practical proposals, but implementation was much delayed and in the end was overtaken by the onset of the First World War.

Marriage and Divorce[59]

The influx of immigrants reopened the issues on marriage that most leaders of British Jewry thought had ended and been decided in the 1850s and 1860s. Jewish marriages had to be certified by approved registrars appointed and supervised by the president of the Board or the West London Synagogue, or they had to take place in a registry office with a subsequent Jewish ceremony. No Jewish marriages outside the consanguinity regulations of English law were permitted, even if they were permissible under Jewish law. A *get* would only be granted if the persons concerned had already been divorced by the civil courts. In other words, English law prevailed and there were no concessions to Jewish law if it differed.

The new immigrants, out of ignorance or maybe even perversity, often did not accept this position and ignored the civil law. Divorce was particularly difficult for those who had married abroad, since documentation might have been lost and the costs of a civil divorce much too expensive. Rabbis were very sympathetic and often gave *gittim* on grounds of mutual consent or desertion, neither of which were grounds in English law, although acceptable under Jewish law. They also performed marriages which could not be certified under English law, for example where a *get* had been issued and not a civil divorce, so that the marriage was in effect bigamous, or where there was consanguinity under English but not Jewish law. The point at issue was important, even fundamental. Should the Board as representing the Jews of Britain try to obtain concessions or should it adhere to its previous policy and try to ensure that the Jews of Britain adhered to the law of the land? It stuck to the latter. As a consequence, the Board spent a lot of its time trying to stamp out irregular marriages and divorces.

At its meeting on 21 November 1888 the Board agreed a proposal to request an Act of Parliament that would make it a felony for Jews to solemnize or contract a marriage without carrying out the formalities required by the English marriage laws. A draft of a bill imposing a penalty on the solemnization of such irregular marriages was agreed by the Board at its meeting on 20 March 1889 and, although some members suggested a delay in putting it forward until the government's Immigration Committee had reported, it was decided to forward the draft bill to the government.[60] In the event the draft bill was not put forward to the government, although the Board had received great support from the chief rabbi, and the Registrar General had approved it in principle. The Board was anxious to obtain the prior support from some Jewish MPs and this was not immediately forthcoming. In March 1892 the Law, Parliamentary and General Purposes Committee reported on the subject again and urged the Board to put the draft bill forward provided they had the support of two of the Jewish MPs, namely Sir Julian Goldsmid and Samuel Montagu, and provided they received an assurance from the Attorney General that the government would assist the Board in passing the bill through Parliament. This report was agreed by the Board at its meeting on 13 March 1892, but

Samuel Montagu objected strongly and as a result it was felt unwise to proceed.[61] This might seem rather undemocratic, but Samuel Montagu, who was president of the Federation of Synagogues, had much more knowledge of – and was probably more sympathetic towards – those getting married clandestinely, and unless the Board had his support in the House of Commons it was unlikely that the Bill would succeed. He was often in dispute with the United Synagogue and one of his concerns was the level of fees they charged for marriages.

Irregular marriages continued and the Board was put under pressure from the Registrar General to take some action. In October 1896 a notice in English and Yiddish was sent to all known synagogues and *chevrot* in Britain with the request that it be should be prominently displayed. The notice explained the circumstances under which a legal marriage could take place and warned that if these were not complied with the parties would not be considered legally married both in Britain and abroad and that their offspring would be considered illegitimate. The notice also pointed out that anyone who received fees for performing an illegal marriage would incur the risk of prosecution for obtaining money under false pretences. Subsequently the Board heard that most of the synagogues exhibited the notice, but none of the *chevrot* replied and that was where the problem resided.

Matters came to a head in 1910 when a Royal Commission on Divorce was established. The Board in its evidence suggested that the *get* was an inducement to desertion rather than a sympathetic way of dealing with the problem after it had arisen. They were quite adamant that the practice of 'foreign' rabbis who carried out marriages and agreed to divorces that were not sanctioned by English law had to be stopped, and there should be legislation imposing a penalty on all those taking part in Jewish divorce proceedings unless there had been a prior divorce through the English divorce courts. Interestingly, they did not propose similar legislation for those involved in irregular marriages as had been mooted in the 1890s, but maybe this was because it was a Divorce Commission or maybe they still had respect for the views of Samuel Montagu, by then the first Lord Swaythling. They were not prepared to request that desertion should be grounds under English law as it was under Jewish law and were not even prepared to argue the legality of what some rabbis were doing in granting a *get*. The view of the Board was challenged by the haham, Moses Gaster, who wrote to the Board stating that the Board should vindicate and defend Jewish law, that divorce was a religious question as only a rabbi could grant one, and no rabbi could be guilty if they were not in breach of God's commandments. He thought the Board had conceived its functions incorrectly and its job was to safeguard Jewish law and to seek solutions by the state when there was a conflict with English law. In other words he sought privileges, which was of course in conflict with the views of those who had fought for and succeeded in obtaining emancipation. This view not to seek privileges had remained a guiding principle of the Board. Not surprisingly the Board rejected the views of the haham. The Commission reported in 1912 and one of its recommendations was that the proposal of the Board for penalties for those involved in irregular Jewish divorces should be adopted.[62] No action was taken by the government on the recommendations of the Commission except for a minor change in the definition of adultery that was enacted in 1923.

Sunday Work and Trading[63]

In Chapter 2 it was explained how the Board had spent a lot of time on two issues concerning work on Sundays. One culminated in the Factory Act of 1878, which permitted Jewish-owned factories and workshops that were closed on Saturdays to employ women and children on Sundays. This was a piece of social legislation to reduce the number of hours worked by women and children, but was often misinterpreted as if it meant that Jewish-owned factories and workshops that were closed on Saturday could be opened on Sunday for all employees. The Board had to issue a number of leaflets to Jewish factory owners to explain this. The employment of men on a Sunday remained restricted by the Sunday Observance Act, commonly known as the Lord's Day Act, but in practice it was very rare for prosecutions to occur under the provisions of this Act due to complex procedural requirements that had been introduced, mainly in the late nineteenth century. The other issue was Sunday trading where bills had been introduced into Parliament seeking to reduce or eliminate trading on Sundays. The pressure for these measures primarily came from the Sabbatarian movements. The Board had always sought exemption for Jewish shops closed on Saturdays, but in fact none of these bills ever reached the statute book.

Special legislation had been introduced in 1836 for bakers and this bore down particularly hard on Jewish bakers who closed on Saturdays and found that the hours on which they could bake and deliver on a Sunday were too restrictive. In fact the legislation was such that on one interpretation they could not bake at all on a Sunday.

Although there were frequent prosecutions for infringements of this Act by Jewish bakers, generally the magistrates were lenient by either refusing to issue a summons or only imposing trivial fines.[64] The position, however, was unsatisfactory, particularly since the Master Bakers Protection Society (a non-Jewish organization who were business rivals of the Jewish bakers) often campaigned against Jewish bakers baking on Sundays and informed on them to the police. From time to time the Board pressed the government to have the law changed to accommodate Jewish bakers who closed their businesses on Saturdays, but without any great success, except to elicit sympathy from the home secretary but no promise to amend the legislation. Following a meeting in 1901 with a delegation from the Jewish Master Bakers Association the Board agreed to approach the Home Office to request special legislation, which would permit Sunday baking by Jewish bakers who did not bake on Saturdays. The response from the Home Office was that whereas the government would not be prepared to introduce such a bill, they would consider favourably a private bill. Accordingly, the Board arranged for such a bill to be drafted and submitted to the home secretary. In the event the introduction of the bill into Parliament was held in abeyance because all prosecutions suddenly ceased.[65] The reason for this is not known but maybe the Home Office had let it be known to the public prosecution officers that they did not support such prosecutions. Whatever the reason, a success for the Board.

Sunday closing re-emerged as an issue in 1905 when Lord Avebury introduced into the House of Lords a Sunday Closing Bill. It was considered by the Board that this would be particularly harmful for Jews who kept their shops closed on Saturdays. The bill proposed to make it illegal to open any shop, sell or offer for sale any goods on Sundays and imposed a rising scale of fines. There were certain exemptions such as the sale of fish, fruit and vegetables before 9 a.m. and dairy products before 9 a.m. and after 4 p.m. The Board did not seek to obtain a total exemption for all Jewish shops that were closed on a Saturday, but only those in a locality where no offence could possibly be given to other local residents. The Board wrote to Lord Avebury making suggestions which would alleviate the position for Jews and also arranged for various Jewish trader organizations in the East End to submit petitions to the House of Lords. The president of the Board appeared as a witness before the Select Committee of the House of Lords. In the event the bill failed to become law.[66]

However, in 1906 Parliament appointed a joint Select Committee, under the chairmanship of Lord Avebury, to consider the subject of Sunday trading and the Board proposed to the government that a Jewish MP should be appointed to this committee. As a result Stuart Samuel was appointed to the Select Committee. A number of Jews were called to give evidence to this committee including the chief rabbi and the president of the Board. In his evidence the president put forward the principle that a Jew who closed his shop and abstained from trade on the Jewish Sabbath should be allowed to open for trade on a Sunday provided he employed only Jewish labour on that day. The report recommended restricting the sale of most goods on a Sunday to only part of the day, and although it did accept the case for special provisions for Jews, these were limited to areas of certain cities that were largely inhabited by Jews, and trade was only permissible until midday on Sundays. The Board was disappointed with the outcome and it was agreed that it would object strongly to any legislation that dealt with Sunday trading on the lines suggested by the Select Committee.[67] No action on the report was taken by the government, but agitation, particularly from Lord Avebury and his supporters, for a Sunday Closing Bill continued.

Sunday closing took on another aspect in 1907 when the Board was approached by the National Hygienic League to support a bill entitled the Weekly Rest Day Bill, which had the objective of a compulsory day of rest for all workers: they saw the issue as a social rather than a religious matter. After some negotiation, the Board agreed to support this bill, which would include a clause to the effect that no Jew who conscientiously kept his Sabbath would be liable for prosecution if he traded on a Sunday so long as it did not unnecessarily annoy his Christian neighbours. The bill was introduced into Parliament in 1908 but failed to become law. In the meantime the Jewish Sabbath Observance Society, an organization of Jewish shopkeepers and stallholders in the East End of London, was discouraged by the Board from taking action in the form of a mass meeting, as the Board considered that this might be injurious to the Jewish cause in the event of Lord Avebury's bill being reintroduced. The Society went ahead nonetheless and the Board refused to participate in the meeting, which was probably just as well as the meeting was noisy and disorderly and ended in chaos.[68]

In 1910 the Board was informed that the government intended to introduce a Shops Bill, which would include a clause restricting Sunday trading. A draft statement was prepared by the Board, which was discussed with the Jewish MPs who were not in the government. Following this meeting a letter was sent to the home secretary, Winston

Churchill, requesting that the bill should contain a clause permitting Jews who closed their shops on the Sabbath to be able to trade on a Sunday up to 3 p.m. provided they did not employ non-Jewish labour on that day. This aroused the ire of the Whitechapel and Spitalfields Costermongers' and Street-Sellers' Union, who represented most of the Jewish street traders in the East End of London. They had long been in dispute with the Board over the 1905 and 1908 bills, partly because they thought the Board's attitude was supine and partly because they did not consider that the officers and officials of the Board properly understood their concerns and the Board's proposals would be harmful to costermongers and street-sellers.[69] In October 1910 the Union decided to bypass the Board and sent a delegation to the Home Office putting its point of view, that was essentially that Sunday Trading should be permitted to all, irrespective of religion. A deputation of the leading Jews in the country, including the president of the Board and the chief rabbi, also met with the home secretary in October, who expressed sympathy.[70] Subsequently an amendment was proposed that Jewish shops could remain open to 2 p.m. but serving Jewish customers only. Although the restriction to Jewish customers only had been mentioned by the Board in its original representations, on further reflection the Board considered this proposal to be unworkable.[71]

In the meantime the Jewish shopkeepers and workers in the East End of London held a mass protest meeting in January 1911. It was a protest against the bill, but it developed into an attack on the Board, whose proposals would force upon them a half-holiday which they could ill afford. The Board had acted against the interests of the Jews who were most in need of its services, and had proposed compromises with the government without having consulted the Jewish public.[72] The organizers of the meeting subsequently decided to form the East London Jewish Shopkeepers Protection Association to take what action they deemed necessary, but as an act of conciliation agreed that any such action should be in consultation with the Board. A mass meeting was held on 10 July 1911 presided over by the president of the Board. A petition was agreed and sent to the home secretary protesting against the Sunday closing provisions of the bill and demanding either that this clause be abandoned or that special provision should be incorporated for Jewish shopkeepers without the requirement that they could only serve Jews.[73] Similar local committees were also established in some of the provincial centres, such as Leeds and Manchester. This pressure proved successful and shortly afterwards an amendment was introduced under which regulations would be made providing that in certain areas and under certain conditions, to be denoted in the regulations, shops could remain open until 2 p.m. on Sundays. It was intimated that these would apply in predominately Jewish areas and there would be no requirement to limit sales to Jews. A victory of sorts to the Board, but it was pyrrhic. The government received such opposition from all sides regarding the Sunday closing provisions of the bill that they were removed before it was enacted.

Shechita Issues
In November 1892, the Board discussed information they had received that a large number of Swiss electors had signed a draft bill that would prohibit the Jewish method of slaughtering cattle (*shechita*) in Switzerland. Under the Swiss constitution either the Federal Assembly would have to consider the measure or it would have to be put to a plebiscite. The Board was very concerned with this, not only on behalf of the Jews of Switzerland but also because of fears that if this measure were to succeed in Switzerland agitation for such a measure might extend to Britain. The Board forwarded to its contacts and newspapers in Switzerland various articles and papers that discussed *shechita* and concluding that it did not cause any more suffering than any other method of slaughter.[74] The bill was rejected in the Swiss National Assembly, but in 1893 a national plebiscite supported the banning of *shechita* and this ban came into force in 1896. It would seem the first such ban anywhere in the world.

The Board's fears that the issue of banning *shechita* might extend to Britain were not in fact realized until 1904, although there had been sporadic attacks on it from time to time. In July 1904 a committee appointed by the Admiralty to assess the adequacy of the nation's meat supply in the event of war and, as part of that remit, to ascertain the most humane method of slaughtering animals for human food, reported adversely on *shechita*.[75] The Board was asked by the Board of Shechita to take steps to counter this.[76] It set up a committee and in July 1805 an extensive and thorough report was presented to the Board. It countered all the points in the adverse Admiralty report and included evidence from leading non-Jewish scientific and medical specialists that the Jewish method was very humane and that the other methods in use in Britain often led to great cruelty. This report was printed and widely circulated. In fact it became of use immediately. In Liverpool the draft by-laws of a new slaughterhouse included a provision that animals should be stunned before slaughter, which would be contrary to *shechita* requirements. The Board forwarded its report to the Liverpool Shechita Board which as a result was able to obtain an exemption from that by-law for the Jewish method of slaughter. The *JC* commented that the Board's report had rendered any adverse legislation almost impossible.[77] In March 1907 the Local Government Board issued a circular on regulations for the slaughter of animals to all local councils, and in it they commended the by-laws of the Liverpool slaughterhouse and drew specific attention to the exemption from stunning for the Jewish method. The Local Government Board had under consideration published a set of recommended by-laws and the Board asked them to include the exemption in them.

In June 1911 a private member's bill, the Slaughter of Animals Bill, was introduced into the House of Commons.[78] This bill was examined by the *shechita* committee of the Board, which was alarmed that one of the clauses would practically prohibit *shechita* and that under another clause there could be problems in licensing *shochetim*. Accordingly they discussed the matter with George Greenwood, MP, the promoter of the bill, and he readily agreed to an amendment exempting *shechita* and for *shochetim* authorized by the chief rabbi or the president of the Board to be exempt from the licensing requirements. The haham, Dr Gaster, protested strongly at this for a variety of reasons, including that he was not one of the persons who could grant the necessary authorization.[79] The Board tried to placate him by changing the authority solely to the president of the Board, who had to act in accord with the Board's Ecclesiastical Authorities (which included the haham). This amendment was agreed by the Bill's promoter, but the haham was not satisfied and through the auspices of the B'nei B'rith tried to get another, to him preferable, amendment passed. This attempt was not successful, but the Board complained that 'such irresponsible interference might involve the community in loss of influence in matters of legislation that would extend far beyond the actual question at issue'.[80] The bill failed to be passed.

In 1913 there was a lot of agitation from branches of the RSPCA that slaughter of animals should always be preceded by stunning. Representatives of the Board met with officials of the RSPCA and were able to convince them that *shechita* should be deemed an acceptable method of slaughter. Subsequently the Board were informed that the proposed model by-laws would contain a provision that stunning should not apply to any Jewish slaughterer licensed by the chief rabbi.[81] There was an ironic epilogue in that several non-Jewish committee members of the RSPCA branch that had first raised the objections to *shechita* had apparently started to purchase kosher meat.

In February 1914 a private member's bill, The Humane Slaughter of Animals Bill, was introduced into the House of Commons. It required that all animals had to be stunned before slaughter and that slaughterers had to have a license granted by the local authority. The Board prepared itself for a long campaign against the bill including a revised and shortened form of its 1905 report and a pamphlet containing the opinions of 457 continental experts on the humanity of *shechita*. It also sought and obtained the support of the RSPCA. In the event the promoter of the bill, Arthur Lee, MP, dropped it through lack of support.[82]

The Burton Manuscript[83]

Sir Richard Burton (1821–90) was a Victorian polymath. He was an explorer, translator, writer, soldier, ethnologist, linguist, poet, hypnotist, fencer and diplomat. He was totally unconventional and well known for his travels and explorations within Asia and Africa as well as his extraordinary knowledge of languages and cultures. He went on the Haj to Mecca disguised as a Moslem. He tried but failed to find the source of the Nile, but was credited with discovering Lake Victoria. He translated the *Kama Sutra*, *The Arabian Nights* and *The Perfumed Garden* into English.

However, he had a darker side to his character, and it is this darker side that involved the Board. In the early 1870s, he wrote a book provisionally titled *The Jew*, which he tried to get published.[84] The book stated as a fact that the Sephardim had a practice of human sacrifice and used the alleged and discredited murder of Father Thomas in Damascus in 1840 as an example. Burton received advice that due to its antisemitic nature, publication was inadvisable and would be harmful to his reputation, particularly as, at the time, he was in the British diplomatic service. He accepted this advice, deciding to attempt publication again after his retirement. He died, however, a few months before retirement. The manuscript then fell into the hands of his wife Isabel, who on her death in 1896 left instructions to her literary executors that it should be burnt. It was not, and her sister Elizabeth Fitzgerald, who was one of her literary executors, was anxious to publish the manuscript.

In early 1897 the Board discussed an advertisement for a book by the late Sir Richard Burton, edited by William Wilkins who was Isabel's editor, entitled *Human Sacrifices amongst the Sephardim or Eastern Jews*, which was about to be published. The Board entered into correspondence with the publishers, editor and the trustees of Isabel's estate, in particular requesting to see a copy of the proposed book.[85] It got nowhere and at a Board meeting on 18 March 1897 it was resolved that if the book was found to be a defamatory libel on the Jewish people, the Board would take criminal proceedings against anyone involved in its publication.[86] The following day the Board's solicitor wrote to Isabel's literary executors pointing this out and asking them to prevent the book's publication. The Board was subsequently told that the book would be published in a much-abridged form. On 16 October 1897, the *Athenaeum* published another advert for the book, still with the same title, but the Board decided to wait until publication before taking any further action. In the event the book, retitled *The Jew, The Gypsy and El Islam*, was published in 1898 and most of the offending antisemitic material had been excised. The Board considered that it was because of its prompt action that the book was modified and were advised that there was no case for legal action against what was actually published.[87]

The manuscript remained with Wilkins although it was unclear whether he had legal title to it. In 1903, Wilkins sold the unexpurgated manuscript of the whole book to a firm of booksellers, who sold it on to Henry Frederick Manners-Sutton, who owned a publishing business. In 1908, Manners-Sutton approached Isabel's executors asking for permission to reprint the book including the expurgated parts. They, and Wilkins' executors, refused so he decided to sell it. In early 1909 the Board purchased the manuscript including the offending and unpublished chapters as well as a galley proof of the unpublished book. One of the conditions of the sale laid down by the literary executors was that the Board would never publish the manuscript.[88] However, Manners-Sutton, who had physical but no longer legal possession of the manuscript, refused to hand it over and in March 1911 the Board took legal action to force him to do so. The court so ordered and at a meeting of the Board on 9 April 1911 the president announced that the Board had the documents and that no doubt they would be suppressed forever.[89] It was probably this statement that subsequently led the Board to refuse anyone access to read the documents. It was argued by Israel Zangwill that by suppressing the book, the Board implied that some corroboration did exist for the 'blood libel'.[90] The *Jewish World* wrote:

The Board of Deputies bought up a book which propagated the Blood Libel not long ago and thereby acted with far less shrewdness. To escape from a libellous work by buying it up has always seemed to us a peculiarly dangerous method of meeting an agitation for the simple reason that it is liable to the worst misconstruction.[91]

It remained in the Board's archives and when these were catalogued in 1978 the file was given the title 'The Burton Book'. In December 1984 Professor Geoffrey Alderman, then a member of the Board, asked for the book to be made available to bona fide scholars but this was refused. In 1986 the new president, Dr Lionel Kopelowitz, wrote to Professor Alderman giving him permission to examine the book under certain conditions. It took another two years before Professor Alderman was able to do so. 'Forever' had lasted seventy-five years.

A few years later there was a remarkable change of policy. At a plenary meeting of the Board in May 2001, the president, Mrs Jo Wagerman, announced that the manuscript was to be auctioned to raise money to enable the Board to obtain new premises. This was a unanimous decision of the honorary officers and the Executive Committee. They had taken advice from worldwide experts on antisemitism and in a letter to Board members the president wrote: 'we were assured unequivocally that its contents, though ridiculous and racist, pose no threat to the Jewish Community of today, either from the extreme right or the Arab world'.[92] Its possible sale created a furore in the Jewish community in Britain and overseas. The issue was not the selling of the 'family silver' but rather that in the wrong hands it could be used to ferment even more anti-semitism. A former president of the Board, Lord Greville Janner, wrote to all deputies informing them that he had been contacted by a benefactor who was prepared to offer £150,000 if the Board withdrew the manuscript from sale. The Board did not do so, as withdrawal would have cost it £40,000 to £50,000 and it had been advised by Christie's that the sale would fetch considerably more than the £150,000 on offer. In the event the book failed to reach its reserve price and was withdrawn. Subsequently the benefactor donated £75,000 to the Board on the understanding that the book would be kept securely at its London offices and only bona fide scholars could have access to it.[93]

The Limerick Boycott[94]

On Monday 11 January 1904, Father Creagh, a Catholic priest, delivered an antisemitic address at the weekly meeting of the Redemptorist

Confraternity in Limerick. He was the spiritual director of the Confraternity and it was considered that his objective was to inflame local prejudice against the Jewish traders in the city. The local Jewish minister at once informed the Board, but before it could take any action Father Creagh delivered another even more vitriolic address on 18 January. This provoked physical violence against Jews in the town and started a ruinous boycott of their shops and businesses. The Board was informed by telegram and the president contacted the undersecretary for Ireland asking for protection for the Jews and punishment for the offenders, and a reply was received that proper protection would be made. Subsequently the Board was informed that the boycott was continuing and there was every likelihood of a continuation of antisemitic and provocative sermons and speeches. On 25 January the Board contacted the chief secretary for Ireland, who was a member of the cabinet, and he advised that there was insufficient evidence to institute legal proceedings against Father Creagh, and that in any event to do so might be counterproductive. Furthermore, he considered that the situation was improving and the Limerick police were giving full protection to the Jews resident there.[95] This proved to be rather complacent since at the end of March the Board was informed that out of the thirty-five Jewish families in Limerick, twenty had been reduced to poverty. The Board wrote to the Lord Lieutenant and to the cardinal archbishop of Armagh. The archbishop, whilst deprecating what had happened, stated that Limerick was outside his area of influence but that he would talk to the bishop of Limerick. The Lord Lieutenant just assured the Board that the police were doing all they could. In April the Board established a fund to aid the victims and to provide legal aid if necessary as well. It also wrote to the bishop of Limerick, but only received an acknowledgement.[96]

Representatives of the Board visited Limerick in May to investigate the position and to assist in the distribution of aid. The delegation found no evidence of excessive profits having been made by the Jews, which had been cited as the *raison d'être* for the boycott. They met with Father Creagh who, despite evidence to the contrary, was adamant that his grievance against the Jews was economic and stated that he intended to continue with his crusade against them. The delegation also met with the leaders of the Protestants in the district who had waged a press campaign in favour of the Jews, and asked them to drop this since it was proving to be counterproductive. Regrettably the boycott continued and many Jewish families, probably about one-third of the total, were forced to leave the city.

Steven Bayme has used this affair as an example of what he has termed the post-emancipation policy of the Board to avoid direct action and rely upon non-Jewish help to defend Jews from attacks, and has suggested that this policy was not good enough.[97] He is right in this instance in that although the Board got a lot of support from some Protestant clergy and organizations and the media, it got very limited support from Catholic clergy and organizations. Bayme does not, though, suggest alternative actions for the Board. On the other hand, he also suggests that the Board's failure to halt the Limerick boycott was one of the reasons why from about 1910 onwards the Board became much more proactive particularly in combating antisemitism.[98]

White Slave Traffic[99]
The Jewish Association for the Protection of Girls and Women was established in 1885 to assist Jewish girls who had been forced into prostitution and to stamp out the very large Jewish involvement in the running of the White Slave Trade. In 1907 the Board established with the Association a Conjoint Vigilance Committee to deal with this issue, and in particular to consider what changes needed to be made to the law, as many weaknesses had been exposed which enabled traffickers to escape penalties. The Board was concerned, in particular, with the likely adverse implications for the Jewish community, as a number of Jews were connected to this vice trade.[100] A report based on a study led by the president of the Board was considered at a conference of the Conjoint Vigilance Committee, the National Vigilance Association and the London Council for the Promotion of Public Morality in 1909. This conference decided to frame bills to carry out the amendments to the law as suggested by the president of the Board.[101] It took considerable time and effort, mainly by the Conjoint Vigilance Committee, to get an appropriate amending Act through Parliament but they succeeded in 1912. The Act did not go as far as the committee would have liked but it did act as a further deterrent to the traffickers.

This is a good example of the Board acting not only to try to eradicate a social evil within the Jewish community but also one within wider society. It would seem that the Board obtained a lot of kudos for its efforts in this area.[102]

The First World War[103]
Despite the *JC*'s banner headline a few days after the outbreak of war – 'England has been all she could be to the Jews; the Jews will be all

they can be to England'[104] – Britain was not all she could have been to the Jews nor were the Jews all they could have been to Britain during the war. The reaction of the Jewish population at the outbreak of the war was mixed. The older established ones responded immediately and with enthusiasm to the call to arms. It was an opportunity to deny the lack of patriotism that was part of the charges of the antisemites. On the other hand, the immigrant community was less than enthusiastic at first, although many did respond and joined the armed forces well before conscription. The issue of Jewish 'slackers' became a national one, and was compounded by the government policy in the first years of the war not to enlist men born in the Russian Empire.

At the outset of the war the Conjoint, and thus indirectly the Board, was faced with a major dilemma. Europe's most antisemitic countries, Russia and Romania, were allies of Britain, and in fighting for the rights of Jews in those countries the Conjoint had cooperated with Germany and Austria-Hungary, now Britain's enemies. For three months the Conjoint did not meet and for much longer than that it did not make any statements. As a result it came under fire from the Jewish press for the lack of clarity of its policy regarding the war and its aftermath. The position was clarified in March 1915 by a statement from the president of the Board that the object of the Conjoint was to seek to secure civil and political rights for Jews in all countries where they were at present denied, and to safeguard such rights when they were jeopardized by the consequences of the war. This statement was warmly welcomed by the *JC*.[105]

Overall the Board did not have a good war. Its first problem was the issue of Jewish enemy aliens resident in Britain. These aliens were not permitted to reside in certain areas and many of them were interned. Appeals were made to the Board that it should make representations to the government that all Jewish aliens – or at least those from Galicia, where their position was ambiguous – should not be treated as enemies, and that the Board should ask the government if it could be made responsible for sifting the cases of Jewish enemy aliens. The Board was not prepared to accept these requests, partly because it was fearful of being accused of disloyalty. Its view was that the issue was generally not one of religion but rather of nationality. Appeals against internment for Jewish aliens were thus left to the B'nei B'rith and the Jewish Friendly Societies, and as a result the Board was out of favour with the immigrant Jewish community. The Board, however, was prepared to help if a grievance arose that was related to the alien being

Jewish. Some Jewish enemy aliens were interned in concentration camps and the Board was asked to help with providing them with kosher food. The Board did attempt to alleviate this situation and even proposed that all Jewish alien enemies should be interned in the same camp to facilitate it. In due course it was agreed that any Jewish internee who so requested could be transferred to a camp in Douglas, Isle of Man, where kosher food would be available. The Board was informed of the detention of a Jewish minister, a Rabbi Heilpern of Gateshead, and it was able not only to secure his release but also, more generally, a regulation that Jewish ministers against whom there was no evidence of their being in touch with the enemies would not be interned. In January 1915, on an initiative from the chief rabbi, the Board suggested to the Home Office that it, in cooperation with the B'nei B'rith, would be prepared to assist all Jewish internees in their applications for help and release.[106] The Home Office agreed to this initiative, which proved of great value to interned Jews. At the request of the government the Board became involved in making special arrangements for Jewish festivals, special food – particularly for Passover – and other religious requirements for members of the armed forces.

In May 1915 new and tougher regulations regarding internment were issued by the government, and the Board was asked by the B'nei B'rith to cooperate with a committee that had been recently established by the B'nei B'rith to give assistance where appropriate to Jewish internees and Jews liable to internment or even deportation. The Board, with only one vote against, declined to do so, mainly because it considered this might be deemed as unpatriotic and, again, that it was not an issue of religion but of nationality. The president remarked that assisting Jewish internees might suggest 'they were putting racial claims before their patriotism'. The Board would help as it had previously done to assist interned Jews with their religious observance but nothing else. This refusal led to a vigorous and hostile response in the Jewish press.[107] Despite this, however, there are indications from subsequent Board minutes and correspondence that the Board did assist a number of Jewish internees and make representations on behalf of a number of Jews threatened with internment or deportation.

Another issue arose in January 1916 when the government announced the introduction of conscription (for unmarried men in January and all men in April) and in May announced proposals for a change in the policy regarding the recruitment of aliens to the armed forces. Previously they had been barred, but the new policy was that those of military age would be able and encouraged to enlist and in due course conscription would be imposed on them unless they agreed to be repatriated to their original countries. For most alien Jews this meant Russia. There was a heated debate on this at a Board meeting in July 1916, with one side arguing that the Board should accept the government's new policy and others deploring this 'forced' repatriation. In the end the argument was resolved by the passing of a deliberately ambiguously worded motion approving the policy of the enlistment of aliens but with no mention of deportation for those who refused. Subsequently there was much confusion regarding this motion, judging by statements and letters in the *JC*. Some, including Herbert Samuel, the home secretary, viewed this resolution as implying support for deportation, but others took the opposite view.

A further strongly-held opinion was that Russian-born alien Jews who enlisted should automatically be naturalized. The result was that a significant proportion of the Jewish community was upset by the Board, which was denounced at many Jewish public meetings.[108] What added to the problem was that there was a widespread view in the country that Jews were shirkers. This issue was made more noticeable by many Jews (not only aliens) appearing before conscription tribunals asking for exemption because they were conscientious objectors or they were *cohanim*. All of this created quite a scandal and split the community, but the Board did not get involved and so was blamed for disingenuousness by all sides. In fact the government put off time and again the deportment provision, but following the first Russian Revolution in February 1917 it legislated for this and, as a result, a few thousand Jewish aliens were sent back to Russia. Many others followed as they considered that the revolution meant that the problems for Jews in Russia were over.

Early in the war there had been a campaign for the creation of a Jewish battalion in the army, but because of hostility from most of the elite of Anglo-Jewry – essentially because they did not like the concept of setting Jews apart as a separate group – nothing came of it. The idea was resurrected again in 1916 by Vladimir Jabotinsky, but initially it also seemed doomed, probably because of hostility from the same groups as before. Then in July 1917 the government announced that it wished to create a Jewish regiment to be called the Jewish Regiment and to have as its insignia the Magen David (Star of David). The Jewish community was split on this issue, but the Board seemed united in its opposition to the proposal. As a result of this opposition, from the Board and from others in the Jewish community, the proposal was modified and instead of a Jewish regiment a Jewish battalion of the Royal Fusiliers was formed, which was subsequently increased to three battalions. Following the formation of the first battalion the opposition faded away, and the battalion became a source of pride among British Jews. At a later stage the insignia of the three battalions was changed to a seven-branched menorah, and they began to become known as the Jewish Brigade or the Judeans but more popularly as the 'Royal Jewsiliers'. The third battalion comprised mainly Jews from Palestine and took part in the final phases of the Palestine campaign; its members included Private David Ben-Gurion, later to become the first prime minister of Israel, and Private Isaac Ben-Zvi, later to become the second president of Israel.[109]

3. FOREIGN AFFAIRS

During the whole of the period covered by this chapter, the Board had essentially delegated its involvement in the affairs of Jews in foreign countries to the Conjoint Foreign Committee. At first, the Board's representatives on the Conjoint only occasionally mentioned issues at Board meetings and there was never any discussion. Later, following frustration expressed by some deputies, a summary of Conjoint activities was tabled at Board meetings, but discussion on them was infrequent and often discouraged by the chair. The agreement between the Board and the AJA gave the Conjoint full executive powers provided the representatives of both bodies agreed.

The Conjoint did not continue with Moses Montefiore's approach to foreign matters, such as direct and personal involvement, and overseas visits to countries following crises involving the local Jewish community were much rarer. Mark Levene has postulated that the Conjoint's approach to foreign matters stemmed from a premise that there was a congruence of interests in the international arena between Britain and British Jews. This premise led to the view that British foreign policy would not only be sympathetic but also make active interventions on behalf of persecuted Jewry abroad. In other words there could be a sort of special relationship between the British Foreign Office and Anglo-Jewry's foreign arm, the Conjoint.[110] In practice this was fine when it suited British foreign policy, but there was only sympathy when it did not suit government policy. Crises affecting Jews in such countries as Morocco and elsewhere in North Africa, Turkey, the Balkans and Persia (Iran) were generally raised with the Foreign Office and had its support, although matters were not always resolved successfully and invariably appeals were made to the British Jewish community for aid to any victims. On the other hand, crises affecting Jews in one of the major powers, in particular Russia, seldom got the full support of the British government. Furthermore, this policy, which was carried out more often by indirect approaches through contacts of members of the Conjoint rather than directly with the Foreign Office, could and did conflict with the general views within the British Jewish community – for instance, the problems of the Conjoint at the start of the First World War.[111]

This chapter deals with only two foreign matters, both of which involved the Board directly as well as the Conjoint. It also includes a third matter that falls between home and foreign affairs, namely Zionism. There were two foreign matters during this period on which, surprisingly, the Board did not take any action or even discuss the situation, at least as far as its records are concerned. The first was the Dreyfus Affair, starting in 1894, and the second the Beiliss blood libel in 1911.[112]

The Eastern Question and the Congress of Berlin
The Eastern Question relates to the foreign policy of Britain vis-à-vis the Balkans and Turkey. In 1875 there was an uprising of Bulgarian Christians attempting to overthrow the oppressive administration of the Turks, leading to a massacre by the Turks of Bulgarian Christians. Disraeli was the prime minister at the time and he was concerned to support and prop up Turkey because of his fear of Russian domination in the area, whereas Gladstone tended to sympathize with the Balkan Christians in their struggle against Turkish rule. Opinion in Britain was split on the matter. The Jewish issue arose because Disraeli was accused of being indifferent towards the massacre of Bulgarian Christians and supporting the Turks because of his oriental racial origins. Indeed some persons considered that the Jewish community in Britain as a whole were unpatriotic in supporting Disraeli's anti-Christian policy and that they were more concerned with the interests of Jewish bondholders.[113] There was much antisemitic sentiment and agitation in the press, the country was split and the Liberal Party, which was in opposition, attacked the policy of the government, sometimes with crude antisemitic accusations. For example, Gladstone referred to Disraeli's Judaic sympathies as influencing his judgement. The Board had not previously kept silent when there had been antisemitic agitation in the press or elsewhere, but it did on this occasion. The reason for

its silence is difficult to understand, particularly as during the debates on the Eastern Question in the Commons a number of Jewish MPs who were members of the Board raised the issue of the antisemitic sentiments that were being expressed in the press and by some of their Liberal colleagues.

Russia eventually declared war on Turkey in 1877, Disraeli sent the British fleet to Constantinople, and as a result both sides sought a peace settlement. The resulting peace settlement was the Treaty of Berlin negotiated at the Congress of Berlin in 1878.[114] This Congress, apart from settling the dispute between Russia and Turkey, considered the position of Jews in the Balkan countries, including Serbia and Romania. The participants at the Congress were Austria–Hungary, Britain, France, Germany, Italy, Russia and Turkey. Disraeli insisted that recognition of independence of any state in the region must depend on a clear promise of social and political equality for the Jews. The Congress proved to be a triumph for Disraeli and British diplomacy. *The Times* commented: 'We may doubt if Britain has ever, on a like occasion, been represented by a Plenipotentiary who has better deserved her thanks both for what he has done and for what he has avoided doing.'[115] Bismarck remarked on Disraeli: 'Der alte Jude, das ist der Mann' (The old Jew, that is the man).[116] The Board can take some credit for this. Directly, and via the Conjoint, it lobbied the government very strongly on behalf of the Jews in the Balkans and indeed it sent a number of representatives to lobby at the Congress itself.[117] Unfortunately, the agreement that the major powers would not recognize a state's independence unless it granted full equality to Jews began to unravel quickly, particularly in Romania.

Pogroms in Russia
On 13 March 1881, Tsar Alexander II was assassinated. It is generally considered that the group responsible, most probably anarchists, included only one Jew. Coincidentally or not, a wave of pogroms swept parts of Russia, commencing in a small way in Elisavetgrad on 16 April 1881 and spreading to Kiev, Odessa and other towns in the Ukraine and, towards the end of the year, to Warsaw. The causes of the pogroms, the perpetrators, and the extent of loss of lives, injuries, rapes, pillage and destruction are still disputed between historians.[118] There is no dispute about the victims – they were all Jews. In May 1882 the new tsar, Alexander III, announced a series of measures (generally now called the 'May Laws') aimed at removing the tension between non-Jews and

Jews. They were mainly restrictive on Jews. They included prohibiting any business activity on Sundays or Christian holidays, preventing Jews from owning land or residing in agricultural areas, and reaffirming again the requirement that Jews could only reside in the Pale of Settlement. In 1890 there was another wave of pogroms and Jews were expelled from Moscow, and in 1903/04 yet another wave of pogroms including the massacre of Jews at Kishinev.

The Board, or rather the Conjoint Foreign Committee, was not slow to react to the 1881 pogroms. Representatives of the Conjoint met with the foreign secretary, Lord Granville, on 24 May 1881, but the government, although sympathetic, refused to interfere in Russia's internal affairs or to make any official representations regarding the pogroms – it considered that it would be 'injudicious and unjustified by international usage to make any remonstrance to the Government of Russia'. Furthermore, Lord Granville thought such interference might be counterproductive, but said he would speak to the Russian ambassador unofficially on the subject.[119] The Conjoint representatives then considered making a public issue of the matter, but decided unanimously that a public meeting was inexpedient. This was reported to the Board at its meeting on 25 May and no disagreement with this view is recorded. Passivity, even deference, remained the response if the Board did not have the support of the government or was out of step with public opinion. This time, however, the Board had misjudged public opinion as there was a nationwide outcry, led by *The Times*, against what had been perpetrated in Russia. An account of the meeting with Lord Granville was given by Arthur Cohen, the president of the Board, to his uncle Sir Moses Montefiore. His response was that the only chance of an appeal reaching the tsar was by a representative of the Board going to Russia and Sir Moses, at the age of 97, volunteered to go himself.[120] This must have been declined, although it is not recorded in any minutes nor is there a record of any discussion at the Board or at the Conjoint of sending a representative to Russia.

On 13 November 1881 a special committee was created to report into the condition of the Jews in Russia.[121] This committee, the Russo-Jewish Committee, was charged with considering and adopting such measures as it might think fit for ameliorating the condition of the Jews in Russia. The committee comprised of five representatives of the Board, five representatives of the AJA and five others, including the chief rabbi, Nathaniel Mayer Rothschild and Lionel Louis Cohen, the president of the Jewish Board of Guardians.

The committee was short-lived and probably did not do much, or so it would seem, as there are no records extant of its meetings. This committee is not to be confused with a committee of the same name, but not involving the Board and established much later, whose responsibilities were to manage and help (financially and otherwise) refugees from Russia, keep them off the books of the Board of Guardians, and try to prevent them becoming a public charge.

An attack on Jews in Warsaw at the end of 1881 stimulated the AJA to demand action from the Russo-Jewish Committee or they would withdraw from it. This stirred the committee into action and it published a report on the persecution of the Jews in Russia, which was issued in pamphlet form and reproduced in *The Times* on 11 and 13 January 1882.[122] As a result of this and other reports it became clear that the public in Britain was appalled at what had been going on in Russia, and the AJA decided that a public meeting protesting against the inhuman treatment of Jews in Russia should be held. This proposal was referred to the Russo-Jewish Committee, which was rather more cautious than the AJA and decided instead to submit a memorandum to the tsar, drawing his attention to the pogroms. Some members of the committee, including the president of the Board, Arthur Cohen, did not feel this went far enough and supported a public meeting as well. Thus the Board jumped on the bandwagon, but a little tardily. Maybe it had been stimulated by some articles in the *JC*.[123] In fact someone had jumped the gun. A member of the council of the AJA, Oswald Simon, wrote a letter to the *Jewish World* on 13 January saying that he had held discussions with leading Christians and they had agreed to hold a meeting to denounce Russia in the name of Christianity. His letter referred to the Russo-Jewish Committee and concluded: 'Fifteen gentlemen of our religion agreed that no public action should be taken. Is that the view of the Jews of Britain or only of their fifteen co-religionist?'[124] A public meeting to protest against the pogroms in Russia was held on 1 February 1882 at the Mansion House, chaired by the Lord Mayor and attended by most of the great and the good. This meeting was followed by meetings in thirty-six other cities, each one presided over by the appropriate Lord Mayor or Lord Provost. As a result of the public meetings a Mansion House Fund was established and more than £100,000 was raised to help refugees from Russia in Britain and elsewhere.

The prime minister, William Gladstone, was approached but he refused to intervene on the grounds that 'the interference of foreign

Governments in such cases is more likely to do more harm than good'.[125] Not the same views as he expressed regarding the Balkan Christians during the Eastern crisis a few years previously, but then the politics were different and he was not in government. This refusal led Baron Henry de Worms, a Conservative MP and president of the AJA, to propose a motion in the House of Commons calling on the government to make representations to the Russian government. This motion was opposed by Arthur Cohen, a Liberal MP, and president of the Board, Nathaniel Mayer Rothschild, a Conservative MP and chairman of the Russo-Jewish Committee, as well as all the other Jewish MPs. The fault line was clear; probably most leaders of Anglo-Jewry did not want to pursue policies that were not supported by the government and were loath to make a public noise on issues that might not have the support of the public at large. In other words, the 'keep your heads down' view still prevailed. On the other hand there was some criticism of the president of the Board by at least a few deputies. At the Board's ordinary monthly meeting on 15 March 1882 the president made a personal statement explaining his position on the persecution of the Jews in Russia. He pointed out that in the House of Commons he had not spoken and acted in his capacity as president of the Board. His view was that any motion urging the government to take action would be inadvisable because it would not improve the conditions of the Jews in Russia; it would irritate the Russian government and would not succeed in persuading the British government to go any further than it had already gone. In the ensuing debate some deputies did not agree with the attitude of the president in the House of Commons, but they did not pursue their disagreement to the extent of censuring the president or demanding a change in policy.[126] There was an echo of this almost exactly seventy-five years later when, during the Suez crisis in 1956, some deputies wanted to censure the then president, Barnett Janner, for voting against the government on a 'no confidence' motion in the House of Commons, and he made a personal statement to the Board. In 1956, however, in contrast to 1882 there was a vote of confidence in the president and it was carried nem. con.[127]

All remained quiet on the Russian front until 1890, at least as far as the Board was concerned. However, in late July 1890 *The Times* published a news item stating that the 'May Laws' first introduced in 1882 would be enforced with new rigour and Jews were to be expelled from cities outside the Pale of Settlement including Moscow and St Petersburg. This was denied by the Russian government, but nonetheless the Conjoint was spurred into action and wrote to the foreign secretary requesting that the British government should do all in its powers to avert the impending oppressive measures against the Jews of Russia.[128] In the House of Commons, one of the ministers in the Foreign Office, in replying to a question, stated that if what had been reported was correct, it was to be deeply regretted but as the matter concerned the internal affairs of Russia, the British government could not interfere. The response to the letter to the foreign secretary was that the Foreign Office had been informed that there had been no such edict. The secretary to the Board published this reply in *The Times* and the *JC*,[129] and this created a dispute within the Jewish community because it was said that by publishing the letter, the Board implied that it accepted that there was no such edict and demonstrated naivety or its lack of information.

Gradually news did emerge confirming the edict and that some pogroms had occurred. The Conjoint and the Board seemed rather quiet, and the initiative for a public protest passed to the Evangelical Alliance, who arranged for the Lord Mayor to hold a public meeting at the Guildhall on 10 December 1890. The Board passed a resolution thanking the Lord Mayor and the Christian community for arranging this meeting and the support they were offering to the Jews of Russia.[130] The public meeting at the Guildhall was attended by even more of the great and the good than the meeting at Mansion House in 1882 following the 1881 pogroms. Various supportive resolutions were passed, but in reality had no effect, since as 1891 progressed the position of the Jews in Russia deteriorated significantly and the expulsions that had been rumoured in July 1890 started happening. Queen Victoria was so moved by what was happening to the Jews in Russia that she wrote to the tsar asking him to put a stop to the barbarous legislation, but her letter was returned apparently unread. It would seem that although the Board was deeply concerned, it was prepared to let any initiatives in this matter be dealt with by the Russo-Jewish Committee (not the one formed by the Board and the AJA in 1881 but a new one resulting from the Mansion House Conference and with no representation from the Board). The AJA, however, was not content with this and requested a joint conference with this committee, and the Board decided to participate. The conference was duly held in October 1891, but it concentrated on an appeal to be made to raise funds for helping Russian Jews, rather than taking any further political steps. In fact it was reiterated that in order to avoid any clash the Conjoint, with the agreement of the Board and AJA, had agreed that all active work in connection with Russian Jewry would be dealt with by the Russo-Jewish Committee.[131] The Board held a special meeting on 13 October 1891 on the subject of this appeal and many noteworthy contributions in words as well as money were made, and a number of resolutions were passed, including one that efforts should be made to dissuade Russian Jews from immigrating to Britain. That seems to have been the end of the Board's involvement with the 1890/91 Russian–Jewish issues. The Board's annual report of 1892, when discussing the Russian issue, concluded:

> As to the probable solution of the Russo-Jewish question, the Board hesitates to pronounce an opinion. The circumstances are unique. Religious persecution has left its blot on almost every century of human history, but it was reserved for the nineteenth century to witness the extraordinary and unparalleled spectacle of a European community of five millions of persons expelled from their home in their native country, and refused an asylum in almost every other land.[132]

Little did they know that the twentieth century was to be even worse.

On 18 April 1903, following a ritual murder allegation, violence erupted against Jews in Kishinev. It lasted three days and about fifty Jews were killed with hundreds injured and much property destroyed. On 13 May 2003 the Conjoint met to discuss the Kishinev riots. Three issues were considered. First, whether a letter should be sent to *The Times* deploring the massacres that had occurred. This was agreed and on 18 May *The Times* published a long letter from the presidents of the Board and the AJA, formally protesting about these riots and the apathetic attitude towards them of the Russian authorities.[133] The second issue was whether a public meeting should be arranged, and the third was whether a public fund to aid the victims should be established. Decisions on these last two issues were postponed. On 21 May the Conjoint met again and decided, nearly unanimously, that no public protest meeting should be arranged but that it would make a public appeal for funds to aid the victims and their families.[134] It seems that the Jews of Kishinev had asked that a pubic protest meeting should not be made, as they feared that this would aggravate the already appalling situation.[135]

These decisions were conveyed to the Board at a meeting on 24 May and there was strong opposition to the decision of the Conjoint not to convene a protest meeting; it is clear from the report in the *JC* that the discussion must have become quite heated at that point.[136] About that time, the Board was very involved with the aliens issue and some deputies feared that a public meeting of Jews could draw unwarranted attention to them. The *JC* was also of the view that it was inappropriate to hold a public meeting and it considered that a meeting at the Guildhall called by the current Lord Mayor, Sir Marcus Samuel, who was Jewish, might pose certain difficulties. On the other hand, the AJA, after a very heated debate, resolved that a public meeting should be held as soon as possible.[137] This was subsequently discussed by the Conjoint, and it again decided that a public meeting was inappropriate; when this was referred back to the AJA, it changed its mind and agreed not to call a meeting. The Board called a special meeting on 28 June to reconsider the matter of a public meeting, but again, after a heated debate, decided not to support one. So once again there was unity – the Board, the AJA, the Conjoint, the Russo-Jewish committee and even the *JC* were all against holding a public protest meeting. Nonetheless, two public meetings were organized, one by a self-appointed committee established by a group of radical former Russian Jews living in the East End of London, who called themselves 'The International Kishinev Massacre Protest Committee', and the other by the English Zionist Federation. Curiously, the Zionist Federation held its meeting in the East End and the East End group held its meeting in Hyde Park. Both were well attended, but had no support from any of the major organizations of Anglo-Jewry. They were a one-off and the protest committee wound up a few months later at the end of July 1903. Nonetheless, Eugene Black is of the view that the issue of protest meetings created a political division within the Jewish community for a generation and led to the formation of a more general Jewish Workers Committee in the East End.[138] The split, or rather splits, must already have been there, but Kishinev acted as a catalyst for the radicals.

The question of whether to take any political action to protest through the British government does not appear to have been discussed at either the Conjoint or the Board meetings. A view was expressed that Russia was a power against which the British government could do nothing, and no deputy dissented from this opinion. This lack of political initiative and refusal to call a public meeting created a lot of adverse comments in the letter columns of the *JC* and one correspondent went so far as to contrast the rather supine nature of the current attitude of the Board with Sir Moses Montefiore, who did not hesitate to go to

Russia and elsewhere when Jews were facing crises. Another complained of the 'masterly inactivity' of the Board and other bodies.[139]

At the end of December 1903, reports reached London that further anti-Jewish riots were about to erupt in Kishinev, probably timed to coincide with the Russian Orthodox Christmas. This time the Conjoint decided to contact the Foreign Office and a letter was sent to the foreign secretary asking him to make representations to the Russian government, requesting it to take measures to prevent a recurrence of the riots at Kishinev.[140] It is not clear if representations were made to Russia by the British government, but it was reported in the press that Christmas in Kishinev passed quietly and the streets were patrolled the whole time by troops. The Board considered that the riots had been adverted as a direct result of the action taken by the Conjoint and the resultant press publicity.[141]

Anti-Jewish riots erupted again in Kishinev and elsewhere in Russia in October 1905. The Board discussed these at its meeting on 19 November 1905 and it was announced by the president that the Foreign Office had been informed, that a relief appeal had been established and the question of organizing a public protest meeting was under consideration. The objects of the relief appeal generated a heated debate, as the Russo-Jewish Committee who were organizing the appeal had stated that the funds could not be used to facilitate the emigration of Russian Jews to Britain. A number of deputies objected strongly to this, but in the end were ruled out of order since it was not a responsibility of the Board to determine the use of these monies. At the first Annual Meeting of the Board on 3 December 1905, great pressure was put on the Board to arrange a protest meeting, and at its meeting on 17 December 1905 the president informed the Board that following various private discussions between the leaders of Anglo-Jewry it had been decided that the Board would call a public protest meeting involving Jews and non-Jews.[142] This meeting was held on 8 January 1906 under the chairmanship of Lord Rothschild. The meeting was very well attended, with speeches by many very important non-Jewish dignitaries, and resolutions protesting the attacks on Jews in Russia were passed on to the Russian Embassy. Regrettably, these had little effect since atrocities against Jews in Russia continued and on more than one occasion they were discussed by the Board, who sought help from the Foreign Office, generally in vain.

Zionism and the Balfour Declaration

Theodore Herzl met a number of deputies and probably some of the leaders of the Board during his visits to Britain, but he never met the Board as a body. The English Zionist Federation was formed in 1899 and fairly early on came to the view that it needed to obtain the support of the major Anglo-Jewish institutions including the Board. According to Stuart Cohen, the EZF embarked on a strategy to infiltrate the Board gradually through the electoral process with the idea that the deputies who supported their objectives would gradually form themselves into an important lobby. One of the founders of the EZF, Herbert Bentwich, was a deputy and so it had at least a toe in the door. Furthermore, the EZF decided that it would involve itself in communal issues that had little if anything to do with the Zionist cause.[143] One early example of this was the organization of a public memorial meeting for the victims of the Kishinev pogrom. Although this was contrary to the Board's policy on this issue, the Zionist protest was deliberately low-key so as not to irritate the Anglo-Jewish establishment too much.[144]

In December 1905 the EZF tried to persuade the Board to participate in an international conference, called the General Jewish Conference, to be held in Brussels to consider the situation of Jews in Eastern Europe, particularly Romania and Russia. The Board declined, and it seems that this may have been because it feared that the Zionists might control the conference.[145] This might have been an early indication that the majority of deputies were probably anti-Zionist and most of the rest non-Zionist. We cannot be sure of this because Zionism or Zionist issues were hardly discussed at the Board or at meetings of its committees until well into the second decade of the twentieth century, but there is some fragmentary and anecdotal evidence in support of this contention. It would seem that most deputies supported the view that the solution to the Jewish problems in Eastern Europe could and should be solved by local economic and emancipation reforms rather than the nationalistic ideas of the Zionists. In 1908 two deputies, Herbert Bentwich and Leopold Greenberg, the managing editor of the *JC*, were accused at a meeting of the Board of making too much of Zionism during an argument over the Jewish vote at a by-election in Manchester. In 1913 the Board castigated the EZF over its efforts to support a public protest meeting in connection with the Beiliss affair, claiming that 'the issues involved could not be properly assessed by the narrow perspectives of an obvious minority group

within the community. The advice tendered by a rowdy bunch of irresponsible fanatics, most of whom had little experience in communal
management, was really irrelevant.'[146]

At the beginning of the First World War, the Zionists, led by Chaim
Weitzmann, decided to open discussions directly with the government
and it was these discussions that led ultimately to the Balfour Declaration in 1917. The Conjoint, as the foreign policy arm of the Board
and the AJA, resented this and in December 1914 pointed out to the
Foreign Office that it was the only body authorized to represent the
views of the Jewish community to government. It went further and
mentioned that it was aware that others representing no one except
themselves had been making representations but they did not speak
for the Jews of Britain. The internal Anglo-Jewish battle lines were
clearly being drawn at the same time as the more general battle lines
were being drawn in Europe. However, initially the concern of the
Conjoint was that it did not want anyone else stepping on its preserves,
as it had not yet appreciated the ultimate significance of Palestine in the
war. A meeting between the Conjoint (whose delegation included the
president of the Board) and the Zionists in April 1915 brought matters
to a head. The Zionists wanted nothing less than the establishment of
a Jewish state, whereas the furthest the Conjoint would go would be the
establishment of some sort of Jewish local government in Palestine,
hedged in with all sorts of restrictions to be imposed on the Zionists.
Thereafter both sides went their own ways.

The 'battle' is well described by Stuart Cohen in his book, *English
Zionists and British Jews*, as well as in Leonard Stein's *The Balfour
Declaration* and James Renton's *The Zionist Masquerade*, and will not
be rehearsed here.[147] The Conjoint side was led by Lucien Wolf, the
secretary to the committee and an avowed anti-Zionist. It is not clear
from the archives as to what extent the Board itself was informed at the
time as to what was going on, but it is certain that the president, David
Alexander, who was also vice-chairman of the Conjoint, was fully in
the picture and involved. In fact the first time the issue was debated
at the Board was in October 1916 when a resolution favouring
the establishment of a Jewish home in Palestine was discussed but
withdrawn.[148]

In mid-May 1917 there was a debate on Palestine at a Board meeting on a motion, proposed by Samuel Daiches, that the Board should
issue a declaration that 'British Jews hope that the historic claims of the
Jewish people to their ancient homeland will be recognised and that

Palestine will be made a Jewish centre.' The debate was heated and in the end the motion was narrowly defeated with twenty-six votes for and thirty-three against.[149] The 'battle' had become increasingly bitter and entered into the public arena, culminating in a statement from the Conjoint published in *The Times* on 24 May 1917. It was headed 'Palestine and Zionism – Views of Anglo-Jewry' and was a total attack on Zionism. The publication of this 'manifesto' became a cause célèbre in the Jewish community, and two of the Board's representatives resigned from the Conjoint. On 17 June the manifesto was discussed at a meeting of the Board and following a most acrimonious debate a resolution was passed disagreeing with the views of the Conjoint and calling upon the Board's representatives on the Conjoint to resign from it forthwith.[150] In less than a month, therefore, the voting had changed and clearly some who had voted against the pro-Zionist resolution in mid-May had changed sides. An analysis of the voting figures indicates that these deputies had not necessarily changed their views on Zionism, but were aggrieved against the leadership for other reasons including not consulting the Board before publishing the 'manifesto'.

The vote, despite subsequent myths, did not in fact indicate that the EZF had achieved its long-term objective of obtaining a majority of deputies since, as we have seen, the motives of those supporting the censure motion were very mixed. Furthermore, many of the deputies who voted for the resolution did so not because they disagreed with the 'manifesto' but because they had not been consulted in advance of its publication.[151] It is clear from subsequent developments that the EZF had not captured the Board and that the majority of deputies remained non- or anti-Zionist.[152] For example, in November 1917, following the Balfour Declaration, the Board passed a motion thanking the government but rejected a motion to cooperate with the EZF in promoting a Jewish National Home.

The censure vote, though, had significance well beyond the resignation of the executives of the Board itself. The Foreign Office decided that it no longer needed to consult the Conjoint and a day or so later the foreign secretary asked Lord Rothschild (who had become the president of the EZF) and Chaim Weizmann to submit a 'formula' for Palestine. The countdown to the Balfour Declaration had begun in earnest. Thus, unwittingly and unknowingly the Board had acted as a catalyst. It also explains in part why the letter from Balfour was addressed to Lord Rothschild and not to the president of the Board, who had hitherto been seen by British governments as the lay leader of Jews in Britain.

Lord Rothschild had just been elected the senior vice-president of the Board, so the Board's *amour-propre* was not dented too much.

NOTES

1. *Jewish Chronicle* [JC], 3 April 1874, p.885.
2. Robert G. Weisbord, *African Zion: The Attempt to establish a Jewish Colony in the East African Protectorate, 1903–1905* (Philadelphia: Jewish Publication Society of America, 1968).
3. William Rubinstein (ed.), *Dictionary of Anglo-Jewish History* (Basingstoke: Palgrave Macmillan, 2010) [Forthcoming].
4. *JC*, 8 May 1874, p.88.
5. BOD, ACC/3121/A/11, pp.410 and 415–17.
6 *JC*, 8 December 1876, p.570; 15 December 1876, p.581; 12 January 1877, pp.4, 5, 7; 19 January 1877, p.4; 26 January 1877, p.5; 23 February 1887, p.4.
7. Archives of the United Synagogue, London Metropolitan Archives [US], ACC/2712/1/1, p.229.
8. *JC*, 16 February 1877, pp.5–6; 23 February 1877 pp.8–9.
9. For an excellent profile of Arthur Cohen, see Israel Finestein, *Jewish Society in Victorian England: Collected Essays* (London: Vallentine Mitchell, 1993), pp.305–26.
10. Ibid., pp.315–16.
11. *JC*, 25 October 1895, p.13.
12. *JC*, 29 November 1895, pp.13–14.
13. Ibid; Rubinstein, *Dictionary of Anglo-Jewish History.*
14. Sharman Kadish, *Oxford Dictionary of National Biography* (Oxford: Oxford University Press, 2004).
15. *JC*, 30 September 1881, p.3.
16. *JC*, 11 January 1889, p.5; 18 January 1889, p.9; 1 February 1889, p.12.
17. *JC*, 21 February 1902, pp.12, 18.
18. *JC*, 20 February 1903, pp.12, 21.
19. *JC*, 10 June 1904, p.7.
20. *JC*, 26 April 1907, p.9.
21. Walter M. Schwab, *B'nai B'rith: The First Lodge of England, A Record of Fifty Years* (Letchworth: Oswald Wolff, 1960), pp.17–18.
22. Ibid., p.27.
23. Ibid., pp.28–31.
24. *JC*, 2 June 1911, p.23; 4 August 1911, p.20.
25. Annual Report of the Board of Deputies (AR), 1908.
26. *JC*, 1 July 1910, pp.3, 17; 8 July 1910, p.29.
27. Stuart A. Cohen, *English Zionists and British Jews: The Communal Politics of Anglo-Jewry, 1895–1920* (Princeton, NJ: Princeton University Press, 1982), p.70, n.51.
28. David Feldman, *Englishmen and Jews: Social Relations and Political Culture 1840–1914* (London: Yale University Press, 1994), pp.363-6.
29. David Cesarani, *The Jewish Chronicle and Anglo-Jewry, 1841–1991* (Cambridge: Cambridge University Press, 1994), p.109.
30. *JC*, 13 October 1911, p.9.
31. Cohen, *English Zionists and British Jews*, pp.66–70, 150.
32. BOD, ACC/3121/A/16, p.82.
33. *JC*, 24 November 1911, p.18.
34. *JC*, 20 October 1911, p.14; 27 October 1911, pp.16, 27; 24 November 1911, pp.8, 14–17; 26 January 1912, pp.8, 17–18.
35. *JC*, 9 February 1912, pp.10, 18–19.
36. *JC*, 10 January 1913, p.12; 14 March 1913, p.11; 2 May 1913, p.21; 27 June 1913, pp.13–14; 31 October, 1913, pp.15–17.
37. *JC*, 9 July 1914, p.15; 24 July 1914, p.13.
38. *JC*, 23 April 1915, pp.7, 12.
39. *JC*, 24 December 1915, p.8; 7 January 1916, pp.8, 13–14; 28 January 1915, pp.8, 12–13.

40. *JC*, 16 June 1916, p.9; 7 July 1916, p.7.
41. *JC*, 30 June 1916, p.6; 10 July 1916, p.22.
42. *The Times*, 24 May 1917, p.5.
43. *JC*, 22 June 1917, pp.5–6, 14–15, 18–20; Elsley Zeitlyn, *The Board of Deputies and the B'nai B'rith* (London: Board of Deputies, 1930); BOD, ACC/3121/A/017/66–7.
44. Stuart Cohen, 'The Conquest of a Community? The Zionists and the Board of Deputies in 1917', *Jewish Journal of Sociology*, 19 (1977), 157–84; Cohen, *English Zionists and British Jews*, pp.260–76; Todd M. Endelman, *The Jews of Britain, 1656–2000* (London: University of California Press, 2002), pp.193–5; Aubrey Newman, *The Board of Deputies of British Jews 1760–1985: A Brief Survey* (London: Vallentine Mitchell, 1987), pp.19–22.
45. *JC*, 24 June 1898, p.27.
46. *JC*, 3 March, 1899, p.19; 10 March 1899, p.3.
47. AR, 1902, pp.25–6, 51–9.
48. *JC*, 29 April 1904, p.16; 27 May 1904, p.10; BOD, ACC/3121/A/15, 22 and 36.
49. Geoffrey Alderman, *Modern British Jewry*, new edn (Oxford: Clarendon Press, 1998), pp.136–7.
50. David Feldman, 'Jews and the State in Britain', in Michael Brenner, Rainer Liedke and David Rechter (eds), *Two Nations: British and German Jews in Comparative Perspective* (Tübingen: M. Siebeck, 1999), p.155.
51. *JC*, 12 May 1905, p.13; 19 May 1905, p.12; 26 May 1905, pp.12, 18; 27 July 1905, p.12; AR, 1902, pp.74, 78 and 83.
52. See, for example, Geoffrey Alderman, *Controversy and Crisis: Studies in the History of the Jews in Modern Britain* (Boston, MA: Academic Studies Press, 2008), p.301.
53. *JC*, 2 November 1906, p.11; BOD. 51st Annual Report (1902), pp.115 and 142.
54. *JC*, 1 March 1907, pp.14–15; 20 March 1907, p.15; BOD. 51st Annual Report (1902), pp.156–7 and 160.
55. *JC*, 25 October 1907, p.22; 15 November 1907, p.20; 22 November 1907, p.20.
56. *JC*, 14 February 1908, p.11.
57. Feldman, 'Jews and the State in Britain', p.155.
58. *JC*, 10 June 1910, pp.5–6, 25; 21 October 1910, pp.5, 16–17; 28 October 1910, p.15; 3 November 1910, p.16.
59. Charles Tucker, 'Jewish Marriages and Divorces in England until 1940', *Genealogist Magazine*, 24, 3 and 4 (1992), pp.139–43.
60. *JC*, 23 November 1888, p.8; 22 March 1889, p.12; BOD, ACC/3121/A/12, pp.480 and 490; BOD, ACC/3121/A/13, pp.1–2.
61. BOD, ACC/3121/A/13, p.144.
62. *JC*, 3 February 1911, p.20; 7 April 1911, pp.32–4; 15 November 1912, p.10. The published report of the Divorce Commission has the reference Cmd 6478–82.
63. A description of the law on Sunday Trading and Sunday Labour as it stood in 1914 can be found in AR, 1915, pp.77–87.
64. *JC*, 21 August 1896, p.12; 4 September 1896, p.21.
65. *JC*, 26 July 1901, p.12; 12 December 1902, p.19.
66. *JC*, 31 March 1905, p.11; 21 April 1905, p.21; 12 May 1905, p.20; David Englander, *A Documentary History of Jewish Immigrants in Britain, 1840–1920* (London: Leicester University Press, 1994), pp.45–8; BOD, ACC/3121/A/15, pp.71, 79 and 88.
67. *JC*, 2 November 1906; BOD, ACC/3121/A/15, pp.123, 132 and 145–6.
68. *JC*, 5 April 1907, pp.8, 19; 12 April 1907, pp.12, 29; 19 April, 1907, p.10.
69. *JC*, 30 July 1909, p.22; 13 July 1910, p.20; 20 July 1910, p.20.
70. *JC*, 28 October, 1910, pp.22–3.
71. *JC*, 19 May 1911, p.25.
72. *JC*, January 20 1911, p.20.
73. *JC*, 14 July 1911, pp.16–19.
74. *JC*, 25 November 1892, p.11.
75. http://www.socialsciences.manchester.ac.uk/disciplines/politics/researchgroups/mancept/workingpapers/documents/shortenCulturalExemptions.pdf.
76. *JC*, 4 November 1904, p.12; BOD, ACC/3121/A/15, pp.45–6.
77. *JC*, 21 July, 1905, pp.8, 12–13.
78. *JC*, 2 June 1911, p.10.

79. *JC*, 11 August 1911, pp.12–13.
80. AR, 1911, p.38; BOD, ACC/3121/A/16, pp.76–9, 84 and 89.
81. *JC*, 1 August 1913, p.30; BOD, ACC/3121/A/16, 136.
82. *JC*, 20 March 1914, pp.21–2; 1 May 1914, p.24; 26 June 1914, p.26; BOD, ACC/3121/A/16, pp.136, 151–2, 175, 180–1 and 201.
83. A description of this subject is contained in Geoffrey Alderman and Colin Holmes, 'The Burton Book', *Journal of the Royal Asiatic Society*, 18, 1 (January 2008), pp.1–13. See also Christie's catalogue, *Valuable Printed Books and Manuscripts*, 6 June 2001, pp.60–4.
84. For a description of the book and its contents see Christie's catalogue, p.61.
85. BOD, ACC/3121/C13/1/4A, p.48.
86. BOD, ACC/3121/A/13, p.398.
87. *JC*, 22 April 1898, p.12; 20 May 1898, p.20.
88. BOD, ACC/3121/A/16, p.1b.
89. BOD, ACC/3121/A/16, pp.6, 16 and 63.
90. Steven Gilbert Bayme, *Jewish Leadership and Antisemitism in Britain* (Ann Arbor, MI: Columbia University Press, 1986), p.255.
91. *Jewish World*, 22 October 1913, p.6.
92. Letter from Board president, Jo Wagerman, to all deputies, 1 June 2001.
93. *JC*, 26 September 2003, p.32.
94. David Simmonds, 'Limerick 1904–1906: The Official Jewish Response', unpublished paper delivered at a conference on 'Jewish Ireland', organized by the Academy for Irish Cultural Heritages, University of Ulster, Coleraine (Belfast, September 2004).
95. *JC*, 26 February 1904, p.14; 25 March 1904, p.16.
96. *JC*, 22 April 1904, pp.12–13; 13 May 1904, p.12; 10 June 1904, p.11.
97. Bayme, *Jewish Leadership and Antisemitism in Britain*, pp.240–7.
98. Ibid., p.256.
99. Lloyd P. Gartner, 'Anglo-Jewry and the Jewish International Traffic in Prostitution, 1885–1914', *AJS Review*, 7 (1982), pp.129–78.
100. Colin Holmes, *Anti-Semitism in British Society, 1876–1939* (London: Edward Arnold, 1979), p.45.
101. *JC*, 17 December 1909, p.20.
102. *JC*, 18 October 1912, p.16; 25 October 1912, p.17; 24 January 1913, p.18.
103. David Cesarani, 'An Embattled Minority: The Jews in Britain During the First World War', *Immigrants and Minorities*, 8 (March 1989), pp.61–81.
104. *JC*, 7 August 1914, p.5.
105. *JC*, 26 March 1915, pp.11, 17;
106. *JC*, 22 January 1915, pp.8–9.
107. *JC*, 18 June 1915, pp.7, 12–14; 25 June 1915, pp.7, 13–14; 2 July 1915, p.6, 15; 9 July 1915, pp.8, 15.
108. *JC*, 21 July 1916, pp.4, 10; 28 July 1916, p.4; 11 August 1916, p.14.
109. Cesarani, 'An Embattled Minority', pp.69–72; Martin Watts, *The Jewish Legion in the First World War* (Basingstoke: Palgrave, 2004); *JC*, 17 August 1917, pp.5, 14–15.
110. Mark Levene, *War, Jews, and the New Europe: The Diplomacy of Lucien Wolf, 1914–19* (Oxford: Littman Library, 1992), pp.4–5; Mark Levene, 'Anglo-Jewish Foreign Policy in Crisis – Lucien Wolf, the Conjoint Committee and the War, 1914–18', *Jewish Historical Studies*, 30 (1987–88), p.181.
111. Ibid., pp.10–11.
112. Deborah Yellin Bachrach, *The Impact of the Dreyfus Affair on Great Britain* (Michigan: University of Minnesota, 1978); Maurice Samuel, *Blood Accusation: The Strange History of the Beiliss case* (Philadelphia: Jewish Publication Society of America, 1966).
113. Edgar Feuchtwanger, '"Jew Feeling" and Realpolitik: Disraeli and the Making of Foreign and Imperial Policy', in Todd M. Endelman and Tony Kushner (eds), *Disraeli's Jewishness* (London: Vallentine Mitchell, 2002), pp.180–97.
114. Lucien Wolf, *Notes on the Diplomatic History of the Jewish Question* (London: Jewish Historical Society of England, 1919), pp.23–34.
115. *The Times*, 15 July 1878, p.9.
116. George Earle Buckle, *The Life of Benjamin Disraeli, Earl of Beaconsfield* (London: John Murray, 1920), p.311.

117. BOD, ACC/3121/A/12, pp.13 and 18; BOD, ACC/3121/C11/1, p.8.
118. See, for example, John Klier and Shlomo Lamboza (eds), *Pogroms: Anti-Jewish Violence in Modern Russian History* (Cambridge: Cambridge University Press, 1992).
119. AR, 1881, p.39.
120. Louis Loewe (ed.), *Diaries of Sir Moses and Lady Montefiore*, a facsimile of the 1890 edition (London: Jewish Historical Society of England, 1983), Vol. 2, p.300.
121. *JC*, 18 November 1881, p.9.
122. *The Times*, 11 and 13 January, 1882, p.4.
123. *JC*, 20 January 1882, p.13.
124. *Jewish World*, 12 January 1882, p.3.
125. H.G.C. Mathews (ed.), *The Gladstone Diaries, Vol. 10* (Oxford: Clarendon, 1990), pp.201–6.
126. *JC*, 17 March 1882, p.9.
127. See Chapter 5.
128. Insert to *JC*, 8 August 1890, p.1.
129. *JC*, 22 August 1890, p.4.
130. *JC*, 21 November 1890, p.7.
131. *JC*, 18 December 1891, p.3.
132. AR, 1892, p.46.
133. *The Times*, 18 May 1903, p.10.
134. This appeal was published in the *JC*, 22 May 1903, p.3.
135. *JC*, 24 March 1905, p.8.
136. *JC*, 29 May 1903, p.14.
137. *JC*, 19 June 1903, p.18.
138. Eugene Black, *The Social Politics of Anglo-Jewry 1880–1920* (Oxford: Blackwell, 1988), p.213.
139. *JC*, 29 May 1903, p.8; 3 July 1903, p.6.
140. *JC*, 8 January 1904, p.10.
141. *JC*, 22 January 1904, p.21.
142. *JC*, 24 November 1905, p.14; 8 December 1905, p.13; 22 December 1905, p.14.
143. Stuart A. Cohen, *English Zionists and British Jews: The Communal Politics of Anglo-Jewry, 1895–1920* (Princeton, NJ: Princeton University Press, 1982), pp.54–5.
144. Ibid., pp.73–6.
145. *JC*, 2 February 1906, p.6.
146. Quoted by Cohen, *English Zionists and British Jews*, p.147.
147. Cohen, ibid; Leonard Stein, *The Balfour Declaration* (London: Vallentine Mitchell, 1961); James Renton, *The Zionist Masquerade* (Basingstoke: Palgrave Macmillan, 2007).
148. *JC*, 27 October 1916, pp.16–17.
149. *JC*, 25 May 1917, pp.10–12; 1 June 1917, p.5.
150. *JC*, 22 June 1917, pp.5, 14–16.
151. See letter to *JC* from Simon Rowson, *JC*, 22 June 1917, p.22.
152. For a detailed analysis of the voting, see Stuart Cohen, 'The Conquest of a Community? The Zionists and the Board of Deputies in 1917', *Jewish Journal of Sociology*, 19 (1977), pp.157–84, 244–50.

4 Decline and Fall of the Old Regime, 1917–1939

As the First World War drew to its close, the position of the Jews in Britain, whilst not precarious in any way, was decidedly uncomfortable. There were more openly antisemitic comments and articles in the press, social antisemitism was on the upsurge, and antisemitism was quite acceptable in many quarters.[1] There were a number of reasons for this. Much of the public saw Jews as shirkers who avoided war service. In fact this was not true, as overall the proportion of Jews who served in the armed forces was greater than in the country as a whole, partly – but only partly – attributable to their younger age distribution. Furthermore, in the East End of London those not serving stood out, often because until the final stages of the war they were ineligible to serve in the armed services through not having been born in Britain. Another reason was that Jews were suspected of supporting Germany and not the Russians, who were British allies. A third reason was that the Bolshevik revolution in October 1917 unleashed much antisemitism because of the allegations that most of the leaders were Jewish. Antisemitism became socially acceptable. For example, there were attacks on *shechita*, and many employers – particularly in the public sector – would not employ aliens, and to a large extent this meant Jews, and other restrictions on aliens impinged particularly harshly on Jews. There were difficulties not experienced previously in obtaining special arrangements for examinations on Saturdays and Jewish holidays, and some private schools and clubs operated severe restrictions against Jews. Obtaining insurance, particularly car insurance, was difficult and for many years the London County Council (LCC) discriminated against Jews in various areas.

It would be wrong to overstate antisemitism in Britain, as compared with the Continent there was virtually no violence against Jews (except in the 1930s by the fascists), no expulsions, no false arrests and bogus trials, no boycotts, no anti-Jewish legislation and no serious antisemitic political parties. Jewish historians of the period remain divided on the significance of this antisemitism, its effect on Britain and on the British Jewish community and its leaders.[2] Nonetheless it was unpleasant to say the least, a feature of Jewish life in Britain, sometimes marginal, sometimes significant, and there is evidence that fascist anti-semitism in the 1930s created great fear among many Jews in the East End of London and elsewhere.[3]

The Board had not only to face up to this antisemitism and decide how to respond, but in this period had also to meet the challenges of the British mandate in Palestine and the promised creation of a Jewish national home there, the rise of Nazism in Germany, and the impact of these issues on Britain and the Jewish communities at home and abroad. What is important is also context. The Board also had to react to social changes in the Jewish community itself. As David Cesarani has so succinctly described: 'During the inter-war years, the Jewish popula-tion of Britain mutated from one that was largely of recent immigrant origin, inner-city and working class into one that was mainly British-born, suburban and middle class.'[4] In a way the community was becoming again what it had been in the 1870s – a settled community. This is not to say that the community was homogeneous and entirely middle class. Significant numbers of Jews, probably about one-quarter of the total Jewish population of Britain, remained in inner-city areas, particularly the East End of London, most in traditional occupations, and the economic slump hit them badly. It was mainly but not exclu-sively this group who felt they were not properly represented by the Board, particularly during the 1930s. Furthermore, the leadership of the Board remained upper middle class, British-born and male. This period was to see a gradual transformation.

Following the First World War, the British economy was weak, lead-ing to severe and prolonged economic depression resulting in mass unemployment, which peaked at 2.7 million (22 per cent of the regis-tered labour force) in 1932, and a financial crisis in 1931 resulting in the abandonment of the gold standard to which Britain had only returned in 1925. Foreign policy was confused to say the least – for example, blowing hot and cold over such issues as appeasement and supporting or otherwise the Jews in Palestine. In determining its actions the Board had also to be aware that, as Bernard Wasserstein has described, 'decisions of importance were still being taken in Pall Mall clubs' and 'the effective-ness of political action by the Anglo-Jewish leadership consequently depended less on its ability to mobilize its constituency than in its access to influential quarters'. He also considers that, 'due to its centralised nature and using its "notable" category of leaders, those with an external, non-Jewish basis of importance', the leadership served the community well.[5]

There are again three parts to this chapter. The first considers the internal structure and workings of the Board: how it tried to meet its internal and external challenges and its critics and how its leadership was gradually transformed from the old elite establishment in 1917 to electing a new president in 1939 who was not only a strong Zionist but was born in Russia. The second part covers the issues the Board dealt with that arose at home, and the third part is again foreign affairs. The Board's reactions to the rise of Nazism is treated as a home issue although its root was in a foreign country, and Palestine is included under foreign affairs although many of the issues were in a sense at home.

1. THE BOARD

Leadership

The June 1917 'revolution' at the Board did not give rise to any real change at the top. Sir Stuart Samuel, MP, a merchant banker, a former Liberal MP and the brother of Herbert Samuel, the home secretary, was elected president, and Lord Rothschild and Sir Philip Magnus were elected vice-presidents – all three were members of the Cousinhood. Nathan Laski was elected honorary treasurer, who although not strictly speaking in the Cousinhood was considered part of the Jewish establishment. He was, though, from Manchester and thus the provinces at last had representation at the highest level on the Board. The *Jewish Chronicle* (*JC*) interviewed Sir Stuart Samuel a few days after he took up office and he remarked that as long as he could remember, the Board had been considered a hopeless body and it was thus very appropriate that he should be elected president, as for the past twenty-two years he had been head of the Home for Incurables.[6]

In 1922 Sir Stuart Samuel retired as president, essentially because he thought the Board needed a younger man and that the president should not occupy the office for more than one triennial session. In fact Sir Stuart served as president for more than three years, as he took over following the resignation of D.L. Alexander in 1917 and was re-elected in the triennial election in 1919. The Board elected Henry Straus Quixano Henriques as president. He was a barrister and had written a number of works on law including in particular *The Jews and the English Law*. He was a past president of the Jewish Historical Society of England and had been chairman of the West London Reform Synagogue. He had been one of the vice-presidents who had resigned in 1917 as a result of the censure vote. He was a few years younger than Sir Stuart and continued in office for a second term, but this was curtailed by his premature death. In fact comparatively few presidents have served for only one three-year term. Lord Rothschild occupied the chair for a few months until a new president was elected. At the beginning of 1926 Osmond E. D'Avigdor–Goldsmid was elected president. He was a banker, a very active local politician and received a baronetcy in 1934. He was already president of the AJA and immediately following his election a motion was set down proposing the amalgamation of the Board and the AJA. D'Avigdor–Goldsmid requested that consideration of this matter should be deferred for six months and it was not raised again. It seems pretty clear that there must have been quite a bit of 'behind the scenes' discussion within the then Jewish establishment on this. He resigned as president at the end of 1932. Bernard Homa, a deputy from 1928 to 1971 representing Strictly Orthodox synagogues and a scourge of the Progressive movements, recorded in his memoirs:

> Sir Osmond d'Avigdor-Goldsmid was the perfect English gentleman, but his contacts with mainstream Judaism were very tenuous. He belonged to the Reform Community. I well remember when he delivered his 'swan-song' at a Board meeting on his retirement in December 1932, he concluded his speech by wishing everyone a Merry Xmas! Surprisingly, only a small minority of those present indicated any astonishment.[7]

On 15 January 1933 Neville Laski was elected President of the Board. This was the first-ever contested election for the presidency. The other candidate was Major Harry Nathan, a Liberal MP at the time and subsequently a Labour MP. The result was 128 votes for Laski and seventy-nine for Nathan.[8] One possible reason for Nathan's defeat was that he was a strong Zionist whereas Laski was a non-Zionist, and at that time Zionists were in a minority on the Board. Neville Laski was a barrister (later a judge) and from a prominent Manchester Jewish family – his father, Nathan Laski, had been a treasurer of the Board and Neville had seconded the censure motion in 1917. The Laski family had been involved in work on behalf of Jewish settlements in Palestine;

thus the Zionists hoped he might support them and he was invited to join the council of the Zionist Federation, an invitation he refused. He was the first president who was not from the Cousinhood, and it was hoped by many that he would complete the revolution at the Board, started in 1917. They were to be disappointed, as his views, opinions and policies remained those of the old Anglo-Jewish establishment. Neville Laski's election was followed fifteen days later by Adolph Hitler becoming Chancellor of Germany. Neville Laski's period of office was dominated by the persecution of the Jews by the Nazis, fascist antisemitism in Britain, the Palestine issue and the disagreements within the British Jewish community as to how best to react to these events. He was president at the start of the Second World War on 3 September 1939.

On 12 September 1939 a meeting was held at New Court, the offices of the Rothschild Bank, of some of the most eminent men of Anglo-Jewry with the object of reorganizing and streamlining the communal leadership in view of the start of the Second World War. The proposal was to establish a committee to be called the New Court Committee with the Board to appoint a committee to cooperate with it. Neville Laski was present at the meeting and supported the proposal. This proposal was debated at a Board meeting on 1 October 1939 and was strenuously opposed by most deputies. It was argued that the Board should never allow itself to become subordinate to any other communal body. It was suggested instead that the Board should appoint an Executive Committee to deal with all matters during the emergency situation and this proposal was unanimously adopted.[9] Despite the end of the emergency in 1945, the Executive Committee has remained as the central committee of the Board.

At the meeting of the Board on 19 November 1939, Laski announced his resignation. It is doubtful if his resignation was due to the rejection of the proposed New Court Committee, which he had supported. The pressure of work on him was enormous and for the last two or three years he had worked virtually full-time for the Board, and his legal practice had suffered as a result. He had been offered an annual honorarium by the Defence Committee but he had refused this.[10] He probably had had enough and was under great stress. There is no evidence whatsoever that he was forced out of office. In fact resignation must have been in his mind by August 1939 as indicated in a letter to him from Cyril Picciotto, dated 10 August 1939, in which Picciotto proposed what should happen to the Defence Committee, should Laski resign the presidency.[11]

To consider what happened next we have to go back a few years. The general secretary of the Zionist Federation, Lavy Bakstansky, considered it vital that the Board of Deputies should move from being non-Zionist at best to supporting the Zionist cause. Lavy Bakstansky was born in Lithuania but his family moved to Palestine when he was a child. He went to London to study at the London School of Economics and following his graduation in 1928 he joined the Zionist Federation as its assistant secretary, and in 1930 was appointed its general secretary, a position he occupied for more than forty years. Gideon Shimoni writes that 'Bakstansky attained a position of extraordinary influence in British Zionist circles by virtue of his powers of persuasion, his organisational genius and fervent devotion to Zionism. He preferred to operate out of the limelight.'[12] In 1934 Bakstansky joined the Board as a deputy and immediately began a process of increasing the number of pro-Zionist deputies with a view to fielding successfully a Zionist candidate for presidency at the triennial elections in 1940; he thought 1937 too soon to be sure of having sufficient support. He chose as the potential candidate Professor Selig Brodetsky, a man of great distinction in Britain and a fervent Zionist. It was thought that such a person would also gain the support of some non-Zionist deputies. Brodetsky was born in 1888 in Russia and came to Britain with his parents in 1893 when he was 5 years old. At the age of 20 he was top of the list of mathematical graduates at Cambridge – the senior wrangler. By 1924 he was professor of applied mathematics at Leeds University and became very active in various Jewish organizations. He was elected to the Board in May 1939 at a by-election to represent the Leeds United Hebrew Congregation and attended his first Board meeting on 15 October 1939. Lavy Bakstansky's was not the first attempt at organizing Zionists on the Board. In 1918 Harry Sacher had suggested to Simon Marks, both of Marks and Spencer fame and leading Zionists and deputies, that the pro-Zionist deputies should form a Zionist party on the Board with whips and endeavour to fill every committee vacancy with Zionists.[13] However, nothing came of this.

In the meantime the Zionists had already had a success in a Board by-election for an honorary officer. In January 1938 the vice-president, Lionel Cohen, resigned due to pressure of other work,[14] not because of the pro-Zionist motion passed by the Board on 16 January 1938 as suggested by some historians.[15] Cohen informed the president in October 1937 that he intended to resign; his letter of resignation was dated December 1937 and announced at the Board meeting on

16 January prior to the vote. In the ensuing by-election Israel Feldman, the candidate put up by the Zionists, narrowly defeated by 127 votes to 121 Otto Schiff, a non-Zionist, despite intensive lobbying for Schiff by Neville Laski.

It seems that in the December 1939 by-election for president, Lavy Bakstansky even contemplated asking Chaim Weizmann to stand, given the circumstances,[16] and because Brodetsky was very reluctant. In the event great pressure was put on Brodetsky and he agreed to be a candidate. Neville Laski went out of his way to prevent Brodetsky's candidature, going so far as to try to persuade Chaim Weizmann and Simon Marks that it would be preferable if the president of the Board was a man of distinction who was more moderate in his Zionist views. He suggested Harry Nathan, who had stood against him in the 1933 presidential election and was then a Labour MP. They rejected this out of hand and Laski then turned to Anthony de Rothschild, head of the Rothschild Bank in Britain. When Brodetsky heard that Rothschild might stand he wavered, but was pressed to continue by Bakstansky who assured him that he had gathered enough votes to ensure his election. Bakstansky had in fact issued a 'three-line-whip' to all Zionist-sympathizing deputies requiring them to attend the election meeting and stating in his letter: 'We are no longer prepared to be governed by a clique from above who have little contact with the masses of Jewry.'[17]

There is an apocryphal story that Brodetsky overheard a leading member of the Jewish establishment mutter that 'we couldn't have a bloody foreigner as leader of Anglo-Jewry' and it was this remark that determined him to stand. There is another story related by Brodetsky in his *Memoirs* that Anthony Rothschild had written to Weizmann asking what had a professor of mathematics to do with the presidency of the Board? Weizmann, who had been the reader in organic chemistry at Manchester University, replied asking Rothschild what a reader in organic chemistry had to do with the presidency of the Jewish Agency.[18] In the event Rothschild withdrew, primarily it seems because he could not face the ignominy of defeat, and the elite realized they were beaten and decided not to put forward another candidate.

Professor Selig Brodetsky was elected unanimously as president at the Board meeting on 17 December 1939, there being no other candidate.[19] He was the first foreign-born president (if we ignore, as we should, that Moses Montefiore was born in Italy whilst his parents were on a visit there) and the first president who was a Zionist. The revolution at the Board that started at the end of the First World War was completed at the start of the Second. The new generation, 'the children of the ghetto', had at last taken power.

Changes Following 1917 Censure Resolution

Following the passing of the resolution censuring the officers and demanding withdrawal of the Board from the Conjoint, that committee was dissolved and the agreement with the AJA terminated. The Board replaced that committee temporarily by a Foreign Affairs Committee, but within a few months an agreement was reached with the AJA and a new joint committee, the Joint Foreign Affairs Committee, was established with Lucien Wolf – the secretary of the old Conjoint – appointed its permanent secretary. In fact, the honorary officers threatened to resign if the agreement was not accepted by the Board.[20] The structure of the Joint was slightly different to that of the Conjoint in that the Board had eleven members (compared with seven on the Conjoint) and the AJA had eight (compared with seven). Thus the Board now had a majority, although Mark Levene has inferred that the AJA really had the ascendancy (due to the dual membership of the Board and the AJA) and made the running.[21] The first constitution of the newly formed Joint specifically stated that the question of Zionism was to be outside the purview of that committee unless specially delegated by both parent bodies,[22] but this was rescinded a few months later.

The president and the others who had resigned because of the vote of no confidence did not give up the anti-Zionist fight. They were among the founders of the League of British Jews, which was established in November 1917 to oppose the idea that Jews constituted a political nation. The League did not in any way try to usurp the Board. At first there was a great deal of animosity between the Board and the League, but this died away as it became clear that the League was not garnering much support. The League, which at its height had no more than about 1,300 members, folded in the late 1920s.

Although there was in effect no change in the nature of the hierarchy of the Board, nonetheless it recognized that some changes in its structure were vital, and rapidly established a committee to consider reforms of the Board. This committee duly reported and made a number of recommendations that largely were supported by the Board, and in January 1919 a new constitution was adopted. One main change was that representation that had been confined to individual synagogues was opened to communal institutional bodies including the United Synagogue, the Federation of Synagogues, a number of Jewish Friendly

Societies, and Oxford and Cambridge Universities, and the Board was given power to agree to the election of deputies by other institutions. This change could be seen as a sort of secularization of the Board, since for the first time secular and non-religious organizations could elect deputies. It is also relevant to note that neither the Zionist organizations nor Jewish Trade Unions were invited to elect deputies. Another change was that female seat-holders could vote for deputies and women be elected as deputies – this was at a time when the suffragette movement in Britain was at its peak in its activities and no doubt the Board was influenced by this. Enfranchising women was a permissive change as each synagogue could decide for itself whether or not to permit its women members to vote and stand for election, and some still do not permit women to vote or stand for election. Although the guidance of the Board on religious affairs remained with the previously defined ecclesiastical authorities (the chief rabbi and the haham) it was provided that this should not affect the rights of action or control regarding its internal affairs of any congregation which did not acknowledge the jurisdiction of these ecclesiastical authorities.[23] By this time it was not only the Reform and Liberal synagogues that were concerned but also some of the strictly Orthodox, like the Union of Orthodox Congregations. There was an animated discussion both at the Board and in the press over a proposed change to the constitution to exclude criminals, bankrupts and moneylenders from election as deputies. In the end it was decided by a narrow majority that moneylenders were acceptable but the other two classes should be excluded.

Mrs M. Model and Mrs M.A. Spielman were elected deputies representing the Union of Jewish Women and attended their first meeting on 19 October 1919. They were the first women deputies to serve on the Board, which thus had women members before the House of Commons. Constance Markiewicz (Sinn Fein) was elected an MP in December 1918 but did not take up her seat, leaving Lady Nancy Astor (Unionist) the honour of being the first woman to take her seat on 1 December 1919. There was an interesting change to the constitution in 1925 when it was agreed that members of university synagogues could vote at Board elections even though under the required age of 21. The Board had bowed to pressure from the students themselves. The Liberal Synagogue joined the Board in 1922 without any of the furore that preceded the admission of the Reform Synagogue in the mid-nineteenth century. It asked for certain changes in the wording of the constitution regarding the non-application of the jurisdiction of the Board's ecclesiastical authorities and after some negotiations these were agreed without any dissent.[24]

Dissentions Within the Board, 1917–39

The period between 1917 and 1939 was marked by dissent from deputies representing the Friendly Societies, who saw themselves as champions of the immigrant and working-class community and did not consider the Board was doing enough for them or representing their views adequately, particularly in relation to discrimination against aliens in the 1920s and in relation to the fight against fascist antisemitism in the 1930s. The Friendly Societies were also concerned with what they considered under-representation on the Board's committees. The Zionists were also continuing to snipe at the Board, trying to get the Board to take a more active stance in support of Zionist aspirations for Palestine. This was all part of their campaign to infiltrate all Jewish institutions that held power and authority.[25]

The rise of Nazism galvanized the Board. Many subcommittees were formed to deal with specific issues related to Nazi Germany, such as refugees, information, parliamentary affairs, public meetings, and coordination with other Jewish movements involved in anti-Nazi activities. Many people who were not deputies but could offer certain expertise were co-opted onto these committees, and other leaders of the community, such as the chief rabbi, were co-opted on to the major committees of the Board.[26] As Bernard Krikler has written, the rise of Nazism presented the Board with a dilemma. As the official representatives of the British Jewish community it considered it should not embarrass the government, which was tending to play down what was happening in Germany. On the other hand, a low-key reaction would alienate the majority of the Jewish community in Britain who demanded a very proactive anti-Nazi stance. In addition, the Board was concerned not to do or say anything that might make matters worse for German Jews. As the issue developed the views on which policy to pursue became irreconcilable and there were major differences of opinion within the Board. As a result the Board's public utterances were often platitudinous and it failed to provide positive leadership to the community at least until 1936.[27]

The ways in which the Board tackled the major issues that arose are discussed in the next section of this chapter. However, it is important to address briefly here the dissentions within the Board on its policy towards fascist antisemitism. The fascist movement held meetings and parades in various parts of the country, but particularly in those areas where there was a large Jewish population. These meetings and parades provoked the Jews to react angrily and violently against them, particularly as this was a means of letting off steam against what was happening in Nazi Germany. The Board decried Jews involving themselves in such events and this policy was criticized by much of the community and parts of the Jewish press at the time, and has been subject to severe criticism by many Jewish historians subsequently. Most of the leaders of the Board were of the view that violent protests at fascist meetings created publicity for the Fascist Party, whereas if they were ignored they might not obtain much attention. They were also of the view that the Fascist Party would not last long and the problems would blow over.

The Board and its officers were, however, not at all unmindful of what was happening and of the effect on Jews in the areas where these fascist activities were being carried out. The reports of the Board and its committee meetings as well as the Board's correspondence files make this clear. Many deputies were unhappy with the Board's policy and the honorary officers were very sympathetic to the Jewish victims in these areas, but the Board stuck to its policy. Not only did this policy fit the Boards's traditional 'low profile' one but also it was much in line with the policy of the government. There could have been other reasons for sticking to this policy as well. The leaders of the Board probably truly believed that a non-confrontational policy would be more effective in countering the fascists, even though they fully understood that in areas like the East End of London the Jewish population was being physically abused and was looking for a physical reaction. Daniel Tilles, in a paper to be published in 2010, has found from his researches that the leaders of the Board had been involved in combating fascism much earlier than previously thought and had been attempting to undermine it as well. The ways they did this could not be disclosed at the time. The paper also indicates that the Board's policy was broader and more vigorous than suggested by most historians of the period.[28] Board policy was formulated by the honorary officers and it is possible that they saw their major objectives as helping refugees from Nazism and trying to alleviate the dire position of the Jews in Germany. Both of these would require help from the government, and the officers did not want to prejudice this by going against government policy on the fascist issue.[29] The situation of the Jewish community in relation to the antisemitic meetings and marches of the fascists, particularly in the East End of London, was a difficult and unhappy one, but it paled into insignificance in relation to what was happening in Germany.

The policies of the Board divided not only the community but the Board as well. For example, on 31 March 1933 the *JC* published a letter from Michael Levy, a deputy representing the Association of Jewish Friendly Societies, complaining about the attitude of the Board's officers at a Board meeting the previous week and stating that 'after fourteen years as a member of the Deputies, I have arrived at the conclusion that the Board does not represent the opinion of Anglo-Jewry, although it may represent the opinion of a miserable minority who are always against coming to the front lest their social standing suffer'.[30] Two large Jewish Friendly Societies were contemplating the formation of a united opposition to the Board, and Simon Marks, a deputy and also chairman of Marks and Spencer, had proposed that Laski resign in favour of Chaim Weizmann.[31] Following the refusal of the Board to get involved in the boycott of German goods campaign, an organization called the Jewish Representative Council for the Boy-cott of German Goods and Services was established in September 1933. One can presume that the use of the word 'Representative' in its title was a deliberate slight to the Board. In 1934 a number of Jewish trade unionists and others formed the Jewish Labour Council to com-bat fascism and in July 1936, in despair at the non-active policy of the Board, they set up the Jewish People's Council against Fascism and Anti-Semitism (JPC).[32] Immediately there was great hostility between the JPC and the Board. Criticism of the Board was not limited to its reaction to fascist antisemitism, but also included complaints against the poor way it had defended Jewish rights such as trading on Sundays and its claim to be fully representative. This latter complaint was that it did not properly represent working- and lower-middle-class Jews. At a Board meeting in 1936, suggestions were raised that the Board should include Jewish trade unions among its institutional members but this was rejected. Another issue that divided the Board was its policy on Palestine. There were constant clashes over Palestine policy between the Zionists who dominated the Board's Palestine Committee and the honorary officers and others in the hierarchy who tended to be anti- or non-Zionist.

Stuart Cohen argues that the perceived inadequacies of the Board's reactions to fascist antisemitism, its feeble representations to the gov-ernment on the fate of Jewish communities abroad and its refusal to join the World Jewish Congress (WJC) (see below), as well as general communal dissatisfaction with the Board, particularly among the second- and third-generation immigrants, put the Board at serious risk of atrophy and decay. It became vital that the Board should take steps to restore its public image.[33] On the other hand, the results in the triennial elections did not indicate any falling-off in demand for representation on the Board. In 1931, 299 deputies were elected representing 219 congregations and institutions, rising to 347 deputies representing 229 constituencies in 1934 and rising again to 387 deputies representing 263 constituencies in 1937. In 1940 the numbers fell to 288 deputies representing 207 constituencies, but this reduction must have reflected the onset of the Second World War.

The World Jewish Congress

The Board was also faced with the establishment of the World Jewish Congress. A motion that it should participate by sending a delegation to a conference on this issue was defeated at a Board meeting on 26 April 1936, but only after some considerable behind-the-scenes lobbying by Neville Laski.[34] The issue arose again in July when the Board was invited to attend a conference of worldwide Jewish organizations to consider the establishment of a worldwide body to act as the future spokesman for diaspora Jewry. The invitation was debated by the Board, but by a narrow majority of only two it decided not to participate. The arguments against were essentially that the Board would appear to be giving up its independence by affiliating to an international Jewish organization; there was concern that such an organization would be dominated by Zionists and thus become a quasi-Zionist organization; and the formation of such a body might give fodder to antisemites who considered that there was a worldwide conspiracy among Jews. There was also concern that the Board would lose its influence with the British government, as it would no longer be seen as a solely British organization.

As a result of this refusal, a significant number of British Jewish organizations (mainly but not exclusively Zionist) held a meeting in London and decided to send twelve delegates representing British Jewry to the worldwide conference in Geneva. The WJC was formally established at that conference and, because the Board had refused to participate, the WJC established a separate British Section, initially housed in the offices of the Zionist Federation in London. Some deputies were among the first honorary officers of the British Section.

Although the WJC did not in principle interfere with the internal affairs of Jewish communities it did lead to much conflict with and within the Board, particularly as from an early stage the WJC made direct representations to the British government on matters affecting world Jewry. The Board consistently made efforts to ensure that the government paid no attention to the WJC on matters relating to British Jewry. It was successful in this probably because the WJC had no real wish to involve itself in these matters. It was not until 1974 that the Board decided to participate in the WJC and as a consequence the separate British Section was dissolved and its functions were taken over by the Board.[35]

2. HOME ISSUES

Aliens and Refugees from the Nazis[36]

The Board was disappointed to find that following the end of the First World War the position of aliens did not improve. Although the war regulations were revoked, a fresh and more stringent order was substituted. Under this order all aliens wishing to enter Britain had to be given leave to land by an immigration officer without any appeal to an Immigration Board. Furthermore, the requirements under which leave to land could be granted could at any time be varied and made more restrictive on the instructions of the home secretary. Registration restrictions for aliens already in Britain were increased and they could be deported without a right of appeal.

In August 1919, the Board requested a meeting with the home secretary, Edward Shortt, on the issue of appeals and this was refused on the grounds that no useful service would be achieved by such a meeting.[37] The government had just introduced a bill to perpetuate in statutory form restrictions on aliens including the denial of rights of hearing and appeal. In fact the expulsion of enemy aliens had been an election pledge in the 1918 general election, as were proposals to make permanent the various restrictions on aliens that had been introduced during the war. These were populist pledges. When the bill was promulgated the Board decided to hold a meeting with Jewish and other MPs, but the MPs were of the view that only one amendment should be sought, namely that no order or deportation should be made unless an appropriate court before which the alien would be able to state his case had issued a certificate. The Board did not consider that this went far enough and sought another amendment so that aliens seeking to land should have the right of appeal to an Immigration Board. Both amendments were moved in the House of Commons by Lionel de Rothschild, and although they were unsuccessful he persuaded the home secretary to agree that he would look into the possibility of some form of appeal in certain circumstances. The Board then sought and obtained a meeting with the home secretary and at that meeting made a number of proposals. Although the home secretary stated that he had great sympathy with the views of the Board, he considered that the national danger (and he probably had in mind sedition and threats from the Bolsheviks) was not yet over and it was not possible at present to constitute bodies for even the purpose of rehearing cases. The bill became law, as the Aliens Restriction (Amendment) Act 1919, and as a result it became almost impossible to secure the right of entry for refugees and even re-entry for those aliens who had left Britain to fight for Russia under the Military Convention Act. The Board considered employing officers at the ports to obtain immediately information on aliens refused leave to land, but financial considerations precluded this.[38] It is important to note that although the Board and, one presumes, much of the Jewish community in Britain were sympathetic to the plight of Jewish aliens and potential immigrants, the measures brought in by the government were popular in the country at large.[39]

The position worsened during 1920 when, according to the Board's annual report, 'A flood of feeling against the Alien and against the Jews has been let loose. At the present time it is a fact that the Alien can be deprived of his freedom, denied the right of remaining here, forced to leave his home, family and business, without trial, without appeal, and without the opportunity of answering or even ascertaining the charge made against him.'[40] What exacerbated the problems for the alien Jews was that all the regulations were published in English only and the Board tried to alleviate this by publishing leaflets in Yiddish and more comprehensible English. Not all government departments were as unsympathetic as the Home Office and, for example, the Ministry of Health asked the Board to issue a pamphlet in Yiddish dealing with the provisions of National Health Insurance for aliens.[41] The Board was successful when it intervened in a number of cases of threatened deportation or what seemed harsh refusals to give permission to land, but most of its interventions came to naught. The position of aliens improved somewhat during 1923 with fewer threatened or actual deportations, although the 'exceptional' legislation was still in force. This improvement can be attributed in part to the fact that the requirements imposed on aliens had

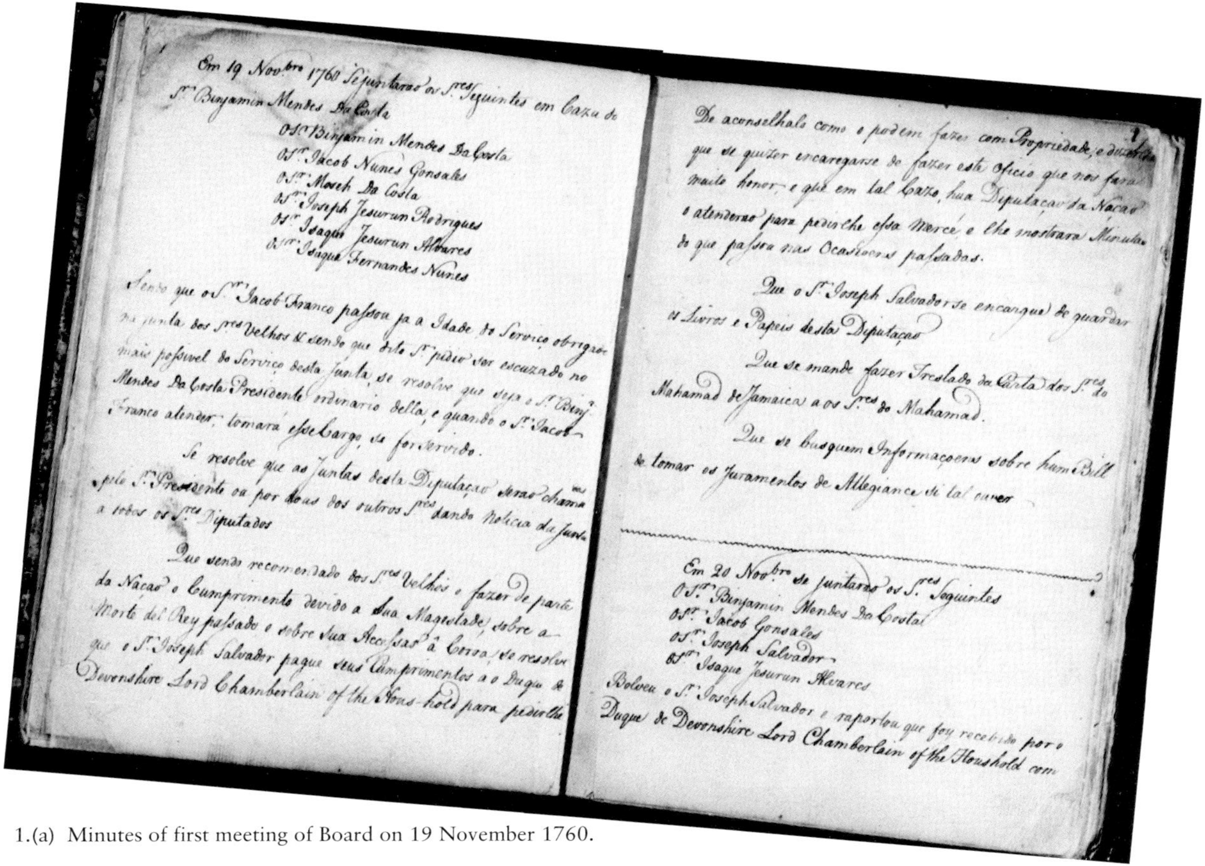

Em 19 Novbro 1760 Se juntarão os Sres Seguintes em Caza do
Sr Benjamin Mendes Da Costa
O Sr Benjamin Mendes Da Costa
O Sr Jacob Nunes Gonsales
O Sr Moseh Da Costa
O Sr Joseph Jesurun Rodrigues
O Sr Isaque Jesurun Alvares
O Sr Isaque Fernandes Nunes

Sendo que o Sr Jacob Franco passou ja a Idade do Serviço obrigrio da junta dos Sres Velhos & sendo que dito Sr pidio ser escuzado no mais possivel do Serviço desta junta, se resolve que seja o Sr Benjn Mendes Da Costa Presidente ordinario della, e quando o Sr Jacob Franco atender, tomara esse Cargo, se for servido.

Se resolve que as Juntas desta Diputação serão chamadas pelo Sr Presidente ou por dous dos outros Sres dando Noticia da Junta a todos os Sres Diputados

Que sendo recomendado dos Sres Velhos o fazer de parte da Nação o Cumprimento devido a Sua Magestade sobre a Morte del Rey passado e sobre Sua Accessão à Corôa, se resolve que o Sr Joseph Salvador paque seus Cumprimentos a o Duque de Devonshire Lord Chamberlain of the Hous-hold para pedirlhe

De aconselhalo como o podem fazer com Propriedade, e dizerlhe que se quiser encarregarse de fazer este Oficio que nos fara muito honor, e que em tal Caso, hua Diputação da Nação o atenderão para pedirlhe essa Mercé, e lhe mostrara Minutas do que passou nas Ocasioens passadas.

Que o Sr Joseph Salvador se encargue de guardar os Livros e Papeis desta Diputação

Que se mande fazer Treslado da Carta dos Sres do Mahamad de Jamaica a os Sres do Mahamad.

Que se busquem Informaçoens sobre hum Bill de tomar os Juramentos de Allegiance si tal ouver

Em 20 Novbro se juntarão os Sres Seguintes
O Sr Benjamin Mendes Da Costa
O Sr Jacob Gonsales
O Sr Joseph Salvador
O Sr Isaque Jesurun Alvares

Bolveu o Sr Joseph Salvador e raportou que foy recebido por o Duque de Devonshire Lord Chamberlain of the Houshold com

1.(a) Minutes of first meeting of Board on 19 November 1760.

2

Jacob Franco

Benj. Mendes DaCosta   Joseph Salvador
Jacob Gonsales   Isaac Jesuran Alvares
Moses DaCosta   Isaac Fernandes Nunes

In the Name of the Community of Portuguese Jews wait on
His Grace the Duke of Devonshire Lord Chamberlain of His
Majesty's Houshold, to desire His Grace would favour them in
humbly representing to His Majesty that His Majesty's most faithful
& loyal Subjects the Portuguese Jews, being so small a Body, have
not had the Honour to address, but have been permitted to testify their
Duty to the Sovereign on his Accession to the Throne; They in the
like manner, most humbly beg Leave to condole with His Majesty on
the Demise of the late King, whose sacred Memory will ever be revere
& to congratulate His Majesty on His Majesty's Accession to the
Throne of these Kingdoms, humbly craving the Continuance of his
Majesty's Favour & Protection, which they hope to merit by an
unalterable Zeal for His Majesty's most Sacred Person, & Service,
& by promoting to the utmost of their Abilities the Benefit of
His Majesty's Realms.

London y.e 21.st Nov.r 1760

To   His Grace the Duke of Devonshire Lord Chambe
       of His Majesty's Houshold. &c. &c. &c.a

1.(b) 'Loyal Address to King George III'.

2. Sir Moses Montefiore at 85.

3. Charles H.L. Emanuel was Assistant Secretary 1893–98, Secretary and Solicitor 1898–1927, and Honorary Solicitor 1927–62.

4. Neville Laski, elected President on 15 January 1933. Neville Laski is on the left being congratulated by Sir Isadore Salmon, a vice-president. In the centre is the defeated candidate Major Harry Nathan.

5. The top table at a Board meeting on 19 February 1933. From left to right, A.G. Brotman (Assistant Secretary), B.A. Zaiman (Secretary), Neville Laski (President), Sir Isidore Salmon (Vice-President), L.G. Montefiore (Joint-Chairman, Joint Foreign Affairs Committee), Lady Spielman (Chairman, Education Committee).

6. The top table at a Board meeting in 1940. From left to right, N.G. Liverman (Treasurer), A.G. Brotman (Secretary), Professor Brodetsky (President), Sir Robert Waley Cohen (Vice-President), L.J. Stein (Joint Chairman, Joint Foreign Affairs Committee), H.S. Schildkraut (Chairman, Aliens Committee).

7. The President's Chair. Legend has it that it was first occupied by Sir Moses Montefiore. The reality is that it was presented to the Board in 1948 by Mr and Mrs Jacques Cohen in commemoration of the establishment of the State of Israel. The Board sold it by auction in 1995 when they moved from Woburn House.

8. Board meeting in April 1952. Rev. Dr Abraham Cohen (President) in the chair.

9. His Royal Highness the Duke of Edinburgh toasting the Board at the celebration of the Board's centenary on 4 April 1960. On his right is Lady Janner and on his left Sir Barnett Janner, President of the Board. (Courtesy of E. H. Emanuel/The *Jewish Chronicle*.)

10. Children in a Jewish school in Tangier celebrate Purim. The school receives a regular grant from the Board's Morocco Relief Fund.

11. Anthony Levine addressing the Provincial Seminar of the Board on the subject of Human Rights. He must have impressed, as shortly afterwards he was elected President of the Leeds Representative Council.

12. Her Majesty The Queen attends a Board dinner in 1977. (Courtesy of Peter Fisher/ The *Jewish Chronicle*.)

13.(a) 'Say No to the PLO'. A mass rally in Trafalgar Square in July 1981, organized by the Board.

13.(b) Leaders of British Jewry meet with Yasser Arafat on 15 December 1993. From left to right, Lord Rothschild, Greville Janner, Sir Sigmund Sternberg, His Honour Judge Israel Finestein (President of the Board), and Yasser Arafat.

14.(a) 'Let my People Go'. Mass rally organized by the Board during the Soviet Foreign Minister's visit to London in October 1970. (Courtesy of The *Jewish Chronicle*.)

14.(b) Natan Sharansky addressing the Board on 28 September 1986. (Courtesy of Sidney Harris.)

15. Their Royal Highnesses the Prince and Princess of Wales celebrate the 225th anniversary of the Board at Hampton Court in 1985. From left to right, Greville Janner (President of the Board), Lady Sylvia Leigh, Princess Diana, Sir Geoffrey Leigh (sponsor of the evening) and Prince Charles. (Courtesy of Sidney Harris.)

16. Prime Minister Margaret Thatcher addresses the Board on 18 February 1990. (Courtesy of Peter Fisher.)

17. Yom Hashoa commemorative meeting at the Holocaust Memorial in Hyde Park, April 1990. From left to right, Dr Lionel Kopelowitz (President of the Board), His Honour Judge Israel Finestein (Vice-President of the Board), Rev. Dr Isaac Levy, Rabbi Hugo Gryn and cantor Simon Hass. (Courtesy of Peter Fisher.)

18. The new Honorary Officers elected in July 1991. From left to right, Aubrey Rose (Senior Vice-President), His Honour Judge Israel Finestein (President), Rosalind Preston (Vice-President) and Ronald Shelley (Treasurer). Rosalind Preston was the first woman elected as an Honorary Officer. (Courtesy of Sidney Harris.)

19. Danielle runs for the Board. In April 1992 Danielle Sanderson, one of Britain's leading marathon runners, competed in the London Marathon wearing the Board's colours. She raised £20,000 for the Board. (Courtesy of Sidney Harris.)

20. A rally organized by the CST and the Board protesting about David Irving's Holocaust denial views.

21. Nelson Mandela addresses the Board in April 2000. On his right is Eldred Tabachnik (President) and on his left Jo Wagerman (Senior Vice-President). (Courtesy of John R. Rifkin, Photographer.)

22. The Board's offices at 6 Bloomsbury Square. From 1817 to 1829 the house was occupied by Isaac D'Israeli, and this is commemorated by a plaque in the middle of the right side. His son Benjamin lived here as a boy. The house was purchased by the Board in 2001, financed in part by a generous donation from Sir Sigmund Sternberg and a legacy from Frances Rubens.

23. Jo Wagerman, first woman President of the Board. (Courtesy of John R Rifkin, Photographer.)

24. The *Jewish Way of Life Exhibition*.

25.(a) Tony Blair, the Prime Minister, dines with the Board in 2005. He is shaking hands with Eleanor Lind and in the centre is Flo Kaufmann, both Vice-Presidents.

25.(b) David Cameron, the leader of the Conservative Party, dines with the Board in June 2006. He is shaking hands with Jon Benjamin, the Director General of the Board, and in the centre are Alison and Henry Grunwald, the President of the Board.

26. Her Majesty The Queen attending a reception in 2006 commemorating the 350th anniversary of the resettlement of Jews in England. Also in the photograph, from left to right, are the Chief Rabbi Sir Jonathan Sacks (now Lord Sacks), Henry Grunwald, President of the Board and Sandra Clark, the Administrative Director of the Board. (Courtesy of Theodore Wood.)

27. The Board's Darfur campaign.

28. Vivian Wineman, elected President on 13 May 2009.

become better known – no doubt the Board's pamphlets had helped – and in part because some of the authorities with responsibility for aliens were more sympathetic, particularly in response to representations by the Board. In 1923, the Board spent a lot of time presenting to the Home Office complaints that there were significant and unnecessary delays in granting Certificates of Naturalisation to many Jewish aliens. Also in June 1923 a deputation from the Board saw the home secretary, William Bridgeman, with a view to ameliorating the position on deportation of aliens. He refused to make any alterations to the existing regulations.

The minority Labour government that took office in January 1924 raised hopes that a more sympathetic response might be forthcoming. A deputation from the Board met with the new home secretary, Arthur Henderson, in May 1924. The president of the Board, Henry Henriques, was particularly aggressive in his opening remarks:

> The regulations under the Aliens Act placed an alien in an inferior position to that of the ordinary person, and this was contrary to the system of law previously obtaining. The old system was to give an alien all the rights of a British subject with the exception of voting power. Most of the aliens had been here before the war and they ought to be exempt from the harassing regulations which put the alien entirely at the mercy of the police. The Home Secretary's powers of deportation, passed in a period of emergency, were powers which previously would not have been dreamed of or tolerated and they were powers that were too great to be left in the hands of any one man. They deprived the alien of power over his own person or property. It was an arbitrary power.'[42]

Sir Stuart Samuel, the immediate past president, added: 'to banish a man without legal trial was antiquated, savage and revengeful'.[43] Arthur Henderson promised to look into the matter and the Board was very optimistic. In the meantime Sir John Pedder, the permanent under-secretary of state in the Home Office, had been at work, and in a minute to the home secretary tried to justify the delay in dealing with applications for naturalization on the grounds that it was necessary for the applicants to have resided in Britain for far longer than the statutory period of five years, since 'Jews do not want to be assimilated into the life and habits of Britain and do not readily identify themselves with this country. Even British born Jews always speak of themselves as a "community", separate to a considerable degree and different from the British people.' Furthermore, he wrote that he did not believe there was a genuine demand for naturalization and that 'it was largely a racket by a number of enterprising solicitors and other agents who make it their business to canvass wholesale for applications from these classes of aliens'.[44] Sir John Pedder drafted the reply to the Board from Arthur Henderson, and it is not surprising that it did not meet any of their demands.[45]

A Conservative government replaced the Labour government in October 1924 and the new home secretary was Sir William Joynson-Hicks. This was very bad news for the Board. Joynson-Hicks was considered by many as reactionary, authoritarian and inflexible,[46] and seemed to have no sympathy for aliens – or, for that matter, Jews. A delegation from the Board met him in February 1925. Every request they made was turned down.[47] These constant rebuffs led the Board to decide to wait its time before approaching government again, and patience brought its reward.

A Labour government was elected in June 1929, and in November 1929 a deputation from the Board saw the new home secretary, John Robert Clynes, and followed up this meeting with considerable correspondence. The result was that several substantial modifications were made to the administration of the aliens' law which eased the situation, particularly concerning deportation and naturalization, all of which had been asked for by the Board. Immigration remained a problem but the Board was assured that applications for leave to land by those seeking refuge from religious persecution would continue to receive sympathetic consideration.[48] Overall, the Board was disappointed although it had realized that the permanent officials at the Home Office had not changed. Pedder was still there and there are two minutes that indicate his attitude. In the first, on the question of asylum, he wrote: 'who are now the religious or political refugees who should receive special consideration? Certainly not the Jews resident in what was once the Russian pale, a simple proof of this being that a very large proportion of the present rulers of Soviet Russia are themselves Jews.'[49] Three days later he wrote: 'Whatever is done at the request of the Jews will not satisfy them, they will always ask for more.'[50]

The position of Jewish aliens in Britain and those Jewish aliens seeking to obtain permission to land became subsumed from 1933 into the issue of refugees from Germany and the more general one of assistance to German Jews. This was discussed at many meetings of the Joint Foreign Committee in 1933, culminating in that committee convening a conference in conjunction with the Alliance Israélite Universelle, the American Jewish Committee, the American Jewish Congress and the Comité des Délégations Juives. As a result, various liaison groups were established to coordinate the actions of Jewish organizations in different countries, and a General Advisory Council for Relief and Reconstruction was established with headquarters in London.

Four main departments of the British government were concerned about the admittance of fleeing German Jews to Britain. The Treasury was concerned with the economic and financial impact of needy immigrants, the Home Office with the fear of an alien invasion leading to an increase in antisemitism, the Foreign Office with the need to placate other countries who might be embarrassed if Britain had too liberal a policy and even object at the implication that their fleeing citizens had to be given refuge, and the Colonial Office worried about the impact on Palestine.[51] The statutory position was that aliens were only given permission to land if they could demonstrate that they were able to support themselves and, until 1938, there was no distinction between aliens as a class and alien refugees. In 1933 a memorandum on behalf of the British Jewish community was presented to the home secretary making proposals regarding Jewish refugees. It contained an undertaking that all costs in respect of accommodation and maintenance for Jewish refugees from Germany would be borne by the Jewish community without ultimate charge to the state. It was signed by Neville Laski, as president of the Board of Deputies; Lionel Cohen, chairman of the Board's Law, Parliamentary and General Purposes Committee; Leonard Montefiore, president of the AJA and a deputy; and Otto Schiff, who was chairman and founder of the Jewish Refugees Committee.[52] This report was never mentioned to the Board and remained secret for some considerable time. The practical implementation was left to the Jewish Refugees Committee.

Initially, and for some time, the Board saw the issue of German refugees as part of the German Nazi problem and believed it would cease if the persecution of Jews in Germany ceased. An international conference of Jewish organizations to deal with German refugees was convened by the Joint Foreign Committee in October 1933 and at that conference Palestine was seen as the pre-eminent territory to absorb the refugees.[53] Following the signing of the 'undertaking' the Board only got involved indirectly in the German refugee issue, normally by cross-membership with other organizations more directly involved, such as the Jewish Refugees Committee, the Jews' Temporary Shelter, the German Jewish Aid Committee and the Central British Fund for World Jewish Relief (CBF). The Aliens Committee received reports from all the organizations involved, discussed them and made suggestions, but did not take an active part as such. The Board was quite happy to let Otto Schiff represent it in negotiations with the Home Office on refugee issues and policy, although the honorary officers did occasionally intervene directly in specific problems. One instance which might illustrate the concerns of Schiff and the Board regarding the nature of the refugees is contained in a minute of a meeting that a delegation of the Board had with the home secretary, Sir Samuel Hoare, on 1 April 1938. Schiff complained that it was very difficult to get rid of a refugee once he had entered and spent some time in Britain and it was important to impose a visa in the case of Austrians, who were mainly shopkeepers and small traders and would prove much more difficult to encourage to leave Britain than the average German. The minutes prepared by the Home Office record the following:

> Sir Samuel Hoare then said he felt bound to point out that it would be necessary for the Home Office to discriminate very carefully as to the type of refugee who could be admitted to this country. If a flood of the wrong type of immigrants were allowed in there might be serious danger of anti-semitic feeling being aroused in this country. The last thing which we wanted here was the creation of a Jewish problem. The Deputation said they entirely agreed with this point of view.[54]

The report to the Board by the delegation makes no mention of this point.[55] This was a few months before *Kristallnacht* and as a result of that and other events the policy of the government changed as did, presumably, that of the Board.

Combating Antisemitism[56]

Early in 1918 a Press Committee was established, under the chairmanship of Lord Rothschild, with the initial object of trying to arrest the growth of antisemitism in the press. One of its first acts was to circulate a pamphlet showing the war services of a number of Jewish leaders in the allied countries. This was a start to its campaign of trying to counter the accusations that Jews were not wholly behind the allies in the war and were 'shirkers'. Although officially the committee's terms of reference did not change, it rapidly took on a role of combating areas of antisemitism wherever they manifested themselves. It was active in the attacks on *The Protocols of the Elders of Zion* when it was published in Britain in 1920 under the title *The Jewish Peril*, and it commissioned and circulated a pamphlet by way of reply entitled *The Jewish Bogey*, written by Lucien Wolf.

In February 1921 a new and enlarged committee to combat anti-semitism was established, composed of representatives of the Board, the AJA, the League of British Jews, the B'nei B'rith, the Maccabeans and the Jewish Historical Society. This was called the Joint Press Committee although its brief was much wider than merely the press. Lord Rothschild was elected chairman of the new committee. It was agreed that the committee could act without reference to its parent bodies in cases of emergency. Reading through the documents relating to the activities of this committee, one is sadly amazed at the large number of antisemitic articles, books and even journals that had to be combated by the committee – often with some success. With the benefit of hindsight there is some irony in the comment in the 1923 annual report of the Board, that a member of the Joint Press Committee – F.L. Emanuel representing the Maccabeans, who was also a member of the British fascist organization – had successfully protested against that organization's exclusion of Jews as members, and against antisemitic remarks by some members. It seems he was able to persuade the fascist organization to state that antisemitism had no part in its programme.[57] This is not entirely surprising since at that time the Italian Fascist Party under Mussolini did not have an antisemitic agenda, and many Jews were members of that party.

In July 1925 the Board decided to withdraw from the Joint Press Committee, despite objections from the Law, Parliamentary and General Purposes Committee, and set up a press committee of its own.[58] As a result the other bodies on the joint committee decided to dissolve that committee. In its 1926 annual report, the Board mentioned that the press committee had met only infrequently, as there had been a considerable decline in the number and importance of antisemitic references in the press. The report did not mention, however, a little spat between some deputies and the Press Committee. It seems that a number of deputies disliked the law and crime reports column in the *JC*, which was published in conjunction with the Press Committee, as in their view it drew unwanted attention to the waywardness of some Jews and could lead to antisemitism. They persuaded the Board to pass a motion asking the Press Committee to discontinue this column. The Press Committee refused to do so on the grounds that publicity might shame the recalcitrant Jews into becoming better citizens. The fall in antisemitic activity seems to have continued, at least as far as the Press Committee and thus the Board were concerned, up until the end of 1932. In that year Sir Oswald Mosley formed a new party, the British Union of Fascists, and in October 1932 wrote to the Press Committee that antisemitism formed no part of the policy of his organization and that antisemitic propaganda was forbidden.[59]

In 1933 matters changed and many antisemitic publications and articles in the press appeared. At first these were dealt with by a sub-committee of the Joint Foreign Affairs Committee but in September 1933 this subcommittee was merged with the Press Committee under a new name, the Press and Information Committee. The committee became active in producing and distributing pamphlets and, in cooperation with the B'nei B'rith, in forming the Central Jewish Lecture committee for supplying speakers to non-Jewish audiences. In the Board's 1934 annual report the Press Committee stated that the sustained efforts of the Nazis to justify their persecution of Jews in Germany and to stimulate antisemitism in Britain had generally been unsuccessful as regards the British press. The Board maintained its view that the Jews in Britain could rely on the state to deal with any anti-Jewish incidents. Following a debate in the House of Commons during which the home secretary had stated that Jew-baiting would not be tolerated in England, the Board discussed the issue only briefly and expressed gratitude to the MPs who had raised the matter. Some historians, for example Gisela Lebzelter, have pointed out that this was in accordance with the Board's general policy of pacification motivated by a sort of 'safety first' attitude.[60] This was also in step with the Board's policy of trying not to get involved in politics, and thus at first it did not condemn fascism as such, and indeed many of the honorary officers were of the view that the British Union of Fascists would not make much of an impact and would not last very long. They were supported in this view by the arguments between Lord Rothermere and Mosley. In January 1934 the *Daily Mail*, owned by Lord Rothermere, came out in support of the BUF, but in July Lord Rothermere publicly dissociated himself from the party on the grounds that he could never support an antisemitic movement. A rally of the BUF at Olympia in June 1934 ended in chaos and violence, and as a result many members left the party and many commentators are of the view that Mosley thereby lost his chance of winning significant mass support.[61]

By 1936 fascist antisemitic activity in Britain had increased to such an extent that there was rising disquiet at the passivity of the Board among many member of the Jewish community, particularly in the East End of London. It was about this time that the *JC*, which had been supportive of the Board's strategy in this area, changed its policy and became for a few months increasingly critical of the Board. During this period the leaders of the Board had become very alarmed at the fascist marches and meetings and the resulting violence in the East End of London and a deputation led by the president met with the home secretary in early July 1936 to discuss the situation. Promises regarding more intensive policing were made. This was welcomed by the *JC*, but even when this became known among many in the Jewish community it was not considered enough, and on 26 July 1936 a conference was convened by two prominent Jewish trade unionists to discuss the formation of an effective defence organization. One hundred and thirty-one delegates representing eighty-seven Jewish organizations were present at that conference and they established the JPC to wage an active campaign against fascism.[62] By coincidence the Board was holding one of its regular plenary meetings on 26 July and at that meeting established a new committee, initially called the Co-ordinating Committee, to unify and direct activities in defence of the Jewish community against attacks made upon it.[63] In 1938 that committee was re-established as the Jewish Defence Committee, charged with responsibility for all antisemitic activities of the Board. The new committee had been formed because many deputies had criticized the lack of leadership of the Board regarding combating antisemitism, and indeed the vice-president, Sir Robert Waley Cohen, had at the previous Board meeting proposed setting up a special committee for this purpose, but had been opposed by the president and advised 'not to exaggerate the nature of the crisis and create feelings of panic'.[64] Almost the first action of the new committee was to appeal to the community at large for funds, and in the letter making the appeal it set out its major task:

> to ensure that through the spoken and written word, and by every appropriate and legitimate means, the calumnies and false allegations against Jews, so sedulously and unscrupulously spread by anti-Jewish organisations and groups, shall be countered by the widest possible dissemination of the facts so that the good name and reputation of the Jews as loyal and law-abiding citizens shall be upheld.[65]

The scope of the committee's work in the first year is evidenced by the fact that nine different leaflets and eleven speakers' notes were issued and 327 meetings were arranged.

It seems, however, that the Board waged war as much against the activities of the JPC as against antisemitism. It condemned the unauthorized activities of the JPC in approaching government departments in 'that these were functions that only the Board was entitled to exercise', and contacted the BBC and *The Times*, who had reported on the JPC, asking them to give no more publicity to the JPC's efforts. The Board refused to send delegates to JPC meetings and not only asked Jewish organizations to boycott a JPC conference on antisemitism on 15 November 1936 but also arranged a conference on the same day, at the same time, on the same subject, and invited the same organizations. In the event it was probably a draw, as the *JC* reported that about seventy organizations were represented at the Board conference and ninety-one at the JPC conference.[66] The Board's objection to the JPC was not only that it usurped the Board's authority and disagreed over strategy but it also had a political dimension. The Board considered that the JPC was a tool of the Communist Party, as a significant number of the JPC's leadership were members of the Communist Party and the party gave the JPC a lot of support.[67] The JPC opposed fascism as such, whereas the Board refused to condemn fascism on political grounds but only on the grounds of antisemitism, the president of the Board, Neville Laski, even pointing out that in Italy Jews were living safely under a fascist regime.

The Co-ordinating (Defence) Committee strategy had four main thrusts.[68] The first was to put pressure on government officials and others in positions of influence and power to consider the interests of the Jewish community in their policies and actions. This was carried out, often discreetly, in the main by the president and the other honorary officers and officials of the Board. Gisela Lebzelter stated that the extent and impact of these consultations were difficult to assess since they were never described in great detail.[69] Nonetheless the reports and minutes of the Board and the Defence Committee indicate some success in this area, but as they do not give examples no assessment is possible.

The second area was a sort of anti-defamation campaign. It combated the statements and allegations of antisemites by publicity, quoting facts and statistics in order to refute the 'information' propagated by antisemites and thus appealing to reason. It continued with the programme of public meetings but these were more focussed and were often held a few hours after and on the same spot as a public antisemitic meeting had been held and refuted what had been said. In addition, as part of this campaign, it produced leaflets trying to correct the negative image of Jews and stressing their patriotism and efforts in the First World War. The campaign was also carried on through the media by giving information to and writing letters to the non-Jewish press. The Board often signed the letters in the names of a number of members of the Jewish community who had agreed for their names to be used for this purpose.

The third area was that of self-criticism so as to reduce what it saw as the causes of antisemitism. This was based on the view, commonly held by many Jews since the enlightenment, that antisemitism was caused by actions and behaviour of some Jews themselves that helped to reinforce common stereotypes. If only these Jews could be re-educated to conform to the norms of society then antisemitism would disappear. A subcommittee of the Defence Committee was established to consider the 'internal causes' of antisemitism and in May 1938 it recommended that a permanent committee should be set up to make the Jewish community aware of the effect of individual malpractices and to cooperate in their elimination. This subcommittee eventually evolved in 1940 into the Trades Advisory Council (TAC), separate from but affiliated to the Board. About fifteen 'Vigilance Committees' were established throughout the country, which followed up all sorts of complaints against Jews, such as Jewish landlords demanding excessive rent, and Jewish employers imposing unfair conditions on their employees. These Vigilance Committees were also charged to watch for any local antisemitic activities and antisemitic items in the local press, to refute these and report back to the Board.

In December 1938 the Board published a guide in English and German for German–Jewish refugees which included not only helpful information on practical problems but also a sort of code of good conduct. All of this was based on a rather simplistic interpretation of the causes of antisemitism and, as pointed out by Professor Selig Brodetsky at a Defence Committee meeting in February 1939, 'the fact that the actions of some Jews were regarded as anti-social did not necessarily produce antisemitism'. This programme did not go down well in the community at large. It was accepted that in many cases of abuse it was not only the Jews but also the non-Jews who offended – it was often 'the culture of the trade'. However, that was no answer and it was felt at the time by many that Jews had to behave more 'ethically', even at some cost to themselves.

The fourth area was a campaign urging the Jewish community not
to attend fascist meetings. This was encouraged by the government on
the grounds that much of the disorder that occurred at fascist meetings
was due to the presence of opposition, and that the meetings would be
much smaller if Jews stayed away. This policy was a continuation of the
low-key policy generally adopted by the Board. As early as May 1933,
Neville Laski, the president of the Board, and the chief rabbi, Dr J.H.
Hertz, had written a letter to the *JC* arguing that the participation by
Jews in disturbances with fascists, whatever the provocation, 'brings
discredit upon the Anglo-Jewish Community, and can only be harmful
to the general cause which we all have at heart'.[70] This element of the
Board's strategy was probably the most unrealistic and had the effect
of adversely provoking many members of the community. It demonstrated how the Board failed to comprehend the feelings of perhaps
most of the community, the effects on the community of the fascist
antisemitic marches and meetings, and how imperative it was among
Jews to demonstrate their feelings publicly. The Board's policy of
'keeping heads down' might have seemed the most effective and was
also supportive of the government's approach, but it really did nothing to assuage the feelings of those Jews most affected by the fascists.

This policy was not supported by all members of the Board. In
September 1936, at a public meeting organized by the Board, Barnett
Janner, already a prominent deputy and to become president of the
Board in 1955, expressed the view that Jews had a right to defend
themselves when slandered by fascist speakers.[71] The Board as well as
the *JC* advised Jews to stay away from Cable Street on 4 October 1936,
and the Board went so far as to have posters displayed in the East End
of London warning Jews against the dangers of being involved in
disorders. However, this advice was ignored by many and in the event
about 100,000 people (including many Jews) confronted and disrupted
a march of about 2,000 to 3,000 fascists. The Board was right: the
confrontation was counterproductive and it was estimated that in the
three weeks following the 'battle', the British Union of Fascists (BUF)
enrolled 2,000 new members, although it seems that these new members fell away fairly quickly. On the other hand, there can be little
doubt that the Jews who participated had a feeling of elation at the
success of the confrontation. Shortly after Cable Street, Neville Laski
had a meeting with Herbert Morrison, a prominent Labour MP and
leader of the LCC. At that meeting Laski expressed his view, which he
said was shared by the Home Office and the police, that 'if everyone

would combine to stay away from fascist meetings no steps more destructive to the fascist movement could be visualised'. The following day Laski arranged, through the offices of his brother Harold Laski, a meeting between Herbert Morrison and Harry Pollitt, the general secretary of the Communist Party. Their objective was to persuade Pollitt to agree to the communists staying away from fascist meetings and parades for a period.[72]

One consequence of Cable Street was the Public Order Act which came into force on 1 January 1937. It banned political uniforms, gave extended powers to the police to restrict processions and substantially increased the maximum penalty from forty shillings to fifty pounds and three months' imprisonment for various offences against 'the peace'. Cable Street also led to attacks by fascists on Jews in the East End and this led to a change of heart at the Board. In 1937 the Board established the London Area Council in the East End to hold meetings, distribute literature and monitor fascist activities. Furthermore, it seems that whilst the Board continued formally to be against active protests by Jews at fascist meetings, the leadership defended these activities at meetings with government ministers, officials and the police.

By 1937 the Board, whilst not complacent, was congratulating itself on the setbacks which antisemitic organizations had sustained during the year. It acknowledged that much of the improvement, particularly in the East End of London, was due to the Public Order Act but felt that it had played a major role. It had arranged several hundred meetings during the year and as a consequence antisemitic organizations had suffered a considerable exposure and consequent loss of prestige.[73] The following year the committee reported that whilst the antisemitic organizations had received a severe setback, there had been a considerable increase in antisemitic propaganda, particularly with regard to Jewish refugees. Renewed efforts were made to counter this, such as many more publications and public speeches.

The Fascist Party in Italy had hitherto not been antisemitic, but when, in 1939, it introduced antisemitic legislation in Italy, the Board recognized that the fight was not only against antisemitism but had to be a political one against fascism as well. It thus sought some sort of accommodation with the JPC. The memorandum to the Board from the Defence Committee concluded: 'The broad effect of this deal would be the liquidation of a somewhat troublesome body and its subordination to the authority of the Board.'[74] However, the Board could not accept the JPC on equal grounds nor would it permit the JPC to be represented on the Defence Committee. The JPC was a single-issue organization whereas the Board was concerned not only with combating antisemitism but also with all issues affecting the entire Jewish community. A merger or takeover did not take place.

How successful was the Board in fighting antisemitism particularly in the 1930s? The BUF never really took off as a major force in British politics. At its peak in July 1934 it reached 50,000 members but declined rapidly to 5,000 in October 1935, rising to 15,500 in November 1936 and to about 22,500 at the start of the Second World War.[75] It is difficult to attribute this failure to any actions of the Board. There is also the question of general antisemitism in Britain, as opposed to antisemitism generated by the fascists. The significance of this in the 1930s is disputed by historians. For example, Colin Holmes, Tony Kushner and David Rosenberg are of the view that there was a great deal,[76] whereas William Rubinstein takes a contrary view and considers antisemitism declined significantly as the 1930s progressed.[77] There is an important caveat even if Rubinstein's analysis of a decline is accepted.

As refugees from Nazi oppression arrived in Britain, particularly in the late 1930s, anti-alienism emerged quite strongly in many areas and circles, and since virtually all the aliens were Jews it was not a long jump to antisemitism. This apart, any decline in general antisemitism during the 1930s must be attributed to a large extent as a result of the news of what the Nazis were perpetrating on the Jews in Germany. The Board can take some credit for this decline, not only by keeping in the public eye the atrocities against Jews in Germany, but also by all the other elements in the strategies employed by its Defence Committee. Overall one can conclude, using the words of Colin Holmes, one of the leading historians of antisemitism in the period, that 'the Board's activities helped in the general containment of the antisemitic campaign of the 1930s'.[78]

Boycott of German Goods[79]

Following the start of the Nazi persecution of Jews in Germany in 1933, a spontaneous movement arose among the Jewish community in Britain to institute a boycott of German goods and services. On 1 April 1933 a complete boycott of Jewish shops and businesses in Germany was announced by the Nazi government. This resulted in pressure on the Board to proclaim a formal counter-boycott, but this was resisted on the grounds that such a policy 'did not seem wise in the circumstances'.[80] Although this statement did not explain the reasons why it was not wise, one can assume that it was partly because the British government was opposed to the boycott and partly because it might be prejudicial to the situation of the Jews in Germany. The matter was debated at a Board meeting on 23 July 1933 and resulted in a majority against formalizing the boycott.[81] Neville Laski was asked by the *Manchester Guardian* why the majority was so narrow and he responded that it was not the quantity that counted but the quality of those who voted against the boycott compared with those who had. When Lord Melchett was co-opted on to the Joint Foreign Committee in July 1933, he was required to renounce his public support for the boycott. In the meantime, a number of boycott committees were established, primarily in the East End of London, and they held a protest meeting on 20 July in Hyde Park, at which about 30,000 people participated, with representatives from all sections of the London Jewish community with the exception of the Board. The Board continued to refuse to get involved and as a result a new organization called the Jewish Representative Council for the Boycott of German Goods and Services (JRC) was established in early September 1933 to coordinate all boycott initiatives. Clearly the Board did not like this and at a Board meeting on 17 September Gordon Liverman, the treasurer of the Board, said that 'considerable harm might result from its claim to speak for British Jewry'. It seems that the concern of the Board's officers was less with the pros and cons of a boycott and more to preserve the position of the Board. The JRC arranged an inaugural conference on 5 November 1933 at which 360 Jewish organizations were represented, but again not the Board.[82]

Pressure on the Board to participate continued and on 18 November 1934 the Board passed a resolution that 'no self-respecting Jew will handle German goods or utilise German services so long as the German anti-Jewish policy endures'.[83] This merely stated the obvious and a boycott never became official Board policy. It considered that a boycott was a matter for individual not collective action. The Board was concerned that the boycott might be prejudicial to the interests of German Jewry and that it might jeopardize the 1933 Transfer Agreement (*Ha'avara*) under which German Jews emigrating to Palestine could realize some assets provided the proceeds were used to buy German goods. The only evidence of success was contained in a report in the *Manchester Guardian* of 7 September 1934 that Leipzig had ceased to be a centre of the world fur trade.[84] On the other hand a boycott was not merely an attempt at creating an economic weapon against Germany; it also had a positive psychological effect on the Jews who participated; as

Leonard Montefiore, the president of the AJA, stated at a Board meeting on 26 March 1933: 'People must express their feelings or they will burst.'[85]

Marriage and Divorce

The issue of women being unable to obtain a *get* (Jewish religious divorce) was raised by the Council for the Amelioration of the Legal Position of the Jewess with the Law, Parliamentary and General Purposes Committee of the Board in 1928. As a result the Board held discussions on the subject with the chief rabbi's Beth Din but no solution was found. Subsequently the Board considered whether some sort of help could be granted to such women by making it a requirement for a civil divorce that a *get* had been granted. It was advised that this would require such a provision to be incorporated into English divorce law and decided not to proceed in this direction. Instead, it wrote to all solicitors and counsel involved in divorce proceedings for Jews, informing them of the position and requesting they do their utmost to assist the women. It also asked the Beth Din to convene an authoritative conference of Orthodox Rabbis to consider the matter and see what steps could be taken to alleviate the problem.[86] No such conference was held. The Board continued to involve itself in difficult situations where recalcitrant parties refused to give or accept a *get* and it seemed that conciliation by the Board might help. Indeed, according to its annual reports, the Board was successful in quite a number of cases. This is a further indication of quiet mediation by the Board in respect of disputes within the community.

Shechita

Despite the success in 1913 and 1914 in fighting off those who had tried to introduce legislation banning *shechita* the Board had to remain vigilant in this area. For example, the Board's annual report for 1923 mentioned that hardly a week passed without the necessity of answering in the press unfair criticism or grossly inaccurate descriptions of the Jewish method of slaughter.[87]

In 1923, a private member's bill that would have required preliminary stunning of animals before slaughter (which is prohibited under Jewish law) gave rise to an interesting discussion and disagreement at the Board. The Board had decided to seek exemption from this requirement and framed the following amendment to the bill:

Provided that nothing in this Act shall apply to any member of the Jewish faith holding a certificate signed by the President for the time being of the London Committee of Deputies of the British Jews as holding a licence from the Jewish Ecclesiastical Authorities to act as a slaughter when engaged in the slaughtering of animals according to the Jewish method.

A number of deputies objected to some of the wording and a revision was made that was supported by the overwhelming majority. It read:

Provided that nothing in this Act shall apply to any member of the Jewish faith holding a certificate signed by the President for the time being of the London Committee of Deputies of the British Jews as a qualified slaughterer when engaged in the slaughtering of animals according to the Jewish method of slaughter if no unnecessary suffering is inflicted.

Note the change from a licence from the ecclesiastical authorities to a certificate from the president of the Board. This was to placate those in the Strictly Orthodox community who did not recognize the ecclesiastical authorities of the Board (the chief rabbi and the haham). In the end the bill lapsed.[88]

Associated with *shechita* were complaints by the Jewish public concerning the price of kosher meat. In 1925 the Board decided to take up this matter and appointed a committee to investigate it. The committee found that the allegations of overcharging by both wholesale and retail butchers were substantiated, but the only action the Board took was to refer the findings to the London Shechita Board – presumably not the action that the Jewish public had hoped for. Clearly the Board considered that competition was vital in that it expressed the view that real improvement would only arise if means were devised to obtain kosher chilled imported beef. The report was sent to the Shechita Board and its reply was entirely negative, although the Board's response implied otherwise.[89] It just did not want to stir up matters too far.

This issue did not go away and in 1927 the Board convened a meeting of representatives of all organizations and butchers involved in the provision of kosher meat. The report to the Board indicated that the views expressed by the various groups were impossible to reconcile, except that all agreed that the embargo placed by the Ministry of Agriculture on the import of Argentine cattle killed on the Continent had the effect of raising the price of home-killed meat. This was an issue for the Board of Shechita, and the Board of Deputies could not interfere. One deputy who attended the conference, Bertram Jacobs, put in a minority report recommending certain ways in which prices could be lowered, but this depended on the attitude of the Shechita Board, which continued to argue that the price of kosher meat was not its responsibility.[90] When the reports were considered by the Board it was proposed and agreed that the Board enter into discussions with the Shechita Board with a view to all kosher meat suppliers and distributors requiring not only the necessary *kashrut* certificate from the Shechita Board but also a certificate from the Board of Deputies as to their general conduct, behaviour and trading methods. The minutes record that the result of the vote on the proposal was greeted with acclamation.[91] The Board thus saw itself as the champion of the Jewish housewife. Regrettably the proposal was snubbed by the Shechita Board and nothing came of this initiative. Reading between the lines of the debates on this whole issue, and on *shechita* as well, it seems that arguments within the London Board of Shechita and between them and other *shechita* boards were being continued at meetings of the Board of Deputies.[92] The issue of the price of kosher meat and other foods has been a perennial one for the Board, which has on a number of occasions established enquiries, but generally without any success, as the Board has no control or sanction over the wholesalers and retailers.

In 1928 a huge dispute erupted in Manchester regarding the licensing of *shochetim*. It would seem that following the 'interference' of certain rabbis from Strictly Orthodox communities in Manchester and elsewhere, the Manchester City Corporation intended to introduce by-laws that differed from the standard model by-laws, in that a *shochet* could be licensed by any rabbi instead of the chief rabbi. The Board was called in to arbitrate and as a result the City Council decided only to accept *shochetim* certified by the chief rabbi.[93]

In 1930 a Slaughter of Animals Bill was introduced which had a clause giving exemption to *shechita* carried out only by *shochetim* licensed by the chief rabbi. This gave rise to much controversy between different factions within the community, particularly among the Strictly Orthodox communities who did not recognize the jurisdiction of the chief rabbi.[94] Reading the letters and minutes in the archives of the Board and elsewhere, on the Manchester dispute and this one, one cannot help but come away with the view that some of the gentlemen involved were less concerned with the provision of kosher meat and poultry to the British Jewish community than with their own egos and the *amour-propre* of the organizations they represented.[95] The Board tried to act as a mediator and was successful in having the licence requirements amended by substituting a 'Rabbinical Commission' for the licensing of shochetim. This bill failed to be passed but in 1932 a similar bill, including the Board's amendment, was introduced and enacted in 1933. The constitution of the Rabbinical Commission gave rise to many problems within the community, but was eventually resolved and has remained unchanged to this day. It is chaired by the chief rabbi, and the Spanish and Portuguese congregations nominate the vice-chairman, six other members representing different main Orthodox congregations and two appointed by the president of the Board to represent provincial communities.

Although the 1933 Act established the Rabbinical Commission, it did not include regulations as to how it should operate and this also gave rise to major difficulties between different sections of the Jewish community. Eventually a document was agreed and signed by the Board and the synagogal bodies on the Commission. Neville Laski wrote on his copy of this agreement: 'I conducted the negotiations under the direction of Sir Osmond and for that reason was asked to be a signatory. I finally reached agreement with Rabbi Munk at 4 a.m. after threatening to leave and actually putting on my hat and coat.'[96] The Act introduced a requirement for casting pens, and the Board made strenuous efforts to ensure that appropriate casting pens were installed in all Jewish abattoirs. In its 1933 annual report, the Board expressed the view that 'with the universal adoption of the Casting Pen wherever Shechita is practised, any unfavourable criticism of the Jewish method of slaughter, based upon the casting, will come to an end'.[97] To a large extent this proved to be the case for many years to come, except for some propaganda stirred up by Nazi-inspired anti-semitic organizations in Britain. Maybe it was this propaganda that led the chairman of the RSPCA to warn the Board in 1939 that 'in the last couple of years there has been growing up a very strong feeling of antagonism towards the continuation of the Jewish method of slaughter in the country'.

Sunday Trading

During this period the Board remained involved with issues regarding Sunday trading. These concerned observant Jews who kept their places of business closed on Saturdays, observant Jews who did not work on

250 Years of Convention and Contention

Saturdays and shops in Jewish areas that wished to open on Sundays. The position was that the Lord's Day Observance Act had fallen into misuse and in practice many shops were open on Sundays, some kept by Christians, and not only in predominantly Jewish areas. There were, however, restrictions by some chief constables in towns where there was a strong Sabbatarian following. During the 1920s many bills regarding trading and work on Sundays and working hours were presented to Parliament, some of which would have impinged adversely on observant Jews. The Law, Parliamentary and General Purposes Committee invariably commented and lobbied on these bills, but in practice none of the bills reached the statute book.

The first such bill to reach the statute book was the Hairdressers' and Barbers' Shops (Sunday Closing) Act, 1930. As a result of lobbying by the Board the Act included a provision that Jewish hairdressers could open on a Sunday provided that they closed on a Saturday and they could choose Friday as their weekly half-day holiday. Apparently, Saturday nights and Sunday mornings were the most profitable times for barbers and, in order to placate non-Jewish barbers, Jewish barbers were not permitted to open during both periods. In 1932 the Board's attention was drawn to certain abuses that had grown out of the exemptions for Jewish barbers. It would seem that some Jewish barbers had established other shops in the same vicinity under their own names or those of a relative, and opened one shop on Saturday night and the other on Sunday, thus capturing all of the most profitable trade. The Board took a very grave view of the situation and condemned the abuses. It was particularly concerned that not only might this lead to a repeal of the exemption clause for Jewish barbers, but also could adversely affect efforts by the Board on behalf of observant Jews for any future legislation.[98] Furthermore, the Board was particularly concerned that this could lead to much antisemitic criticism. These abuses continued and, in 1934, the Board wrote to all establishments who had appeared to participate in this abuse, and in December 1934 convened a meeting where it decided that if, as a result of these abuses, an amendment to the Act were to be made, the Board would maintain the principle that the concession in the Act was in the interests of those Jews whose real concern was the observance of the Sabbath and would lobby accordingly. The Board appointed a subcommittee to watch and deal with any developments in the matter.[99] The subcommittee had mixed success; some barbers cooperated whist others ignored the strictures from the Board.

In 1936 the Shops (Sunday Trading Restriction) Bill was introduced into Parliament by a private member, but obtained the support of the government as a result of pressure from shop workers and the Sunday Observance League. Essentially the object was to bring about a ban on shops opening on Sundays, but the Bill had a number of exceptions, including one which permitted Sunday trading up until 1 p.m. for Jewish shops which closed on Saturday. The Board considered this concession inadequate and lobbied for an extension. This was extended to 2 p.m., but even this was considered inadequate and would cause hardship for observant Jewish traders. Further extension was refused despite representations from the Board and the bill was enacted in July 1936 to become operative on 1 May 1937. The Board was asked to assist in drafting the regulations governing the procedures of the Jewish Tribunal required to be set up under the Act to investigate any alleged contraventions of the provisions applicable to Jewish traders, and also to establish the Tribunal itself. A separate Retail Meat Dealers' Shops (Sunday Closing) Act was introduced at much the same time and had a clause enabling Jewish kosher butcher shops which closed on Saturday to open on Sunday, but without an early closing restriction. It did not apply to poulterers who came under the Shops (Sunday Trading Restrictions) Act.[100] It would seem that a number of Jewish shopkeepers were charged with contravening both Acts, as although they closed on Saturday they remained open on Friday after the Sabbath commenced. These cases were brought before the Tribunal and in most cases were decided adversely to the shopkeeper, who either had to close early on Friday or lose the licence to trade on Sunday.[101]

Charities

For a number of years the Board had been concerned with defalcations and abuse in the conduct of some Jewish charities, and the existence of some bogus charities. In addition a large number of charities were badly administered and mismanaged. The Board's concern was not only for the Jewish community, but also that these abuses could become known and provide ammunition for antisemites. It is thus not entirely surprising that it was in 1935 that the Board decided to tackle the matter. It asked Jewish accountants to volunteer as honorary auditors to charities that had no auditor. This had a little success but matters remained unsatisfactory. As a consequence the Law, Parliamentary and General Purposes Committee established a subcommittee to look into the issues and in February 1937 this committee recommended that the Board should establish a system of registration of Jewish charities.[102] The recommendations were agreed in July 1937 and in December 1937 the Board created a Charities Registration Committee as a subcommittee of the Law, Parliamentary and General Purposes Committee. In order to be registered, a lot of detailed information had to be submitted to the Charities Registration Committee, including accounts audited by a qualified professional accountant. Accounts had to be submitted each year in order for registration to be renewed. A charity so registered was permitted to use the words 'Registered with the Board of Deputies' on its appeals and other publications. The scheme met with wide support and by the end of 1939 more than 100 charities had been registered. In 1954 the registration position was strengthened when the chief rabbi announced that any charity requesting the chief rabbi's patronage would have to be registered with the Charities Registration Committee of the Board.[103]

There is some indication in the correspondence that black humour was around in the very difficult and trying days of the late 1930s. One of the volunteers as an honorary auditor was Harold Langham, who applied on 25 February 1935 using his firm's notepaper headed 'Langham, Son & Co.'[104] The file indicates that he took on a few charities but refused at least one. When registration started, the Charities Registration Committee asked Jewish accountants to volunteer to join the selection panel on a pro bono basis. Harold Langham, by then a deputy, applied to be on this panel in a letter dated 19 May 1938, again using his firm's notepaper but this time with the heading 'Goldfine, Langham & Co.' In this letter he wrote: 'You will see from the above that my practice is now in "Non-Aryan" hands.'[105]

Harold Langham had not finished with the committee. In June 1938 he submitted a proposal that the Board should set up a body to administer for charities its subscriptions and donations.[106] This would have the effect of easing the administrative burden on many charities who found this task onerous and would have a number of other advantages, such as economies of scale and facilities for streamlining the recovery of income tax. The proposal was referred to the Charities Registration Committee who commended it to the Law, Parliamentary and General Purposes Committee. That committee said that a decision on its adoption should be left to the whole Board. The matter appeared on the Board's agenda a number of times in late 1938 and early 1939, but on each occasion discussion was deferred to the next meeting because of lack of time. Eventually it was discussed at a Board meeting on 19

March 1939 when the scheme was proposed by Harold Langham and seconded by A.S. Diamond, the chairman of the Law, Parliamentary and General Purposes Committee. The views expressed were mixed but it became clear that there was neither a consensus for or against the proposal. In the end it was decided to adjourn the discussion because of other pressing matters.[107] The war intervened and it was never reintroduced. Lavy Bakstansky participated in the debate on the proposal and thought the scheme was an excellent one, but did not go far enough. The concept was developed and a scheme introduced by the Jewish National Fund (JNF) (with which Bakstansky was closely connected) in the early 1950s under the name 'KKL Charitable Trust'. Thus a proposal that was considered first by the Board, but not roceeded with, was introduced by the JNF and benefited the JNF rather than the Board.

3. FOREIGN AFFAIRS

For the whole of this period, foreign affairs were dealt with by the Joint Foreign Affairs Committee, generally under the chairmanship of the president of the Board. A major part of its activities was dealing with significant outbreaks of antisemitism that occurred in many countries in Europe and sometimes beyond. On many occasions the Joint had to appeal to the British government for help and generally they intervened, although it has to be questioned as to how effective intervention by Britain was in practice. The best that can be said is that it had a restraining influence. The Joint also made representations directly to the countries involved and took many measures to assist Jews and Jewish communities that were in serious trouble, sometimes with good results, but more often not.

This section will only deal with some of the major issues that arose and involved the Joint Foreign Affairs Committee, such as the Russian Revolution, the Versailles Peace Conference, and Palestine. It will not deal in detail with the myriad of antisemitic manifestations abroad and the attempts of the committee to alleviate them, except to mention that the volume of work undertaken by the committee in this area was immense. Huge pressures were put on the British government by the committee and the Board to take action and make protests against the anti-Jewish actions taken by the Nazis between 1933 and 1939. The committee and the Board cannot be criticized for lack of effort, as their activities in this respect were vast, but they were very rarely instrumental in persuading the British government to take diplomatic or other action. The many delegations to the government got 'tea and sympathy' but seldom anything more. In fact the first time the British government denounced the atrocities against the Jews in Germany was on 31 October 1939, after the war had started.[108] In addition the committee and the Board lobbied the 'good and the great' in Britain and held meetings and published leaflets, and so on, in an effort – often with success – to persuade influential people and the public at large to protest against the persecution of German Jewry. The sections headed Foreign Affairs (until 1926) and Joint Foreign Committee (from 1927) in the annual reports of the Board are a very impressive and contemporary summary of Jewish issues that arose in many countries and the efforts of the Joint Foreign Affairs Committee to deal with them. Until 1930 they were written by Lucien Wolf and thereafter from time to time by the secretaries of the Joint. They are not a pleasant read.

The Russian Revolutions[109]

The February Revolution in 1917 was greeted enthusiastically by Jews in Britain. The hierarchy of the Board had been discouraged by Lucien Wolf from any immediate statement of support, on the grounds that it would be presumptuous of the Conjoint Foreign Affairs committee to pre-empt any statement by the British government. This view prevailed.[110] The committee's dilemma was that Russia, with its antisemitic regime, was one of Britain's allies. This dilemma was resolved almost at a stroke as one of the first acts of the Provisional government was to abolish all racial and religious disabilities. On publication of this decree, the leaders of the Conjoint committee sent a telegram to the new Russian prime minister, Prince Lvoff, informing him of the appreciation of all the Jewish communities of the British Empire for this act.[111] At the Board meeting on 22 April 1917 the president, in a written statement due to his absence owing to illness, warmly welcomed the revolution, and implied that it was partly due to the efforts of the Board for the emancipation of the Jews in Russia! The leaders of the Board came under considerable fire from many deputies for their delay in announcing support for the revolution, and it was suggested that a special meeting of the Board should have been held and that a public meeting should also have been held to enable the Jewish public to express their joy at the events in Russia. Rabbi Dr Daiches said that a proper resolution worthy of the Board should be passed. In the event a motion approving the actions of the Conjoint

Foreign Affairs committee was agreed, but with the additional words proposed from the floor 'that this Board expresses its deep and heart-felt joy at the Revolution, which has liberated the Russian nation, and with it, its Jewish citizens'.[112]

The joy did not last long, because the Bolshevik October Revolution cast a dampener. Although most Jews in Britain were on the side of the moderates there were quite a few Jews among the leaders of the Bolsheviks and this caused significant antisemitism in Britain and elsewhere, as Jews were accused as the creators of Bolshevism and communism. Furthermore, a number of Jews in Britain supported the Bolsheviks and were not only members of the British Communist Party, but some were among its leaders. In fact a number of Jews left Britain to return to Russia in addition to those who were already there having been 'repatriated' by the British government to serve in the Russian army. What compounded the problem was that in March 1918 Lenin signed a peace pact with Germany, which was seen in Britain as a betrayal of the allied cause. Anti-Bolshevism became a cover for antisemitism.[113] In April 1919 a letter was published in the *Morning Post*, signed by ten 'leading' Jews of Britain. They were in fact the leaders of the League of British Jews and none of them were members of the Board. The letter seemed to pass a slur on foreign Jews resident in Britain, implying that it was they, and only they, who supported Bolshevism. This letter was discussed at a Board meeting on 29 April 1919 and it passed a resolution deprecating the letter and repudiating, on behalf of the British Jewish community, any sympathy with Bolshevism.[114] This was going too far because, as just mentioned, there were many British Jews, primarily among the immigrant population, who supported or had a lot of sympathy for communism, but in any case most of this group probably did not consider the Board represented them.

Paris Peace Conference – The Minorities Treaties[115]
As the First World War drew to its close, the Board, through the Joint Foreign Affairs committee, became involved in the settlement of Jewish questions arising out of the war. It asked the foreign secretary to make a public statement that the emancipation of the Jews in Eastern and South-Eastern Europe would be included in the post-war settlement. It received a positive response that the government would do everything in its power to secure a just and permanent settlement of the Jewish question throughout the regions concerned. Following the armistice in November 1917,

the committee sent a memorandum to the foreign secretary reviewing all the Jewish issues that should be resolved as part of the political reconstruction of Europe and proposing a text giving full emancipation to all religious and other minorities be incorporated in each Peace Treaty. Simultaneously it established a secretariat in Paris under Lucien Wolf, the secretary of the committee, to ensure proper Jewish representation at the Peace Conference. These negotiations were long and arduous but in the end there seemed to be great success. In its report for 1919 the Board stated that its hopes for the emancipation of seven million Jews in Eastern Europe had been completely fulfilled.

The Board could take a lot of credit for this outcome. It had successfully negotiated treaties that placed Jews in a position of complete equality with their fellow citizens in all countries in Europe, where previously this had not been the position. The Board was not sanguine as it pointed out that 'the proof of the pudding was in the eating' and success depended on the objectives of the treaties being properly fulfilled and goodwill on all sides. It also noted, probably partly as a result of these treaties, that there was serious unrest in many regions in Europe, and indeed the British government established a commission under the chairmanship of Sir Stuart Samuel, the president of the Board, to examine the problems in Poland.[116] Lucien Wolf had had a bad war – he was suspected of not being a proper patriot because of his antagonism to Britain's ally, Russia – but he had a good peace. However, as Patrick Finney has pointed out, these treaties were devised by the major powers, of which Britain was arguably the most powerful, and were foisted upon the new states. These new states 'bitterly resented the imposition of the minorities treaties as a violation of their newly won and jealously guarded sovereignty'.[117]

As the Board foresaw, it was not easy. The Joint Foreign Affairs committee rapidly became involved in the problems besetting the Jewish communities in Europe that arose as a result of the redrawing of the map and splitting up the Austrian–Hungarian, Ottoman and Russian empires, one consequence of which was that the unity of a number of Jewish communities, for example in Poland, was destroyed. Furthermore, nationalism was once more on the rampage, and Jews are nearly always scapegoats in such circumstances. Antisemitic disturbances were widespread.

The newly formed Joint Committee became involved with trying to quell the antisemitic outbursts in Eastern Europe, and with Jews who became refugees as a result of the redrawing of frontiers. The committee was also involved with the newly formed League of Nations concerning the application of the League's guarantee of the rights of minorities as covered in the various peace treaties. There was some success in this area. In 1921 it was agreed that aggrieved minorities could make direct appeals to the League, and the president of the Board was appointed to examine such appeals (from Jews and non-Jews) and, if these were well founded, to bring them before the council of the League. Furthermore, the committee was involved in the drafting of the rules of procedure of the new International Court of Justice which was to have jurisdiction in all disputes under the Minorities Treaties.

Palestine

Initially it was decided that matters relating to Palestine would not be dealt with by the Joint Foreign Affairs Committee, but within a few months this ruling was changed and that committee became responsible for such matters. Its first act was to prepare and issue a statement of policy which was agreed by the Board and the AJA. The statement approved the Balfour Declaration, but made it clear this was on the understanding that nothing in that letter implied that Jews constituted a separate political nationality all over the world, nor that Jews outside Palestine owed any political allegiance to its government. The statement set out a number of points that should be taken into account in framing the new structure in Palestine, and in particular recommending that it should be mandated to Great Britain. This statement, which the Joint stated was on behalf of the Anglo-Jewish Community, was presented to the Paris Peace Conference on 14 April 1919.[118] In April 1920 the mandate was conferred on Britain by the League of Nations, but it would be stretching a point to attribute this solely to the proposal of the Board. Dr Schneir Levenberg considered the attitude of the Board towards Zionism in the 1920s as non-Zionist, giving 'general support to the mandate but not deeply involved in furthering the advance of the Jewish national home'.[119] He was right, as there were few discussions on Palestine at meetings of the committee and the Board. This was almost certainly because non- and anti-Zionists were in the majority and the Zionists preferred to pursue their activities through other organizations.

This changed on 4 February 1929 when the English Zionist Federation wrote to the Board asking it to convene a conference 'to demonstrate the desire of the Anglo-Jewish Community to play its part in giving effect to the British Mandate for Palestine and to associate itself with other important Jewish communities in entering the Jewish Agency'. The reason the Board was asked to participate in the Jewish Agency was that Chaim Weizmann, who was to be the first president of the Jewish Agency, was of the view that the Board was the most representative and influential non-Zionist body in Anglo-Jewry.[120] The invitation was accepted, the conference held in April and the result was that the Board agreed to appoint six (subsequently increased to seven) persons to represent the British Jewish community on the Jewish Agency.[121] The attitude of the hierarchy of the Board can best be illustrated in the words of D'Avigdor-Goldsmid, the president, at the conference: 'As an Englishman I feel that so long as the British Government holds the mandate for Palestine, it is our bounden duty to assist in the development of the country.'[122] The persons recommended as the seven representatives on the Jewish Agency resulted in an intemperate attack at a Board meeting on 21 July 1929 by a deputy, S. Finburgh, on the president, who he claimed had selected the names himself and imposed them on the Board. The president vacated the chair and indicated that he saw the issue as one of confidence in himself. The debate became quite acrimonious, but in the end peace was restored and no vote taken.[123] The Jewish Agency was formally established in August 1929 by the World Zionist Organisation (WZO) as a partnership between the WZO and non-Zionist Jewish leaders, and in effect to be the representative organ of World Jewry to assist in theestablishment of a Jewish National Home in Palestine. As a consequence the Board also formed a Palestine Committee to be esponsible for the Board's policy on Palestine.

No sooner had the Palestine Committee been created than Arab riots broke out in Palestine. These resulted in a special meeting of the Board on 5 September 1929 when resolutions were passed and sent to the prime minister, colonial secretary and all MPs and peers, expressing sympathy with the victims and associating the Board with the High Commissioner's condemnation of the riots. The resolution also called on the government to restore order and punish the guilty, and welcomed the government's statement that the riots in no way affected its policy to establish a Jewish National home in Palestine.[124] Maybe it did not, but in May 1930 the government suspended a number of immigration certificates that had already been allotted to the Jewish Agency. In June 1930 the Board discussed this suspension and passed resolutions regretting this decision by the government and urging the government to release the certificates. A deputation from the Board met with the colonial secretary, Lord Passfield, who made it clear that the mandate did not envisage a Jewish State but only a Jewish National Home in Palestine, and that there had to be a limit on Jewish immigration based on the absorptive capacity of the country.[125]

As a result of this abortive meeting, the Board participated in a conference on 26 July 1930 organized by the Jewish Agency, and supported a resolution registering a strong protest against the attitude of the government. The majority of deputies were not Zionists, but the suggested limitation on immigration to Palestine and the implied breaking of the pledge in the Balfour declaration aroused even this group to fury. In October, the government issued a White Paper on Palestine which, according to the Board's annual report, 'roused the whole of Jewry to a fever of indignation'. The White Paper resulted in the Board holding a special meeting on 16 November 1930, which reaffirmed a resolution passed at the normal Board meeting on 26 October that 'the Board records its profound conviction that the policy outlined in the White Paper on Palestine is contrary to the spirit of the mandate and a breach of public pledges made in the name of England by successive British Governments and welcomes the pronouncements, written and spoken, of the leading statesmen of the Conservative Party, Mr Lloyd George and General Smuts, to the same effect'. This clearly had some effect as the government appointed a subcommittee of the cabinet to enter into negotiations with representatives of the Jewish Agency, including the president of the Board.[126]

This seems to have been the first occasion since its foundation when the Board took a public political stance against the government and in support of the Opposition. This also indicates how far the Board had changed regarding Zionism since the events of 1917. From the Board's point of view the negotiations proved successful, in that the prime minister issued a letter of 'clarification' on 13 February 1931 to Chaim Weizmann that met most of the Jewish objections to the White Paper and effectively abrogated it. It seems to have been at least partly due to this success that D'Avigdor-Goldsmid, the president of the Board, was elected chairman of the Council of the Jewish Agency in July 1931 – not only an honour but also a position of considerable influence for the Board.

Towards the end of 1933, the British government announced a policy to deport illegal Jewish immigrants in Palestine. Most Zionist deputies demanded that the Board should protest formally to the government. As a result, in January 1934 Neville Laski and Lionel Cohen met with the

Secretary of State for Foreign Affairs, Sir Philip Cunliffe Lister, and the
minutes of their meeting indicate that they told the Secretary of State
that 'their object was to discourage any idea of a formal deputation
from the Board of Deputies'. It would seem that a few months later
Laski made an offer to the Secretary of State to 'spy' on the Jewish
Agency.[127] It is not clear whether his object was to ingratiate himself
and the Board with the Colonial Office or, as Geoffrey Alderman has
suggested, to influence the British government against the political
aims of the World Zionist movement.[128] William Rubinstein, who has
examined the documents on which this claim is based, states that Laski
never used the term 'I will inform' (i.e. 'spy') and merely offered to
provide an alternative Jewish viewpoint on Palestine.[129]

In April 1936, following repeated Arab attacks on Jews and their
property in Palestine, the British government appointed a Royal Commission to enquire into the working of the mandate and investigate the
causes of the unrest. The Board was not asked to give any views to the
Commission, nor did it do so. However, the Palestine Committee put
forward to the Board a resolution supporting the government's policy of
trying to maintain the mandate and permit continuing Jewish immigration. This was opposed by Sir Robert Waley Cohen, a vice-president,
but the resolution was passed by a large majority.[130] The report of the
Commission, generally referred to as the 'Peel Report' after the name
of its chairman, was published on 7 July 1937. One of its main
conclusions was that the demands of the Arabs and the Jews were
irreconcilable and as a consequence it recommended that Palestine be
partitioned into a Jewish state, a British-controlled enclave including
Jerusalem and a corridor to Jaffa, and an Arab state consisting of Transjordan and the rest of Palestine. On the same day as the report was
published the British government announced its support in principle
for partition. Thereafter great pressure, mainly from the Arab side, was
mounted against partition, coupled with disarray and some resistance
to partition within the Zionist movements. Following a further study by
what was known as the Woodhead Commission, which had a 'hidden
agenda' to report unfavourably on partition (which it did), Britain
formally abandoned partition as its policy in November 1938.[131]

The Board discussed the Peel Report at its meeting on 25 July 1937
and the views expressed were mixed, but generally most deputies who
spoke were against partition.[132] Following the appointment of the
Woodhead Commission it held a full discussion on Palestine at its
meeting on 16 January 1938. After an animated debate it passed nearly

unanimously three resolutions: it regretted the long period of delay in formulating the British government's final policy; called for the re-establishment of 'economic absorptive capacity' as the criterion for immigration; and declared opposition to any solution which relegated Jews to a permanent minority status in Palestine. It proposed the establishment of a Jewish Dominion in Palestine within the British Commonwealth.[133] Although the Woodhead Report and the consequential formal abandonment of partition by the British government was discussed at meetings of the Palestine Committee and the Board, no actions were taken. Concern had shifted to trying to get the government to relax its policy regarding the admission of Jews, and in particular refugees from Germany, to Palestine. A government-led Conference on Palestine was held in February/March 1939, and although it was meant to be trilateral, in the event there were two bilateral conferences – one between the government and Arab representatives and the other between the government and Jewish representatives.

The Board was invited to participate and was represented by Dr Israel Feldman. No agreement was reached and as a result the government, as it had warned at the outset of the conference, imposed its own solution. On 17 May 1939 it issued a White Paper which, inter alia, provided for the establishment of an independent Palestinian state within ten years, the admission of 'only' 75,000 Jews within the next five years and the suspension of Jewish immigration thereafter (unless the Arabs consented), and for sales of land to be at the discretion of the High Commissioner in a limited zone and prohibited elsewhere. The Board discussed the White Paper four days later at its meeting on 21 May 1939, and in the debate a speech by Sir Robert Waley Cohen, a vice-president, included the now much-quoted phrase: 'I appeal to the Government to reconsider a proposal which is as unworthy of the history of the British Empire as it is false to its high place in the vanguard of civilisation.'[134] The Board passed the following resolution unanimously:

> The Board of Deputies of British Jews, having considered the statement of policy issued by HM Government (Cmd 6019) is of the opinion that the proposed termination of the development of the Jewish National Home represents a fundamental departure from the pledges given and the obligations accepted in the Balfour Declaration and the Mandate for Palestine and expresses the view that the policy set out in the White Paper is unacceptable.

The Board earnestly appeals to HM Government to reconsider its policy and to carry out the terms of the Balfour Declaration and the Mandate for Palestine.[135]

The government did not change its mind and in mid-July announced the cessation of all legal immigration to Palestine because of the continuation of illegal immigration. This resulted in a furious riposte by the Board at its meeting on 16 July.[136] Seven weeks later Britain declared war on Germany.

NOTES

1. For a full discussion of this, see Tony Kushner, 'The Impact of British Anti-Semitism, 1918–1945', in David Cesarani (ed.), *The Making of Modern Anglo-Jewry* (Oxford: Basil Blackwell, 1990), pp.191–208.
2. See, for example, Geoffrey Alderman, *Modern British Jewry*, new edn (Oxford: Clarendon Press, 1998); Todd M. Endelman, *The Jews of Britain, 1656 to 2000* (London: University of California Press, 2002); Colin Holmes, *Anti-Semitism in British Society, 1876–1939* (London: Edward Arnold, 1979); Gisela C. Lebzelter, *Political Anti-Semitism in England, 1918–1939* (Basingstoke: Macmillan, 1978); W.D. Rubinstein, *A History of the Jews in the English-Speaking World: Great Britain* (Basingstoke: Macmillan, 1996).
3. Kushner, 'Impact of British Anti-Semitism, 1918–1945', p.194.
4. David Cesarani, *The Jewish Chronicle and Anglo-Jewry 1841–1991* (Cambridge: Cambridge University Press, 1994), p.133.
5. Bernard Wasserstein, 'Patterns of Jewish Leadership in Great Britain during the Nazi Era', in Randolph Braham (ed.), *Jewish Leadership During the Nazi Era* (New York: Institute for Holocaust Studies, 1985), p.31.
6. *Jewish Chronicle [JC]*, 20 July 1917, p.6.
7. Bernard Homa, *Footprints on the Sands of Time* (London: author, 1990).
8. BOD, ACC/3121/A/26, p.33.
9. BOD, ACC/3121/A/30, p.129.
10. Neville Laski Papers, MS134/AJ33/148.
11. Ibid., MS134/AJ33/9.
12. Gideon Shimoni, 'Selig Brodetsky and the Ascendancy of Zionism in Anglo-Jewry (1939–1945)', *Jewish Journal of Sociology*, 22 (1980), p.130.
13. S. Levenberg, *The Board and Zion: An Historical Survey* (London: Rare Times, 1985), p.58.
14. Annual Report of the Board of Deputies (AR), 1938, p.32.
15. For example, Alderman, *Modern British Jewry*, p.312; Endelman, *The Jews of Britain 1656 to 2000*, p.218.
16. Shimoni, 'Selig Brodetsky and the Ascendancy of Zionism', p.132.
17. Aubrey Newman, *The Board of Deputies of British Jews 1760–1985: A Brief Survey* (London; Vallentine Mitchell, 1987), p.29.
18. Selig Brodetsky, *Memoirs: From Ghetto to Israel* (London: Weidenfeld & Nicolson, 1960), pp.194–5.
19. BOD, ACC/3121/A/19, p.149.
20. Levenberg, *The Board and Zion*, p.59.
21. Mark Levene, *War, Jews, and the New Europe: The Diplomacy of Lucien Wolf, 1914–1919* (Oxford: Littman Library, 1992), pp.157–8.
22. BOD, ACC/3121/A/017, p.92.
23. BOD, ACC/3121/A/017, pp.110–13.
24. BOD, ACC/3121/A/018, p.12.
25. David Cesarani, 'The Transformation of Communal Authority in Anglo-Jewry, 1914–1940', in Cesarani (ed.), *Making of Modern Anglo-Jewry*, p.124.
26. Ibid., p.64.
27. Bernard Krikler, *Anglo-Jewish Attitudes to the Rise of Nazism* (1968), p.39, unpublished manuscript available in the Wiener Library, London.
28. Daniel Tilles, '"Some Lesser Known Aspects": The Anti-Fascist Campaign of the Board of Deputies of British Jews, 1936–40', in Geoffrey Alderman (ed.), *The Jews in Britain* (Boston: Academic Studies Press). [Forthcoming, probably 2010.]
29. There is no evidence for this, nor would there be, since the leaders of the Board would have

discussed it discreetly with government ministers or senior civil servants in the confines of the Pall Mall clubs.

30. *JC*, 31 March 1933, p.43.
31. Cesarani, 'The Transformation of Communal Authority', p.127.
32. Lebzelter, *Political Anti-Semitism in England, 1918–1939*, pp.139–40.
33. Stuart A. Cohen, 'Selig Brodetsky and the Ascendancy of Zionism in Anglo-Jewry: Another View of his Role and Achievements', *Jewish Journal of Sociology*, 24, 1 (June 1982), p.28.
34. Sharon Gewirtz, 'Anglo-Jewish Responses to Nazi Germany 1933–39: The Anti-Nazi Boycott and the Board of Deputies of British Jews', *Journal of Contemporary History* 26, 2 (April 1991), p.269.
35. Josef Fraenkel, *The History of the British Section of the World Jewish Congress* (London: Leicester University Press, 1976).
36. The alien issues, particularly as they affected Jews after the First World War, are well described in David Cesarani, 'Anti-Alienism in England after the First World War', in *Immigrants and Minorities*, 6 (1987), pp.4–29. There are many works regarding German refugees and Britain, with many of the authors disagreeing with each other. One work that the interested reader might like to consult is Louise London, *Whitehall and the Jews, 1933–1948: British Immigration Policy, Jewish Refugees and the Holocaust* (Cambridge: Cambridge University Press, 2000).
37. AR, 1919, pp.23–4.
38. Ibid., pp.29–30.
39. See, for example, the first two chapters of Susan Kingsley Kent, *Aftershock: Politics and Trauma in Britain, 1918–1931* (Basingstoke: Palgrave, 2008).
40. AR, 1920, p.25.
41. Ibid., p.33.
42. BOD, ACC/3121/A/18, p.115.
43. Ibid.
44. Cesarani, 'Anti-Alienism in England', p.17; The National Archive, Public Records Office [NA PRO], HO 45/24765/17/A, 28 May 1924.
45. BOD, ACC/3121/C2/1/3.
46. H.C.G. Mathews and Brian Harrison (eds), *Oxford Dictionary of National Biography* (Oxford: Oxford University Press, 2004).
47. Cesarani, 'Anti-Alienism in England', pp.18–20.
48. AR, 1930, pp.42–3, 61–6; AR, 1931, pp.34–5, 53–6; BOD, ACC/3121/A/023, p.49.
49. Cesarani, 'Anti-Alienism in England', pp.21–2; NA PRO, HO 45/24765/56/D, 11 December 1929.
50. NA PRO, HO 45/24765/56/E, 14 December 1929.
51. Anthony Sherman, *Island Refuge: Britain and Refugees from the Third Reich 1933–1939* (London: Frank Cass, 1994), pp.15–16.
52. NA PRO, CAB 24/239, CP 96/33.
53. AR, 1933, pp.57, 63–5.
54. NA PRO, HO/213/42.
55. BOD, ACC/312/A/29, p.227.
56. Much of this section has been based on Lebzelter, *Political Anti-Semitism in England, 1918–1939*.
57. AR, 1923, p.59; BOD, ACC/3121/A/018, p.99.
58. BOD, ACC/3121/A/017, p.129.
59. BOD, ACC/3121/A/26, p.17.
60. Lebzelter, *Political Anti-Semitism in England, 1918–1939*, p.139.
61. Ibid., pp.92–3, 105–7.
62. Ibid., p.140; Elaine R. Smith, 'Class, ethnicity and politics in the Jewish East End, 1918–1939', *Jewish Historical Studies*, 32 (1990–92), p.360.
63. BOD, ACC/3121/A/28, p.122.
64. Ibid, p.111.
65. AR, 1936, p.56.
66. *JC*, 20 November 1936, pp.19–20.
67. Nigel Copsey, *Anti-Fascism in Britain* (Basingstoke: Macmillan, 2000), p.53.
68. Lebzelter, *Political Anti-Semitism in England, 1918–1939*, p.144.
69. Ibid.
70. *JC*, 12 May 1933, p.33.
71. Neil Barrett, 'The Threat of the British Union of Fascists in Manchester', in Tony Kushner and Nadia Valman (eds), *Remembering Cable Street: Fascism and Anti-Fascism in British Society* (London: Vallentine Mitchell, 2000), p.68.
72. Anglo-Jewish Archives, MS134/AJ33/89 and 90.
73. AR, 1937, p.68.

74. Archives of the Community Security Trust [CST], C/6/1/1/1, p.170.
75. Rubinstein, *History of the Jews in the English-Speaking World*, p.316.
76. Holmes, *Anti-Semitism in British Society, 1876–1939*; Kushner, 'Impact of British Anti-Semitism, 1918–1945', pp.191–208; David Rosenberg, *Facing up to Antisemitism: How Jews in Britain Countered the Threats of the 1930s* (London: JCARP Publications, 1985), pp.15–30.
77. Rubinstein, *History of the Jews in the English-Speaking World*, pp.287–331.
78. Holmes, *Anti-Semitism in British Society, 1876–1939*, p.200.
79. Sharon Gewirtz, 'Anglo-Jewish responses to Nazi Germany', pp.255–76.
80. AR, 1933, pp.54–5.
81. BOD, ACC/3121/A/26, p.89.
82. Gewirtz, 'Anglo-Jewish responses to Nazi Germany', pp.259–60.
83. BOD, ACC/3121/A/27, p.79.
84. Krikler, *Anglo-Jewish Attitudes to the Rise of Nazism*, p.71.
85. BOD, ACC/3121/A/26, p.56.
86. BOD, ACC/3121/A/021, pp.94–5, 102–3; BOD, ACC/3121/A/022, pp.6, 12, 19–20, 28, 43, 54, 60.
87. AR, 1923, p.52.
88. Ibid., pp.55–6.
89. BOD, ACC/3121/A/019, p.105; BOD, ACC/3121/A/020, pp.21, 31.
90. BOD, ACC/3121/A/021, pp.52–3.
91. Ibid., p.68.
92. Ibid., p.103.
93. Ibid., pp.110–14, 119.
94. See Endelman, *The Jews of Britain 1656 to 2000*, pp.221, 249.
95. There is an indication of this in the correspondence annexed to the *Special Report on the Slaughter of Animals* of the Law, Parliamentary and General Purposes Committee of 29 June and 21 July 1931, BOD, ACC/3121/A/25, pp.6–7, and the minutes of the Board meeting of 27 July 1931, BOD, ACC/3121/A/25, pp.10–117.
96. Anglo-Jewish Archives, MS134/AJ33/210.
97. AR, 1933, p.49.
98. BOD, ACC/3121/A/26, pp.3, 7 and 8.
99. AR, 1934, pp.36–7.
100. AR, 1936, pp.32–3.
101. AR, 1938, pp.35–6.
102. BOD, ACC/3121/A/28, p.108.
103. AR, 1954, pp.37–8.
104. BOD, ACC/3121/C3/2/1/2. The son in the original name of the firm was aged 1 at the time and did not know of the partnership with his father until he found this correspondence in the archives some seventy-four years later!
105. BOD, ACC/3121/C3/2/1/3.
106. BOD, ACC/3121/C3/1/4.
107. BOD, ACC/3121/A/30, p.90.
108. Gewirtz, 'Anglo-Jewish responses to Nazi Germany', p.267.
109. An in-depth study of the impact of the Russian Revolution on the British Jewish community is contained in Sharman Kadish, *Bolsheviks and British Jews* (London: Frank Cass, 1992).
110. Ibid., pp.64–5.
111. AR, 1917, p.26.
112. *JC*, 27 April 1917, pp.11–12.
113. Alderman, *Modern British Jewry*, pp.238–9, 251, 253; Rubinstein, *History of the Jews in the English-Speaking World*, pp.201, 212–13.
114. BOD, ACC/3121/A/017.
115. The diplomatic moves regarding Jews and the post-First World War peace treaties, particularly those of Lucien Wolf, are described in Levene, *War, Jews, and the New Europe*, pp.34–6.
116. AR, 1919, pp.41–4; BOD, ACC/3121/A/017, p.129.
117. Patrick B. Finney, '"An Evil for All Concerned": Great Britain and Minority Protection after 1919', *Journal of Contemporary History*, 30 (1995), pp.533–4.
118. Ibid., pp.44–6.
119. Levenberg, *The Board and Zion*, p.59.
120. This is the view of Israel Finestein, but I have been unable to find confirmation from other sources, including Weizmann's diaries. Following the agreement of the Board to appoint representatives, Chaim Weizmann sent a telegram to the president which read: 'Delighted clear demonstration of English Jewry's determination participate in development Jewish Palestine as realisation Balfour Declaration', BOD, ACC/3121/A/022, p.118.

121. BOD, ACC/3121/A/022, pp.80, 83–4, 94, 118, 122.
122. Levenberg, *The Board and Zion*, pp.30–1.
123. BOD, ACC/3121/A/023, p.35.
124. AR, 1929, pp.40–3.
125. AR, 1930, pp.37–9.
126. Ibid., pp.39–40.
127. Cesarani, 'Transformation of Communal Authority', p.133.
128. Alderman, *Modern British Jewry*, p.272.
129. Rubinstein, *History of the Jews in the English-Speaking World*, p.285.
130. BOD, ACC/3121/A/28, p.24.
131. Itzak Galnoor, *The Partition of Palestine: Decision Crossroads in the Zionist Movement* (New York: State University, 1995), pp.53–4.
132. BOD, ACC/3121/A/29, p.147.
133. BOD, ACC/3121/A/29, pp.203–4.
134. BOD, ACC/3121/A/30, p.108.
135. Ibid., pp.108–9.
136. Ibid., p.126–7.

5 Zionists Take Control, 1939–1964

At the start of the Second World War in September 1939, the Jews in Britain overwhelmingly supported the government. This was in contrast to the situation at the start of the First World War in 1914 when there was some ambiguity, particularly from East European Jews in Britain. This was due to Jewish animosity towards Russia, which was Britain's ally, and friendliness towards Germany, which was Britain's enemy. Furthermore, in 1939 there was a significant number of Jews able to join the armed forces as virtually all Jews of military age had been born in Britain, in contrast to the position at the start of the First World War. The Association of Jewish Ex-Servicemen (AJEX) set up a committee, in conjunction with the Board, to organize a national recruiting campaign, which proved to be highly effective and hundreds of Jews were encouraged to volunteer for the armed forces.[1] The Jews of Britain fought to defeat Nazism, but also they hoped that declaration of war would end antisemitism in Britain. It did not during the first few months, the so-called 'phoney war', as government policy towards fascist and other antisemitic groups remained inadequate. In a report, the Board remarked on a marked increase in antisemitic propaganda at this time. Government policy changed in May 1940 when the invasion of Britain became a distinct possibility, and most fascist leaders as well as outspoken antisemites were interned.[2]

This change in policy coincided with the appointment of Winston Churchill as prime minister, and the Jews in Britain greatly welcomed his appointment. Churchill had always been seen as a friend of the Jews, and he ousted from the government virtually all the appeasers and those who had reneged on their promises to the Jews regarding Palestine. As the war proceeded, however, Jewish priorities began to change. The priority of the government was consistently to win the war, whereas as news of the Holocaust began to emerge, the priorities of the Jews changed to that of the rescue of the Jews of Europe. To the Jews the future of Palestine was of vital importance, whereas to the government it was at best a secondary matter. As Winston Churchill stated in October 1943: 'Everything for the war, whether controversial or not, and nothing controversial that is not *bona fide* needed for the war.'[3]

The war brought on a multiplicity of problems for the Board, many of which it had not previously confronted. These included not only the Holocaust, but also the evacuation of children and whole families; internment of alien Jews, mainly refugees from Nazi Germany; the destruction by bombing of many buildings occupied or used by Jews, particularly in the East End of London; and the question as to how the Board could and should operate in wartime conditions.

With the ending of the war, the events in Palestine leading to Britain relinquishing the mandate and the establishment of the State of Israel became major issues for the Board and created tensions with the British government, but the re-emergence of antisemitism and of the Fascist Party in Britain filled much of the agenda as well. Following the establishment of Israel, the Board, as the leading representative for British Jewry, found itself in the position of having to comment on Israel and on the policies of the Israeli government. This created tensions within the Board, and between the Board and many members of the community who did not always share the Board's support for Israeli actions and policies. Internal disputes within the Board occupied a fair amount of time and perhaps reached their peak with the tabling of a 'no confidence' motion against the president for his voting action in the House of Commons during the debates on the 1956 Suez crisis.

Since the end of the Second World War, there have been many major conflicts within the British Jewish community. Geoffrey Alderman has labelled it as 'A House Divided' and 'Mismanagement and Fragmentation', Chaim Bermant published a book entitled *Troubled Eden*, Todd Endelman has termed the post-war period as 'The Fracturing of Anglo-Jewry', and Vivian Lipman has termed it 'Polarization and Decline'.[4] Israel Finestein tended to differ and wrote: 'Division is no stranger to Jewish history.'[5] Bill Rubinstein does not see anything new in these disputes, but does see the loss of a separate and distinctive British Jewish identity over the last forty or so years.[6] Disputation is endemic to Jews. This book is concerned solely with the role of the Board and only touches on these issues to the extent that they involved the Board. Similarly, the acrimonious debate between British Jewish historians as to the actions or lack of them by British Jews and their institutions concerning the Holocaust has been ignored, except to the extent that it involved the Board.[7] As Todd Endelman, in reviewing the responses of the Anglo-Jewish leadership to the Holocaust, has concluded: 'Retrospective attacks on the behaviour of communal leaders reveal, in the end, more about the historians making them and *their* concerns than they do about the agonizing days of World War II and the unprecedented challenges it presented.'[8]

1. THE BOARD

Leadership

At the start of the Second World War, the Board established an Executive Committee for the duration of the war with powers to act if necessary without recourse to the full Board, should it not be practicable to convene Board or Committee meetings. The committee was to consist of the honorary officers, the chairman of the Law, Parliamentary and General Purposes Committee, the joint chairmen of the Joint Foreign Affairs Committee, and five other members elected by the Board, and the committee itself had the power to co-opt up to three additional members. It co-opted Anthony de Rothschild, the Marchioness of Reading and Harry Sacher and invited two former presidents – Sir Osmond D'Avigdor-Goldsmid and Neville Laski – to attend its meetings. Lavy Bakstansky ensured that he was a member of the Executive Committee as part of his strategy to effecting Zionist control of the Board. In practice, the worst fears of the Board were not realized and it was able to hold its meetings regularly throughout the war. The Executive Committee proved a success and when the war ended, it was decided not to close that committee as had been envisaged in 1939.

Following the election of Selig Brodetsky as president, the anti- and non-Zionists on the Board and in the community generally were concerned that the Board would become part of the Zionist camp, whereas the Zionists thought that they were a long way down the road of 'capturing' the Board. Both sides were to be surprised. In fact, in his acceptance speech at the Board meeting on 17 December 1939 Selig Brodetsky told the deputies:

> As a Zionist I realise there are other Jews who have other views about Jewish problems, and I consider it the primary function of anybody who directs the activities of an organisation like the Board of Deputies to conduct the affairs with due regard to the views of all sections of the Board ... I hope that when the time

came to examine my behaviour during the coming months you would find that it was possible for a convinced Zionist to be just as impartial and objective and fair in the conduct of the affairs of a mixed body as a convinced non-Zionist or a convinced anti-Zionist.[9]

Actions speak louder than words and he was true to his words. Within a few days, he co-opted Anthony de Rothschild, a leading non-Zionist, on to the newly formed Executive Committee. Some months later Anthony de Rothschild wrote to him complaining about a particularly pro-Zionist speech he had made implying that assimilation represented a capitulation on the part of the Jewish people. In his reply, Brodetsky emphasized that on this occasion he was not speaking as the president of the Board but as a leading Zionist and he would always keep these two roles separate.[10] When in May 1943 Lavy Bakstansky was busy behind the scenes reorganizing the committee chairmen and structures, Brodetsky wrote to him insisting that Sir Robert Waley Cohen, a leading non-Zionist, be retained as vice-president.[11] Sir Robert was defeated in the election, but the tone of that correspondence indicated that Brodetsky was no tool of the Zionists and there was not much love lost between him and Bakstansky. Neither was much love lost between Sir Robert and Bakstansky. Following a particularly acrimonious debate between the two at a Board meeting on 6 November 1942, Brodetsky wrote to Waley Cohen on 9 November 1942 upbraiding him. In reply Waley Cohen wrote: 'I do not know anything and I am afraid I care less, about Mr Bakstansky's personality, but I do feel that it is most unfortunate that a whole time paid secretary of a political organisation in the community should be allowed by that organisation to sit on the Board.'[12]

Selig Brodetsky was re-elected unopposed in 1943 and retired from the presidency at the end of the triennial session in 1949 to take up an appointment as president of the Hebrew University in Jerusalem. His resignation gave the Zionist group on the Board a problem as to whom to select as their candidate. They considered asking Lord Nathan, who had been the unsuccessful candidate against Neville Laski in the 1933 election, but he would only agree if he were unopposed and there was no certainty of this. They also considered Barnett Janner, one of the vice-presidents and a Labour MP, but they were concerned that he might find a conflict between his loyalties to the Labour government and to the Board, particularly if differences arose over Israel. In the event they settled on the Rev. Dr Abraham Cohen, who was the minister of the main Birmingham Synagogue, which he represented on the Board. He was a strong supporter of the World Jewish Congress and a member of the Zionist group. The other candidate was Israel Feldman, a vice-president, who although a Zionist was strongly opposed to the activities of the Zionist group on the Board and the World Jewish Congress. There was a hard-fought election and the *Jewish Chronicle* (*JC*) came out strongly for Dr Feldman.[13] In the event, Dr Cohen was elected by 130 votes to 115. Had the thirty-eight deputies from the Liberal and Reform synagogues and other groups not withdrawn from the Board a few months previously (see below), it is very likely that Dr Feldman would have been successful, since all of the withdrawing deputies were opposed to the Zionist group on the Board. This was the first time in the history of the Jewish community in Britain that a religious leader had become the lay leader of the community. It has not been repeated.

Dr Cohen was re-elected unopposed in 1952 but he decided to retire after his second term of three years and in June 1955 Barnett Janner, MP, was elected president. He defeated Israel Feldman by 187 votes to eighty-two. This time there were no concerns about any conflict of loyalty between the Board and the government as by then Labour was in opposition. However, before too long the issue of conflict of loyalty arose in connection with the Suez crisis. Barnett Janner was a solicitor, a Liberal MP from 1931 to 1935 and a Labour MP from 1945 to 1970. He was knighted in 1961 and created a life peer in 1970.

Barnett Janner was re-elected president unopposed in the 1958 and 1961 elections and in the July 1964 triennial election he stood again as president for what would have been his fourth three-year term of office. Alderman Abraham Moss, a businessman and leading local politician from Manchester, defeated him by 155 votes to 140.[14] It was also a defeat for Lavy Bakstansky and the Zionist group, whose candidate Barnett Janner was. It was the first, and so far only, time that an incumbent president was challenged and defeated in a bid to be re-elected, and the *JC* referred to it as a 'turning point'.[15]

Zionists 'Capture' the Board

In late 1942, the Board agreed that the normal triennial elections of deputies would take place in 1943 despite the prevailing wartime conditions. Bakstansky thought that it was now opportune for the

Zionists to 'capture' the Board. Gideon Shimoni has suggested a particular reason why Bakstansky was anxious to obtain Zionist control of the Board at this time. In May 1942, a special World Zionist Conference was held at the Biltmore Hotel in New York. This conference issued what became known as the Biltmore Declaration, often referred to as the Biltmore Program. It demanded that after the war a Jewish Commonwealth should be established in Palestine and that to achieve this, certain powers, such as immigration, should be transferred by Britain (as the mandate authority) to the Jewish Agency. Britain would retain sovereignty over Palestine until a Jewish majority had been established. The Zionist Federation considered it was essential in discussions with the British government that the representative body of British Jews (i.e. the Board of Deputies), should be unequivocally in favour of this.[16]

Bakstansky organized the Zionist deputies already on the Board into a group termed the Zionist Progressive Group. This was a harbinger of what subsequently developed into a number of different 'groups' with differing views and differing allegiances and policies and generally each acting in unison, rather akin to political parties in Parliament. Other groups included the Independent Group, consisting of deputies who disagreed with the policies or disliked the actions of the Zionist group; there was the Orthodox Group, essentially deputies representing Strictly Orthodox congregations; even for a time a Communist Group; and a group of deputies from constituents of the United Synagogue.[17] The Zionist group became known colloquially as the 'caucus', at first a disparaging name given to it by its detractors but subsequently used by friends and foes alike. It seems that the caucus had the practice of holding a meeting immediately prior to the regular Board meetings and entering the hall where the main meeting was being held as a group and often a little late. One wag is reputed to have called out when they entered, 'They have received their instructions now.'[18]

After establishing the Zionist group Bakstansky then addressed the forthcoming triennial elections. His objective was to swamp the Board with Zionist supporters and his strategy had three strands. In synagogues and institutions that already had a full complement of deputies he sought to ensure that they elected deputies who were Zionists. In those that did not have a full complement he arranged for additional suitable candidates to come forward. Finally, he persuaded many synagogues to join the Board for the first time. He did not do this quietly but with full publicity in the Jewish press. It was open and not surreptitious. The *JC* strongly opposed the domination of a Zionist bloc on the Board, and feared that it would divide the community and devalue its representations to the government. A few days before the elections there was a leader on the subject and it ended with a rallying cry:

> We urge every member of a synagogue or other constituent to stamp on the plots and factions, to exercise courageously and independently his voting right, and to employ it only in support of a candidate not chained to a party machine but determined to work in accord with his conscience and the charge of his constituents, for the general communal good. The carefully approved 'yes man' of this or that party or group should be plainly informed that there is no place for him at the Deputies of British Jews. This is the fight of every individual Jew, a fight for the future of the Community and of many Jews beyond these islands. To shirk it would be not merely blameworthy, but black treachery.[19]

Despite this, Bakstansky's strategy was overwhelmingly successful. The number of synagogues and institutions represented increased from 207 to 274 and the number of deputies from 288 to 459, and the majority were committed Zionists. There were numerous complaints about election irregularities and the Board formed a special subcommittee to examine these and make recommendations for future changes. It found that irregularities had occurred but they were no different and probably no more numerous than those that had occurred in the past – a sort of whitewash. It did, however, propose certain administrative changes that would provide better machinery for future elections and amendments to the constitution to limit 'canvassing' and similar activities during elections. The *JC* was highly dissatisfied and very critical of the findings and recommendations of the subcommittee, and published an editorial headed 'Tinkering with the Trouble':

> So the Community will have to form its own opinion as to why the victim, which in this case is the whole Board, is, if not dead, in a state of serious decline so far as its representative character and general reputation is concerned. The cause, indeed, is obvious. Until all this buying and selling of seats is done away with and, what is much more important, until steps are taken to eliminate party organisation and caucus activity, and to make the 'capture' of the Board impossible, the Board will continue to decline in prestige.

Men of character will not for long waste their time attending
Board meetings at which most if not all-important decisions have
been settled beforehand by two or three individuals in a caucus
office, enforcing their will by the block vote majority of disci-
plined nonentities.[20]

The changes recommended by the subcommittee were agreed by the
Board, which did not decline, and the 'caucus' continued.

Following the 1943 triennial elections, all the committees, with
exception of the Shechita Committee whose work was taken over by
the Law, Parliamentary and General Purposes Committee, were
reconstituted with Zionist caucus members forming a majority on each
committee. Whereas Brodetsky was re-elected unopposed as president,
only one of the two candidates of the caucus for vice-president,
Professor Samson Wright, was elected; their other candidate, Barnett
Janner, was narrowly defeated by Israel Feldman, one of the incumbents.
Gordon Liverman, the incumbent treasurer, defeated the caucus
candidate, Isaac Landau, by 162 votes to 161. Thus the caucus did not
have an absolute majority among deputies, and it was not until the
1949 election for honorary officers that they succeeded in obtaining a
clean slate. Indeed, they might not even have succeeded then had it not
been for the withdrawal from the Board of a number of groups who
were opposed to the caucus. The agreement with the Anglo-Jewish
Association with regard to foreign affairs, which had lasted from 1878
with a short break in 1917, was terminated at the first meeting of the
new Board in 1943, although not without a difficult debate and by
a majority of only 154 to 148 with thirty-seven abstentions. A new
Foreign Affairs Committee of the Board was established.[21]

All of this manoeuvring and particularly the dissolution of the Joint
Foreign Affairs Committee led to a lot of acrimony and controversy in the
Jewish community, not only among non-Zionists but among Zionists as
well. The *JC* was highly critical and Brodetsky was clearly upset. His aim
was to try to be objective and impartial and Bakstansky's policies militated against this. On 23 June 1943, ten days before the meeting that
cancelled the agreement with the AJA, Brodetsky wrote to Bakstansky:

As you know I have repudiated the idea of what is called 'capturing' the Board ... The strength of the opinion of British Jewry
on any Jewish issue, and particularly on what is most vital to both
of us, namely the Jewish future in Palestine, will largely depend
upon the extent to which one can say that this opinion is the

result of free and open discussion at the Representative Institution of the Community. I believe that the decision of the community will be most powerful if we have those who oppose our view inside the Board.[22]

It seems that for some months after the elections Board meetings were turned into Zionist demonstrations, such that at the conclusion of the Board meeting on 12 September 1943 Brodetsky remarked:

The work of this Board and the work of the community as a whole has in the last couple of months been pushed to a very low level by considerations which are based on all sorts of interests, most of which have nothing whatever to do with the interests of the community. I must say that, as far as we are concerned in the office, it is impossible to get on with any job. Our time is taken up with irrelevancies ... This is how the energy of the community is being used up at the present moment, and at a time when we are told that something like four million Jews have been exterminated in Europe.[23]

Indeed the controversy reached such a pitch that Brodetsky considered resigning in October 1943, but did not do so because of a sense of responsibility and as he did not want to bring the disagreements between himself and the leaders of the caucus out into the open.[24]

World Jewish Congress and the AJA
Disagreements between the Board and the British section of the World Jewish Congress erupted in late 1943. Brodetsky was in a difficult position since not only was he president of the Board but he was also a vice-president of the British Section of the WJC. The British Section of the WJC continued to make representations to the British government on matters involving Jews outside Britain, in the main Palestine and Europe, and this was resented by many deputies who felt that the Board should have a monopoly in any lobbying with the government. Correspondence and negotiations continued for a number of months, but in March 1944 a sort of modus vivendi was agreed. It provided for regular exchanges of information between the Board and the British Section of the WJC and stated that the Board was recognized by the WJC as the representative body of British Jewry and authorized as such to make representations on behalf of the Jewish community in the United Kingdom in regard to both internal and foreign affairs.[25] Note

that it did not preclude the British Section of the WJC lobbying the government with regard to Jews outside Britain, and furthermore the agreement stated that each body should retain its freedom of action. Dissension continued.

At the same time as these problems arose with the WJC there were issues with the AJA, which did not accept the dissolution of the Joint Foreign Affairs Committee quietly. Brodetsky tried to reach some sort of compromise, but the AJA set up its own General Purposes and Foreign Committee and the Foreign Office agreed to its request that it could continue to place its views before the foreign secretary. There is some irony in the fact that the president of the AJA and chairman of that committee was Leonard Stein, who was a former member of the Board's Executive Committee, and the AJA delegations to the Foreign Office often included Neville Laski, a former president of the Board, and Sir Robert Waley Cohen, a former vice-president. The *JC*'s concern that the Board's representations to government would be devalued was borne out in a memorandum on the implications of the Board elections and the break with the AJA from Harold Beeley, the Foreign Office's expert on Jewish Affairs, circulated to his colleagues in August 1943. He concluded:

> views on the future of the Jews in foreign countries, notably on the continent of Europe and Palestine, will be put before HMG by two distinct bodies with different outlooks – the one elected by a wide constituency but controlled in the last resort by an international organisation with a single objective, the other representing a small upper class of assimilated British Jews.[26]

Gideon Shimoni, commenting on this memorandum, makes the point that, as a result, the Foreign Office would no longer attach overwhelming importance to the views of the Board, which would always be conveniently counterbalanced by the conflicting views of the AJA. Thus the 'capture' of the Board might even have been counterproductive.[27]

Some sort of agreement was reached between the Board and the AJA in March 1944 that there would be a regular exchange of information and they would try to reach agreement over post-war policies. This latter matter proved insurmountable due to differences regarding the future of Palestine, and there were a number of quite acrimonious clashes. From mid-1946 the deputies from the AJA ceased to attend Board meetings and subsequently the AJA withdrew its representation on the Board. Its main reason was that the Board had not agreed to the reconstitution of the Joint Foreign Committee.[28] Concern over the activities of the 'caucus', and that the present method of electing committees did not afford adequate opportunities for the expression of minority views, was shared by many deputies and by much of the Jewish press as well. The honorary officers were mindful of these concerns and in 1947 they set up a subcommittee to consider new methods of setting up committees so that they included places for deputies representing groups with minority views. The deliberations of this subcommittee were overtaken by another controversy of an entirely different nature.

Liberal Synagogues Marriage Secretaries

In 1946 a number of Liberal synagogues applied to the Board for permission to appoint marriage secretaries and a subcommittee was established to consider this. The statutory position was that the president of the Board had the power to do so in respect of a secretary of a 'Synagogue of persons professing the Jewish religion'. Under the Board's constitution the president had first to obtain a certificate from the Board's ecclesiastical authorities – the chief rabbi or the haham – to the effect that the synagogue in question was one of persons professing the Jewish religion. The subcommittee reported that three out of four of its members were of the view that a precedent had been established in 1935 when the chief rabbi had issued such a certificate for the main Liberal Synagogue in St John's Wood, London.[29] In an interview at that time with Bernard Homa, the chief rabbi stated that he had been pressurized to do so by Sir Robert Waley Cohen, a vice-president of the Board, in view of the prevailing 'Hitlerite climate', and subsequently he had regretted his action and had declined to grant any further certificates for Liberal synagogues.[30] It would seem that the three did not know of this later retraction and were of the view that the original certificate encompassed all Liberal synagogues since they were affiliated to the main one. As a safeguard they proposed that the part of the constitution that dealt with the appointment of marriage secretaries should be amended by adding after the words 'Ecclesiastical Authorities' the words 'or in the case of a Liberal Synagogue by a certificate from the President of the Liberal Jewish Synagogue, St John's Wood Road, London'.

The minority voice on the subcommittee was Dr Bernard Homa, a leader of the Orthodox Group on the Board, who argued strongly against the proposition. After some discussion the Board decided not to take an immediate decision but to ask Dayan Lazarus, the deputy chief rabbi, to issue certificates for all Liberal synagogues on the same lines as the late chief rabbi had done for the St John's Wood Synagogue. The reply signed by all the members of the Beth Din was uncompromising; it stated that 'the Board of Deputies, which comprises an overwhelming majority of representatives of Orthodox communities, is not permitted in Jewish law to give authority to Liberal synagogues to solemnise marriages'.[31] It was decided that before proceeding with discussing the proposed amendment to the constitution, the president should meet with all sides and attempt some sort of reconciliation. This failed, the proposed constitution change was defeated by seventy-eight votes to sixty, and the president then informed the main Liberal Synagogue that he was not able to appoint marriage secretaries for the other Liberal synagogues.[32] The Liberal Synagogue movement decided to consult its lawyers and it also attempted, unsuccessfully, to have a clause added to a Marriage (Consolidation) Bill that was going through Parliament in 1949 to extend to the Liberal Synagogue the statutory powers already conferred on the West London Synagogue (Reform) to certify secretaries for marriages for itself and its affiliated synagogues.

The position was not resolved either by legal action or by the Board agreeing the previously proposed amendment of the constitution and, as a result, the Liberal synagogues withdrew from the Board, as did the West London and most other Reform synagogues in support of the Liberals. The Spanish and Portuguese Synagogue, the founders of the Board, and the Union of Jewish Women also withdrew their membership as a protest that arrangements for representation of minority groups on committees had not yet been realized. The Reform and Sephardi synagogues in Manchester did not withdraw – an illustration of the individualism of Manchester Jewry. All of these withdrawals took effect immediately prior to the triennial elections in May 1949. In total, including those of the AJA, thirty-eight deputies represented the synagogues and institutions that withdrew. None of the deputies who resigned was a member of the caucus and thus the caucus position was much strengthened.

Return of the Seceders
Following his election as president in 1949, Dr Abraham Cohen made it one of his first priorities to try to resolve the issues that had led to the secessions from the Board. This took up a lot of his time, dealing as he had to with very entrenched views on all sides. For example, the Orthodox Group was determined that the Liberals must not be

accepted as 'persons professing the Jewish religion' whereas the Liberals were equally determined that they should be. The communists' group saw this issue as getting back at the old Jewish establishment, and there were some who wanted to use the issue as a test of the credentials (and backbone!) of the recently appointed new chief rabbi, Dr Israel Brodie.[33] Negotiations took two years, and in 1951 the president was able to announce that an agreement had been reached with the seceding synagogues.[34]

The first issue was the relationship between the Board and other organizations, and the fear among some of the seceding group that it was much too dominated by the Zionist organization and that some deputies might even be trying to affiliate the Board with the WJC. A statement was made that the Board, as the representative organ of British Jewry, while free to cooperate with other organizations, was independent of any form of outside control and would reflect the largest possible measure of common agreement. It was also stated that no resolution for the affiliation of the Board with any other body would be considered except by a special meeting of the Board.

On the question of groups it was agreed that deputies could combine into groups with like-minded views, but there must be no improper pressure on deputies in recording their votes or in the election of Board committees.

The third issue was the lack of means of representation of minority groups on committees. It was agreed that in order to make committees more representative of the Board as a whole, the single transferable vote (STV) method of proportional representation should be adopted for a trial period. In practice this method was used for committee elections in 1952, 1955, 1958 and 1961. After reviewing the results of those elections the Board came to the view that there was no compensating advantage outweighing the cumbersome procedure and expense involved in the STV method, and it reverted to the direct 'first past the post' method. The STV method was introduced again in May 1997 for the election of honorary officers and committee (strictly speaking division) members. It was used for the election of the president in 2009, since for the first time ever there were more than two candidates.

The fourth issue, the thorniest, was the appointment of marriage secretaries for Liberal synagogues. It was emphasized that the constitution stated that the Board should consist of representatives of Congregations of Jews and, as the Liberal Jewish Synagogue was clearly one, the Board would welcome the return of their synagogues to the Board. In view of the difficulty of finding a solution to the problem of marriage secretaries for Liberal synagogues which would be recognized as honourable to both sides, it was agreed that the Board would support special parliamentary legislation as the means of achieving this purpose, which was the route adopted by the Reform synagogue in 1852. This was in reality a splitting of hairs. The distinction between 'a synagogue of persons professing the Jewish religion', as required to obtain a certificate from the chief rabbi to enable the president of the Board to appoint a marriage secretary, and a 'Congregation of Jews', as required to have representatives on the Board, is indeed a very fine one.

Appropriate changes were made to the Board's constitution, suitable legislation for marriage secretaries was enacted in 1958,[35] and the seceding synagogues and the Union of Jewish Women, but not the AJA, rejoined the Board in November 1951.[36] Thus ended an episode that, with the benefit of hindsight, does not cast a particularly favourable light on some members of the British Jewish community, but the Board could once again claim to be the only fully representative body of all British Jewry.

Censuring the President
On 29 October 1956 Israeli forces invaded Egypt. On 30 October Britain and France demanded that both Israeli and Egyptian forces agree a ceasefire and issued a twelve-hour ultimatum to both sides. Israel accepted but Egypt refused and hostilities continued. On 31 October British and French planes attacked airbases in Egypt and on 5 November began to move troops into the Suez Canal Zone at Port Said and Suez. Under pressure from the United States and threats from the Soviet Union, Britain, France and Israel agreed to a ceasefire commencing at midnight on 7 November. On 1 November, the Labour Party tabled a 'no confidence' motion in the House of Commons, reading: 'This house deplores the action of Her Majesty's Government in resorting to armed force against Egypt in clear violation of the UN Charter.' Note that there was no mention of Israel in the motion. No Jewish MP spoke during this debate but all seventeen Jewish Labour MPs (including Barnett Janner, the president of the Board) voted for the no confidence motion.

No public statements appear to have been made by Board, honorary officers or executives in the early days of the war. However, a lot must have been going on behind the scenes, as many deputies publicly expressed their objection to the way the Labour Jewish MPs, and in particular

Barnet Janner, had voted. On 15 November there was a joint meeting of
the Executive and the Eretz Israel Committees of the Board. This was
convened to consider a motion of censure against the president for his
voting in support of the Labour Party censure motion. Curiously, the
president was in the chair. He stated that, after consultation with the
chief rabbi and other leading personalities in the community, he had concluded it would not be in the best interests of the community to discuss
publicly the question of his compatibility as president and as an MP. In
other words, let us brush the matter under the table. The meeting determined otherwise. Those present decided to face up to the issue and tabled
their own motion expressing full confidence in the president.[37]

On Sunday 18 November 1956 the Board met and when the censure
matter was reached the president handed over the chair to the senior
vice-president. There followed a very lively and acrimonious debate.
Those against the president, and by inference supporting the government's policy, claimed that the British intervention was of help to Israel
and quoted in support a remark by Moshe Dayan, the Israeli chief of
staff, that the intervention had reduced Israeli casualties. The other side
claimed that this remark had been taken out of context and Moshe
Dayan had also stated that Israel would have completed her action on
schedule without the Anglo-French intervention. Furthermore, the
British action might well be to Israel's disadvantage in the long term.
Barnett Janner was permitted to make a personal statement. His main
points were that the issues of Israel and the actions of the British government were distinct from each other; that Israel could not be regarded
as an aggressor; that the British government had failed to establish legal
grounds for its use of force; and that the vote of no confidence in the
House of Commons did not deal with the Israel situation at all. This
speech was heavily applauded and clearly swung the meeting. In the
event the motion of confidence in the president was passed without
opposition, with an added proviso that the resolution was not to be
taken as an expression of opinion of the Board either in favour of or in
opposition to action taken by the government.[38]

The Bicentenary
As the Board approached its bicentenary in 1960, the anticipated
celebrations were marred somewhat by a leader in the *JC* in September
1959. It suggested the Board wasted too much time on gestures to
Israel and debating foreign issues on which it no longer could have any
influence. Furthermore, it lacked the machinery to enforce decisions it

took on home issues, relying on the power of persuasion which was somewhat lacking. The article concluded that 'thus far the Board has failed to make a satisfactory adjustment to the changed conditions of the mid-twentieth century'.[39] It must have been some relief when at the celebration banquet on 4 April 1960 the Duke of Edinburgh included the following passage in his speech: 'Throughout history the fate of minorities has always been uncertain, but in the Board of Deputies of British Jews the Jewish community has had a fearless and devoted protector, and the community's present standing in the British Isles is largely due to the Board's unremitting efforts.'[40]

2. HOME ISSUES

Evacuation

The war led to evacuation from the major cities of Britain, mainly children on their own (both those with parents who remained in the cities and refugee children) but also whole families, sometimes without husbands who were serving in the armed forces. It became apparent that there were many organizations and individuals prepared to help the Jewish refugees in different ways and what was needed was some sort of centralized coordination. This was rapidly appreciated by the Board and on 5 November 1939 it called a conference of representatives of organizations engaged in aiding evacuated persons. This conference established a Central Jewish Committee for Problems of Evacuation under the chairmanship of A.G. Brotman, the secretary of the Board, to coordinate the different organizations involved.[41] There were few, if any, Jews living in the reception areas where evacuees were sent and the committee was faced with the problem of ensuring that communal life was properly organized in these areas. This included finding and providing facilities for religious worship, organizing the religious education of children, finding hostels for children, hiring halls for religious and educational purpose, ensuring that kosher food was available and – if appropriate – kosher canteens, social and welfare work and trying to maintain good relations between evacuees and the resident population. The Central Committee also had to provide ministers and other suitable workers in the reception areas. With the intensification of air raids (the Blitz) their work expanded to coordinate the various forms of immediate help that the different Jewish organizations were best in a position to give.

Early in 1940 the government established a scheme for evacuating children to Canada, other Dominions and the United States. The Board contacted Jewish organizations in all the countries concerned and arranged with them for all Jewish children to be housed in Jewish homes. The Board established a committee to deal with all such Jewish refugees and this committee was recognized by the government.

The increase in evacuation because of the Blitz, particularly of whole families in contrast to the earlier phase which was mainly children on their own, led to a great extension of the work required in the reception areas and funds were needed to enable that work to be undertaken. Accordingly, at the end of 1940, the Board launched an appeal to provide the essential services to maintain organized communal life in the reception areas.[42] It was agreed that the Executive Committee would allocate the funds based on recommendations from the Central Committee. The following extract from the 1940 report of the Board gives a picture of what was involved:

> While the Jewish evacuees found in their new billets considerable sympathy from their hosts, there were also factors present which were likely to cause friction; for there was not only the difference of environment, but also differences associated with upbringing and habits and ways of living.
>
> Experience derived from the evacuation in the previous year – which was largely of children – showed that these possible causes of friction could be removed or avoided by the appointment of tactful persons who could not only explain the hosts to the guests and vice versa, but who could see that the Jewish evacuees should as soon as possible get back to some semblance of their former communal life, and have as far as possible provision for religious worship and for the religious teaching of their children, and facilities for obtaining Kosher food and for social activities.
>
> The Central Committee for Problems of Evacuation, therefore, extended its work considerably, and appointed a number of liaison officers, Ministers, and qualified laymen and women in the reception areas. The aim of these workers was to help each individual community to organise itself at the earliest possible moment.[43]

Regrettably, in 1942 it became necessary to reorganize a lot of work in the reception areas so that it could be carried out by voluntary workers. This was because the Central Committee had to terminate the employment of a number of paid employees due to lack of funds. On the other hand, a number of the new communities established by evacuees had become self-sufficient. In addition, the secretary of the Board and other employees of the Board took on extra work to assist the reception areas. From 1943 the need for providing the essential services reduced with the return home of many evacuees. Many left London again in 1944 with the onset of the attacks by flying bombs but by then most of the required infrastructure was in place and the new communities as well as many provincial ones were able to meet the situation very satisfactorily. The Central Committee wound up its activities in March 1945.

What this indicates is that an organization such as the Board can play a significant role in the social organization of the community, in addition to its lobbying and similar activities.

Internment[44]

The outbreak of war created a problem for Jewish refugees in Britain who came from Germany or one of its allies and became technically 'enemy' aliens. Special tribunals were set up which divided these aliens into three classes – (A) interned, (B) free but subject to certain restrictions, and (C) refugees from Nazi oppression who were treated as friendly aliens and were free without special restrictions. There were very few Jews in class (A) but some in class (B) whom it was hoped would be reclassified as (C). The majority of Jewish refugees were in class (C). However, following the fall of France in May 1940 the policy was changed to internment of all 'enemy' aliens. As a result most Jewish male refugees were interned as well as most of the women in category (B). The Executive Committee determined that the Board's policy would be that, subject to the paramount considerations of the country's security, all those interned should be released whose release would involve no danger to the country.[45] All actions of the Board would be in concurrence with that principle and it made this clear to the government and its advisory committees on internment matters. At the same time the Board concerned itself with the conditions in the internment camps and the morale of those interned, many of whom were close to panic. The Board tried to ensure that those interned were provided with suitable kosher food, full arrangements for Passover observance and the holding of regular religious services, which were normally organized by the internees themselves.

The government established a number of committees to deal with problems associated with internment and the Board asked, in view of the large number of Jews among the internees, that one or two Jewish refugees with special knowledge of the problems and with impeccable credentials should be co-opted on to two of these committees. Despite the chairmen of both committees being in favour of the proposal, it was turned down by the government.[46] One of the two committees was called the Asquith Committee, from the name of its chairman, Mr Justice Asquith. Its responsibility was to examine the whole policy, suggest changes and examine all cases referred to it by the home secretary. By the end of 1940, as a result of recommendations from the Asquith Committee, the government had issued three White Papers that listed categories of persons that could be released. These related essentially to the nature of the internee's occupation, including those with academic distinction and those who had made an outstanding contribution to art, science, learning or letters.[47] Although the Board considered these categories too limited and the principle of selection by category unsatisfactory, in that the ordinary, perfectly reliable person not in any of the selected categories could not obtain release, nonetheless a large number of Jews were released.

The other committee where the Board tried for representation was the Lytton Council of Aliens, named after its chairman, Lord Lytton, a former governor of Bengal. This committee was concerned with welfare inside the camps. The Board made many recommendations to this committee regarding the Jewish internees and most were accepted. The Board's annual report for 1940 remarked that by the end of 1940 there had been great improvements in camp conditions. On the other hand, the Board tended to be defensive when it came to its advice to German refugees. In a circular to German refugees issued in May 1940 the Board advised them not to speak German in public, not to push in queues and not to tell Englishmen that things were done better in Germany. What might have stimulated this circular, which was similar to one issued in January 1939 by the Central Committee for Jewish Refugees, was a letter dated 14 May 1940 from Gordon Liverman, the chairman of the Defence Committee, to A.G. Brotman, the secretary of the Board, expressing concern at the thoughtless behaviour of refugees in the areas where they concentrated such as Hampstead and Golders Green.[48] By the end of 1943 virtually all Jews who had been interned had been released.

Antisemitism
Despite knowledge of what was happening to the Jews in Europe and the internment in Britain of the leading fascists and their sympathizers,

antisemitism persisted in Britain throughout the war.[49] Following the outbreak of war, the Defence Committee had to reorientate and curtail its work, although it noted that antisemitic propaganda was still being quietly propagated. Open-air meetings were suspended in May 1940 as soon as the government took action to prevent antisemitic meetings and intern most of the leading fascists. As the news concerning the fate of the Jews in Europe became known during 1942, there was much sympathy from all sections of the non-Jewish population as well as demands on the government to try to save the threatened Jewish population in Europe. In contrast, though, there was an increase in antisemitism, which the Board tried to combat in various ways, in particular by supplying material for lectures and articles as well as providing speakers and publishing pamphlets. Allegations were made that Jews were responsible for many commercial malpractices and breaches of wartime regulations, and the Board approved a resolution that it would assist the authorities in dealing with those guilty of such malpractices.[50] It decided to go even further and on 1 November 1943 a conference was arranged by the Board and attended by over a hundred leaders of synagogues. This conference resolved that persons failing to maintain the highest standards of conduct in social and business relationships should be barred from being elected to any communal office, and that all ministers and honorary officers of congregations should not attend functions such as weddings or bar-mitzvahs which were ostentatious, extravagant or out of keeping with the austerity of the present times.[51] It is difficult to judge the effectiveness of this, particularly regarding election to office and non-attendance at ostentatious functions, but issues of the *JC* were peppered with announcements like 'austerity lunch' or 'shiur followed by austerity kiddush'.

The Board had become so concerned at the increase in anti-semitism, particularly in the media,[52] that it established a subcommittee in October 1943 to consider whether it should request legislation making defamatory statements against the community a punishable offence. The subcommittee reported in May 1944 that no action should be taken. This was accepted by the Executive Committee but rejected by the Board as a whole, and it was agreed to establish a Standing Committee on Communal Libel to keep the question of legislation under review and to contact other interested bodies in this area.[53] This Standing Committee issued a report to the Board in July 1945. The majority of its members recommended that criminal law should be amended, and defamation and similar statements should become a punishable offence. A minority added that in their view civil law should also be amended to include libel of communities. The Board accepted the majority view.[54] Before action could be taken the government set up a committee, known as the Porter Committee, to consider the issue of community libel. The Board made written and oral representations to this committee dealing with the position of the Jewish community vis-à-vis antisemitic and fascist propaganda. The Board's view was that the existing law of seditious libel was an inadequate safeguard. The Porter Committee reported in 1948 and rejected any change in the libel laws. It agreed that the Jewish community had a legitimate grievance, but it maintained that the existing law was sufficient to afford protection.[55] The Board did not accept this view and decided to continue pressing its case for a change in the libel laws. In 1952 the Board was particularly disappointed when the Anti-Defamation Act, promoted by Harold Lever, MP, did not include provision for the protection of communities against libel and slander, despite strong efforts by the Board to have suitable protective clauses incorporated in it. Concern in this area increased with the proliferation of antisemitic publications of all sorts, most of which fortunately had a short lifespan.

One of the ways in which the Defence Committee operated was to encourage the establishment of District Committees in provincial towns and suburbs of London. In 1944 a Metropolitan Area Committee was established to coordinate the work of the London suburban committees and a Provincial Liaison Committee established as a liaison with the Provincial Defence Committees. There was a subtle but important difference between the provincial and London suburban committees. The provincial committees were generally a subcommittee of the Representative Council in towns where such a council operated or independent committees in other towns. The suburban London committees were subcommittees of the Board's Defence Committee. A lesson had clearly been learnt from the 1930s where there had been too much centralization and not enough delegation; now there were a large number of separate committees with the Board acting only as a coordinator. At the same time the Defence Committee increased its staff, and the activities of the Central Lecture Committee were expanded and it appointed an organizer in addition to its secretary. It also started recruiting observers, whose task it was to observe any local antisemitic activity and report this to the appropriate committee. The Board was gearing up for what it foresaw as the old fascist parties resuming their activities.[56]

It did not have long to wait. The end of the war in 1945 saw the re-emergence of the fascist parties and other antisemitic groups. Sir Oswald Mosley, the leader of the British Union of Fascists, later the Union Movement, announced, on his release from internment and house arrest, that he had not changed his political views, and antisemitic activities resumed. These activities started with antisemitic publications, but public meetings soon followed. In particular, the BUF began to hold regular open-air meetings in areas where it had operated before the war, such as Bethnal Green and Ridley Road, Dalston. The Board countered these by holding its own meetings in the East End and Hyde Park in liaison with AJEX.[57] The speakers at these meetings concentrated on attacking the fascist parties and their policies. The Board's policy remained as it had been in the 1930s to encourage Jews to stay away from the fascist meetings. The Board was totally opposed to the use of violence, and it took the position that if the agitators provoked hostility leading to physical confrontation, it was the responsibility of the authorities to deal with the situation.[58]

Not all in the community were content with this seemingly passive approach. In March 1946 the '43 Group' was established by forty-three Jewish ex-service men and women who were present at a meeting called to consider how to counteract the rise of new fascist groups in a more dynamic way than the Board.[59] In his book on the 43 Group, Morris Beckman mentions that in February 1946 there were 'fourteen identifiable fascist groups operating on the streets and inside schools and halls in London'.[60] The 43 Group was a very proactive organization, attacking fascists, breaking up meetings, destroying stocks of antisemitic books and infiltrating the fascist movement. It was effective and broke up in 1950 when it considered its work completed. The Board did not support it, indeed it deplored its activities and resented its claim to represent communal opinion.[61]

In 1946 and 1947 the problems of Palestine and the terrorist occurrences there aggravated antisemitism in Britain and there were many disturbances including rioting and looting in a number of provincial cities. The advantage of developing local Defence Committees, who were on the spot immediately, was clearly apparent. Overall the Board's approach to combating antisemitism remained a mixture of holding open-air meetings, organizing lectures (more than 500 were delivered to more than 200 non-Jewish organizations alone in 1947) and training speakers, and preparing and distributing booklets, pamphlets and leaflets. Close contact was maintained with the appropriate authorities and meetings were held with the home secretary and others from time to time.[62]

In 1949 the BUF started on a campaign of violent antisemitic agitation and many of its meetings were followed by marches leading to disorder and assaults on Jews. The Defence Committee urged the Home Office to ban such processions under the Public Order Act and to implement Section 5 of that Act regarding provocative statements. This was resisted by the authorities at first, but later some action was taken – political processions were banned, it was accepted that under Section 5 it was not necessary for Jews to be present at a meeting or a disturbance to be created for an offence to be committed, and additional police protection was afforded in the areas where there was most violence. The Board was able to claim some credit for this. For example, when the issue was debated in the House of Commons on 7 December 1949, mention was made of the helpful information the Home Office had received from the Board. The advice of the Board to the Jewish community remained to stay away from fascist meetings, but if they did attend not to give publicity to the meetings by heckling. The Board claimed that this had produced excellent results with a significant reduction from 1950 onwards in the number of such meetings and the number attending. The Board's 1951 report mentioned Mosley's move to Ireland, and although it attributed this to a significant decline in the support for the Union Movement in Britain it did not claim credit for it.[63] The Board did, however, claim credit for foiling an attempt in 1952 by the fascists to make the Stamford Hill area a second 'Ridley Road'. The president wrote to all synagogues in the area warning Jews against attending fascist meetings and arranged for AJEX to hold a series of meetings to explain the value of ignoring fascist meetings.[64] The Union Movement held a few meetings, but when these failed to raise much support it withdrew.

All remained relatively quiet on the antisemitic front for a few years with the attention of the fascists being diverted towards the immigration of black people leading to race riots in 1958. The Board came out with a forthright statement condemning these disturbances.[65] However, the quietness on the antisemitic front did not last, and in 1959/60 there was a spate of swastika and other antisemitic daubings on Jewish communal buildings and other properties associated with Jews. This was combined with threatening telephone calls and messages to prominent members of the community. It was estimated that by the time the daubings died down there had been 160 different incidents in about sixty different localities. A delegation from the Board discussed the matter with the home secretary, who assured them that the police would make strenuous enquiries and try to convict any persons found to be involved. These inquiries indicated that those responsible were mainly youngsters, that the spread was imitative, and those involved had no connection with antisemitic organizations. Much more serious was the formation of the British National Party (BNP) in 1960 with an avowed antisemitic policy. The BNP organized meetings and promoted anti-semitic literature. Some of its members were convicted of insulting behaviour at the Lord Mayor's Show when they had protested against the election of a Jewish Lord Mayor.

In 1962 the BNP split and its leader, Colin Jordan, formed the National Socialist Movement, which decided to flex its antisemitic muscles. It announced a mass rally in Trafalgar Square with the slogan: 'Free Britain from Jewish Control'. A delegation from the Board met with the Metropolitan police and pointed out that although the Board always advised the community to stay away from such meetings, the provocative slogan might make such advice ineffective. The police thought that there would be no trouble but that if any did result they could deal with it. They were wrong. There was considerable disorder, the meeting was brought to a halt on three occasions and had to be stopped by the police after two hours. There were many arrests, including a few Jews, and Jordan and his deputy were charged under Section 5 of the Public Order Act. The home secretary subsequently announced that the government felt that its existing powers were sufficient. The Board was less sanguine and seems to have been right. Further meetings were held by different fascist organizations in London and elsewhere and they all led to disorder. The president of the Board and the chief rabbi met with the home secretary, who promised to review the existing legislation, but despite this promise and a number of amend-ments to the current law proposed by some MPs no changes reached the statute book.

It is important to put this antisemitic activity in its context. The fascist parties did not engender any support from the public at large. Indeed the public reaction, judging by editorials and letters to news-papers and statement from many important non-Jewish organisations, was particularly hostile to the antisemites and supported the Board in demanding effective legislation.[66]

A Public Order Bill was published early in 1963 but it created no new offences, as had been demanded by the Board and many MPs, although it increased the penalties for breaches of the existing Acts. The Board issued a detailed critique of this bill. It did not consider that the bill would be effective, and was disappointed that incitement to racial hatred was not to be made an offence. The Board also wanted much wider coverage of the offence of incitement to include not only public order but also to include printed matter.[67] Despite support for the Board's views from all sides in Parliament, the bill was enacted substantially unchanged. Following its success in the 1964 general election, the Labour Party included in the Queen's Speech its intention to take action against racial discrimination. The Board welcomed this and hoped that the promised legislation would include provisions to cover incitement to contempt and hatred of persons on the ground of their colour, race and religion.[68]

Antisemitism of a different nature emerged at the end of November 1963. Lord Mancroft was forced to resign as a director of the Advisory Board of the Norwich Union Insurance Society, as a result of pressure from the Arab Boycott Committee. Essentially this committee had the object of organizing a boycott of exports from Israel and of companies with business in Israel, but it had spread its tentacles wider. This issue was immediately taken up by the Board, first by a letter to the president of the Norwich Union, and subsequently by a meeting between the officers of the Board and the directors of Norwich Union. As a consequence the Norwich Union invited Lord Mancroft to return. He refused. It is clear from the Norwich Union statements that the Board had some influence on its decision, but no doubt it was also influenced by the outcry in the media. The Board's report on the incident ascribes to the Norwich Union a miscalculation of the probable commercial advantage and a misjudgement of public reaction rather than racial prejudice.[69]

Trades Advisory Council

In 1938 an ad hoc committee known as the Trades Advisory Council (TAC) was set up to advise the Defence Committee on trade practices and related matters. It met infrequently, but in 1940 it was reconstituted as a semi-autonomous body separate from the Board and with its own constitution, honorary officers, secretariat and an executive committee comprising mainly leading Jewish businessmen. The report recommending this change in structure gives only one reason – that the TAC would be more effective.[70] However, in order to attract leading businessmen to the TAC executive committee it was probably necessary that it should be at least semi-autonomous rather than a committee of the Board. The membership of the TAC encompassed Jewish traders, industrialists and professional men. Its aim was to fight antisemitism arising out of trade, commerce and industry. It concerned itself particularly with removing the causes of friction between Jewish and non-Jewish businesses, and also with relations between employer and employees. It was involved with discrimination against Jews by employers, and complaints involving Jews and non-Jews, including misrepresentation in trade advertisements and defamatory statements in newspapers.[71]

The Board did not cut the umbilical cord and the TAC remained affiliated to it. The Board agreed to make a regular grant to the TAC, two members of the TAC were co-opted on to the Defence Committee and the Defence Committee was represented on the Council and Executive Committee of the TAC. From time to time the relationship between the Board and the TAC became a little fraught. This was particularly so in 1942 when the Board became concerned at some of the activities of the TAC which had not been reported to it. In particular, the TAC had been in negotiations with the Citizens' Advice Bureau and the National Council of Social Affairs with a view to arranging co-ordination with regard to Jewish trade issues. Many deputies thought that this was stepping on matters that were the Board's preserve.[72] The TAC was obliged to affirm the authority of the Board on all matters of policy, including trade policy, and it was agreed that all publicity connected with the TAC should in future be made by the Board. The number of co-opted representatives of the TAC on the Defence Committee was increased to four, and six representatives of the Board were appointed to the Executive Committee of the TAC.[73]

Thereafter all seemed to be working well, as exemplified by the comment in the 1946 annual report of the Board that 'Harmonious and close relations between the Defence Committee and the TAC continue. Both organizations are in constant touch and exchange information as well as pass on to each other cases which call for action in their respective fields.'[74] However, in 1951 the affairs of the TAC were again considered by the Board as the result of agitation and rumours reflecting on the TAC administration, which followed the resignation of Alec Nathan from its chairmanship. The rumours included financial mismanagement and the suggestion that there was undue left-wing political influence on the TAC. The political issue arose because there were at least two communists on the TAC executive committee and the general secretary,

Maurice Orbach, was a left-wing Labour MP. This was at the height of the Cold War and at a time when McCarthyism was rampant in the United States. The Board decided to set up an inquiry to survey and report on the circumstances leading to the resignation of the chairman, to investigate the allegation of undue political influence and generally to examine the work and practice of the TAC.[75] The committee of inquiry was established with Dr Cohen, the president, as chairman and Councillor M.P. Greengross, Arnold Levy and Sidney Silverman, MP, as members. Midway through its investigations Arnold Levy resigned because the rest of the committee would not agree to his request that a financial investigation should be conducted by an independent firm of accountants. The committee had held meetings with the auditors and had advice in this area from three expert witnesses, and the majority on the committee had concluded there was no evidence of any financial irregularities, but Arnold Levy considered there was a need to investigate further.[76] As a result four reports were eventually submitted to the Board: the report of the committee, observations from Arnold Levy on that report, comments from the rest of the committee on Arnold Levy's observations and, finally, Arnold Levy's comments on the committee's comments on his observations.[77]

At about the same time as the Committee of Inquiry was established, the Law, Parliamentary and General Purposes Committee set up a subcommittee to enquire into the exact status of the TAC and its relationship with the Board and to ascertain to what extent the Board was responsible for the functioning of the TAC and for its policy. It also submitted a report to the Board and in addition there was an addendum from Harry Samuels, a member of the subcommittee.

Thus in December 1951 the Board had to consider six documents on the TAC – four from the inquiry and two from the Law, Parliamentary and General Purposes Committee. The Committee of Inquiry considered that Alec Nathan, the national chairman of the TAC, had resigned because of difficulties and disagreements between himself and the secretariat and there was nothing untoward. It blamed the chairman, whereas Arnold Levy put the blame on the secretariat. Although two members of the Executive Committee of the TAC were avowed communists, there was no evidence of any attempt to influence the TAC in the interests of communism. Arnold Levy accepted this but was concerned that the General Secretary of the TAC was a Labour Party MP, and there was evidence that he only recruited for the office supporters of the Labour Party. The committee and Arnold Levy agreed that the TAC was doing an excellent job, but should stick to its remit, as it often went beyond it. The report from the Law, Parliamentary and General Purposes Committee indicated that there had been no agreed change in the relationship between the TAC and the Board, even though the rights of the Board to control the policy of the TAC on matters outside its particular province had to an extent been ignored for some time. This gives us a clue as to one of the reasons why the Board was getting so agitated – that is, that the TAC must have been stepping on matters that the Board considered its own.

The upshot was a series of recommendations to the TAC that it was asked to accept and include in a revised constitution. These were: that the TAC was a non-political body under the ultimate control of the Board, that the TAC should confine its tasks to trade matters, and that the Board should continue to have the right to appoint its representatives on the Finance and General Purposes Committee of the TAC, which would present annual accounts to the Board. Furthermore, it agreed Harry Samuels's addendum which expressed the right of the Board to make such enquiries as it thought fit into the administration and expenditure of the TAC. After some very difficult negotiations the TAC accepted the Board's proposals and amended its constitution accordingly.[78]

Relationships remained good until 1957 when the TAC changed its constitution without any prior notification or discussion with the Board. The Board was quite aghast at this and acrimonious discussions were held with the TAC. The upshot was that an agreement was reached confirming the principle that, although the TAC was autonomous, it accepted the supervision of and jurisdiction of the Board in the sphere of general policy. Furthermore, any change in its constitution must not be effected without the joint agreement between the Board and the TAC, provided that the approval of the former would not be unreasonably withheld.[79] Clearly the parent did not want to let go of control of its offspring and the child wanted complete independence even to the extent of treading on the parent's preserves. In 1992 the TAC was effectively dissolved and its work transferred back to the Board.

Education

At the beginning of 1944 the Board turned its attention towards education. What stimulated this was the Education Bill then going through Parliament. Two provisions of this bill were seen as giving enhanced opportunities for religious education. One enabled religious denominations to establish and maintain day schools under conditions more favourable than hitherto, and with generous state aid. Israel Finestein has commented that this provision fostered the fashionability of such education and offered the Jewish community significant tangible support for the extension of its schools systems.[80] Under another provision, children in non-denominational state maintained schools would be permitted to attend classes for religious instruction in their religion during the school day, even if this meant withdrawing from other classes. These provisions applied to both primary and secondary schools. The importance of this bill was such that in January 1944 the Board invited R.A. Butler, the president of the Board of Education and a cabinet minister, to address it on the implications of the proposed legislation. In the course of his speech he remarked: 'never has there been such a time in the history of the Jews, never such a diaspora, and never such suffering in their history. Therefore it is more than ever important that the Jews should concentrate their energies on bringing up their children and young people in the tradition of Hebraism.'[81]

As a consequence of the bill, the Board decided to re-establish an Education Committee in May 1944. The committee was to act as a liaison between the Board and Jewish educational bodies in the community but not to be concerned with the conduct and administration of Jewish religious education itself,[82] a sort of coordinating role. Subsequently the committee extended the scope of its work by including a responsibility to assist in furthering the highest standards of Jewish education. The committee also assumed the responsibility for trying to ensure special arrangements for Jewish students when examinations were due to be held on a Saturday or Jewish festivals. Another issue with which it concerned itself was trying to resolve difficulties experienced by some Jewish children being required to attend Christian services and lessons and obtaining permission to be absent from school on Saturdays and Jewish festivals. This latter issue sometimes involved Jewish teachers as well. The Board was generally successful in these areas but there were difficulties with some schools, particularly those that are termed nowadays as 'faith schools'. Some schools had fixed quotas for the number of Jewish children. The Board studied this issue and concluded that in general this was not deliberate anti-Jewish discrimination but merely a desire on the part of governors of Christian faith schools to maintain the Christian tradition of their school.

One of the first acts of the committee was to conduct a survey of all the organizations concerned with Jewish religious education encompassing the Orthodox, Reform and Liberal synagogues. The object was to establish the current situation of Jewish education in Britain, and thus the committee would be able to examine ways in which the Board could be of assistance in securing necessary funds and encouraging a greater number of children to participate. This latter point was particularly important since a survey in 1943 had indicated that only 40 per cent of Jewish children of elementary school age were receiving any formal Jewish education, albeit that the survey had been conducted during the war and many children were, as a result, receiving private tuition. Unfortunately, the results of the survey were not as comprehensive as had been hoped and the report recommended that the committee engage an expert educationalist and a statistician to carry out a more thorough survey, but this could not be undertaken for financial reasons.

In 1945, the chief rabbi convened a conference on the future organization of Jewish religious education. The Board representatives at that conference tried unsuccessfully to persuade all those present to agree that on issues involving the government and other authorities, the bodies concerned with Jewish education should consult together and present a united front. The conference agreed that Jewish religious education in Britain should be organised by the creation of two bodies – a London Board for Jewish Religious Education and a Central Council for the rest of the country. The Board was to be represented on both bodies, but the Strictly Orthodox communities declined to participate and the Reform and Liberal communities were excluded from both bodies. It is interesting to note that in 1948 the Board attempted to arrange a conference of all bodies associated with Jewish education for promoting and encouraging such education, but the London Board, the Central Council and the Orthodox Board declined to participate. As a result the conference was cancelled and instead the Board proposed a Jewish Education Week. This was cancelled on the advice of the chief rabbi, as he considered that it would be difficult for the Board to intervene in matters of Jewish religious education due to the vast denominational differences within the community.[83] It seems that the message had got through to the Board, because in 1952 it called a meeting concerning prayers and religious instruction in schools and limited attendance at that meeting to representatives of the London Board of Jewish Religious Education, the Central Council for Jewish Religious Education and the Board of Orthodox Jewish Education, excluding the Reform and Liberal bodies. The issues were ones with which these latter communities must have been concerned and which were in a sense non-controversial, and it is surprising that there does not seem to have been any protest from these bodies, maybe because at that time they had just rejoined the Board.

Jewish Book Week

On 2 December 1948, Lord Justice Cohen, the president of the Jewish Historical Society, convened a conference under the auspices of that society. The object of the conference was to consider how best to encourage the revival of interest in Jewish books. Those present at the meeting were representatives of Jewish institutions interested in cultural matters, including the Board of Deputies. Jacques Cohen, the chairman of the Central Jewish Lecture Committee of the Board, informed those present that the Board was in the process of organizing a 'Jewish Book Exhibition' (subsequently that exhibition was referred to in minutes of the Board and in the *JC* as Jewish Book Week). The conference decided to establish a Jewish Book Council with the purpose of encouraging the revival and establishment of Jewish libraries by synagogues and other institutions and to advise in the selection of Jewish books by municipal and other non-Jewish public libraries. In June 1949, the Jewish Book Council elected an Executive Committee with Dr George Webber, a member of the Executive Committee of the Board, as its chairman.[84]

Jewish Book Week opened on 17 October 1949 with Dr Abraham Cohen, the president of the Board, in the chair; Lord Justice Cohen, the immediate past president of the Jewish Historical Society of England, delivered the opening speech. In that speech he paid tribute to the late Jacques Cohen (who had recently died) and who had been the inspiration behind that Jewish Book Week.[85] Prior to the Second World War, there had been a Jewish Book Week in Glasgow in 1937 and in Manchester in 1938, both organized by Women's lodges of the B'nei B'rith. Thus, one cannot attribute to the Board the organization of the first Jewish Book Week in Britain, but it was responsible for its postwar revival.

Although the report to the Board on Jewish Book Week concluded that 'It is hoped that it will be the forerunner of annual functions of this kind and on a scale commensurate with the importance of the subject',[86] the Board did not arrange another book week. The mantle seems to have been passed by the Board to the Jewish Book Council. George Webber, the chairman of the Jewish Book Council, was a very close friend of Jacques Cohen and it is likely that they had discussed a continuation of Jewish Book Week. The first Jewish Book Week under the auspices of the Jewish Book Council was held in November 1952. It has continued as an annual event ever since and has become one of the most important cultural events in the British Jewish calendar.

Shechita

In 1947, the Board decided to re-constitute its Shechita Committee as the issue of banning *shechita* had arisen in Australia and Rhodesia (now Zimbabwe) and there were concerns that the adverse press campaign in these countries might spread to Britain.[87] This was a wise decision as in 1948 there were attacks on *shechita* in a number of local newspapers, a number of Animal Humane Societies started a campaign against *shechita* through leaflets and all of this culminated in questions being asked about *shechita* in the House of Commons and an anti-*shechita* motion being debated in the House of Lords. The Board was very active in refuting all of these attacks and reissued a leaflet explaining the Jewish case. It also convened two conferences on the subject, and the results were somewhat disquieting. The government had made it clear that it would be issuing an order that *shechita* was permissible provided an approved casting apparatus was used. At the conferences it emerged that a number of communities were carrying out *shechita* without the use of a casting pen; this was a pen into which the animal was led and then was rotated for the purpose of slaughter. Arrangements were made with the Ministry of Food to distribute meat from centres which carried out *shechita* with a pen to neighbouring communities who did not have a pen and were unable, for one reason or another, to install one.[88]

The agitation against *shechita* itself continued into 1949, particularly by the National Council of Justice to Animals and the Scottish Society for the Prevention of Cruelty to Animals, resulting in the question being raised in a large number of borough councils throughout Britain. The Board was very active in refuting the allegations and revised pamphlets were printed and distributed very widely.[89] The government took a lot of heat out of the debate by announcing that from 1 January 1950 *shechita* would be prohibited except where an approved casting pen was used. The Board, together with the London Shechita Board, was involved in the design of an improved casting pen and in finding suitable manufacturers. Unfortunately, the special versions of the new machines for the smaller communities were not installed by 1 January 1950, and those communities, with the help of the Board, had to make special arrangements for the supply of kosher meat in the interim.[90]

Despite this, agitation against *shechita* continued and the Board had to be alert and active in refuting it. There was an important development later in 1950 that had long been advocated by the Board. A National Council of Shechita Bodies was established with overall responsibility for assisting all the local *shechita* organizations in all areas relating to *shechita*, and the Board's activities in this area became limited to defending the right to practise *shechita* and to counter any attacks against its continuance whether in the press, in Parliament or elsewhere.[91]

3A. THE HOLOCAUST AND THE CREATION OF THE STATE OF ISRAEL

The two most important matters affecting World Jewry since the establishment of the Board, namely the Holocaust and the creation of the State of Israel, occurred in the early years covered by this chapter. The Board, however, was in the intolerable position of being unable to take any real action regarding the Holocaust and in a very difficult and non-influential position concerning the policy of the British government with regard to Palestine.

The Holocaust
In January 1942, the Board declared that the policy of the Nazis with regard to Jews was one of ruthless extermination.[92] It had not given the Nazis the benefit of the doubt prior to this, but had been hesitant about confirming it. The Board realized that there was nothing it could do to stop the slaughter as such, but it could alert public opinion to what was going on in the rather vain hope that this might deter the Nazis, particularly with threats of war crime indictments when the war was over. The Board asked the government to use all that was in its power to assist rescue and held a series of meetings with ministers and officials suggesting ways and means of achieving rescue and finding asylum for those rescued or who had escaped.[93] On 27 October 1942 the Board organized a public protest meeting at the Albert Hall, with the archbishop of Canterbury in the chair, at which the continuing atrocities against the Jews by the Nazis was condemned. In November 1942 the Board set up a Consultative Committee consisting of representatives of the Jewish Agency, the British Section of the WJC, and the Agudas Israel, as well as the chief rabbi and Jewish members of the Polish and Czech governments in exile in London. The object was to

coordinate the activities of the various Jewish organizations in Britain involved with the Holocaust. It met frequently, but seems to have achieved little except for bickering between the different member organizations.[94] Due to this infighting it lasted only six months. The fact that there was no coordination in the memoranda and deputations to the government by different Jewish organizations in Britain probably made no difference one way or the other, but no doubt created a bad impression in government circles.[95]

A special meeting of the Board was held on 9 December 1942, which culminated in the passing of a resolution of sympathy to all the victims and calling on all governments to give asylum to all who manage to escape. Just over a week later Anthony Eden, the foreign secretary, announced in the House of Commons that the government had received irrefutable evidence of the mass slaughter of Jews by the Nazis in occupied East Europe. The House rose in sympathy and stood in silence, a demonstration unparalleled in the history of the House of Commons.[96] Two weeks later on 31 December 1942, Eden chaired the first meeting of a cabinet committee to consider arrangements for new Jewish refugees, at which the home secretary, Herbert Morrison, stated that he could not agree to the admission of more than 1,000 to 2,000 refugees to Britain.[97]

The year 1943 proved disappointing for the Board with regard to all the proposals and pressures on the government to try to assist in the escape of Jews and facilitate shelter in neutral and other countries for Jews who escaped or were rescued. The government, whilst sympathetic, continually stated its view that whilst attempts would be made to aid escape, the only real solution was victory of the allies. An Anglo-American conference was due to be held in Bermuda on the question of how to deal with Jewish refugees who had managed to escape, and the Board requested that there should be a Jewish member of the British delegation, but this was refused.[98] The conference was held in private and no organizations were admitted. The Board had submitted a comprehensive memorandum of proposals to the government in advance of the conference, but there was no indication in the rather brief and bland report on the conference whether these had been considered. The proposals of the conference were, in fact, kept highly confidential,[99] possibly because the delegates were ashamed of them. In July 1943, the Board passed a resolution expressing concern and disappointment at the outcome of the Bermuda conference.[100] That was probably all that it could do since it had neither power nor influence – nor, it would seem, ideas that were compatible with the government's war policy. The Board, however, had remained protective of its position and continued to oppose those who seemed to interfere with what it saw as its exclusive right to raise matters with the government. In January 1944 Rabbi Dr Solomon Schonfeld, the presiding rabbi of the Union of Orthodox Hebrew Congregations, who had been successful in rescuing hundreds of Jews from Europe, persuaded a very large group of MPs and members of the House of Lords, in particular the archbishop of Canterbury, to support a motion calling upon the government to find temporary refuge in Britain or in territories under its control for Jews who managed to escape. It would appear that the motion was never passed, because it was sabotaged by a campaign led by the Board. The Board's action was defended by Brodetsky on the grounds that 'the intervention of an unauthorised individual, however well intentioned, in a situation of this sort, naturally brings confusion and may have damaging effects'.[101]

On the one hand, 1944 proved better in one respect, in that much of the territory occupied by the Nazis was liberated but, on the other hand, the full scale and horror of the atrocities perpetrated against the Jews of Europe was revealed. The Board, whilst still active in trying to facilitate rescue for the Jews remaining under Nazi control, began to concentrate on relief for the survivors and on putting pressure on the British government to enable those who wished to go to Palestine to be admitted there. As the war drew to a close in 1945 the Board published two booklets – *The Jews in Europe: Their Martyrdom and Future* and *The Jews in Europe – Their Post-War Situation*. These were part of a PR effort to explain the situation and what had happened to the world at large, and obtain help in the massive relief work that was now needed.

A number of Jewish historians have criticized the Anglo-Jewish leadership in general and the Board in particular for doing little to save the Jews of Europe during the Second World War.[102] However vigorous these criticisms might seem, it is important to stress, as has Pamela Shatzkes, that the critics have never explained what else the Board could have done, other than perhaps lobbying the government with greater skill and pressure, given that the government consistently refused to divert any resources from its main and only aim of the fastest possible victory.[103] Furthermore, this distracting pressure from the Anglo-Jewish leadership must have been an irritant to the government. For example, Bernard Wasserstein quotes a remark made in September 1944 by a senior official in the Foreign Office, after he had received a submission from the Board urging measures to help Jews in Hungary and Romania: 'In my opinion a disproportionate amount of the time of this office is wasted in dealing with these wailing Jews.'[104] There is a view, as developed by Richard Bolchover, that if a proper and detailed feasibility study had been commissioned by the Board on how rescue could be achieved, and the results of this study presented in a forceful way to the British government by a united front of all the major Jewish organizations, something might have been achieved.[105] On the other hand, William Rubinstein has argued very cogently that almost certainly nothing could have been done to rescue any significant numbers of Jews.[106]

Establishment of the State of Israel

The policy of the Board towards the future of the Jews in Palestine was contained in the Board's statement on post-war policy issued in November 1944.[107] In essence its objective was that *undivided* Palestine should become, after a period of transitional government, a Jewish state or Commonwealth and that there should be no restrictions on Jews who wished to settle there. Furthermore, as soon as the war finished, the United Nations should make arrangements for the speedy transfer to Palestine of all Jewish survivors of Nazi persecution who wished to settle there. The Board hoped that the Jewish state would be within the British Commonwealth. There was no mention of the Arab population of Palestine, but it was stated that the constitution of the new state would guarantee the equality of rights of all citizens irrespective of race or religion. The rights of the respective religious authorities concerning the Holy Places should be guaranteed internationally.[108]

At almost the same time the Board issued a statement regarding terrorism in Palestine. It deplored all acts of terror carried out in Palestine by a small number of Jews who were not representative of the majority of Jews in Palestine, and it deplored the attempts at placing the responsibility for these deeds upon the Jewish population of Palestine or even upon the Jewish people as a whole.[109]

Following the end of the war the Board concentrated its efforts in trying to persuade the new British government to abrogate the 1939 White Paper and to ease entirely the restrictions on Jewish immigration to Palestine. In particular the Board demanded that the government grant immediately, as a matter of urgency, 100,000 immigration certificates. In October 1945 it asked for an interview with the prime minister, Clement Attlee, but this was refused. On 13 November 1945 the foreign secretary, Ernest Bevin, announced that the White Paper restrictions on immigration would continue and an Anglo-American

Committee of Enquiry would be established to consider Jewish refugees
and Palestine. The Board was incensed at this, which it saw at best as
procrastination and at worst as a change in Labour Party policy from
supporting the establishment of a Jewish state towards appeasement of
the Arabs. The Board issued a hard-hitting indictment of the British
government's policy in the whole area of dealing with the Jewish dis-
placed persons in Europe, and its reneging on the promises made by
previous governments on Palestine.[110] It drew no comment or response
from the government.

The Board submitted written evidence to the Anglo-American Committee of Enquiry and the president gave oral evidence. In the main the
written and oral evidence elaborated the principles laid down in the
1944 Statement of Policy. In February 1946 the Board passed a resolution by seventy-nine votes to seventy-three, condemning a member
of the Board, Colonel L.H. Gluckstein, who in the course of giving
evidence to the Anglo-American Committee had attacked the character of the Board by stating that it was not representative of the Anglo-
Jewish Community. No sanctions were taken against that deputy.[111]
The report of the Committee included a recommendation that
100,000 certificates be issued immediately, but it failed to deal with
the Palestine issue as a whole. The Board welcomed the first but
regretted the second. The British government ignored the first and was
satisfied with the second, as it could continue as it had been doing.

Following the announcement in 1946 that Britain was terminating
its mandate in Transjordan and recognizing the independence of that
country, the Board issued a statement condemning the action of the
government, in particular pointing out that the Balfour Declaration
applied to the whole of Palestine including land east of the Jordan.
The Board were clearly in a militant mood vis-à-vis the government's
policy towards Palestine and it refused an invitation issued in September
1946 to attend a conference on Palestine convened by the government.
The Board did so mainly on the grounds that the Jewish Agency had
refused to do so. Many other Jewish bodies who were invited also
refused to attend. A major reason for the refusal of Jewish organizations
to attend this conference was because of various repressive measures
(including imprisonment) that had been taken by the British administration in Palestine against leaders of the Jewish Agency, the Vaad Leumi
(the representative Council of Jews in Palestine), and many others in
Palestine. A dispute erupted over these refusals in the community at
large and in the Board in particular. Thirty deputies tabled a resolution

that the Board should accept the invitation but this was not supported by the majority, who passed an amended resolution that the Board would only send representatives to the conference provided the Jewish Agency was represented there.[112] It was not, so no representatives of the Board attended. The Board had in fact given up hope that the British government would, of its own accord, accept the establishment of a Jewish State in Palestine and would fulfil the proposals of the Anglo-American Committee to grant 100,000 certificates for Jews to enter Palestine. The Board's strategy lay in trying to influence British public opinion in favour of its objectives, but regrettably this was countered by the various acts of terrorism in Palestine, which the Board consistently condemned.

The conference took place in late 1946 but without any representatives from any Jewish organization. In February 1947 the British government informed the Board of new proposals that it intended to submit to the United Nations, having given up on finding a solution itself. These proposals in effect amounted to an annulment of Britain's undertaking under the Balfour Declaration: Palestine was to be a UN trusteeship for five years, followed by the establishment of an independent Palestine State, and restrictions on immigration to Palestine were to be maintained. The Board was asked to express its views on this new policy, which it totally rejected. In the event the government decided to submit the problem to the United Nations, but without recommending any particular solution. The United Nations established a Special Committee to consider the matter and, in July 1947, the Board submitted a memorandum to this Committee proposing the establishment of a state with a Jewish majority and with the right of all Jews to immigrate and settle there. When the Special Committee reported, the Board supported its recommendations for a Jewish state in a partitioned Palestine, although it regretted the exclusion of Jerusalem and a few other places of historical importance to Jews from the areas proposed to be allocated to that state.

All was not plain sailing as far as the media were concerned and in November 1947 the Palestine Committee remarked upon 'the partial and, at times, unfair attitude of some sections of the British Press and the BBC towards the Jews in the new situation created by the decision of the Assembly'.[113] *Plus ça change plus c'est la même chose!* This 'bias' in reporting continued into 1948 and the Board noted that the attitude of a large part of the British press and occasionally the BBC was unfriendly to the Jews in Palestine, and it made several approaches to try to ensure fair representation of the news of events in Palestine. This was not easy because of the difficult relations between Jews and British troops in Palestine and the often-resulting violence.

At its meeting on 21 December 1947 the Board welcomed the decision of the United Nations on 29 November 1947 to implement the proposals for a Jewish state in a partitioned Palestine, and its resolution included the following:

> The Board wishes to pay a heartfelt tribute to the British people and its great sons who brought about the Balfour Declaration and who helped materially in the development of the Jewish National Home. It prays that this fulfilment of Jewish hopes will be accompanied by the strengthening of the traditional friendly ties between the British and the Jewish peoples.[114]

3B. FOREIGN AFFAIRS

Foreign affairs of the Board continued to be dealt with by the Joint Foreign Committee (in partnership with the AJA) until 1943, and thereafter by the Foreign Affairs Committee of the Board. The Palestine Committee dealt with Palestine and from May 1948 with Israel, changing its name to the Eretz Israel Committee in 1949.

From the start of the war there was a 'sea change' with regard to the approach of the Board to foreign matters. Hitherto it had tended, and indeed preferred, to act independently of all other organizations, both those in Britain and in particular those overseas. The Board now began to get involved with international Jewish bodies and thereafter much of its actions were through these bodies. There are a number of reasons for this change. During the war it became impossible for the Board to continue to involve itself directly with most countries in Europe. Following the war the world had altered and was essentially divided into two power blocks (one headed by the United States and the other by the Soviet Union) plus many non-aligned countries. Britain was a leading member of one of the blocks, but its power in the world had diminished. The days when the Board could approach the British government concerning problems affecting Jews in a foreign country, with the expectation that the government would take some action, had passed. The Board also no longer saw itself as the leading Jewish representative organization in the world; it recognized that there were others of at least equal stature in particular in the United States.

The most important reason for the change in the Board's approach to foreign issues, though, was probably the transformation in the leadership of the Board. The previous leaders of the Board were essentially insular in their outlook whereas the new leaders were already involved in international Jewish bodies, such as the World Jewish Congress and the World Zionist Organisation. These new leaders considered that the Board had much to gain by becoming less of an island.

It is perhaps surprising that as early as the end of 1939, and before the full brunt of the Holocaust, the Board discussed how best to prepare constructive proposals as to the future of the Jews in Europe after an allied victory. It had informal consultations with the Alliance Israelite Universelle, the American Jewish Committee, the AJC and the WJC. Representatives of the Joint Foreign Affairs Committee went to Paris in early 1940 for a meeting convened by the Alliance of various Jewish organizations, where it was agreed that a unified approach to Jewish problems was essential. This was perhaps the first step in the change of attitude of the Board to sister organizations elsewhere as it had hitherto generally stood aloof from such meetings and cooperation. It will be recalled that some sixty-four years earlier, in 1876, the Board had refused an invitation from the Alliance to participate at an international conference in Paris to consider joint action regarding attacks on Jews in Turkey and Serbia, on the grounds that the Board would continue to rely on the British government to look after the interests of Jews in foreign lands. Following the fall of France, the Joint Foreign Affairs Committee continued contact with the American Jewish organizations on both current issues and ideas for the future.

In August 1942, a special conference was held in London to consider the likely Jewish post-war problems and, as a result, certain principles were formulated and contact was made with the equivalent organizations in Australia, Canada, New Zealand, South Africa and the United States.[115] A memorandum on the issues involved was submitted to the government minister dealing with post-war issues, and the committee held meetings at the Foreign Office and with the representatives of other countries in London. The Joint Foreign Affairs Committee became a member of the Council of British Societies for Relief Abroad, whose task it was to plan the work of relief in European countries after their liberation from German occupation. Special Jewish units were formed, under the umbrella of a special committee established by the Joint Foreign Affairs Committee called the Jewish Committee for Relief Abroad, to help in this prospective relief effort and training was given to the volunteers including lessons in Yiddish. The Board, or rather the Joint Foreign Affairs Committee, had found a role for itself in the very difficult circumstances where there was precious little it could do. Activity in this area continued following the dissolution of the Joint Foreign Affairs Committee and its replacement by the Board's Foreign Affairs Committee, which promoted the formation in Britain of a Jewish Relief and Rehabilitation Organisation which would be able to work with similar Jewish organizations in other countries and with the recently formed United Nations Relief and Rehabilitation Administration (UNRRA).

On 19 November 1944 the Board agreed a statement on post-war policy in relation to general post-war Jewish problems and Palestine. This policy was prepared and agreed after detailed discussions with the AJA and the European branch of the WJC. In essence the policy was a proposal to the British government and the about-to-be-established United Nations that Jews as individuals should be able to live as equals with their fellow citizens in all countries, and that a Jewish Commonwealth should be established in Palestine.[116]

Following the end of the war, the Board involved itself in making representations regarding Jews in the negotiations of the various peace treaties as well as making representations to the British government concerning the various war crime trials. The Foreign Affairs sections of the annual reports of the Board for the years 1944 to 1947 include an excellent contemporary report of what had been happening in each European country occupied by the Nazis and make very sombre reading. The peace treaty negotiations were generally conducted through the Co-ordination Board (see below) and the main principles included the following:

(a) There should be redress for the wrong suffered by the Jews.

(b) Discriminatory legislation against Jews should be abrogated and fascist organizations dissolved. There should be laws banning antisemitic and anti-racial activities.

(c) Persons who committed crimes against Jews should be regarded as guilty of war crimes and crimes against humanity and punished accordingly.

(d) There should be fundamental human rights freedoms without discrimination as to race, sex, language, religion or place of birth.

(e)   Provisions for restitution of individual and communal property. Transfer of heirless and unclaimed property of Jewish victims to an appropriate Jewish body for the purposes of Jewish reconstruction, rehabilitation and resettlement.

(f)   The right of emigration of Jews from ex-enemy territories with the right to transfer their property and assets to their new place of settlement.[117]

Most of these principles are in the various Human Rights Conventions published from 1948 onwards and one suspects that these treaties formed the basis of the principles enunciated by the Co-ordination Board. These principles were incorporated into the various peace treaties, although as with the treaties following the First World War, many of them fell apart, particularly in countries that found themselves on the eastern side of the Iron Curtain.

In December 1944 the president and secretary of the Board visited the United States to make closer contact with American Jewish organizations with a view to coordinating with them in policy and action on post-war Jewish issues. It was agreed with the AJC and the WJC that a committee should be set up of representatives of the three organizations to work out means whereby consultation and coordination between themselves and other appropriate Jewish bodies could be secured.[118] In 1945 a tripartite agreement was made between the Board, the AJC and the WJC, and secretariats in London and New York were established in order to ensure full coordination and consultation between the three bodies. In 1946 the tripartite agreement group prepared an application under the name 'Co-ordinating Board of Jewish Organisations' to the Economic and Social Council of the United Nations (UNESCO) to be recognized by that organization as a consultant body. The members of the group hoped that the Conseil Representatif des Juifs de France (CRIF) and the South African Board of Deputies would join with them, but CRIF did not. What stimulated them was that another Jewish group had beaten them to the gun. The WJC had already achieved recognition on its own account. The 'Consultative Council' consisting of the AJA, the Alliance from France and the American Jewish Committee had already applied for this status, and had asked the Board to join its group, but this had been rejected. Agudas Israel also applied for individual recognition. Thus, four different Jewish bodies applied for and obtained recognition status from UNESCO. In 1950 a fifth Jewish organization, the World Union for Progressive Judaism, was granted consultative status. There was, therefore, cooperation but rivalry as well.

The Co-ordinating Board, with the acronym CBJO, which consisted of the Board, the American Jewish Conference, the South African Jewish Board of Deputies and the WJC, was granted consultative status by UNESCO in August 1947. Strenuous efforts were made by the Board to try to ensure at a minimum some sort of cooperation between the four Jewish consultative bodies to UNESCO, and in 1948 it was agreed by all of them that there should be regular meetings of representatives of each of the four bodies and that when representations were necessary they should be coordinated. In 1948 the AJC was dissolved and in 1949 it was replaced on the Co-ordinating Board by the American B'nei B'rith. The work of the Co-ordinating Board was quite substantial; in addition to its involvement in peace treaties it also made representations to and attended meetings of the United Nations itself, UNESCO, the Human Rights Commission of the United Nations, UNICEF, the Conference of International Non-Governmental Organisations and many others.

The Board was approached in February 1954 by the AJA to agree to the establishment of permanent machinery for consultation on all aspects of foreign affairs. This was discussed by the Foreign Affairs Committee, which took the view that it would be a derogation from the Board's responsibilities in this area to establish permanent machinery for consultation with any self-constituted and sectional organization.[119] The Board, however, felt that some form of coordination might be possible and later in the year arranged a meeting with representatives of the AJA, the British Section of Agudas Israel, the British section of the WJC and the World Union of Progressive Judaism. Not much progress was made in 1954 but in March 1955 the Board approved draft proposals for coordination suggested by the Foreign Affairs Committee. The draft started with a statement that the Board, because it was the only elected representative body of British Jewry, was alone authorized to make representations to the government in the name of British Jewry. It was prepared to consult with the other four organizations from time to time and to this end was prepared to co-opt on to its Foreign Affairs Committee one representative from each body. Any organization which dissented from the committee's decision on any issue and decided to make separate representations to government on that issue must make it clear that it was acting only on its own behalf. Judging by the lack of any further meetings on the subject, one can only assume that the other organizations were not overjoyed with the draft proposals.[120] In fact nothing came of this, but from time to time the Board called meetings of other British Jewish organizations to discuss matters affecting foreign affairs where it felt a common approach to government was highly desirable.

In 1957 the formation of yet another body was proposed for action in the field of world Jewish affairs. It was proposed by Nahum Goldmann, the president of the WJC, and would include not only the Board but also a number of Jewish representative organizations from many countries. It was essentially to be an organization to cover information-gathering, to provide a forum for the exchange of views, and to coordinate action on world Jewish problems, although joint action could take place – but only if there was unanimity by all involved. It was to operate for two years, and if successful it would replace the WJC. The Board accepted the invitation to participate on the understanding that it would not affect the independence of the Board.[121] The first meeting took place in January 1958 and included representatives from the Board, the American Jewish Committee, the B'nei B'rith, the Canadian Jewish Congress, CRIF, the Delegacion de Asociaciones Israelitas Argentinas, the Executive Council of Australian Jewry, the Jewish Labour Committee of America, the South African Board of Deputies and the WJC. At the end of the two-year trial period it was agreed that the organization, under the name Conference of Jewish Organisations (COJO), should continue on the same lines as before, but the WJC did not dissolve as had been part of Nahum Goldmann's proposal. In 1963 COJO spawned yet another organization, the World Council of Jewish Education (WCJE), to supervise the setting up and maintenance of a bureau or bureaux of Jewish education. The Board agreed to participate in this and responsibility was passed to the Education Committee of the Board.[122]

By the end of 1964 we find that the Board was participating in no fewer than six international Jewish organizations, namely CBJO, COJO, WCJE, the Jewish Restitution Successor Organisation (JRSO), the Conference of Jewish Material Claims Against Germany (called the Claims Conference), and the Memorial Foundation for Jewish Culture.

Israel

Immediately following the establishment of the State of Israel on 14 May 1948, the Board directed much of its activity to trying to dissuade the British government from supplying officers, training, arms, material and other assistance to some of the invading Arab armies. At the same time it tried to refute the intense propaganda against Israel emanating in the main from Arab sources. A letter was published in *The Times* on 8 June 1948 on behalf of the Board, pointing out that the State of Israel can have no claim upon the allegiance of Jewish citizens of other countries however concerned they may be for its welfare and progress and that 'we as citizens of this country can have no political relationship with the State of Israel'.[123]

The relationship between the Board and Israel caused much discussion and friction. Some deputies deprecated any action by the Board which might have the appearance of intervening in the internal affairs or external relations of Israel, because Israel was technically a 'foreign' country. Early in 1949 the chairman of the Eretz Israel Committee suggested that that committee should follow and discuss developments in Israel and where considered necessary make representations to the British government. The committee's object should be to strengthen the links of friendship between the people of Britain and the people of Israel and to further the peace, independence and prosperity of Israel. There was no dissent from this view at the Board meeting, nor was there any discussion on what attitude the Board might adopt with regard to the actions and policies of the government of Israel, whether or not it agreed with them. In practice, and certainly in the early years of the state, the Board either worked quietly behind the scenes on matters that were of concern to sections of the British Jewish community, for example the importation into Israel of trefa (non-kosher) meat, and the National Service for Women Bill when it was before the Knesset (the Israeli Parliament). The Board only publicly came out in support of Israel when it thought that either the media or even the statements of the Foreign Office did not properly reflect the matter, for example the Israeli attack on the Arab village of Qibya in October 1953. In this latter issue the Board did not support or dissent from the action of the Israeli government but pointed out the background and the previous attacks by Arabs on Jews in Israel.[124] Some objections were expressed at Board meetings that even this quiet behind-the-scenes diplomacy was interference in matters within the jurisdiction of the Israeli government, but these objections do not appear to have been a majority view, as they were never raised as a substantive matter at a Board meeting.[125] Another issue affecting Israel was the arms race and in particular armaments sent to Arab countries. Delegations from the Board frequently saw the ministers responsible in the British government to express their concerns.

Soviet Union and Eastern Europe

After the war it was mainly only countries in the Eastern Bloc for which the Board made representations to the British government regarding Jews in those countries. Jewish communities in the Soviet Union, and rapidly in the other countries in Eastern Europe, became isolated from Jewish life in the world outside. In the Soviet Union, Jews – particularly writers and journalists – who showed interest in matters outside the country were labelled as 'bourgeois cosmopolitans'. At first immigration to Israel was permitted from most countries, excluding the Soviet Union, but gradually severe restrictions were imposed everywhere. The Board was deeply concerned with anti-Jewish show trials, for example in Prague in 1952, and the so-called Jewish doctors trial in Moscow in 1953, but the only action it took, or was able to take, was passing resolutions condemning these trials and holding public meetings. These were effective in getting the media onside and protesting at these developments in countries behind the Iron Curtain. Following the death of Stalin in March 1953 it seemed to the Board and other Jewish organizations that the position would ease somewhat, which it did.

This better situation did not last very long, as towards the end of the 1953 a number of Jews were arrested in Romania and Hungary on fabricated charges. The Board hoped that public opinion and public protests would have some influence on the authorities in those countries, and in May 1954 it passed a resolution condemning what was going on and gave a lot of publicity to this.[126] The resolution was sent in a letter to the Romanian Embassy, but no reply was received. The Board might have been right about the effect of public opinion as, shortly after public protest meetings had been held in a number of countries, some of the prisoners were released. The Board decided to defer holding a public meeting in London in the hope that further releases might take place. The Board was right. Not only were more prisoners released, but also in one or two eastern European countries the conditions for emigration to Israel were eased.

The year 1957 held mixed fortunes. The two leaders of the Soviet Union, Bulganin and Khrushchev, visited London, but they could not or would not find the time to meet a delegation from the Board.[127] The Suez crisis in 1956 had created a hostile attitude from the Soviet Union towards Israel with adverse effects on the Russian Jewish population. On the other hand, a number of Jews were able to escape from Hungary following the October 1956 rising, and some refugees were given

asylum in England and assisted by the community, including the Aliens
Committee of the Board.

NOTES

1. Henry Morris, *The AJEX Chronicles* (London: AJEX, 1999), p.22.
2. W.D. Rubinstein, *A History of the Jews in the English-Speaking World: Great Britain* (Basingstoke: Macmillan, 1996) pp.342–3.
3. Quoted by Bernard Wasserstein, 'Patterns of Jewish Leadership in Great Britain during the Nazi Era', in Randolph Braham (ed.), *Jewish Leadership During the Nazi Era* (New York: Institute for Holocaust Studies, 1985), p.41.
4. Geoffrey Alderman, *Modern British Jewry*, new edn (Oxford: Clarendon Press, 1998), pp.321–410; Chaim Bermant, *Troubled Eden: An Anatomy of British Jewry* (London: Vallentine Mitchell, 1969); Todd M. Endelman, *The Jews of Britain, 1656 to 2000* (London: University of California Press, 2002), pp.229–56; Vivian Lipman, *A History of the Jews in Britain since 1858* (Leicester: Leicester University Press, 1990), pp.242–3.
5. Quoted at a Memorial Meeting for Israel Finestein held on 19 November 2009, by his nephew Colin Lang from an article in *Academy*, the journal of the Inter-University Jewish Federation (IUJF).
6. Rubinstein, *History of the Jews in the English-Speaking World*, pp.364–427; William Rubinstein, 'The decline and fall of Anglo-Jewry?', *Jewish Historical Studies*, 38 (2002), pp.13–21.
7. See, for example, Richard Bolchover, *'British Jewry and the Holocaust*, 2nd edn (Oxford: Littman Library of Jewish Civilization, 2003); Rubinstein, *History of the Jews*, pp.349–63; Pamela Shatzkes, *Holocaust and Rescue: Impotent or Indifferent? Anglo-Jewry 1938–1945* (Basingstoke: Palgrave, 200); Meir Sompolinsky, *The British Government and the Holocaust: The Failure of Anglo-Jewish Leadership* (Brighton: Sussex Academic Press, 1999); Bernard Wasserstein, *Britain and the Jews of Europe, 1939–1945* (Oxford: Oxford University Press, 1988).
8. Endelman, *The Jews of Britain, 1656 to 2000*, p.226.
9. *Jewish Chronicle* [JC], 22 December 1939, p.6.
10. Selig Brodetsky Papers, Hartley Library, Southampton University, MS119/AJ3.
11. Ibid.
12. BOD, ACC/3121/B5/2/2, part 4.
13. *JC*, 24 June 1949, p.12.
14. BOD, ACC/3121/A/41, p.46.
15. *JC*, 19 June 1964, pp.6, 11.
16. Gideon Shimoni, 'Selig Brodetsky and the Ascendancy of Zionism in Anglo-Jewry (1939–1945)', *Jewish Journal of Sociology*, 22 (1980), pp.36–7.
17. Israel Finestein, *Scenes and Personalities in Anglo-Jewry, 1800–2000* (London: Vallentine Mitchell, 2002), pp.256–60.
18. Related to me by Israel Finestein.
19. *JC*, 14 May 1943, p.10.
20. *JC*, 24 March 1944, p.10.
21. BOD, ACC/3121/A.32, pp.89–90.
22. Brodetsky Papers, MS119/AJ3.
23. BOD, ACC/3121/A/32, p.116.
24. Shimoni, 'Selig Brodetsky and the Ascendancy of Zionism', pp.42–3; BOD, ACC/3121/A/32, p.122.
25. BOD, ACC/3121/A/32, p.195.
26. The National Archive, Public Records Office (TNA, PRO), FO 371/36741.
27. Shimoni, 'Selig Brodetsky and the Ascendancy of Zionism', p.51.
28. BOD, ACC/3121/A/34, p.6.
29. BOD, ACC/3121/A/33, p.170.
30. Bernard Homa, *Footprints on the Sands of Time* (London: author, 1990) p.150.
31. BOD, ACC/3121/A/33, p.180.
32. BOD, ACC/3121/A/35, p.12.

33. See, for example, a report in the *JC*, 25 November 1949, p.9; see also Homa, *Footprints on the Sands of Time*, pp.150–4.
34. BOD, ACC/3121/A/36, pp.20–3.
35. Alderman, *Modern British Jewry*, p.361.
36. Annual Report of the Board of Deputies (AR), 1951, pp.16–17.
37. AR, 1956, pp.97–100.
38. Ibid., p.101.
39. *JC*, 25 September 1959, p.22.
40. AR, 1960, p.17.
41. BOD, ACC/3121/A/30, p.191.
42. BOD, ACC/3121/A/31, p.30.
43. AR, 1940, p.25.
44. David Cesarani and Tony Kushner, *The Internment of Aliens in Twentieth Century Britain* (London: Frank Cass, 1993); Ronald Stent, *A Bespattered Page? The Internment of His Majesty's 'most loyal enemy aliens'* (London: Andre Deutsch, 1980).
45. BOD, ACC/3121/A/31, p.4.
46. Stent, *A Bespattered Page?* p.207.
47. Ibid., p.212.
48. BOD, ACC/3121/C2/3/3/1.
49. Tony Kushner, 'The Impact of British Anti-Semitism, 1918–1945', in David Cesarani (ed.), *The Making of Modern Anglo-Jewry* (Oxford: Basil Blackwell, 1990), pp.192–4.
50. BOD, ACC/3121/A/31, pp.153–4.
51. AR, 1943, p.28.
52. Wasserstein, *Britain and the Jews of Europe*, pp.116–7.
53. BOD, ACC/3121/A/32, pp.126, 132, 226, 241.
54. BOD, ACC/3121/A/33, pp.29–32.
55. BOD, ACC/3121/C4/4.
56. AR, 1944, pp.22–3.
57. Nigel Copsey, *Anti-Fascism in Britain* (Basingstoke: Macmillan, 2000), p.82.
58. Morris, *AJEX Chronicles*, p.29.
59. Morris Beckman, *The 43 Group*, 2nd edn (London: Centerprise, 1993), pp.24–6.
60. Ibid., p.14.
61. Endelman, *The Jews of Britain, 1656 to 2000*, p.233.
62. Copsey, *Anti-Fascism in Britain*, p.95.
63. AR, 1951, p.30.
64. AR, 1952, p.29.
65. BOD, ACC/3121/A/39, p.62
66. BOD, ACC/3121/A/40, pp.195, 198–9 and 107 (second part).
67. Ibid., pp.163, 173.
68. BOD, ACC/3121/A/41, p.85.
69. AR, 1963, pp.17–19.
70. Archives of the Community Security Trust [CST], C/6/1/1/2, pp.189–91, 200–1.
71. This description of the TAC has been extracted from http://archives.ucl.ac.uk/special collections.
72. BOD, ACC/3121/A/31, p.168.
73. BOD, ACC/3121/A/35 pp.17, 24, 29.
74. AR, 1946, p.31.
75. BOD, ACC/3121/A/35, pp.180, 184.
76. BOD, ACC/3121/A/36, pp.14, 31, 44.
77. Ibid., p.71; BOD, ACC/3121/G4/11–13.
78. BOD, ACC/3121/A/36, pp.70, 100.
79. BOD, ACC/3121/A/38, pp.15, 173.
80. Finestein, *Scenes and Personalities*, p.73.
81. *JC*, 14 January 1944, p.5.
82. BOD, ACC/3121/A/32, p.218.
83. AR,1948, p.23.
84. Archives of the Jewish Memorial Council, London Metropolitan Archives, ACC/2999/43/1.
85. AR, 1949, p.30; *JC*, 14 October 1949, p.12; *JC*, 21 October 1949, p.5.

86. CST, C6/1/1/3, p.362.
87. BOD, ACC/3121/A/34, pp.42–3.
88. Ibid., pp.132, 158, 168.
89. Ibid., p.195; BOD, ACC/3121/A/35, p.38.
90. Ibid., p.79.
91. AR, 1950, pp.37–9.
92. BOD, ACC/3121/A/31, pp.151–2.
93. Many of the meetings are recorded in TNA, PRO, FO/371/30885.
94. *JC*, 25 December 1942, p.8; Shatzkes, *Holocaust and Rescue*, pp.39–42.
95. Shatzkes, *Holocaust and Rescue*, p.41.
96. *The Times*, 18 December 1942, p.4.
97. Wasserstein, *Britain and the Jews of Europe*, p.183.
98. Ibid., p.190.
99. Ibid., p.200.
100. BOD, ACC/3121/C2/2/5/1.
101. *JC*, 29 January 1943, p.5; 5 February 1943, p.6.
102. See Note 3, above.
103. Shatzkes, *Holocaust and Rescue*, pp.261–7.
104. Wasserstein, *Britain and the Jews of Europe*, p.351.
105. Bolchover, *British Jewry and the Holocaust*, pp.151–6.
106. Rubinstein, *History of the Jews in the English-Speaking World*, p.358.
107. BOD, ACC/3121/A/32, pp.249, 251.
108. Ibid., p.249.
109. Ibid.
110. AR, 1945, pp.33–7.
111. BOD, ACC/3121/A/33 pp.83–4.
112. AR, 1946, pp.33–5.
113. AR, 1947, p.43.
114. Ibid.
115. BOD, ACC/3121/A/32, p.16.
116. Ibid., pp.249, 251.
117. AR, 1946, pp.45–6.
118. BOD, ACC/3121/A/32, p.282.
119. BOD, ACC/3121/A/37, p.65.
120. Ibid. p.156.
121. BOD, ACC/3121/A/38, pp.71, 118.
122. BOD, ACC/3121/A/40, p.155.
123. *The Times*, 8 June 1948, p.5.
124. AR, 1949, p.23; AR, 1951, p.28; AR, 1953, pp.24–6.
125. AR, 1954, pp.25–6.
126. BOD, ACC/3121/A/39, p.90.
127. BOD, ACC/3121/A/38, p.59.

6 Towards the Twenty-first Century, 1964–1996

The last third of the twentieth century accentuated and accelerated some trends among the Jewish population of Britain that had been evident since the end of the Second World War. The number of Jews in Britain declined from a peak of about 420,000 in 1955 to about 300,000 in 1995.[1] The reasons for this fall are a mixture of low fertility rates and consequential smaller families (except among the Strictly Orthodox), emigration (including aliya to Israel) exceeding immigration (including *yerida* from Israel), intermarriage and assimilation, and a decline in synagogue marriages from nearly 2,000 in 1965 to fewer than 900 by 1996.[2] Furthermore, Jewish society had become much more pluralistic, as had the general population of multicultural Britain. This is illustrated by a change in the relative membership of synagogues according to religious adherence, with a move from the centre to the wings. For example, in London between 1970 and 1990 the membership of the Progressive synagogues increased from 21 per cent to 29 per cent of synagogue-affiliated Jews, and the Strictly Orthodox increased from 3 per cent to 9 per cent, whereas the Central Orthodox declined over the same period from 76 per cent to 62 per cent.[3] (See Introduction for definitions of these groups.) It was, however, much more than a numbers game. The Progressives were determined to get recognition of their religious authorities and obtain acceptance not only as Jews but also as practising the Jewish religion; on the other hand, the Strictly Orthodox were equally determined not to concede an inch in this regard. The Board became the battlefield, with both wings flexing their muscles and threatening to leave the Board unless changes were made to the constitution regarding the ecclesiastical authorities of the Board. This battle resulted in most of the Strictly Orthodox and some Central Orthodox communities leaving the Board in 1971, as they could not support the compromise worked out with the Progressive movements. Most of the synagogues that left have

never returned, and thus for the last forty years most of the Strictly
Orthodox congregations, about 10 per cent of the Jews in Britain, have
not been represented on the Board. The proportion of Jews in Britain
not associated with any synagogue decreased from 34 per cent in 1967
to 30 per cent in 1995.[4] Many of these persons are represented on the
Board through their membership of Jewish institutions who have
deputies on the Board.

In general, the Jewish population in Britain prospered during this
period, particularly during the Thatcher years, but the economic
recession during the 1990s had a significant adverse impact leading to
financial problems for the Board as well as other Jewish institutional
bodies and charities. To the rescue of the community came a very small
group of wealthy Jewish philanthropists, who became known as the
'funding fathers'. As Geoffrey Alderman has explained, this new group
of Jewish moneyed benefactors differed from their predecessors in the
nineteenth and early twentieth centuries by not involving themselves
in the governance of the major Jewish institutions. They have ignored
these institutions (often because they did not wish to get involved in
their parochial politics) and have wanted and achieved direct control
on how their money is spent.[5] They wished to make decisions as they
saw fit, particularly in social welfare, education and Jewish defence,
without representative machinery or democratic procedures.[6] There
was thus a coterie of unelected leaders. Israel Finestein, during his presidency of the Board from 1991 to 1994, tried to harness these men to
support the Board and its activities by proposing to co-opt some onto
appropriate Board committees, but this proposal was rejected by the
Board, much to his and the *Jewish Chronicle*'s (*JC*) disappointment.[7]
This rejection no doubt contributed to the establishment of the Jewish
Leadership Council in 2003, a non-elected body of Jewish leaders from
institutions, including the Board, and prominent individuals in the
community.

The concerns of Jewish women in respect of their subordinate
status and the impact of certain Jewish laws, in particular those of
divorce, became a major issue during this time. The matter was essentially one for the Orthodox synagogues as women are treated in exactly
the same way as men in the Progressive movements. Strictly speaking,
this was not an issue for the Board as it was essentially one of Jewish law
and its interpretation. The Board had admitted women deputies from
1919, although many synagogues were very slow in permitting women
to stand or vote in their elections – and even in the 2009 elections a few

synagogues did not allow women to vote or stand for election as a deputy. The first woman chair of a Board committee was elected in 1925 – Mrs M.A. Spielman on the Education Committee. The first woman honorary officer was Rosalind Preston, elected a vice-president in 1991, and in 2000 Jo Wagerman was elected the first woman president. In 1991, the chief rabbi asked Rosalind Preston to head an enquiry into the role of women in the Anglo-Jewish community. The report was an excellent one, but progress has been slow in respect of the recommendations addressed specifically to the religious authorities. The Board devoted a plenary session to the enquiry's findings and, as a result, established a Women's Issues Action Group.[8]

For most Jews in Britain, the welfare of Israel became of paramount importance. A National Opinion Poll (NOP) in 1970 showed that 80 per cent of British Jews supported a Jewish state and a survey conducted in 1973/4 found that Zionism 'seems to be the new focal point of Jewish identity'.[9] There was almost overwhelming support for Israel during the Six-Day War in 1967, during the war of attrition and during the Yom Kippur War of 1973. Views were somewhat mixed during the first Lebanon war in 1982, but wholehearted support and concern welled up when Israel was subject to attacks by scuds during the first Gulf War in 1991. The Board reacted to all of these with resolutions and public meetings in support of Israel although they were somewhat muted during the Lebanon war. Following the Six-Day War, a number of Jews in Britain were disturbed by the continuing occupation of the West Bank and Gaza, particularly when settlements began to be built in those territories. This mood was accentuated, particularly among liberal-thinking members of the community, by the election of right-wing governments in Israel from 1977. When in 1978 a Peace Now movement developed in Israel as a result of the visit of Anwar Sadat, a sister movement grew up in Britain. These concerns and the calls for peace initiatives were generally not endorsed by the Board, which tended to follow what it perceived as the views of the majority of Jews in Britain – that is, unconditional support for Israel. It was correct in that the allegiances of British Jews did not change – a survey of Jewish opinion in the 1990s found that 81 per cent of British Jews had a moderate-to-strong attachment to Israel,[10] which was much the same percentage that the NOP found in 1970. This percentage included many Jews who were attached to Israel but had concerns and doubts about the policies of the Israeli government.

After the 1967 war, the far left, including the left wing of the

Labour Party, turned very much against Israel. (In fact much of the far left, in particular the Communist Party, had always been anti-Zionist although there were periods when it suited them to support Zionism and Israel.[11]) The Jews were no longer the underdogs. They were seen as aggressors. This criticism of Israel seemed to legitimize a dislike of Jews, even though many Jews did not support the policies of the Israeli governments. Many members of Britain's rapidly growing Moslem community saw this as an opportunity to attack Israel, or rather the Jews in Britain whom they saw as Israel's supporters and advocates.[12] Threats and actual attacks were made on synagogues and other places where Jews might gather, and security became a major issue and activity for the Board.

1. THE BOARD

Leadership

Alderman Abraham Moss was elected president of the Board on Sunday 14 June 1964, but sadly died suddenly six days later on Saturday 20 June. In accord with the constitution, the Law, Parliamentary and General Purposes Committee appointed the senior vice-president, Solomon Teff, as president until an election was held. Alderman Moss had promised reforms to the Board including imposing a maximum of two terms for a president and a revision to the election and constituency system. It remained to be seen if his successor would carry out these and other reforms. The *JC*, which had forecast the end of the caucus because of Barnett Janner's defeat, was wrong, at least for the time being. The caucus dominated the 1964 elections to Board committees such that AJEX threatened to resign from the Board, as its candidates had been unsuccessful in the election to the Defence Committee because of block voting by the caucus.[13] It is interesting to note that for this election the Board had reverted to the 'first past the post' system instead of the single transferable vote proportional representation system that had been used for the previous four elections. The threatened withdrawal of AJEX was avoided by the Board agreeing to co-opt two of its members on to the Defence Committee.[14] In the by-election for a new vice-president to replace Solomon Teff, the caucus candidate, Councillor Samuel Davies, was elected. It is clear that the *JC*'s obituary on the caucus was premature.

On Sunday 18 October 1964 the Board elected Solomon Teff as president; he was unopposed. Solomon Teff was a solicitor and had been a deputy since 1922. On the Friday prior to his election the *JC* told him what reforms he needed to introduce in order for the Board to be more effective, more representative and more accepted by the community at large. These included radically revising the constituency system for the election of deputies, reducing the number of deputies, getting rid of the 'rotten boroughs', and reducing the number of committees. In his opening address, the new president did not refer to these proposals as such but promised to hold discussions to see how to improve the image of the Board and make it more effective. He subsequently pointed out that he was already 72 and did not intend to seek re-election at the end of his three-year term.[15]

Reforms took a long time in coming. In January 1966 the Board approved proposals to limit the period of office of honorary officers and committee chairmen to six years.[16] The object of the change was rejuvenation and the hope that the Board would thus have younger honorary officers. Solomon Teff kept to his word and stepped down as president at the triennial election in July 1967. In a fiercely fought election, Alderman Michael Fidler from Manchester defeated Victor Mishcon by 129 votes to 112. Victor Mishcon was the candidate of the caucus, but Michael Fidler won because of his superior organization, the almost complete support of provincial deputies (many of whom were members of the caucus and thus ignored the three-line whip) and because he had had longer service on the Board.[17] Michael Fidler was a businessman and active in both local and national politics.

After this election, the Board embarked on a period of uncontested elections for the presidency. Michael Fidler was re-elected unopposed for a second term in 1970, the same year that he was elected a Conservative MP. Sir Samuel Fisher was elected unopposed in 1973 and for a second term in 1976, having been elevated to Lord Fisher of Camden in 1974. Samuel Fisher was a businessman and leading local politician. He was the first mayor of Camden in 1965/66, knighted in 1967 and made a life peer in 1974. He was followed by Greville Janner, the son of Barnett Janner, a barrister and Labour MP, who was elected president unopposed in 1979 and re-elected unopposed for a second term in 1982. He received a life peerage in 1997. This sequence of unopposed elections ended in 1985 when both vice-presidents stood and Dr Lionel Kopelowitz, a physician from Newcastle, narrowly defeated Martin Savitt by 241 votes to 227. Lionel Kopelowitz was re-elected unopposed in 1988 and in 1991 was succeeded by a vice-president, His Honour Judge Israel Finestein, who defeated the senior

vice-president Eric Moonman. Israel Finestein was a QC and a Crown
Court Judge from 1972 to 1987. He was twice president of the Jewish Historical Society of England and the author of a number of books
on British Jewish history. Judge Finestein served for only one term –
he could not stand for re-election in 1994 as he was then over the age
of 72 and not eligible under the constitution. He was succeeded in
1994 by Eldred Tabachnik, who defeated Jerry Lewis in the election.
Eldred Tabachnik was a QC and became a Recorder in 2000.

Representation

The *JC* continued expressing its concern over the lack of reform
and, in a leader regarding Solomon Teff stepping down, concluded:
'Today the Board is bogged down by the inadequacies in its system of
representation.'[18] This matter of the width of representation was raised
by Leo Abse, a Labour MP, in a letter of 16 February 1968 to the *JC*,
in which he decried the 'Board of Deputies founded on an outworn
synagogal basis' for failing to give intelligent young diaspora Jews mean-
ingful leadership.[19] At the Board meeting on the following Sunday
he was given short shrift by the president, who pointed out the lack of
intelligentsia in the House of Commons and thought the Board was
widely representative.[20] Abse's theme was taken up by Dr Hans Kimmel, who published an article in *Jewish Public Affairs* that was highly
critical of the Board's representation being essentially limited to synagogue members elected at poorly attended AGMs. He proposed that
the majority of deputies should be elected by all Jews on a constituency
basis using postal votes. His article included an open letter to the new
president, Michael Fidler.[21] There does not appear to have been
any reply to the letter and there is an absence in the archives of any
discussion of the article at the Board or at any committee meetings.
Dr Kimmel died on 6 October 1970 and there is no mention of his
proposal to the Board in his obituary in the *JC*.[22] Many similar proposals have been made from time to time to widen the franchise and
thus make the Board more representative, in particular to have some
sort of general election among all Jews in Britain. Bill Rubinstein has
commented on these as follows:

> One should, however, not look at such proposals as necessarily a
> panacea: there would be very difficult questions of who is a Jew
> for the purposes of such elections; big and powerful institutions,
> especially the synagogues, would obviously organize the most

successful electoral campaigns, to the exclusion of independents and 'fringe' groups; there would be a danger of the election of extremist delegates; and there would be a constant diversion of resources to the electoral process, and probably even more public acrimony than at present. In all likelihood, a reformed Board of Deputies would adopt policies similar or identical to those of its predecessor.[23]

In a footnote, he mentions that in Australia one-half of the representatives to the New South Wales Board of Deputies are elected by direct community franchise, but only 3,000 out of a community of 35,000 to 40,000 bother to vote. What these critics had drawn attention to was that the Board was becoming much less representative; indeed, as previously mentioned, about 30 per cent of the Jews in Britain at the time were not affiliated to any synagogue and thus had no means of being represented on the Board, other than those who were members of Jewish institutions that have representation on the Board. Bill Rubinstein might be right that broadening the franchise would be difficult and might not achieve anything, but the Board chose not to try or even to consider it.

The Clause 43 Conflict

These constitutional issues were nothing compared with what happened next. The Orthodox (both Strictly and Central) had had a series of conflicts with the Progressives. These arose because of religious differences. The Judaism practised by the Orthodox, described as 'rabbinic Judaism' by historians, developed following the destruction of the Temple in 70 CE and the subsequent dispersion of the Jews from Judaea (Israel). Orthodox Judaism is predicated on the acceptance of the divine origin of both the written law (the Torah) and the oral law (as recorded in the Talmud and codified in the *Shulchan Aruch*). The Progressives do not acknowledge the divine origin of the oral law and over the years have changed and discarded many of the laws and observances of Orthodox Judaism. As a result, the Orthodox do not consider that the Progressives practise authentic Judaism. This has given rise to a multiplicity of issues including the validity of Progressive conversion, marriage and divorce. The Progressives had been unhappy with a number of ways in which they felt the Board had treated them as second-class citizens. In particular, there had been the refusal to acknowledge their marriage secretaries because of the refusal of the chief rabbi to certify them as 'congregations practising the Jewish religion', as discussed in Chapter 5. By the late 1960s their numbers had grown and they were now more than 20 per cent of synagogue-affiliated Jews. They decided to flex their muscles.

The issue that brought the conflict to a head at the Board was a clause in the constitution (Clause 43) which stated that in all religious matters the Board was to be guided by its ecclesiastical authorities,[24] which were defined in another clause (Clause 50) as the chief rabbi and the haham. It was Clause 43 that had delayed the entry into the Board of the Reform synagogues until 1886, when an additional sentence had been added making it clear that any decision taken by the Board would not represent the opinion of any congregation that did not accept the jurisdiction of the Board's ecclesiastical authorities. This addendum subsequently enabled both the Liberal and most Strictly Orthodox synagogues to join the Board, as none of them accepted the chief rabbi's jurisdiction. The Progressives were not only anxious that their religious authorities would be consulted, but there was also a hidden agenda – it was important that these authorities should be named in the constitution, as this would give some sort of recognition to them. This latter point is confirmed in an article by Chief Rabbi Jakobovits in the *JC*, in which he wrote: 'But when the Progressives subsequently revealed what they really intended was communal recognition for their "religious authorities" rather than mere consultative status ...'[25]

During Solomon Teff's presidency, these concerns of the Progressives led to the formation of a small committee, known as the Teff Committee, to look into the Clause 43 matter as well as other issues that were dividing the different religious communities. No steps were taken, and it was decided to defer the issue in view of the impending appointment of a new chief rabbi to replace Israel Brodie.[26] Following his election as president in 1967, Michael Fidler made some sort of commitment to have Clause 43 amended and held consultations with the Progressives and later with the new chief rabbi, Immanuel Jakobovits. Eventually a number of proposed amendments to Clause 43 were agreed by the chief rabbi and the Progressives. In April 1970, the Orthodox Group on the Board[27] became aware of these discussions and the proposed changes to the constitution. The group objected to three phrases in the draft and the Progressives agreed to two of them being removed, but refused to excise the third phrase which included the words 'consultation with their respective religious authorities' with regard to congregations not accepting the authority of the chief rabbi or the haham. One can see why, since their hidden objective was to get their religious authorities mentioned in the constitution. The Orthodox Group could not agree to this, as it would mean recognition of the rabbinic leaders of the Progressive movements as Jewish religious authorities. This proposed amendment, however, was acceptable to the chief rabbi, since in his view the wording did not accord any religious recognition of the Progressives.[28]

On 26 July 1970 the Board debated the proposed amendment, including the phrase objected to by the Orthodox Group. Bernard Homa, one of the leaders of the Orthodox Group, and S.S. Levin, a deputy for the United Synagogue, moved the deletion of the offending words but this was defeated by 112 votes to sixty-three. The amendment was approved by 129 in favour and seventy against, but it failed to get the necessary two-thirds majority.[29] This meant it would have to be resubmitted the following month when a simple majority would have sufficed, but it was not resubmitted due to the holiday period.[30] An analysis of the voting figures indicated that deputies representing Central Orthodox synagogues, such as the United and the Federation, had been split – some voting in favour of the new clause and others against.[31] All the Progressive deputies voted for the amendment and all the Strictly Orthodox deputies voted against the change.

There followed many acrimonious meetings and discussions between the different parties, including an ad hoc committee of deputies from the Strictly Orthodox and Central Orthodox synagogues, the honorary officers, the chief rabbi, the haham, and representatives of the Progressive synagogues. At a meeting on 22 March 1971 between representatives of the Orthodox Group and the Progressives, it appeared that some sort of agreement in principle had been reached. In essence, the words 'their Jewish religious authorities' would be replaced by 'their appropriate authorities'. Both sides had to obtain approval from their principals. The Orthodox Group decided not to oppose the new wording in the interests of maintaining unity at the Board, whereas the Progressives insisted that the words 'religious leaders' or 'religious authorities' had to remain.[32] This is not surprising. What is surprising is that the representatives of the Progressives at the meeting on 22 March agreed to drop those words, but perhaps they were not privy to the hidden agenda.

Impasse. Two deputies, Freddie Landau, the treasurer of the United Synagogue and also a member of the New London Masorti Synagogue, and Ashe Lincoln, representing the New London on the Board, then requisitioned a special meeting of the Board for 23 May 1971 with the purpose of deleting Clause 43 in its entirety. This proposal, which, if passed, would have created major problems within the Board when Jewish religious matters had to be considered, was opposed not only by the Orthodox Group but also by the honorary officers and was defeated by 110 votes to sixty-six.[33] Discussions between all the groups resumed and on 13 July 1971 agreement seemed to be in sight when the Orthodox Group agreed not to oppose an amendment including the words 'their respective religious leaders', provided that an explanatory statement was made at the Board meeting and published in the annual report. This statement was to the effect that the change had only been agreed by the Orthodox Group in order to avoid a break-up of the Board and 'it must be clearly understood that the basic tenets of the Torah make it impossible for orthodoxy to recognise the religious leaders of the Progressives as Jewish religious authorities or as exponents of authentic Judaism'. This was conveyed to the Progressives, but five days later, at the next meeting of the Board on 18 July 1971, the Progressive deputies did not turn up and held their own meeting. The Board sent its secretary, Abraham Marks, as an envoy to ask the Progressives to come to the main meeting. They refused and subsequently it became known that they had agreed that they would secede from the Board by 31 October 1971 unless the constitution was amended suitably.[34]

The threat of secession by the Progressives stimulated the honorary officers of the Board to act quickly, and they proposed to both sides a form of wording almost identical to that previously agreed by the Orthodox Group, but without the safeguard. Much correspondence and many meetings then ensued but without any agreement, and on 15 October 1971 the president wrote to each deputy with a proposed amendment including the words 'and the Board shall consult with those designated by such groups of Congregations as their respective religious leaders for this purpose on religious matters in any manner whatsoever concerning them'.[35] The Orthodox Group decided to boycott the Board meeting on 24 October 1971, as did most of the deputies of the Federation of Synagogues and many deputies from other Central Orthodox communities. The amendment was approved overwhelmingly on a show of hands, with only seven voting against the amendment.[36] A few weeks later all the deputies representing the Strictly Orthodox synagogues and the Federation of Synagogues resigned – about eighty deputies. Technically, they had to remain until the end of the triennial session in May 1973. The annual report of the Board for the year ending 30 April 1972 made clear that whenever the ecclesiastical authorities were approached pursuant to Clause 43, the Board could only act in accordance with the guidance received from them and that the only religious authorities recognized by the Board were these ecclesiastical authorities, but that a consultative procedure had been provided for those sections who do not come under the jurisdiction of these authorities.[37] This confirmed assurances given by the honorary officers to the chief rabbi and haham, and on which they had based their assent to the amendment to Clause 43. It still did not satisfy the Strictly Orthodox, but it satisfied the Federation and in April 1973 its deputies returned.

In December 1984, because of a disagreement between the leadership of the Board and the chief rabbi on the practical application of the amended Clause 43 (by then Clause 74), the Board adopted a code of practice regarding this clause. It was proposed by the United Synagogue and supported by most deputies representing Central Orthodox synagogues. This code made the guidance the Board receives from its ecclesiastical authorities mandatory and, as a result, the Machzike Hadath and a few other Strictly Orthodox congregations rejoined the Board, and at the age of 84 Bernard Homa returned as a deputy.[38] The Progressives voted against the code of practice, but made less fuss than in the Clause 43 debates, particularly as the new code allowed them to make separate representations to government should their position differ widely from that of the Board and could not be reconciled.[39] In the end the Progressives had succeeded with their hidden agenda, since the constitution now included reference to their religious authorities, and these authorities could, but did not have to, be consulted. Harold Langdon, in a paper published in 1979, considered it was:

> A battle that had to be won if we [*sic* – the Progressives] were to remain on the Board of Deputies and play our full part in the mainstream of Jewish life. It shows we are no longer second-class members of a secular organisation claiming to represent all Jews. We are no longer 'congregations of Jews' only for the purpose of communal activity; our synagogues are Jewish synagogues, and our Rabbis are religious leaders.[40]

The Progressives were not, however, happy with the code of practice introduced in 1984; as Langdon wrote: 'What is the use of consultations if the guidance of the ecclesiastical authorities is mandatory?'[41]

The Board could not find a compromise that satisfied all sides and as a result lost in membership an important part of the British Jewish community. Given the entrenched positions of the two main protagonists it probably was a conflict where there could not be a satisfactory resolution.

World Jewish Congress

No sooner had the Board dealt with a major crisis at home than it was faced with an important international matter. Britain had decided to enter the European Community in 1973, and the Board had to consider the implications of this for the way it operated with regard to foreign affairs. In January 1973, the Board, together with the WJC, arranged a conference in London of representatives of the leading Jewish communities in Europe. As a result, the WJC issued a further invitation to the Board to join the WJC, and the Board established a subcommittee on 26 February 1973 to consider this invitation and hold discussions with the WJC.[42] These discussions included how to safeguard the independence of the Board, the issue of the Board's relationship with the British government if it became a member of an international body, and the effect on the Board's position with other international bodies such as COJO and CBJO. On 26 March 1973, the president of the WJC, Dr Nahum Goldmann, wrote to the president of the Board confirming that if the Board were to join:

1. In any case, when there was a conflict between the constitution of the Board and that of the WJC, the Board's view would prevail.
2. All approaches to British government would only be made by the Board.
3. In approaches to the EEC, the Board could make separate representations in the name of British Jewry.
4. In all items affecting the Jewish religious interests, the Board would represent the views of British Jewry.[43]

These terms were acceptable to the Board and at a special meeting of the Board on 20 January 1974 the recommendation of the Executive Committee that the Board should become a National Participant of the WJC was agreed by 224 votes to twenty-eight.[44] Thus ended a saga that had started in 1936 when the Board refused an invitation to join the WJC, partly because it thought that joining an international body would lead to a hostile reaction in Britain, particularly from antisemites, and partly because it wanted to protect its own sole access to the British government. The world – as well as personalities and the Board's political objectives – had changed.

Number of Deputies

As a result of the dispute over Clause 43 and the withdrawal of deputies by the Strictly Orthodox congregations, the chief rabbi and the United Synagogue became concerned that the Board might come under the dominance of the Progressives. The United Synagogue had always placed limits on the number of deputies each constituent synagogue could elect and these numbers were generally much lower than the numbers permitted under the constitution. As a consequence of its concern that the Progressives might come to dominate the Board, from 1976 onwards the United Synagogue relaxed this restriction and encouraged constituent synagogues to elect their full permitted quota. This explains why the number of deputies increased from 432 in 1973 to 667 in 1985. This overwhelming number of 667, more than the number of MPs, attracted criticism in the Jewish press and was of concern to the honorary officers. The president, Dr Lionel Kopelowitz, asked the Law, Parliamentary and General Purposes Committee to examine the position. They recommended quite drastic changes. Synagogue representation should be reduced from one deputy for every 200 members, with no upper limit, to one deputy for every 400 members with a maximum of five; deputies from central synagogal organizations should be reduced from twenty-four to fourteen; Commonwealth representation should be ended; and the number of deputies from institutions should be reduced except for women and youth, where there should be an increase.[45] After difficult and acrimonious debates, the proposals were accepted. In the 1988 elections, the number of deputies elected fell to 448, back to the position in 1973. The Central Orthodox still had a good majority compared with the Progressives, but in order to ensure some control the United Synagogue formed its deputies into a group. Discipline in this group was not strong and members often did not vote in accord with their orders, particularly in elections for officers and committee members.

Reorganization

The question of examining the structure and running of the Board had been raised by Dr Kopelowitz at a Board meeting in late 1973, and on 14 August 1974 the Executive Committee established a working party to consider the structure, functions and administration of the Board. The terms of reference were to examine, report and make recommendations on the functions of the Board, including an examination of its objects, the basis of its representation, its functions and methods of procedure and work.[46] In an interview with the *JC*, Lord Fisher explained that this study had always been one of his objectives, since 'for more than forty five years there had been no examination of the Board and whether it was doing things that it should not and not doing things that it should'.[47] Membership of the working party did not include the honorary officers or chairmen of Board committees and it was under an independent and impartial chairman, Jack Wolkind, who was the town clerk and chief executive of Tower Hamlets.[48] The working party thus became known as the Wolkind Working Party.

The report of the working party was received by the Executive Committee in April 1976 and it was generally expected that it would be circulated and discussed by the Board shortly afterwards. It was not. The Executive Committee found the report disappointing. It did not deal with what the Board did (as Lord Fisher had hoped) but rather with its structure and how it operated. Nor did it deal with the representative nature of the Board and how representative of the Jewish community it really was, as had been advocated by the *JC* and other critics. It recommended, without specifying how, an increase in the representation of women and younger persons. The Executive Committee did not like the report since the recommendation was to disband that committee and replace the committee structure of the Board with a four-departmental organization reporting to a committee of the honorary officers (increased from four to five or six).[49] The Executive Committee held dozens of meetings discussing the recommendations and it was not until December 1977 that the report, plus counter-recommendations from the Executive Committee, was sent to Board members. It was discussed at a special Board meeting on 5 February 1978, but the results at that meeting were inconclusive and further meetings on it were held in July and October 1978, resulting in only a few rather minor changes to the operation of the Board. Transformation would have to wait.

The wait was a long time, in fact until 1993. The Board's annual report for 1993 was headlined 'A Year of Change',[50] but as far as the structure and running of the Board were concerned, change did not happen. Much time was spent considering proposals from the honorary officers to reform the Board's structure. The aim was a leaner, streamlined and more efficient and effective Board. The proposals were to reduce the number of deputies, reduce the number and size of committees and reduce the number of plenary sessions. It is clear that change was needed – there were more than 400 deputies, and twelve committees with membership ranging between fifteen and thirty. These proposals were approved in principle in June but when the required amendments to the constitution regarding a reduction in the number of deputies and fewer plenary sessions were presented to a plenary session of the Board in December 1993, they failed to obtain the necessary two-thirds majority after a very heated debate.[51] As a result, it was decided to defer consideration of the proposals to streamline the committee structure. The whole issue was reconsidered in the early months of 1994, and the proposals to reduce the number of deputies and plenary meetings were again rejected. However, the number of committees was reduced to eight and their size reduced, but the number of vice-presidents was increased from two to three.[52]

Early in 1995, the United Synagogue and the Progressive group considered that major changes to the operation of the Board were vital. Indeed, in June 1994 the United Synagogue had threatened to withdraw its six deputies from the Board if changes were not made.[53] This threat was particularly serious as, if carried out, it would almost certainly be followed by withdrawal of deputies from most United Synagogue constituent synagogues, and the numbers were such and the financial consequences so severe that such a move would almost certainly have led to the demise of the Board. In October 1995, the Executive Committee decided to appoint a firm of management consultants to propose ways of streamlining the Board's decision-making structure and improving management performance and the general running of the Board.[54] A wise move, since, as has been found in many other organizations both business and institutional, change is difficult to achieve when generated internally and difficult to resist when recommended by external consultants.

The recommendations of the consultants, the Chelms Management Consultancy, were agreed by the Board in June 1996 and implemented following the triennial elections in 1997.[55] In essence, the committee structure was dissolved and the work of the Board divided into four divisions – Defence and Group Relations, Community Issues, International, and Financial and Organisation – each headed by an honorary officer with eight elected deputies as members. No deputy could serve on more than one division. Each division would have the power to organize committees to carry out its work. A much smaller Executive Committee (reduced from thirty to eleven members) would have overall responsibility under the chairmanship of the president. The recommendations also included a restructuring of the responsibilities of the professional management of the Board under an enhanced role for the director general. The report did not recommend any changes in the number of deputies but proposed that the Board must review how it can involve the major community organizations who have never been or are not currently members of the Board. It also proposed that the number of plenary sessions should be reduced to eight. In essence, it was hoped that these changes would give a clearer focus to the activities of the Board and 'transform it into a modern organisation which is democratic, efficient, effective and accountable'.[56]

2. HOME ISSUES

The 'Jacobs' Affair[57]

The period covered by this chapter started with the Board's involvement in an episode that exemplified the religious splits within the British Jewish community.

In 1959, Rabbi Dr Louis Jacobs was appointed by the chief rabbi, Israel Brodie, as tutor and lecturer at Jews' College, with some sort of indication from the College Council that when the then principal retired in the very near future he would take over. Louis Jacobs was one of the foremost rabbis in Britain, a leading Jewish scholar, an excellent teacher and renowned preacher. In 1956, he had written a book entitled *We Have Reason to Believe*, which was essentially intended to answer some of the questions that had concerned his congregants over the years. In some circles, however, many of the points made were considered heretical. When the principal retired, Jacobs was not appointed and, when it became clear that the chief rabbi would not agree to his appointment, he resigned. This was followed by the resignation of the honorary officers and some members of the College Council. In 1962, the chief rabbi explained that he could not appoint Jacobs due to 'his published views'.[58] In 1964 Jacobs's previous post as minister of the New West End Synagogue became vacant, and by a unanimous vote of its Board of Management he was invited to return. The appointment required a certificate from the chief rabbi, and he refused to issue such a certificate unless Jacobs retracted some of the remarks in his book and other statements he had made that seemed to question the divine inspiration of the Torah. He refused. The Board of Management of the New West End Synagogue, supported by an overwhelming majority vote of its members, decided to appoint Jacobs without a certificate. The Council of the United Synagogue dismissed the Board of Management and replaced it with its own nominees.[59] The result was that a significant number of members of the New West End resigned and formed a new independent synagogue called the New London, which was eventually housed in the former St John's Wood Synagogue.

The Board now entered the scene. The New London Synagogue applied to join the Board and was admitted without any problem. In 1965, it applied to the Board to have its secretary appointed as a marriage secretary. The president of the Board, as was required, requested a certificate from the chief rabbi stating that the synagogue was 'a congregation of persons professing the Jewish religion'. Although the New London was able to provide certain assurances, these were considered insufficient and the chief rabbi refused to issue a certificate.[60] It looked as if the Liberal synagogues saga of the late 1940s was going to be replayed. However, matters took a different turn. Chief Rabbi Brodie retired and in 1967 the new chief rabbi, Dr Immanuel Jakobovits, issued the necessary certificate and the president of the Board was able to appoint the synagogue's secretary as a marriage secretary.[61] Dr Jakobovits had accepted an assurance from Rabbi Jacobs that he would not allow any marriage to be performed that was not in conformity with the halacha, in particular that both parties to the marriage were born Jewish or if they had converted then the conversion was under the auspices of an Orthodox Beth Din.[62]

Antisemitism and Security
Antisemitic incidents in 1965 were the most serious for many years. Brondesbury Synagogue was virtually destroyed and there were arson attempts on a number of other synagogues in London and the provinces as well as Jewish schools and kosher butcher shops. There were also swastika and other antisemitic daubings and some attacks on individual Jews. The Defence Committee and AJEX sprung into action and organized a comprehensive security system for the protection of synagogues and other Jewish premises throughout the country. Some arrests and convictions were made and the evidence was that most of those involved in the incidents were members of fascist organizations such as the National Socialist Movement.[63]

A consequence of these incidents was the formation in 1966 of a new group called the Jewish Aid Committee of Britain (JACOB) claiming to present an alternative and more vigorous policy for Jewish defence to that of the Board. The group published a pamphlet entitled *With a Strong Hand*.[64] It claimed that the Board was too complacent and consistently underestimated the danger of fascist organizations operating in Britain. Its members did not consider themselves as rivals to the Defence Committee but rather a 'ginger group'.[65] In April 1966 they wrote to each deputy encouraging them to meet with members of the JACOB committee for private discussions. Their objective was not to re-place the Board in the area of Jewish defence, but rather to elect a new, virile and young leadership of the Defence Committee. The Defence Committee countered JACOB by issuing a leaflet entitled *Defence with Responsibility*,[66] denying that its approach was passive and arguing, as it had always done, that violence against fascists resulted in unnecessary publicity. JACOB considered this much too simplistic as it failed to take into account other factors such as the quality of leadership of fascist organizations and their ability to exploit certain situations.[67] Nigel Copsey points out that in the event both sides could claim they were right. The support for the main fascist party, the Union Movement, was negligible at the 1966 General Election, but shortly thereafter most of the fascist parties combined to form the National Front, which began to cash in on the immigration issue.[68] JACOB did not obtain much support from the deputies and the group eventually wound up.

By the late 1960s security had become a major issue for the community. There were attacks on Jews as well as Jewish buildings, such that it was not only necessary to protect Jewish buildings, such as synagogues and schools, but protection was also needed for Jewish functions. As a result, the Board agreed on the merger of several different groups and organizations into the Community Security Organisation (CSO), a separate organization but closely associated with the Board. This became responsible for defence and security for the British Jewish community as well as monitoring those opposed to the community. In conjunction with the CSO, the defence department of the Board examined the media for antisemitic reports, articles, statements and programmes. In addition, the whole country was covered by regional and local security officers who were advised, and if necessary trained, by the CSO.

In the mid-1970s the National Front won a significant level of support in local elections in London and the Midlands.[69] The Anti-Nazi

League (ANL) was established in late 1977 to resist this advance of the National Front and many Jews joined. In its first year it recruited nearly 50,000 members and was regarded as the largest extra-parliamentary movement since the Campaign for Nuclear Disarmament (CND) in the 1960s.[70] However, the ANL was considered anti-Israel, particularly as a result of the influence on it by activists from the Trotskyite Socialist Workers Party, and this deterred the Board from collaborating with it.[71] Martin Savitt, the chairman of the Defence Committee, remarked: 'The league is an organisation whose motives are primarily political and inimical to the interests of Israel and World Jewry.'[72] In fact this issue divided the Jewish community and on 27 October 1978 the *JC* commented: 'Public debate and the correspondence columns of this newspaper suggest that no issue in recent years has so divided Jewish public opinion as the arguments for and against supporting the Anti-Nazi League campaign against the National Front.'[73] The *JC* advocated some sort of umbrella body that would enable the Board to support the ANL's campaign, but nothing came of it. There also might have been another reason for the Board's reluctance to collaborate with the ANL. The Board had always eschewed violent and active confrontations with fascist organizations, and these were among the main tactics of the ANL.

By the 1980s, the threats to the community came not only from antisemites but also much more so from those opposed to Israel who identified Jews in the diaspora as supporters of Israel. It was during this period that the nomenclature 'anti-Zionist' began to be used to describe these groups. In fact the Board's annual report for 1991 identified three primary and two secondary sources of hostility to the Jewish community. The three primary ones were what the report termed the far right, the extreme Moslem fundamentalists and the campaigning anti-Zionists.[74] The secondary sources were the extreme left and 'social' antisemitism. Thus the Board believed it was faced with not only securing the community from and monitoring the activities of the 'traditional' antisemites such as the fascist groups, but also some anti-Israel groups as well. Another factor entering the equation in the late 1980s was the campaign to deny the Holocaust, led by David Irving. The CSO and the Board had to monitor this group and take appropriate action. They did so in 1991 when they persuaded the home secretary that Fred Leuchter, a leading Holocaust denier, who had entered Britain surreptitiously, should be deported.[75]

Although the National Front had shifted its main targets away from

Jews, nonetheless the Board continuously monitored its activities and opposed all its actions. There was a lot of concern as the May 1994 local elections approached, and the Board took the initiative in forming the United Campaign against Racism (UCAR). This attracted broad support across both the political and religious spectra. UCAR organized a public meeting where pledges were made to oppose racism and keep the race issue out of politics. Those present at the meeting included Michael Howard, the home secretary, and Tony Blair, the shadow home secretary. The problem with the Board's initiative was that there was little grass-roots support and one observer at the meeting reported that there were more people on the platform than in the audience.[76]

In January 1995, the work of the CSO was transferred to the Community Security Trust (CST) that had been established for this purpose in November 1994. The CST was established as a charity to take advantage of new charity regulations that permitted security organizations to obtain charitable status. Such a structure would also more readily attract donations from the Jewish public. The following statement was made in the 1995 annual report of the Board:

> Working in co-operation with the police and other statutory authorities, the CST provides all sections of the Jewish community with a range of services, including physical security, the provision of security advice, materials and training, and monitoring and assessing the intentions and capabilities of the community's enemies. It is the CST that now deals with security and defence and produces all defence related reports for, and on behalf of, the Board, which retains responsibility for political defence and group relations matters. The CST will continue to work closely with the Board on all defence matters.[77]

The Board had thus dispensed with one of its primary services to the Jewish community in Britain. Strictly speaking, this was not quite the first time, since in 1950 following the establishment of a National Council of Shechita Boards, the Board's activities regarding *shechita* became limited to defending the right to practise *shechita*, and the Board were no longer involved in its day-to-day matters.

Race Relations Legislation
Following the return of a Labour government in the October 1964 general election, it was announced in the queen's speech at the opening

of Parliament that the government intended to take action against racial discrimination. The Board had been pressing for such legislation and immediately established an ad hoc committee to examine the issues, and this committee drafted a memorandum which was presented to the home secretary on 14 January 1965.[78] The Race Relations Bill was published in April 1965 and included two sections that the Board considered of particular importance to the Jewish community. Section 3 made it an offence to intend to stir up hatred against 'any section of the public in Great Britain distinguished by colour, race or ethnic or national origins' by the publication or distribution of written matter which was 'threatening, abusive, or insulting'. Alternatively, to use in a public place or at a public meeting words which were 'threatening, abusive or insulting', when the material distributed or the words used were likely to stir up hatred against a section of the public on such grounds. Section 4 made it clear that not only were words spoken at a public meeting which were intended or likely to 'provoke a breach of the peace' made an offence, but also the display of signs or written material which would have the same effect.[79]

After examining the Bill, the Board's major concerns were that religion was absent from any of the categories of persons who were to be given protection, that the necessity to prove 'intent to incite' on the part of the accused person might make prosecution very difficult, and that there should be an absolute curb on spoken and written racist propaganda. These concerns were raised with the home secretary, who made it clear that it was the intention that Jews would be covered, and this assurance was given at all stages during the debates in Parliament.[80] The other concerns of the Board would be considered as the bill proceeded but no satisfactory amendment was made. One late change was that the clauses imposing criminal sanctions against discriminatory practices were removed and replaced by a conciliation procedure. In November 1965 the Race Relations Act was enacted, and generally welcomed by the Board.[81]

The proof of the pudding was going to be in the eating, and certain racist groups immediately found a let-out in that the ban on publication of offensive literature was for publication to the public at large, whereas these groups formed book clubs and published to these clubs. The Board alerted the government to this, and other circumventions and amendments were promised. This emphasizes the point that the Board has to be continuously on the alert in this area as in others. Nonetheless, despite this 'loophole' the Board was particularly pleased to note a significant diminution in racist and antisemitic literature and speeches. Furthermore, there had been a number of successful prosecutions of offences under the act. There was, however, some concern when the 1967 report of the Race Relations Board was published and it drew attention to some uncertainty as to whether or not Jews were covered. The government announced that it intended to legislate if necessary to remove this uncertainty.[82] The following year the government confirmed its view that Jews were covered by the Act.[83]

Sunday Trading

The 1994 Sunday Trading Act permitted general opening of shops on Sunday, but those over a certain size were limited to six hours of opening. The Board was successful in obtaining exemption from this limitation for Jewish shops that closed on Saturday. The panels, which were organized under the auspices of the Board to deal with Sunday trading for Jewish shops under the former legislation, became redundant. The 1994 Act resolved an issue that had been plaguing the Board for many years. In the 1970s, evasion of the Sunday trading laws had become quite widespread and non-Jewish traders had used Jewish partners to obtain registration for Sunday trading even though these partners had little or any involvement in the business or in its financial returns. A solution had been adopted under some regulations introduced in 1979 that gave the Board power to vet the applicants before they could apply for an exemption certificate. The machinery for such vetting had been heavily criticized, but with the 1994 Act, it became redundant.[84]

3. FOREIGN AFFAIRS

Foreign affairs continued in the main to be conducted through the various international organizations of which the Board was a member, such as such as COJO and CBJO. In 1975 the Board established yet another committee for international affairs. This was the United Nations Association Jewish Affiliates Co-Coordinating Committee, and it was comprised of representatives of British Jewish organizations affiliated to the United Nations Association.[85] The honorary officers of the Board and members of the Foreign Affairs Committee were assiduous in attending a great number of meetings throughout the world on behalf of the Board and thus the British Jewish community.

Aden

In 1967 the Board was responsible for the rescue and resettlement of the small Jewish community in Aden. Following independence, the Jews in Aden were in extreme danger from terrorist activity. Sir Barnett Janner, the chairman of the Foreign Affairs Committee, contacted the Foreign Office and was able to obtain work vouchers for Adeni Jews who wished to emigrate to Britain and to facilitate arrangements for those who wished to emigrate to Israel. The Foreign Office instructed the high commissioner to give full protection to the Jewish community whilst it remained in Aden. In April 1967 the Board arranged the evacuation of all the remaining Jews; fifty-two were flown to Israel and eighty to Britain. In fact the Board's secretary, Abraham Marks, flew out to Aden in a specially chartered plane to supervise the evacuation. Those who came to Britain were accommodated at first in the Jews' Temporary Shelter and were given assistance and advice by the Board.[86]

Israel

Israel was the responsibility of the Eretz Israel Committee that changed its name to the Israel Committee in 1980. Much of its time was spent considering developments in Israel and arranging visits there by delegations from the Board. It was in constant touch with senior government leaders in Israel and discussed with them matters of interest and concern to Jews in Britain. It was very common for senior Israeli government ministers to address the Board on their visits to Britain. The Board consistently complained to the British government when the government took action or a government minister or official made a statement that was considered against the interests of Israel. For example, in 1969 the Board objected very strongly to Britain voting in favour of a United Nation's resolution on the Al Aksa mosque fire that seemed to implicate Israel, and protested strongly about the speech on this subject by Lord Caradon, the British permanent representative to the United Nations.[87] Similarly, the Board praised British government actions or statements that seemed to favour Israel.[88]

The Board sprang into action during the 1967 crisis and Six-Day War. A public meeting was convened by the Board on 30 May and attended by more than 1,000 people. The meeting was addressed by the president and other officers and senior members of the Board and concluded with the chief rabbi reciting a psalm. The Executive and Eretz Israel Committees seemed in almost continuous session: they met on 1 June, 4 June, 7 June – the day hostilities commenced – and 8 June. A number of statements were issued following the war, all expressing support for the actions taken by Israel; these no doubt reflected the views and opinions of the vast majority of Jews in Britain.

In advance of the United Nations meetings on the Middle East situation, the Board was clearly concerned with the likely attitude of the British government. On 12 October the Board sent a cable to the prime minister and foreign secretary asking for confirmation that government policy would include full recognition of Israel by all her neighbours, agreed permanent frontiers and free navigation through all international waterways. This request was prefaced by this sentence: 'Cognisant of past experience and bitter lessons, vagueness and appeasement we would welcome assurances that HMG's policy continues based upon guarantee following fundamental and just interests of Israel.' The reply from the foreign secretary, George Brown, dated 27 October, confirmed that this would indeed be the British policy, but added that in addition there had to be a just settlement of the problem of the old and new refugees and that there should be no territorial aggrandizement as a result of war. The upshot was the United Nations Security Council Resolution 242, tabled by the UK and adopted unanimously. It included the three policy points made by the Board as well as reference to refugees, and in the English version referred to 'withdrawal from territories', a phrase that subsequently gave rise to much misunderstanding and disagreement, due to different interpretations of the words, that has not yet been resolved. The Board expressed some disquiet with some of the resolution's provisions, and in response the British government pointed out that the Israeli government, although it regarded the resolution as less than ideal, did not express disquiet at its provisions and was prepared to acquiesce in it.[89] The Board was very active during and following the Yom Kippur War in 1973. In particular, it entered into lengthy correspondence with the British government over what it considered the government's less than impartial policy, pointing out that it appeared more concerned with oil than with a just settlement.[90]

In 1975, the Board wrote to Yitzhak Rabin, the prime minister of Israel, expressing regret at the manner in which the ceremony of re-interring the remains of Lord Moyne's assassins in Israel was handled. They were treated as heroes and the Board pointed out 'that terrorism, in whatever form, was indivisible and Anglo-Jewry could not afford to take an equivocal stand on the issue, no matter what the nature of the particular circumstances prevailing in any given instance'.[91] When this matter was raised at a Board meeting on 20 July 1975, the president stated that it was in the best interests of the community that it should not be discussed.[92] This is one of the few occasions where there has been some formal criticism of Israel by the Board, although at Israel Committee and Board meetings many deputies have criticized some aspects of Israeli government policies.

Soviet Jewry

The ousting of Nikita Khrushchev and his replacement by Leonid Brezhnev and Alexey Kosygin in October 1964 did not improve the position of Jews in Russia. The Board continued to make public statements on the discriminatory treatment of them, and delegations regularly visited the Foreign Office to keep it fully informed of what was happening. The policy of the Board was reiterated at a special Board meeting on 16 May 1965 and at a normal plenary meeting on 24 June 1965 as 'to approach the matter with the greatest care and responsibility and to utilise both private diplomacy and reasoned public protest until such time as the Jews in the USSR were accorded full cultural, religious and humanitarian rights'.[93] There was some evidence that the continued worldwide bad publicity in this area had some effect and it was reported to the Board that a number of apologias were published in Soviet journals.[94] Even the British Communist Party was embarrassed and in May 1966 issued an appeal to the Soviet authorities to avoid these 'impermissible crudities' which could be exploited by antisemites.[95]

Premier Kosygin was due to visit Britain from 6 to 13 February 1967 and the Board asked him to receive a delegation, but this was refused. Consequently the Board sent him a memorandum on 9 February countersigned by all the leading Jewish organizations in Britain. The memorandum reiterated the favourable position of Jews in the Soviet Union before the Second World War and the atrocities perpetrated by the Nazis. It appealed that he should permit proper provision for Jewish educational and cultural facilities, arrangements to be made for synagogues in cities with Jewish populations and permission for Soviet Jewry to have contact with Jewish communities in other parts of the world.[96] There was no reply, although there was an unconfirmed rumour that the baking of matzot had been permitted in some towns. A delegation from the Board saw the Soviet ambassador in April, but this did not appear to do any good since anti-Jewish and anti-Israel publicity continued and about forty Jews were refused exit permits for Israel.[97]

Efforts to obtain some amelioration for the position of Soviet Jewry continued and, at the request of the Board, the prime minister, Harold Wilson, raised the matter during his visit to Moscow in February 1968. He had no success.[98] In June 1969 the Board convened a national conference on Soviet Jewry. The object was essentially to draw the media and the British public's attention to the plight of Soviet Jews, and the proceedings were published on 10 December, Human Rights Day, under the title *Light on Soviet Jewry*.[99]

From the late 1960s the Board devoted much of its time to Soviet Jewry. It issued dozens of press releases and held many press conferences and public meetings as well as meetings with government and leaders of the Opposition, MPs and non-Jewish national and international bodies thought to be sympathetic, and issued appeals to various Soviet authorities, government ministers and ambassadors as well as the United Nations. In 1971 the Women's Campaign for Soviet Jewry was established. It was commonly called 'the 35s' as it was founded by a group of women in support of Raiza Palatnik, a Jewish prisoner in Russia who was aged 35, as were many of the original participants at the first meeting of the group. It was an independent committee and often came into conflict with the Board, as many Board members did not like the committee's method of campaigning.[100] On the other hand, many leaders of the Board, including Barnett Janner, Greville Janner and Victor Mishcon, supported its objectives and methods.[101] In December 1971 the Board formed a special committee called the Soviet Jewry Action Committee, in fact a subcommittee of the Foreign Affairs Committee.[102] One of its first actions was to establish a 'link-up scheme' whereby Soviet Jews who wished to receive messages were twinned with families from Britain. This scheme was subsequently taken over by the 35s and became their 'adoption and twinning programme'.[103]

From January 1972 the Board published a weekly information bulletin titled *Soviet Jewry Bulletin*.[104] All of these activities were connected with the general deterioration of the position of the Jews in the Soviet Union, appeals from individual or groups, particularly those trying to leave for Israel, and those arrested. For example, in June 1970 a number of Jews were arrested in Leningrad on charges of anti-Soviet activity and treason and in November more Jews were arrested for an alleged attempt to hijack a plane.[105] In December 1975 the National Council for Soviet Jewry was established by the Board as a coordinating body for Soviet

Jewry work in Britain. Many deputies were concerned that this body would abrogate the authority of the Board and could be taken over by militant activists whom the community would never endorse or support.[106] In fact almost the opposite occurred, because within a year Doreen Gainsford, the chair of the 35s, resigned as vice-chairman of the National Council because it was not active enough.[107]

Action on all fronts continued until the late 1980s when glasnost and perestroika replaced oppression as far as the Jews of Eastern Europe were concerned, although even before the era of Mikhail Gorbachev more than 300,000 Jews had succeeded in obtaining exit visas. Until the Soviet archives for the period are opened, it is not possible to judge what effect the lobbying by the Board and other bodies and the actions of the 35s and similar groups had on the Soviet government's policies towards Jews. It certainly provided the Jews in Britain with a cause which united them and offered them something to demonstrate about and gave comfort and hope to the Jews in Russia and behind the Iron Curtain. There is an unfounded proposition that the Women's Campaign for Soviet Jewry (the 35s) helped to bring about the downfall of communism.[108]

NOTES

1. Marlena Schmool, 'A Hundred Years of British Jewish Statistics', *Jewish Year Book Centenary Edition* (London: Vallentine Mitchell, 1996), p.viii.
2. Geoffrey Alderman, *Modern British Jewry*, new edn (Oxford: Clarendon Press, 1998), pp.321–6, 409. W.D. Rubinstein, *A History of the Jews in the English-Speaking World: Great Britain* (Basingstoke: Macmillan, 1996), pp.418–9.
3. These figures have been extracted from Marlena Schmool and Frances Cohen, *British Synagogue Membership in 1990* (London: Board of Deputies, 1993), p.25, adjusted for membership of Masorti synagogues.
4. BOD, ACC/3121/A/42, p.153; Schmool, 'Hundred Years of British Jewish Statistics', p.xv.
5. Alderman, *Modern British Jewry*, pp.379–88.
6. Israel Finestein, *Scenes and Personalities in Anglo-Jewry, 1800–2000* (London: Vallentine Mitchell, 2002), p.22.
7. Discussion with Judge Finestein on 2 September 2009.
8. Myrella Cohen, 'After the Preston Report', *Jewish Year Book 1997* (London: Vallentine Mitchell, 1997), pp.lxiv–lxv.
9. Alderman, *Modern British Jewry*, p.342.
10. Marlena Schmool and Frances Cohen, *A Profile of British Jewry: Patterns and Trends at the Turn of the Century* (London: Board of Deputies, 1998), p.29.
11. See Colin Shindler, 'How the Left turned on Israel', *JC*, 25 December 2009, pp.6 and 8.
12. Rubinstein, *History of the Jews in the English-Speaking World* pp.375–80.
13. *Jewish Chronicle* [JC], 17 July 1964, p.1.
14. *JC*, 7 August 1944 p.10.
15. *JC*, 16 October 1964, p.6; 23 October 1964, p.12; 30 October 1964, p.17.
16. BOD, ACC/3121/A/41, p.183.
17. *JC*, 7 July 1967, pp.1, 18.
18. *JC*, 23 December 1966, p.6.
19. *JC*, 16 February 1968, p.8.

20. BOD, ACC/3121/A/42, p.158.
21. Hans Kimmel, 'The Structure and Regime of the Board of Deputies of British Jews', *Jewish Public Affairs*, no. 4 (February 1968), pp.1–4.
22. *JC*, 16 October 1970, p.22.
23. Rubinstein, *History of the Jews in the English-Speaking World*, p.417.
24. Laurence Rigal and Rosita Rosenberg, *Liberal Judaism: The First Hundred Years* (London: Liberal Judaism, 2004), pp.170ff.
25. *JC*, 26 February 1971, p.23.
26. BOD, ACC/3121/A/42, p.31.
27. As mentioned in the Introduction, the Orthodox Group consisted of deputies from the Strictly Orthodox synagogues.
28. Abba Bornstein and Bernard Homa, *Tell it in Gath, British Jewry and Clause 43: The Inside Story* (London: Private, 1972), pp.12–13, 30–1.
29. BOD, ACC/3121/A/44, p.25.
30. Annual Report of the Board of Deputies (AR), 1970, p.40.
31. Bornstein and Homa, *Tell it in Gath*, p.15.
32. Ibid., pp.20–1.
33. BOD, ACC/3121/A/44, p.144.
34. Rigal and Rosenberg, *Liberal Judaism*, p.170.
35. The letters were published in AR, 1972, pp.5–7.
36. BOD, ACC/3121/A/44, p.179.
37. Ibid., p.7.
38. Bernard Homa, *Footprints on the Sands of Time* (London: author, 1990), pp.159–60.
39. Rigal and Rosenberg, *Liberal Judaism*, p.171; Meir Persoff, *Faith Against Reason: Religious Reform and the British Chief Rabbinate 1840–1990* (London: Vallentine Mitchell, 2008), p.355.
40. Quoted in Persoff, *Faith Against Reason*, pp.354–5.
41. Ibid., p.356.
42. BOD, ACC/3121/A/45, pp.137, 151, 162.
43. BOD, ACC/3121/A/46, p.96.
44. AR, 1973–76, p.62; BOD, ACC/3121/A/46, p.97.
45. *JC*, 26 June 1987, p.8.
46. AR, 1973–76, p.59; BOD, ACC/3121/A/47, pp.153, 161, 177.
47. *JC*, 17 January 1975, p.19.
48. BOD, ACC/3121/A/47, p.153.
49. *JC*, 3 February 1978, p.8; 10 February 1978, pp.8, 16; 17 February 1978, p.22.
50. AR, 1993, p.5.
51. BOD, Minutes of Board meeting on 19 December 1993.
52. BOD, Minutes of Board meeting on 17 April 1994.
53. *JC*, 10 June 1994, p.1.
54. BOD, Executive Committee report of October 1995 and approved by Board in Minutes of Board meeting on 22 October 1995, p.4.
55. BOD, Minutes of Board meeting on 19 May 1996, pp.2–5.
56. BOD, *Final Report to the Board of Deputies: The Study 'A Process for Managing Change'*, 15 April 1996.
57. Louis Jacobs, *Helping with Inquiries: An Autobiography* (London: Vallentine Mitchell, 1989).
58. Ibid., p.139.
59. Ibid., pp.159–68.
60. BOD, ACC/3121/D/1/81, letter from Chief Rabbi dated 11 May 1965.
61. BOD, ACC/3121/A/42, p.85.
62. Homa, *Footprints on the Sands of Time*, p.221; Jacobs, *Helping with Inquiries*, p.185.
63. AR, 1965, pp.40–2; AR, 1966, pp.34–5.
64. *With A Strong Hand* (London: Narod Press, 1966).
65. *JC*, 22 April 1966, p.11.
66. *Defence with Responsibility* (London: Board of Deputies, 1966).
67. Nigel Copsey, *Anti-Fascism in Britain* (Basingstoke: Macmillan, 2000), pp.110–11.
68. Ibid., p.112.
69. David Cesarani, *The Jewish Chronicle and Anglo-Jewry, 1841–1991* (Cambridge: Cambridge University Press, 1994), p.241.

70. Copsey, *Anti-Fascism in Britain*, p.115.
71. Ibid., p.147.
72. *JC*, 6 October 1978, p.25.
73. *JC*, 27 October 1978, p.20.
74. AR, 1991, p.32.
75. Ibid.
76. Copsey, Anti-Fascism in Britain, p.177.
77. AR, 1995, p.16.
78. BOD, ACC/3121/A/41, p.100b.
79. AR, 1965, p.44.
80. For example, see BOD, ACC/3121/A/41, p.133.
81. AR, 1964, p.39; AR, 1965, pp.43–6.
82. AR, 1967, p.26.
83. BOD, ACC/3121/A/43, p.33.
84. Geoffrey Alderman, 'Jews and Sunday Trading: The Use and Abuse of Delegated Legislation', *Public Administration*, 60 (March 1982), pp.99–100; BOD, ACC/3121/C/13/9/3.
85. BOD, ACC/3121/A/48, p.189.
86. AR, 1967, pp.12, 18.
87. AR, 1969, pp.14–15.
88. Ibid., p.15
89. AR, 1967, pp.14–17.
90. AR, 1973–76, pp.68–72.
91. BOD, ACC/3121/A/48, p.172.
92. Ibid., p.183.
93. AR, 1965, pp.38–9; BOD, ACC/3121/A/41, pp.130–2, 137.
94. AR, 1964, p.36.
95. AR, 1966, p.32.
96. BOD, ACC/3121/A/42, pp.70ff.
97. AR, 1967, pp.23–4.
98. AR, 1968, p.18.
99. AR, 1969, pp.21–2.
100. See Daphne Gerlis, *Those Wonderful Women in Black: The Story of the Women's Campaign for Soviet Jewry* (London: Minerva Press, 1996).
101. Ibid., p.24.
102. AR, 1972, p.23.
103. Gerlis, *Wonderful Women in Black*, pp.22, 91.
104. BOD, ACC/3121/A/45, p.22.
105. For example, see AR, 1970, pp.23–9 and all subsequent reports until 1988.
106. BOD, ACC/3121/A/49, pp.2–3, 7–11.
107. Gerlis, *Wonderful Women in Black*, p.23.
108. Ibid., pp.182–8.

7 Looking Forward and Looking Back

The new millennium had an explosive start. On 11 September 2001 there was the destruction of the twin towers of the World Trade Centre in New York; in 2002 Operation Defensive Shield in the West Bank; in 2003 the Iraq War; in July 2005 the London bombings; in 2006 Israel's second Lebanon war; and in 2008 Operation Cast Lead in Gaza. Each of these events gave rise in Britain to anti-Zionism and antisemitism, and the three events directly involving Israel led to much uneasiness in the British Jewish community and to what was seen by most Jews in Britain as distorted media reporting. It is much too soon to put these, as well as other recent matters involving the Board, into proper perspective. For this reason, part one of this chapter, which brings this history up to the Board's 250th anniversary in 2010, only includes issues that may be seen by future historians as of some significance. Part two of this chapter is a review of the last 250 years, highlighting the major matters and criticisms concerning the Board since its inception.

1. LOOKING FORWARD, 1997 TO 2010 AND BEYOND

In June 1997 Eldred Tabachnik was re-elected unopposed as president. His first priority was to implement the changes in the Board's structure that had been agreed in the previous year. This was quite a mammoth task as the old committee structure had been replaced by four divisions, each headed by an honorary officer with eight deputies to be elected to serve on them as well as a reorganization of the responsibilities of the staff. The changes would appear to have been carried out smoothly, although the 1997 annual report mentioned that there had been some hiccups, but they had been swiftly sorted out. The report stated that the result of the changes had led to 'a fresh, streamlined and revitalised Board', and that 'there was an increased involvement and excitement about the work of the Board, not only by the deputies and staff, but also in the wider community, since a number of major institutions that had hitherto declined to be represented on the Board now did so'.[1] Twelve months later the 1998 annual report stated: 'Overall the new arrangements represent a distinct improvement, with a much clearer system for enabling us to achieve our priorities and goals.'[2] One of the objects of the changes was a leaner organization, and this seems to have been achieved. Furthermore, the number of deputies has fallen from 362 immediately before the changes to the most recent figure of 267, a reduction of just over 25 per cent. There has also been a reduction in the number of congregations that are represented on the Board, mainly in regional congregations. This is a reflection of the decline in the number of Jews in many parts of the country outside London, which in itself offers challenges to the British Jewish community and the Board.

In 2000, the Board celebrated the new millennium by electing, unopposed, its first woman president. Jo Wagerman had been head teacher of the JFS from 1985 to 1993, was appointed an OBE in 1992 and had been a vice-president of the Board from 1994. Jo Wagerman decided not to stand for a second term in 2003 due to poor health, and Henry Grunwald was elected, unopposed, to replace her. He is a QC, specializing in criminal law, and had been a vice-president of the Board from 1997. He was appointed an OBE in 2009. He was elected, again unopposed, for a second term in 2006. The 2009 election for president was unique. For the first time ever there were more than two candidates – in fact four. It was decided to use the single transferable vote system for this, to ensure that the winning candidate was supported by more than half the deputies. In the event, Vivian Wineman, a solicitor and senior vice-president of the Board since 2006, was successful.

Judging by the archived documents and the annual reviews of the Board there has been no let-up in the Board's activities in recent years. On the contrary, the work seems to have increased. The reorganization in 1996/97 came at a good and necessary time. There were a host of issues to occupy the Board in addition to all the usual 'routine' and regular matters, but three particular ones might prove to be of some significance.

Shechita

In 2003 the Board, together with the National Council of Shechita Boards, the Campaign for the Protection of Shechita and the Union of Orthodox Hebrew Congregations, established a campaign for the protection of *shechita* called Shechita UK, under the chairmanship of the then president of the Board.[3] It was hoped that by centralizing and coordinating the defence of *shechita* it would add more impetus to the lobby and would avoid what had happened in the past when a number of different Jewish groups lobbied separately and with different proposals. It was a particularly apposite time to establish such a body, since earlier in the year the Farm Animal Welfare Council had published a report calling for mandatory pre-stunning and the abolition of the current statutory exemption for meat killed by *shechita* or halal.[4] The recommendations in this report, which would have had the effect of banning *shechita*, were rejected by the government. Thanks were due, it would seem, to the lobbying by Shechita UK. Furthermore, the government acknowledged the scientific evidence submitted by Shechita UK that demonstrates that *shechita* is a humane method of animal slaughter.[5]

Concern on *shechita* issues moved to the European Community, where there was a threat of legislation that could have led to the banning of *shechita* throughout the EU. Because of these concerns and the need to lobby on a European-wide basis, Shechita UK was instrumental in the establishment of Shechita EU early in 2009. This has proved successful. Thanks to the lobbying of Shechita EU plus other organizations, the European Parliament voted in May 2009 to legalize *shechita*. This has to be ratified, and there are other hurdles to conquer. It was a significant victory for Shechita EU and the other members of the lobby.

Jewish Leadership Council

The Jewish Leadership Council (JLC) was established in 2003. It is comprised of the most senior lay leaders of the major institutions in the British Jewish community. Membership includes the chairs and presidents of synagogue movements and leaders of the main charities, welfare organizations and representative bodies, as well as a number of Jewish VIPs and individual leaders. It is not an elected body like the Board, although many of its members who are chairmen or presidents of major Jewish institutions are themselves elected into those positions. The first chairman of its executive committee was Henry Grunwald, president of the Board, and on his retirement Vivian Wineman, his successor as Board president, was elected to that office. The rules of the JLC provide for the chairman of its executive committee to be the president of the Board, unless otherwise agreed. Henry Grunwald wrote in the 2003 annual report of the Board that the aim of the JLC is 'to enhance the long-term effectiveness of Jewish communal representation and ensure greater consultation between key communal organisations and leaders. The Board remains the central representative body for the Jewish community and the Council has been formed to support our work and the work of other organisations within the community.'[6]

It is much too soon to say how the relationship between the Board and the JLC will develop, what tensions between them might emerge, and whether in time the JLC might wish to assert itself in areas that have hitherto been the prerogative and province of the Board.

Israel

The Board's policy towards Israel is a difficult area. In the latest constitution, it is stated that the Board shall 'Take such appropriate action as lies within its power to advance Israel's security, welfare and standing'.[7] The position is quite clear – the Board supports Israel but in no way does it represent Israel. It has not been slow to protest when it considers the British government, or more particularly the media, seems to have been biased against Israel. However, it is in the area of its statements regarding actions of the Israeli government that it has come under fire from some elements in the Jewish community in recent years. In its 1997 annual report, the Board stated: 'Whilst supporting the State of Israel and its right to exist, the Board has never been afraid to criticise where necessary.'[8] Yet where such criticism has been levied, the matters have been relatively minor and the criticisms muted. On major issues, the Board's public statements have tended to be supportive of Israeli government policies. Where the consensus view of the Board is against particular policies of the Israeli government it never publicly states this, but uses other and quiet channels with Israel to put over its views. The Board's position is particularly difficult in that the government, the media and the British public at large view it as the spokesperson for British Jewry.

In recent years the disagreements with some of the Board's statements on Israel, or sometimes a lack of a statement, have been articulated more strongly, mainly because of the disquiet felt by some members of the British Jewish community with the actions of Israel in Lebanon, the West Bank and Gaza.[9] On the other hand, there are many in the community who take the opposite view and consider that the Board does not stand up properly for Israel and is too concerned with not offending the British government.[10]

2. LOOKING BACK, 2010 TO 1760

As one looks back over the past 250 years of the life of the Board, a number of themes emerge which are discussed briefly in this final section.

Protection
A major feature of the activities of the Board is the protection it has afforded not only to the Jews of Britain but also to Jews in other countries. In its early years the Board's examination of new laws that might impact on Jews was a little sporadic, but with the creation of the Law, Parliamentary and General Purposes Committee in 1854 it has been relentless in its scrutiny. It is probably fair to say that virtually every piece of proposed legislation or regulations have been examined where there is a likelihood that they might affect Jews, and where necessary and appropriate representations have been made. This is particularly so in the area of religious observance. The Board has been vigorous, and successful, in protecting the rights of Jews to practise their religion without any hindrance. Examples are manifold, ranging from the defence of *shechita* to ensuring that alternative arrangements are made for observant Jewish examinees when examinations coincided with the Sabbath or Jewish festivals. Dates of elections have even been changed to enable observant Jews to record their votes. From the mid-nineteenth century the Board has generally taken the view that Jews should be subject to the same rights and privileges as all other citizens, and should have no special privileges other than any specifically required in order to observe their religion. Where Jewish law was more 'liberal' than English law, for example on marriage, subject to the 'prohibited degrees' and divorce in the nineteenth and early twentieth centuries, then English law must prevail and no special privileges must be sought.

The Board has also been relentless in dealing with any manifestation of antisemitism. At first this involved refuting allegations in the press, in books and other media, and even on occasions threatening or taking legal action, and taking appropriate action when prominent individuals made antisemitic comments. The scope of combating antisemitism extended in the 1930s with the activities of the fascist organizations, and defence of Jews and the Jewish community against attacks on persons as well as on Jewish buildings became a mainstream activity leading to the establishment of the Defence Committee. There are many reasons why antisemitism in Britain has not been as virulent as in other countries and why there has never been overt persecution, and it is likely that the activities of the Board have played a significant part in this.

As early as its second meeting in November 1760, the Board considered a request from an overseas Jewish community for assistance regarding certain problems it was facing. The Board took action and has never stopped since in helping Jewish communities in foreign countries. The heydays were the period when Sir Moses Montefiore was president and Jewish communities everywhere contacted the Board when they had problems. At this time Britain was one of the Great Powers and the Board was generally able to involve the British government, which was of significant help. Dealing directly with problems in foreign countries continued until the Second World War, but thereafter there was a change, and the Board adapted to this change. Britain was no longer the power that she had been, and the Jews of Britain were no longer the leaders in world Jewish affairs; the power of both Britain and its Jews had shifted to the United States. The Board recognized this, and thereafter foreign affairs have generally been dealt with through membership of various international Jewish organizations. Nonetheless, foreign activities continue to be a mainstream activity of the Board.

Conflicts

The first ever meeting of the Board led immediately to a confrontation between the Sephardim and the Ashkenazim, who considered they had been overlooked and slighted, in that they had not been asked to sign the dutiful address to King George III. This was 'papered over', but was a sign of things to come. The Board has been a centre of disputes and conflicts, not only within the Board between various groups and factions but also between the Board and other members and groups in the British Jewish community. The other side of the coin is that on a number of occasions, particularly in the nineteenth and early twentieth centuries, the Board – or in particular its honorary officers – has been a conciliator in disputes within the Jewish community.

With the benefit of hindsight, many of these conflicts might seem trivial, and the positions adopted by adversaries indicate obstinacy and even denting of amour propre, rather than important points of principle. However, all these matters should be viewed in the context of the times in which they occurred and there was often much more to the dispute than appeared on the surface. For example, the denial of membership of the Board in 1853 to deputies who were members of

Orthodox as well as the Reform synagogues might now seem sheer cussedness or narrow-mindedness, but it was of fundamental importance to many at that time. It was considered by many who were advocating Jewish entry into Parliament that the Board should not adopt entry requirement dependent on religious principles, whereas others saw it as an attempt by the Reform synagogue to obtain recognition.

Representation

Initially the Board only had representatives of the Bevis Marks Sephardi Synagogue. Representatives from two of the London Ashkenazi synagogues were 'in attendance' until 1812 when their representatives became full members. By 1835, when Sir Moses Montefiore became president, only four synagogues, all London based, were members, but he set about widening the scope of membership. Even so, it was some considerable time before most synagogues were members, and in 1919 the Board recognized that many British Jews were not represented and extended membership to 'approved' Jewish institutions. The Board was slow to admit Reform synagogues, and its members, as well as the Strictly Orthodox synagogues, had difficulties with accepting that the ecclesiastical authorities of the Board were the chief rabbi and the haham, whose authority they did not accept. Representation in this sense was and remains a problem. Currently about 30 per cent of Jews in Britain are not members of synagogues and, although many of these will be members of institutions that are represented on the Board, nonetheless there remain a large number who are not directly or indirectly represented on the Board. Probably most are indifferent except perhaps when they claim that the Board does not represent their views. Most Strictly Orthodox synagogues are no longer represented on the Board, following their walkout in 1971. This is the fastest-growing sector of the Jewish population in Britain and currently covers about 10 per cent of the Jewish population. This group, although not represented on the Board, enjoys the benefits of the Board's efforts to ensure there are no difficulties for those who wish to practise strict religious observance.

Representation in another sense has always been an issue for the Board. In its first constitution in 1835, the Board proclaimed that it was the sole representative body for Jews in Britain. This monopoly was in a way accepted by the government when in 1836 the president of the Board was given statutory powers to certify which Jewish synagogue secretaries or officials could be licensed to certify marriages.

This power was not contested at first, but the Board's self-proclaimed monopoly on making representations to government was disputed. As a consequence, in 1838 the Board gave way and passed a motion that no members of a synagogue or of the Board were precluded from exercising their influence with the government for the promotion of their civil rights. Thereafter many individuals and Jewish institutions attempted to 'muscle in' on the Board's monopoly of making representation to the government, sometimes without a fight from the Board and sometimes with a battle. The Board has always been zealous to maintain its position in this regard, but is now content to point out that it is the sole elected representative body of British Jewry, whilst no longer trying to prevent other Jewish organizations from making their own representations on specific issues. This is recognized by the government and others who seek and consider views from other Jewish organizations on specific issues.

A third sense of representation is the views presented by the Board. The views might often reflect the majority views of the British Jewish community, but this is not the object. The Board has to offer leadership, which it has not always done. Generally, the view of the Board is a consensus of the views of the deputies, although often this has been limited to the honorary officers and, on occasions, to the president himself. The danger to the president of going out on a limb was highlighted in 1917 when the president was censured for a letter he wrote to *The Times* on behalf of British Jewry, expressing an anti-Zionist viewpoint. The objection of most deputies was not to the sentiment but that he had not consulted them first.

Low Profile

As mentioned in Chapter 1, in its early years the Board decided on a number of occasions to take no action or very low-key action on matters brought to its attention. It was suggested that this was because it had inherited the seventeenth-century British Jewish position that Jews had nothing to fear if they kept a low profile and were law-abiding and peaceable. Following emancipation in the mid-nineteenth century, some historians have taken the view that there was some sort of unwritten 'emancipation contract' that implied the same. There is no real evidence of this and it could well be a myth, encouraged by those whose agenda it helps. The tactics of the Board seem, on the evidence available, to have been pragmatic, and it chose how to deal with each issue depending on the method most likely to bring success, although its choice was not always flawless. The choice was often low-key where the Board considered quiet diplomacy as more likely to obtain a positive result than shouting from the rooftops. Many of the successes of the Board have been through determined but low-key action,[11] although on the other hand there are also examples of high-profile action by the Board.[12]

There are many examples of occasions when the Board was reluctant to go too far against what it deemed as general public opinion in Britain, or did not wish to be seen to offend the government, but there are examples of the opposite as well, indicating again a more pragmatic approach.[13]

NOTES

1. Annual Report of the Board of Deputies (AR), 1997, p.3.
2. AR, 1998, p.4.
3. AR, 2003, p.17.
4. Ibid.
5. AR, 2005, p.17.
6. AR, 2003, pp.3–4.
7. *Constitution of the Board of Deputies at 21 September 2008*, clause 3 (c).
8. AR,1997, p.8.
9. See, for example, *The Times*, 1 December 2009, p.39.
10. *Jewish Chronicle*, 20 November 2009, p.35.
11. For example, such as its defence of *shechita* and obtaining concessions for Jews with regard to Sunday trading and working hours.
12. For example, the Damascus Blood Libel, the events in Romania in the 1860s and 1870s, the attack on the 1905 Aliens Bill and the subsequent protests against how it was being implemented, the attacks on the government's Palestine policy in 1930 and on the 1939 Palestine White Paper, and the very recent protest regarding the British government's response to the Goldstone Report on Operation Cast Lead in Gaza.
13. For example, the approach of the Board to the pogroms in Russia in the 1880s is a case in point. The Board's policy vis-à-vis the fight against antisemitism and the fascist parties in the 1930s is another example. The actions taken by the Board against the 1905 Aliens Bill is an illustration of not only high-profile action, but also action that ran counter to general public opinion in Britain.

Epilogue

HAS THE BOARD BEEN GOOD FOR THE JEWS?

When I started researching and writing this book I could be ranked among the cynics and sceptics as regards my attitude to the Board. I have spent the best part of the last two years being immersed in the primary and secondary literature of and about the Board, as well as having discussions with many current and former honorary officers. I am no longer a cynic and no longer sceptical. The Board at times did not get things right and some of its internal conflicts seem, with the benefit of hindsight, rather petty. There clearly have been disappointments. On the other hand, many of the actions of the Board have been important and successful, and the work of the honorary officers, the deputies and the staff impressive. The Jews of Britain need a representative body and the Board has fulfilled that function effectively, warts and all. Overall, the Board has been of considerable value not only to the Jews of Britain, but also to those in many other countries as well. כל הכבוד (*kol hakavod*).

Appendix 1

The First Constitution of the Board which was approved on 7 March 1836[1] is as follows:

1. That this meeting is convinced it would be of essential advantage to the interests of the Jews of Britain, that in all matters touching their political welfare they should be represented by one Body, and inasmuch as the general Body of Deputies have long been recognised as their representatives, it is highly desirable for the general good that all the British Jews should so acknowledge them, having a sufficient number of Members from each Congregation to ensure the accordance of their proceedings with the general wishes of the Jews.

2. That this Body be entitled 'Deputies of the British Jews' and composed of the following Members:

   7 Deputies from the Portuguese Synagogue
   7 Deputies from the Great Synagogue
   4 Deputies from the Hambro Synagogue
   4 Deputies from the New Synagogue

3. That in all cases which may tend to protect and promote the welfare of the Jews, the Deputies shall be authorised to adopt such measures as they may deem proper, in order to obtain such objects.

4. That the meetings of the Deputies shall at all times be summoned by the President.

5. That whenever a requisition signed by five members of the Jewish Deputies shall be presented to the President for the

purpose of calling a meeting, and stating the object for which such meeting is desired, the President shall convene such meeting within seven days of the receipt of the Requisition.

6. That the summonses to all Meetings shall be sent to each Deputy at least three days prior thereto, except in cases of exigency. And if on requisition, the object of the intended meeting shall be stated.

7. That at all meetings seven shall form a quorum.

8. That all questions shall be decided by show of hands, and that whenever the numbers shall be equal, then, and in such case only, shall the president vote, which he shall be required to do.

9. That all expenses for conducting the affairs of the deputies shall be defrayed in the following manner:

1/3 by the Portuguese Synagogue
1/3 by the Great Synagogue
1/6 by the Hambro Synagogue
1/6 by the New Synagogue.

10. That whenever any Congregation of Jews in the United Kingdom shall be desirous of sending their Deputies for the purpose of uniting with this Body, such Deputies shall be admitted as part of the Deputies of the British Jews, and shall be required to furnish such proportion of the expenses as shall be considered equitable.

11. That the Deputies representing the above mentioned Synagogues shall be furnished with copies of this form of Constitution, which they shall present to their respective Synagogues for their approval, and to be confirmed by their authority in writing, signed by the Secretary of each Synagogue, and which intimation shall also convey to the Deputies the name of their respective Representatives.

12. That the Synagogues sending Deputies shall every five years proceed to a new election of Deputies, and the names of

those so elected shall be communicated to this Body, by the Secretaries of the different Synagogues.

NOTE

1. BOD Minute Book 2, pp.94–6.

Appendix 2

NUMBER OF DEPUTIES

Year	Synagogues/ Institutions Represented	Number of Deputies
1760	1	7
1778	1	10
1812	4	18
1835	4	22
1850	8	28
1853	35	58
1856	18	31
1859	15	25
1880	26	38
1901	51	65
1904	70	87
1907	97	114
1910	106	123
1913	113	129
1916	137	143
1919	185	251
1922	189	266
1925	200	276
1928	214	308
1931	219	299
1934	239	347
1937	256	377
1940	207	288

NUMBER OF DEPUTIES

Year	Synagogues/ Institutions Represented	Number of Deputies
1943	274	459
1946	275	437
1949	258	415
1952	263	432
1955	267	430
1958	264	405
1961	251	389
1964	252	407
1967	250	413
1970	256	431
1973	264	432
1976	270	533
1979	270	526
1982	270	554
1985	268	667
1988	244	448
1991	234	406
1994	220	362
1997	204	324
2000	221	383
2003	203	306
2006	203	288
2009	187	267

NOTES

1. The Ashkenazi Synagogues are not included until 1812, when they became full members of the Board.
2. From 1919 onwards, some institutions as well as synagogues were able to elect Deputies.

Appendix 3

1760–64	Benjamin Mendes da Costa
1764–84	Joseph Salvador
1784–1801	Moses Isaac Levy
1801–04	Naphteli Bazevy
1805–17	Raphael Brendon
1817–29	Moses Lindo
1829–35	Moses Mocatta
1835–38	Moses Montefiore
1838 (October to November)	David Salomons *
1838–40	I.Q. Henriques*
1840 (May to July)	Sir Moses Montefiore
1840–41	Hananel de Castro*
1841–46	Sir Moses Montefiore
1846 (March to August)	David Salomons* (later Sir David)
1846–1855	Sir Moses Montefiore
1855 (April to December)	Isaac Foligno*
1855–57	Sir Moses Montefiore
1857 (February to September)	Isaac Foligno*
1857–62	Sir Moses Montefiore
1862–68	Joseph Meyer Montefiore*
1868 (June to November)	Sir Moses Montefiore
1868–71	Joseph Meyer Montefiore*
1871–74	Sir Moses Montefiore
1874–80	Joseph Meyer Montefiore

PAST PRESIDENTS

1880–95	Arthur Cohen, QC, MP
1895–1903	Sir Joseph Sebag Montefiore
1903–17	David Lindo Alexander, KC
1917–22	Sir Stuart Samuel
1922–25	Henry S.Q. Henriques, KC
1925–26	Lord Rothschild (acting)
1926–33	Osmond D'Avigdor-Goldsmid (later Sir Osmond)
1933–39	Neville Laski, KC
1939–49	Professor Selig Brodetsky
1949–55	Rev. Dr Abraham Cohen
1955–64	Barnett Janner, MP (Sir Barnett from 1960 and subsequently Lord Janner)
1964 (June)	Alderman Abraham Moss
1964–67	Solomon Teff
1967–73	Alderman Michael Fidler, JP
1973–79	Alderman Sir Samuel Fisher (subsequently Lord Fisher)
1979–85	Greville Janner, QC, MP (subsequently Lord Janner)
1985–91	Dr Lionel Kopelowitz, JP
1991–94	His Honour Judge Israel Finestein, QC
1994–2000	Eldred Tabachnik, QC
2000–03	Jo Wagerman, OBE
2003–09	Henry Grunwald, QC, OBE
2009–	Vivian Wineman

*Pro tem in the absence abroad of Sir Moses Montefiore.

Appendix 4

PAST CHIEF EXECUTIVES

Dates	Position	Name
1837–41	Secretary	Sampson Samuel
1841–68	Solicitor and Secretary	Sampson Samuel
1869–98	Solicitor and Secretary	Lewis Emanuel
1898–1927	Solicitor and Secretary	Charles H.L. Emanuel*
1927–31	Secretary	J.M. Rich
1931–33	Secretary	B.A. Zaiman
1934–64	Secretary	Adolph Brotman
1964–76	Secretary	Abraham Marks
1977–91	Chief Executive	Hayim Pinner
1991–2004	Chief Executive**	Neville Nagler
2005–	Director General	Jon Benjamin

*   Remained as Solicitor until his death in 1962.
**   Director General from 1996.

Glossary

Ashkenazim	Jews of Central and Eastern European origin.
Beth Din	Jewish Ecclesiastical Court. There is not a common one for all synagogues in Britain, but each major group of synagogues has its own.
brit milah	Circumcision of eight-day-old baby boy.
chevrot	Small religious societies and small synagogues.
get	Divorce under Jewish Law.
gittim	Plural of *get*.
haham	Spiritual leader of the Sephardi community.
halacha	Jewish religious law.
herem	Excommunication or ban on an individual or group.
kashrut (kosher)	Jewish dietary laws.
kehilla	Semi-autonomous Jewish community, mainly in Central and Eastern Europe.
Kiddush	In the sense that it is used in this book it means a reception following a Jewish religious service or ceremony.
kol hakavod	Literally: all honour to you. Idiomatically: great job.
Kristallnacht	Literally 'Night of the Broken Glass'. It refers to 9–10 November 1938 when, in Austria and Germany, mobs led by the Nazis destroyed hundreds of synagogues, broke into and looted Jewish-owned shops, businesses and other property, and attacked thousands of Jews.
Mahamad	Lay leaders of the Sephardi synagogues.
Marranos	Jews (and their descendents) who had been forcibly converted to Christianity in Spain and Portugal, but had maintained their Judaism secretly. Also referred to as *Conversos* and New Christians.

maskilim	Supporters of the European Jewish enlighten-ment movement.
matzot (matza)	Unleavened bread, eaten by Jews during Passover.
Sephardim	Jews of Spanish/Portuguese origin.
shechita	The Jewish method of slaughtering animals.
shiur	A group under a leader studying a text generally from the Talmud.
Shulchan Aruch	A codex of Jewish law. It is considered by the vast majority of orthodox Jews to be the most authoritative compilation of Halacha since the Talmud.
Talmud	A record of rabbinic discussions of Jewish law, ethics, customs and history. It comprises more than sixty volumes compiled during the third to fifth centuries CE.
Yiddish	A Jewish language derived mainly from High German and Hebrew. The lingua franca of Jews of Eastern Europe.

Bibliography

PRIMARY SOURCES

Annual Reports of the Board of Deputies.
Archives of the Board of Deputies (BOD), London Metropolitan Archives.
Archives of the Community Security Trust (CST), Shield House, London NW4 2BZ.
Archives of the Jewish Memorial Council (JMC), London Metropolitan Archives.
Archives of the United Synagogue (US), London Metropolitan Archives.
Hansard
Jewish Chronicle (JC)
Jewish World
Neville Laski Papers, Hartley Library, Southampton University.
Selig Brodetsky Papers, Hartley Library, Southampton University.
The Jewish Year Book.
The National Archive, Public Records Office (TNA, PRO), Kew, London.
The Times
Voice of Jacob
Wolf-Mowshowitch Papers, YIVO, New York.

SECONDARY SOURCES

Alderman, Geoffrey, 'Jews and Sunday Trading: The Use and Abuse of Delegated Legislation', *Public Administration*, 60 (March 1982), pp.99–100.
Alderman, Geoffrey, *The Jewish Community in British Politics* (Oxford: Clarendon, 1988).
Alderman, Geoffrey, *Modern British Jewry*, new edn (Oxford: Clarendon, 1998).

Alderman, Geoffrey, *Controversy and Crisis: Studies in the History of the Jews in Modern Britain* (Boston, MA: Academic Studies Press, 2008).

Alderman, Geoffrey and Holmes, Colin, 'The Burton Book', *Journal of the Royal Asiatic Society*, 18, 1 (January 2008).

Bayme, Steven Gilbert, *Jewish Leadership and Antisemitism in Britain* (Ann Arbor, MI: Columbia University Press, 1986).

Beckman, Morris, *The 43 Group*, 2nd edition (London: Centerprise, 1993).

Bermant, Chaim, *Troubled Eden: An Anatomy of British Jewry* (London: Vallentine Mitchell, 1969).

Bermant, Chaim, *The Cousinhood: The Anglo-Jewish Gentry* (London: Eyre & Spottiswoode, 1971).

Black, Eugene C., *The Social Politics of Anglo-Jewry, 1880–1920* (Oxford: Blackwell, 1988).

Black, Gerry, *JFS: The History of the Jews' Free School, London, since 1732* (London: Tymsder, 1998).

Bolchover, Richard, *British Jewry and the Holocaust*, 2nd edition (Oxford: Littman Library of Jewish Civilization, 2003).

Bornstein, Abba and Homa, Bernard, *Tell it in Gath: British Jewry and Clause 43, The Inside Story* (London: Private, 1972).

Brodetsky, Selig, *Memoirs: from Ghetto to Israel* (London: Weidenfeld & Nicolson, 1960).

Brook, Stephen, *The Club: The Jews of Modern Britain*, paperback edition (London: Constable Press, 1989).

Cesarani, David, 'Anti-Alienism in England After the First World War', *Immigrants and Minorities*, 6 (1987), pp.5–29.

Cesarani, David, 'An Embattled Minority: The Jews in Britain During the First World War', *Immigrants and Minorities*, 8 (1989), pp.61–81.

Cesarani, David, *The Jewish Chronicle and Anglo-Jewry, 1841–1991* (Cambridge: Cambridge University Press, 1994).

Cesarani, David (ed.), *The Making of Modern Anglo-Jewry* (Oxford: Basil Blackwell, 1990).

Cesarani, David, and Kushner, Tony, *The Internment of Aliens in Twentieth Century Britain* (London: Frank Cass, 1993).

Cohen, Myrella, 'After the Preston Report', *Jewish Year Book 1997* (London: Vallentine Mitchell, 1997), pp.lxiv–lxv.

Cohen, Stuart A., 'The Conquest of a Community? The Zionists and the Board of Deputies in 1917', *Jewish Journal of Sociology*, 19 (1977), pp.157–84.

Cohen, Stuart A., *English Zionists and British Jews: The Communal Politics of Anglo-Jewry, 1895–1920* (Princeton, NJ: Princeton University Press, 1982).

Cohen, Stuart A., 'Selig Brodetsky and the Ascendancy of Zionism in Anglo-Jewry: Another View of his Role and Achievements', *Jewish Journal of Sociology*, 24, 1 (June 1982), p.28.

Colquhoun, Patrick, *Treatise on the Police of the Metropolis*, 6th enlarged edn (London: Mawman, 1800).

Copsey, Nigel, *Anti-Fascism in Britain* (Basingstoke: Macmillan, 2000).

Copsey, Nigel and Tilles, Daniel, 'Uniting a Divided Community? Re-appraising Jewish Responses to British Fascist Antisemitism, 1932–39', *Holocaust Studies*, 15, 1–2 (Spring/Summer 2010) [Forthcoming].

Emanuel, Charles H.L., *A Century and a Half of Jewish History: Extracted from the Minute Books of The London Committee of Deputies of British Jews* (London: George Routledge, 1910).

Emden, Paul H., *Jews of Britain: A Series of Biographies* (London: Sampson Low, Marsten and Co., 1943).

Endelman, Todd M., *The Jews of Britain, 1656 to 2000* (London: University of California Press, 2002).

Englander, David (ed.), *A Documentary History of Jewish Immigrants in Britain, 1840–1920* (London: Leicester University Press, 1994).

Feldman, David, *Englishmen and Jews: Social Relations and Political Culture 1840–1914* (London: Yale University Press, 1994).

Feldman, David, 'Jews and the State in Britain', in Michael Brenner, Rainer Liedke and David Rechter (eds), *Two Nations: British and German Jews in Comparative Perspective* (Tübingen: M Siebeck, 1999).

Feuchtwanger, Edgar, '"Jew Feeling" and Realpolitik: Disraeli and the Making of Foreign and Imperial Policy', in Todd M. Endelman and Tony Kushner (eds), *Disraeli's Jewishness* (London: Vallentine Mitchell, 2002), pp.180–97.

Finestein, Israel, 'Sir Moses Montefiore: A Modern Appreciation', *Jewish Historical Studies*, 29 (1988).

Finestein, Israel, *Jewish Society in Victorian England: Collected Essays* (London: Vallentine Mitchell, 1993).

Finestein, Israel, *Anglo-Jewry in Changing Times: Studies in Diversity 1840–1914* (London: Vallentine Mitchell, 1999).

Finestein, Israel, *Scenes and Personalities in Anglo-Jewry, 1800–2000* (London: Vallentine Mitchell, 2002).

Finestein Israel, *Studies and Profiles in Anglo-Jewish History: From Picciotto to Bermant* (London: Vallentine Mitchell, 2008).

Finney, Patrick B., '"An Evil for All Concerned": Great Britain and Minority Protection after 1919', *Journal of Contemporary History*, 30 (1995), pp.533–4.

Fraenkel, Josef, *The History of the British Section of the World Jewish Congress* (London: Leicester University Press, 1976).

Frankel, Jonathan, 'Demanding Leadership: The Russian-Jewish Question and the Board of Deputies of the British Jews, July 1842 – February 1846 (with Documents)', in *Transition and Change in Modern Jewish History: Essays presented in honour of Shmuel Ettinger* (Jerusalem: Merkaz Zalman Shazar le-toldot Yiśra'el: ha-Hevrah ha-historit ha-Yiśre'elit, 1987), pp.xxxi–lxxi.

Frankel, Jonathan, *The Damascus Affair: 'Ritual Murder', Politics, and the Jews in 1840* (Cambridge: Cambridge University Press, 1997).

Galnoor, Itzak, *The Partition of Palestine: Decision Crossroads in the Zionist Movement* (New York: State University, 1995).

Garrard, John A., *The English and Immigration 1880–1910* (London: Oxford University Press, 1971).

Gartner, Lloyd P., 'Anglo-Jewry and the Jewish International Traffic in Prostitution, 1885–1914', *AJS Review*, 7 (1982), pp.129–78.

Gartner, Lloyd P., 'Emancipation, Social Change and Communal Reconstruction in Anglo-Jewry, 1789–1881', *Proceedings of the American Academy for Jewish Research*, 54 (1987), pp.73–116.

Gartner, Lloyd P., *The Jewish Immigrant in England 1870–1914*, 3rd edition (London: Vallentine Mitchell, 2001).

Gerlis, Daphne, *Those Wonderful Women in Black: The Story of the Women's Campaign for Soviet Jewry* (London: Minerva, 1996).

Gewirtz, Sharon, 'Anglo-Jewish Responses to Nazi Germany 1933–39: The Anti-Nazi Boycott and the Board of Deputies of British Jews', *Journal of Contemporary History*, 26, 2 (April 1991), pp.255–76.

Gilam, A., *The Emancipation of the Jews in England, 1830–1860* (New York: Garland, 1982).

Gilam, Abraham. 'The Burial Grounds Controversy between Anglo-Jewry and the Victorian Board of Health, 1850', *Jewish Social Studies*, 45 (1983), pp.147–56.

Gould, Julius and Esh, Shaul (eds), *Jewish Life in Modern Britain: Papers and Proceedings of a Conference held at University College, London on 1st and 2nd April, 1962, by the Institute of Contemporary Jewry of the Hebrew University, Jerusalem under the auspices of the Board of Deputies of British Jews*.

Green, Abigail, 'Rethinking Sir Moses Montefiore: Religion, Nationhood, and International Philanthropy in the Nineteenth Century', *American Historical Review*, 110, 3 (June 2005), pp.631–58.

Green, Abigail, *Moses Montefiore: Jewish Liberator, Imperial Hero* (Cambridge, MA: Harvard University Press, 2010) [Forthcoming].

Gutwein, David, *Divided Elite: Economics, Politics, and Anglo-Jewry, 1882–1917* (London: E.J. Brill, 1992).

Henriques, H.S.Q., *The Jews and the English Law* (Oxford: Augustus M. Kelley, 1908).

Henriques, H.S.Q., *Jewish Marriages and the English Law* (Oxford: Bibliophile, 1909).

Holmes, Colin, *Anti-Semitism in British Society, 1876–1939* (London: Edward Arnold, 1979).

Homa, Bernard, *Footprints on the Sands of Time* (London: author, 1990).

Hyamson, Albert M., *The Sephardim of England: A History of the Spanish and Portuguese Jewish Community 1492–1951* (London: Methuen & Co., 1951).

Hyamson, Albert M., *The London Board for Shechita, 1804–1954* (London: London Board for Shechita, 1954).

Itzkowitz, David C., 'Cultural Pluralism and the Board of Deputies of British Jews', in Richard Davis and Richard J. Helmstadter, *Religion and Irreligion in Victorian Society: Essays in Honour of R.K. Wells* (London: Routledge, 1992), pp.85–101.

Jacobs, Louis, *Helping with Inquiries: An Autobiography* (London: Vallentine Mitchell, 1989).

Kadish, Sharman, *Bolsheviks and British Jews: The Anglo-Jewish Community, Britain and the Russian Revolution* (London: Frank Cass, 1992).

Katz, David S., *The Jews in the History of England* (Oxford: Clarendon, 1996).

Kent, Susan Kingsley, *Aftershock: Politics and Trauma in Britain, 1918–1931* (Basingstoke: Palgrave, 2008).

Kershen, Anne J. and Romain, Jonathan A., *Tradition and Change: A History of Reformed Judaism in Britain, 1840–1995* (London: Vallentine Mitchell, 1995).

Kimmel, Hans, 'The Structure and Regime of the Board of Deputies of British Jews', *Jewish Public Affairs*, no. 4 (February 1968), pp.1–4.

Krikler, Bernard, *Anglo-Jewish Attitudes to the Rise of Nazism* (1968), unpublished manuscript available in the Wiener Library, London.

Kushner, Tony (ed.), *The Jewish Heritage in British History: Englishness and Jewishness* (London: Frank Cass, 1992).

Langham, Raphael, 'The reaction in England to the kidnapping of Edgardo Mortara', *Jewish Historical Studies*, 39 (2004), pp.79–101.

Langham, Raphael, *The Jews in Britain: A Chronology* (Basingstoke: Palgrave, 2005).

Laski, Neville, *Jewish Rights and Jewish Wrongs* (London: Soncino Press, 1939).

Lebzelter, Gisela C., *Political Anti-Semitism in England, 1918–1939* (Basingstoke: Macmillan, 1978).

Levenberg, S., *The Board and Zion: An Historical Survey* (London: Rare Times Ltd., 1985).

Levene, Mark, 'Anglo-Jewish Foreign Policy in Crisis – Lucien Wolf, the Conjoint Committee and the War, 1914–18', *Jewish Historical Studies*, 30 (1987–88), p.181.

Levene, Mark, *War, Jews, and the New Europe: The Diplomacy of Lucien Wolf, 1914–1919* (Oxford: Littman Library, 1992).

Levin, Salmond S., *A Century of Anglo-Jewish Life, 1870–1970* (London: United Synagogue, 1970).

Liberles, Robert, 'The Origins of the Jewish Reform Movement in Britain', *AJS Review*, 1 (1976), pp.121–50.

Lipman, Sonia and Lipman V.D. (eds), *Jewish Life in Britain, 1962–1977: Papers and Proceedings of a Conference held at Hillel House, London, on March 13, 1977, by the Board of Deputies of British Jews and the Institute of Jewish Affairs.*

Lipman, Sonia and Lipman V.D. (eds), *The Century of Moses Montefiore* (Oxford: Littman Library, 1985).

Lipman, V.D., *Social History of the Jews in England, 1850–1950* (London: Watts & Co., 1954).

Lipman, V.D. (ed.), *Three Centuries of Anglo-Jewish History: A Volume of Essays* (London: W. Heffer & Son, 1961).

Lipman, V.D., *A History of the Jews In Britain since 1858* (Leicester: Leicester University Press, 1990).

Loewe, Louis (ed.), *Diaries of Sir Moses and Lady Montefiore*, a facsimile of the 1890 edition (London: Jewish Historical Society of England, 1983).

London, Louise, *Whitehall and the Jews, 1933–1948: British Immigration Policy, Jewish Refugees and the Holocaust* (Cambridge: Cambridge University Press, 2000).

Manning, Bernard Lord, *The Protestant Dissenting Deputies* (Cambridge: Cambridge University Press, 1952).

Massil, Stephen, 'Naphtali Hart Myers (1711?–1788): New Yorker and

Londoner', unpublished paper presented to the Jewish Historical Society of England on 17 December 2009.

Mathews, H.C.G. and Harrison, Brian (eds), *Oxford Dictionary of National Biography* (Oxford: Oxford University Press, 2004).

Morris, Henry, *The AJEX Chronicles* (London: AJEX, 1999).

Newman, Aubrey, *The Board of Deputies of British Jews 1760–1985: A Brief Survey* (London: Vallentine Mitchell, 1987).

Persoff, Meir, *Faith Against Reason: Religious Reform and the British Chief Rabbinate 1840–1990* (London: Vallentine Mitchell, 2008).

Picciotto, James, *Sketches of Anglo-Jewish History*, revised and edited with a prologue, notes and an epilogue by Israel Finestein (London: Soncino Press, 1956).

Pollins, Harold, *Economic History of the Jews in England* (London: Littman Library, 1982).

Rigal, Laurence and Rosenberg, Rosita, *Liberal Judaism: The First Hundred Years* (London: Liberal Judaism, 2004).

Romain, Jonathan A., *Anglo-Jewry in Evidence: A History of the Jews of England through Original Sources and Illustrations* (London: Michael Goulston Education Foundation, 1985).

Rosenberg, David, *Facing up to Antisemitism: How the Jews in Britain Countered the Threats of the 1930s* (London: JCARP Publications, 1985).

Rosenzweig, Alexander, *The Jewish Memorial Council: A History 1919–1999* (London: JMC, 1998).

Roth, Cecil, *A History of the Jews in England*, 3rd edn (Oxford: Oxford University Press, 1978).

Rubinstein, W.D., *A History of the Jews in the English-Speaking World: Great Britain* (Basingstoke: Macmillan, 1996).

Rubinstein, W.D., *Britain's Century: A Political and Social History 1815–1905* (London: Arnold, 1998).

Rubinstein, William D., 'The Decline and Fall of Anglo-Jewry?', *Jewish Historical Studies* 38 (2003), pp.13–21.

Rubinstein, W.D. and Rubinstein, Hilary L., *Philosemitism: Admiration and Support in the English-Speaking World for Jews, 1840–1939* (London: Macmillan, 1999).

Rubinstein, William (general ed.), Jolles, Michael and Rubinstein, Hilary (eds), *Dictionary of Anglo-Jewish History, Volume 2* (Basingstoke: Palgrave Macmillan, 2010) [Forthcoming].

Salbstein, M.C.N., *The Emancipation of the Jews in Britain: The Question of the Admission of the Jews to Parliament, 1828–1860* (London: Littman Library, 1982).

Salomon, Sidney, 'Board of Deputies of British Jews, 1760–1960', *Jewish Affairs*, 15, 11 (October 1960), pp.4–9.

Schmool, Marlena, 'A Hundred Years of British Jewish Statistics', *Jewish Year Book Centenary Edition* (London: Vallentine Mitchell, 1996).

Schmool, Marlena and Cohen, Frances, *British Synagogue Membership in 1990* (London: Board of Deputies, 1993).

Schmool, Marlena and Cohen, Frances, *A Profile of British Jewry: Patterns and Trends at the Turn of the Century* (London: Board of Deputies, 1998).

Schwab, William M., *B'nai B'rith: The First Lodge of England, A Record of Fifty Years* (Letchworth: Oswald Wolff, 1960).

Shaftesley, John M. (ed.), *Remember the Days: Essays on Anglo-Jewish History presented to Cecil Roth by members of the Council of the Jewish Historical Society of England* (London: Jewish Historical Society of England, 1966).

Shatzkes, Pamela, *Holocaust and Rescue: Impotent or Indifferent? Anglo-Jewry 1938–1945* (Basingstoke: Palgrave, 2002).

Sherman, Anthony, *Island Refuge: Britain and Refugees from the Third Reich 1933–1939* , 2nd edn (Ilford: Frank Cass, 1994).

Shimoni, Gideon, 'Selig Brodetsky and the Ascendancy of Zionism in Anglo-Jewry (1939–1945)', *Jewish Journal of Sociology*, 22 (1980), p.130.

Sompolinsky, Meier, *The British Government and the Holocaust: The Failure of Anglo-Jewish Leadership* (Brighton: Sussex Academic Press, 1999).

Stent, Ronald, *A Bespattered Page? The Internment of His Majesty's 'most loyal enemy aliens'* (London: Andre Deutsch, 1980).

Tilles, Daniel, ' "Some Lesser Known Aspects": The Anti-Fascist Campaign of the Board of Deputies of British Jews, 1936–40', in Geoffrey Alderman (ed.), *The Jews in Britain* (Boston: Academic Studies Press) [Forthcoming, probably 2010].

Wasserstein, Bernard, 'Patterns of Jewish Leadership in Great Britain during the Nazi Era', in Randolph Braham (ed.), *Jewish Leadership During the Nazi Era* (New York: Institute for Holocaust Studies, 1985), pp.29–43.

Wasserstein, Bernard, *Britain and the Jews of Europe, 1939–1945* (Oxford: Oxford University Press, 1988).

Watts, Martin, *The Jewish Legion in the First World War* (Basingstoke: Palgrave, 2004).

Weisbord, Robert G., *African Zion: The Attempt to establish a Jewish*

Colony in the East African Protectorate, 1903–1905 (Philadelphia: Jewish Publication Society of America, 1968).

Williams, Bill, *The Making of Manchester Jewry, 1740–1875* (Manchester: Manchester University Press, 1976).

Wolf, Lucien, *Notes on the Diplomatic History of the Jewish Question* (London: Jewish Historical Society of England, 1919).

Zeitlyn, Elsley, *The Board of Deputies and the B'nai B'rith* (London: Board of Deputies, 1930).

Index

179

Nathan, Lord, *see* Nathan, Major Harry

National Insurance Bill (1911), *see under* Parliamentary Legislation

New Synagogue, *see* Synagogues

New London Synagogue, *see* Synagogues

New West End Synagogue, *see* Synagogues

Newman, Aubrey, 89

Newton, Moses Levy, 17

Nicholas I, Tsar, 19, 56, 59

Norwood, 16–17

Nunes, Isaac Fernandes, 11

O

Orbach, Maurice, 202

Orthodox Synagogues, *see* Central Orthodox Synagogues

Oven, Joshua van, 16

P

Palatnik,Raiza, 250

Palmerston, Lord, 54–6, 58

Parliamentary Legislation, Acts: Aliens Act 1905, 75, 92–3, 143; Aliens Restriction (Amendment) Act 1919, 142; Conventicle Act 1664, 9; Corporation Act 1661, 34; Dissenters Chapel Act 1855, 45; Factory Act 1878, 51, 52–3, 97; Hairdressers' and Barbers' Shops (Sunday Closing) Act 1930, 160; Internment Act 1850, 47; Lord's Day Observance Act 1677, 52–3, 97–8, 160; Marriage Act 1753, 40; Marriage Act 1836, 40, 41, 44; Marriage Act 1856, 31; Marriage Registration Act 1836, 24, 40; Matrimonial Causes Act 1835,25, 40–1, 42; Military Convention Act 1917, 142; Public

Order Act 1937, 153, 198, 199; Race Relations Act 1965, 245–6; Religious Disabilities Act 1846, 36–7, 48; Retail Meat Dealers' Shops (Sunday Closing) Act 1936, 161; Shops (Sunday Trading Restrictions) Act 1936, 161; Sunday Trading Act 1994, 246; Test Acts 1673 and 1678, 34; Toleration Act 1688, 37; Workshop and Factory (Jews) Act 1871, 52; Bills: Aliens Bill (1904) 91–2; Bakehouse Bill (1914), 86–7; Catholic Relief Bill (1829), 35; Education Bill (1944), 203; Elementary Education Bill (1870), 50; Emancipation Bill (1837), 41; Factories Amendment Bill (1870), 52; Hours of Labour Regulation Bill (1867), 51; Humane Slaughter of Animals Bill (1914), 1914; Income Tax Bill (1842), 39; Internment Bill (1843), 46; Jewish Naturalization Bill (1753), 10; Marriage (Consolidation) Bill (1949), 187; Matrimonial Causes Bill (1857), 43; Metropolitan Internment Bill (1850), 46; National Insurance Bill (1911), 81; Poor Law Amendment Bill (1834), 39; Port of London Bill (1908), 93; Public Order Bill (1963), 199; Shops Bill (1911), 85, 99; Slaughter of Animals Bill (1911), 83, 85, 102; Slaughter of Animals Bill (1930), 158; Sunday Closing Bill (1905), 98–9; University Test Bill (1869), 38; Weekly Rest Day Bill (1907), 99

Passfield, Lord, 169

Pedder, Sir John, 93, 143–4

Peel, Sir Robert, 36, 39

Phillips, Benjamin, 28

Picciotto, Cyril, 132

Picciotto, James, 37, 45

Scenes and Personalities
in Anglo-Jewry 1800-2000
Israel Finestein

'Israel Finestein, offers a fascinating combination of scholarly detachment and an insider's knowledge of the rough and tumble of Jewish communal life.'

Professor John D. Klier, *University College London*

2002 224 pages
978 0 85303 443 5   cloth £35.00/$69.95
978 0 85303 442 7   paper £17.50/$32.95

Studies and Profiles
in Anglo-Jewish History
From Picciotto to Bermant
Israel Finestein

'Israel Finestein's writings on Anglo-Jewish history are characterized by their learning, their lucidity and by their humanity and insight.'

Dr David Feldman, *Birkbeck, University of London*

2008 280 pages
978 0 85303 577 0   cloth £40.00/$74.95

British Chief Rabbis 1664–2006

Derek Taylor

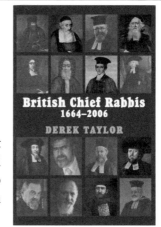

'Derek Taylor has told an important and fascinating story. I hope it will encourage the younger generation to feel pride in the community to which they belong.'

From the Foreword by **Rabbi Dr Abraham Levy, OBE**

2006 472 pages
978 0 85303 610 1   cloth £47.50/$79.50
978 0 85303 611 X   paper £19.95/$35.00

Jewish Parliamentarians

Derek Taylor and Greville Janner

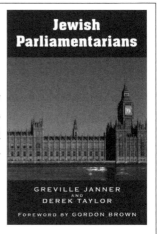

'... this comparatively small community has always supported our country admirably and has shown that an ethnic and religious group can do so without sacrificing their historical traditions.'

From the Foreword by **Gordon Brown**

2008 240 pages
978 0 85303 819 1   cloth £35.00/$59.95
978 0 85303 817 7   paper £16.95/$32.95

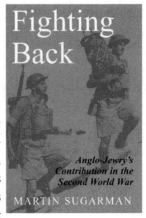

Jewish Year Book
2010
Elkan Levy and Derek Taylor (Eds)

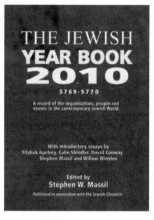

What do you want to know about the
Jewish community in Britain? For 115
years the answers have been found in
The Jewish Year Book; the institutions,
the organisations, the charities their
contact details and a who's who of the personalities.

Also provided are the dates that matter in the Jewish calendar,
the award winners, the anniversaries and the obituaries along
with an overview of the position of Jews in countries outside
Britain, what is happening in Israel and the times in 2010 for
festivals and Sabbaths all over the country along with a 30 year
Jewish calendar.

Plus a series of articles which look back over the year gone by
and the centuries gone by.

The Jewish Year Book has always been meticulous in its
research and widespread in its coverage.

When you want to know the answer on anything to do
with the Jewish community, your best chance is to find it in
The Jewish Year Book.

2010 480 pages
978 0 85303 901 3   cloth   £35.00/$64.95

Jewish Culture and History

Editors: Nadia Valman
            Tobias Brinkmann
Deputy Editor: Tony Kushner
Reviews Editor: Nathan Abrams

Jewish Culture and History is an inter-disciplinary refereed journal which brings together the best of current research in Jewish social history with innovative work in Jewish cultural studies. The journal includes cutting-edge research by younger scholars as well as the work of established specialists. Together with research articles and book reviews, it regularly reproduces selected primary materials from archives, private collections and lesser-known resources for the study of Jewish culture and history.

The journal explores previously neglected areas of the Jewish experience in different cultures and from a range of different perspectives. Its interests include: popular culture, film and visual culture, music, media, cultural representations of Jews, Jewish/non-Jewish relations, Jewish literature in all languages, intellectual, social, political and cultural histories, historiography, gendered histories of Jews, class, consumption and lifestyles, and cultural geographies.

Volume 12 2010 ISSN 1462-169X
Three issues per year: Summer, Autumn, Winter
Individuals £45/$75 Institutions £150/$260

Vallentine Mitchell is a long established international publisher of books of Jewish interest and Middle Eastern Studies, both for the scholar and the general reader. Subjects covered include Jewish history, culture and heritage, religion, modern Jewish thought, biography, reference and the Holocaust. We hope that among our past and present titles you will find much of interest. Vallentine Mitchell also publishes the journals *Jewish Culture and History* and *Holocaust Studies: A Journal of Culture and History*.

Our new and forthcoming publications include several important and eagerly awaited titles.

Visit our website

www.vmbooks.com

to read blurbs, see jackets and journals and more.

Vallentine Mitchell